Manhood, Citizenship, and the National Guard: Illinois, 1870–1917

Eleanor L. Hannah

The Ohio State University Press
Columbus

Copyright © 2007 by The Ohio State University.
All rights reserved.

Library of Congress Cataloging-in-Publication Data

Hannah, Eleanor L.
  Manhood, citizenship, and the National Guard : Illinois, 1870–1917 / Eleanor L. Hannah.
    p. cm.
  Includes bibliographical references and index.
  ISBN-13: 978-0-8142-1045-1 (cloth : alk. paper)
  ISBN-13: 978-0-8142-9125-2 (cd-rom)
  1. Illinois. National Guard—History—19th century. 2. Illinois—Militia—History—19th century. 3. Masculinity—Illinois—History—19th century. 4. Citizenship—Illinois—History—19th century. 5. Illinois. National Guard—History—20th century. 6. Illinois—Militia—History—20th century. 7. Masculinity—Illinois—History—20th century. 8. Citizenship—Illinois—History—20th century. 9. Sociology, Military—Illinois. I. Title.
  UA170.H35 2007
  355.3'70977309034—dc22
                                    2006029311

Paper (ISBN: 978-0-8142-5725-8)
Cover design by Dan O'Dair.
Type set in Goudy.

Contents

	List of Illustrations	v
	Acknowledgments	vii
	Introduction	1
Chapter 1	Illinois Militia Revival in the 1870s	17
Chapter 2	Manhood and Citizenship on Display	41
Chapter 3	Confused Missions: The First Twenty Years of Strike Duty, 1870–90	78
Chapter 4	New Training Practices, Drill Competitions, and the Rise of Sharpshooting	103
Chapter 5	Death, Manhood, and Service in the Spanish American War	133
Chapter 6	Lessons Learned: The ING and Strike Duty, 1894–1916	157
Chapter 7	The Pursuit of State and Federal Support	185

Appendixes:
A Occupations Named by Members of the First Infantry, ING, 1890–1903 — 217
B Occupations Named by Members of Co. A, Third Infantry, ING, 1899–1908 — 218
C Incidents of Strike-Related Active Duty on the Part of the ING, 1877–1904 — 219
D Precipitating Event for Request for State Intervention in Coal Strikes, 1877–1908 — 220
E ING Membership vs. Days of Strike Policing, 1874–1911 — 221
F Selected ING Officers, 1874–90: Military Histories of Officers with Five to Six Years of Service in Their Current Rank — 222

G	Illinois Volunteer Forces: Service beyond the United States, 1898–99	226
H	Illinois Volunteer Forces: Enlisted Losses while in Service, 1898–99	227
I	State and Federal Appropriations per Guardsman, by State, 1897	228
J	Maps Showing Distribution of Illinois Militia Companies by City, 1874 and 1876	229
	Notes	231
	Bibliography	279
	Index	293

Illustrations

Photographs

Figure 1   First Infantry football team, 1897. Courtesy of the Chicago Historical Society. Photographer: Unknown. iCHi-39232.   45

Figure 2   "Off with the Old Loves and On with the New," *Illinois State Journal*, July 17, 1898.   55

Figure 3   White and African American members of the First Division, ING, at Camp Lincoln, ca. 1895. Courtesy of the Chicago Historical Society. Photographer: D. H. Spencer. iCHi-26577.   69

Figure 4   Members of the Third Infantry, playing cards at Camp Lincoln, 1903. Courtesy of the Abraham Lincoln Presidential Library. Photographer: Guy Mathis, Guy Mathis Collection.   119

Figure 5   Ladies visiting the Third Infantry at Camp Lincoln, 1903. Courtesy of the Abraham Lincoln Presidential Library. Photographer: Guy Mathis, Guy Mathis Collection.   119

Figure 6   ING members in costume (many in ladies' undergarments) at Camp Lincoln, 1904. Courtesy of the Abraham Lincoln Presidential Library. Photographer: Guy Mathis, Guy Mathis Collection.   120

Figure 7   Captain Clarke's Midway Squad, Company E, First Regiment, Camp Lincoln, ca. 1895. Courtesy of the Chicago Historical Society. Photographer: Unknown. iCHi-39236.   121

Figure 8   Soldiers firing with "Texas grip" at Camp Logan, Winthrop Harbor, Illinois, 1899. Lt. Cary T. Ray, standing; five men of the Second Infantry, firing. Courtesy of the Chicago Historical Society. Photographer: Unknown. iCHi-39219.   130

Figure 9	Fourth Infantry leaving Savannah, Georgia, for Cuba, January 3, 1899. Courtesy of the Abraham Lincoln Presidential Library. Photographer: Unknown.	145
Figure 10	First Infantry troops entering their Armory, returning from the Spanish American War, September 10, 1898. Courtesy of the Chicago Historical Society. Photographer: E. Hergt. iCHi-39625.	146
Figure 11	Company I, First Infantry, at Calumet during railroad strikes, 1894. Courtesy of the Chicago Historical Society. Photographer: Unknown. iCHi-39229.	163
Figure 12	Pana-Virden strikes, ING members escorting a train, 1898. Courtesy of the Abraham Lincoln Presidential Library. Photographer: Unknown.	173
Figure 13	ING members patrolling the stockade at Virden, 1898. Courtesy of the Abraham Lincoln Presidential Library. Photographer: Unknown.	174
Figure 14	African American Officers of the Eighth Infantry, Camp Lincoln, 1903. From left to right, top row: Edward S. Miller, unidentified man, James S. Nelson. Bottom row: Major Allen A. Wesley, Colonel John R. Marshall, James H. Johnson. Courtesy of the Abraham Lincoln Presidential Library. Photographer: Guy Mathis, Guy Mathis Collection.	197
Figure 15	New Eighth Infantry Armory, 1915. Courtesy of the Chicago Historical Society. Photographer: Chicago Daily News. Glass negative DN-0064686.	205

Graph

Figure E.1	ING membership vs. days of strike policing	221

Maps

Figure J.1	1874 distribution of state militia companies in Illinois by city.	229
Figure J.2	1876 distribution of state militia companies in Illinois by city.	230

Acknowledgments

One of the questions I have been asked most frequently in the course of working on this book is how I came to select the history of the militias and National Guards as the subject of my research. The answer that I have always been pleased to give is that my interest in the militias and the National Guards developed when I was a student at Kalamazoo College, in Kalamazoo, Michigan, while taking my required junior seminar as a history major. I was just back from my foreign study experience in Madrid, and the seminar that year was devoted to the Gilded Age and the Progressive Era. I loved my time in Spain and decided to select the Spanish American War for my research paper. My professor, David Strauss, suggested that I check out the local depository of the archives of the state of Michigan. I found almost *four hundred* letters in their Spanish American War collection. That this remarkable collection was available to me was a twist of fate. One of the handful of National Guard regiments to make it to Cuba in time to participate in the brief period of fighting on the island was from southwestern Michigan, where my college is located.

Those letters were my first real contact with extensive primary documents, and I found them engrossing. I was completely taken in by the young men who wrote home to the sugar-beet farming fathers of Paw Paw and their shopkeeping mothers of Grand Haven, detailing their newly acquired, first-hand experiences with war. I decided to make these young men the subject of my senior paper, and I approached one of the archivists at the main state archive in East Lansing for assistance with my project. When I told him of my plans, he told me that everyone knew about the Michigan 33rd and suggested that I look into the Michigan Naval Militia.

So I did. What I discovered in the process was not only a love of primary research, but much that interested me in this particular story as well. I became fascinated that the young men of privilege (for that is who formed the Detroit companies of the Michigan Naval Militia) should devote such time and effort in peacetime to creating a naval reserve that was clearly unsought by the Navy or its supporters in Washington, DC.

Later on, the state of Michigan archivist was kind enough to remember me and my project, and he invited me to submit a proposal to the Michigan sesquicentennial military history lecture series. Late in my senior year I gave my first academic paper to an audience that consisted of two National Guard officers, my parents and siblings, and one good friend, Molly Horrigan, who hung around over spring break to hear me. Professor John Wickstrom welcomed me back to "K" many years later as a newly minted Ph.D., for which I will always be grateful.

I carried my interest in the phenomenon of the late-nineteenth century National Guards into graduate school at the University of Chicago and in time decided to make the Guards the subject of my dissertation. My advisers, Kathleen Conzen and Michael Geyer, were quick to pick up on my enthusiasm and offered invaluable advice, criticism, and encouragement, from proposal through defense and after. I owe the most profound thanks to Kathleen Conzen for her guidance and support over the course of many years. During my time at Chicago, I also received help and counsel from Neil Harris, Tom Holt, Rashid Khalildi, Ron Inden, Rachel Fulton, Bill Novak, and Leora Ausslander. George Chauncey read a few chapters-in-progress and gave me some excellent suggestions. I also owe a debt of gratitude to the participants of the various workshops of which Chicago's graduate program is justly proud. The participants and speakers from Feminist Theory Workshop that ran in the late 1980s and early 1990s shaped my thinking more than I realized at the time, and to Sheri Ortner in particular I want to say, many, many years later, that I understand now the purpose of reclaiming the hag, in a way that was impossible for someone as young as I was then. I also owe tremendous thanks to the members of the Graduate Student Reading and Writing Workshop and the Social History Workshop, whose comments much improved the chapters I submitted there, and contributed to my growth as a scholar and an historian.

Many friends and fellow students read and reread portions, or the entirety, of the dissertation. I must especially thank Alexandra Gillen, from whom I learned the basics of the Little Red Schoolhouse program, and whose generous time and commentary on my work I can never fully acknowledge or repay. I would also like to thank Maureen Harp, Kate Chavigny, Julie Hessler, Nyan Shah, Elizabeth Dale, Kathy Brosnan, Mort Ames, Lendol Calder, and Fred Bietler. I am also grateful to Nahum Chandler, Kate Hamerton, Alex Dracolby, Andrew Cohen, David Tanenhaus, and Mark Schmeller. Sally Schuler and Stuart Glennen offered friendship and so much more, and Sally began my very first databases, a gift of her time that has grown substantially in importance to this project over the years.

Beyond Chicago, I would like to thank in particular John Shy, David Montgomery, and Jerry Cooper—all of whom provided information and encouragement at crucial moments. Military historians have never known quite what to do with me, as a social historian interested in the peacetime National Guards, but they have nonetheless offered help and support along the way, particularly at The Ohio State University Graduate Student Conference in Military History. Labor historians have also been stumped, more than once, by my interest in the "bad guys," but again they have offered support and advice when I needed it, and I would like to thank in particular the participants and organizers of the Pullman Centennial History Conference, from whom I learned so much. I would also like to thank Jodie Vandenberg-Daves, Kurt Liechtle, Victor Macias-Gonzalez, Mari Trine, and Sharon Wood their conversation, friendship, and advice, as historians and as colleagues. In Minnesota I have profited from the suggestions of the Twin Ports Historians, including Neil Storch, Pat Maus, and Dick Huddleson. I am also grateful to Tim Hoogland of the Minnesota Historical Society for his support and encouragement.

The research for my dissertation was supported by a U.S. Army Center for Military History Doctoral Fellowship, and by the Harry Barnard Dissertation Fellowship of the University of Chicago. I also received much help from the staff of the National Guard Association of the United States, whose headquarters are located in Washington, DC. Archivists at the Illinois State Archives, the Chicago Historical Society, the Abraham Lincoln Presidential Museum and Library, the National Archives—particularly at the old Suitland Annex—all provided assistance and encouragement at key moments.

A small research grant from Kalamazoo College, and a more substantial Grant-in-Aid from the University of Minnesota allowed me to complete the databases that undergird a number of my conclusions about who was in the ING over the years, and I am very grateful for the support. I would like to thank all of the students who handled data entry over the years, in particular Sam Litman who did far more than most because of his generosity of spirit and his interest in the project's outcome.

As the project wended its way from dissertation to book, I have many more people to thank. Jerry Cooper's extensive knowledge of the National Guards enriched my own when he offered his support and his insightful commentary as a manuscript reviewer. Colleagues at the University of Minnesota Duluth, whose friendship, counsel, and advice have enriched the book include Anna-Marie Roos, Mitra Emad, Deborah Plechner, Larry Knopp, Krista Twu, Pat Farrell, Scott Laderman, and Rosemary Stanfield-Johnson. Members of the Feminist Pedogogy workshop, including Beth Bartlett, Maureen Tobin-Stanley, Joan Varney, and Gesa Zinn have been a source of strength and wisdom, for which I am very grateful. Stacey Stark, director of the Geographic Information Sciences Laboratory at the University of Minnesota Duluth, prepared the maps that appear in the appendix of this volume. I must also thank Sandy Crooms and Maggie Diehl at The Ohio State University Pres, who took my manuscript and turned it into the book before you.

Finally I must thank my family for all their support—emotional and otherwise—over the years. My aunt and uncle, Mary and Mike Curzan, housed and fed me more than once as I visited the national archives, and they offered excellent advice and friendship along the way. My siblings, John, Mary, and Rachel, have been excellent cheerleaders. My parents, Robert and Susan Hannah, made all of this possible—and to them I offer my deepest and most heartfelt thanks.

My husband, Drew Digby, read every page of this book so many times that he knows it as well as, if not better than, I do myself, and his loving criticism and commentary have to a large degree shaped the final product. And last, but hardly least, our sons Shaw and Bruck have given me much joy, even as their lives have been shaped by the rhythms of this book.

Introduction

In the last three decades of the nineteenth century, American men of all ages, ethnicities, and economic positions seized on the antebellum tradition of the volunteer militia company as a vehicle to negotiate and act out their crucial concerns of manhood and citizenship. The resolution of the first concern depended on the definition, meanings, and behaviors assigned to the concept of manhood, a conception that was itself undergoing rapid mutation as a consequence of industrialization.[1] The resolution of the second, the issue of citizenship, was, if anything, more difficult to achieve than a secure verdict on the meaning of manhood. Where citizenship was previously clearly linked with and dependent on the definition of white manhood, in the postwar decades that coupling was fracturing under a variety of strains.[2] The scattered old-style volunteer militia companies were not necessarily the solution to either problem, but new members quickly discovered that volunteering to serve with their local militia company could supply meaning to either question, and often to both questions, of manhood and of citizenship. As the militia evolved into the National Guard over the next three decades, members grew ever more articulate about the connections they drew between their volunteer service, their citizenship, and their manhood, and the ways these connections secured their identities as men and as citizens.

Not many historians currently view the nineteenth-century state militias in the context of contemporary debates over manhood or citizenship—perhaps because the National Guards are today so clearly an integral part of the regular military, perhaps because most historians encounter the nineteenth-century National Guard only briefly as it is being dismissed as a tool of management in labor-capital disputes, if they ever encounter the militias at all. But most late nineteenth-century state militias, or as they eventually called themselves, state National Guards, did not enjoy the patronage of their state governments, or especially of the federal government, to any significant or reliable degree until *after* their members had made the case for the importance of their movement to the nation.³ Volunteers brought the National Guards into existence before their states found a use for them, and long before their states were willing to support them generously. National Guard members gave their personal time and provided their own money to build their movement from scattered companies into an integrated and organized all-volunteer reserve army, and they did it virtually unaided by state or federal agencies or cash. Considering these points, how did this organization that is today so casually, if mistakenly, accepted as a natural part of the nineteenth-century landscape come to be? Why were so many men willing to volunteer so much of their time and effort to the creation of an unsought—and, from many points of view, unwelcome—reserve army? The short answer is obviously because the volunteers wanted to. Uncovering the complex of concerns that created that desire is the purpose of this study. In brief, the National Guard movement is best understood as one of a host of associations and organizations late nineteenth-century American men devised to help them negotiate their location and purpose in the strange new world of industrial Capitalism.

The National Guards were unique among those organizations, however, in the ways they explicitly linked manhood and citizenship through the figure of the citizen-soldier. They were also unique for the ways they linked older men and young men, middle-class men and working-class men, men from a wide range of ethnic backgrounds, and even white and African American men through their voluntary membership in the same larger organization. The Civil War served as the touchstone that created this unusually accommodating and broadly based organization. The Union Army, in particular, provided a rationale and a model for the volunteers to use as they built a new organization on top of older, antebellum militia traditions. The Civil War also emerged as one of the increasingly dominant images of male coming-of-age in the later half of the nineteenth century.⁴ Many Americans came to see the war as a rite of passage, as the moment when millions of American boys, not least the newly freed slaves-cum-Union-soldiers, became men as a result of their battlefield experiences. In addition, many Americans came to perceive the war itself as a coming-of-age moment for the nation, even as a millennial moment, when a young nation reconfirmed its commitments to freedom, liberty, and equality.⁵ It was also, of course, the ultimate argument for full African American citizenship.⁶ A powerful blend of patriotism, nationalism, violence, and gunplay fueled these ideas and presented acute challenges to all Americans in the long postwar peace. How were young men to come of age without a battlefield testing of their own? How were men who felt most alive during the bloody war years to hold onto that image of themselves? How were African American men to retain and enlarge the gains of their service in the Union Army?

The antebellum model of volunteer militia companies provided an obvious and convenient place for all these men to look when seeking a resolution to their specific personal concerns; the companies could be at once a rite of passage, a link to the past, and an expression of citizenship. Once gathered there, the new postwar volunteers discovered that they shared enough of a language and vision of soldiering and its importance to both manhood and citizenship that they could create and sustain a larger single organization that would house and shelter them all while each pursued his own more particular agenda. Postwar militia volunteers built an organization that could allow all of these groups to prosper, not only in the sense that each saw in the institution a way to validate or claim an identity that was otherwise difficult to realize, but also in their ability to gain from the proximity to others with similar visions. They discovered a synergy that allowed and even forced them to create an entirely new sort of volunteer reserve army and then press it upon an ambivalent nation.

The history of the Illinois National Guard (ING) from 1870 to 1917 is an excellent subject for a study aimed at recovering the complexity and importance of the development of the National Guards. Because each has its own quirks, no one state militia can replicate the experiences of all of them, but for a variety of reasons, the ING contains within itself examples of nearly every kind of incident that any other state militia experienced. Thus, in one sense, the ING is quite unrepresentative. However, it also means that the ING can function as an extremely useful stand-in for the whole of the disparate state National Guard experiences of the late nineteenth and early twentieth centuries. The ING of these decades contained within itself great diversity—racially, ethnically, economically, and regionally—and its members devised ways to function successfully together without cracking along ethnic or racial lines. Because of the diversity of membership, a study of the ING offers the rare opportunity to examine the ways in which both ethnicity and race functioned within a single organization. The ING is particularly interesting with regard to the persistence of its African American members. Only Ohio and Massachusetts had as long and as steady an African American presence in their state forces, and in the case of Massachusetts, African

American Guardsmen were always a tiny minority. Neither Pennsylvania nor New York, to name two states often put forward as models for understanding the whole of the National Guards in this period, can boast a similar record of African American membership.[7] The record of the Eighth Illinois United States Volunteers, composed entirely of African American men, during the Spanish American War in particular, is among the more interesting and significant African American military experiences of the entire era. Because its members were entirely African Americans, up to and including their colonel, the Eighth Illinois USV was the object of tremendous scrutiny, as it was treated as a test case for the capabilities of African American commissioned officers—as much by African Americans themselves as by any other set of observers.[8]

The ING also engaged in the full range of National Guard activities during this period, from strikes to race riots, through civic parades and social activities to wartime service, in a way that few other individual state guards did. The Massachusetts NG, for example, never served in a strike after 1877, and even the Pennsylvania, New York, and Ohio NGs saw significantly less strike service than the ING.[9] As a result, ING officers and men grappled with strike service more intensely and over a longer period of time than any other state NG members. Their uniquely intensive experiences provide a deep body of evidence from which to understand how strike service shaped the development of the National Guards as a whole across the time period. This experience, nevertheless, is necessarily strongly rooted in the very local nature of strike service, and it is a story that can be fully explored only by close examination of the ways individual instances of strike service, within a single organization within a single state, built over time into a body of opinion and action.

The state of Illinois provided the ING much less financial support than either New York or Massachusetts, to pick two other prominent and well-funded state forces of the era, provided their state militia organizations, and the ING's relative impecuniousness is another area in which their distinctiveness makes them a useful source for understanding the larger National Guard movement.[10] Given the ING's lower levels of state funding, individual ING company members turned to their communities for fund-raising and supported lobbying efforts at both the state and federal levels. Their need for funds forced them to articulate often and regularly what their purpose and appeal was. A second, and related, result was the prominence of ING officers in the national-level lobbying organizations as they turned early and consistently toward the federal government, seeking support for their organization and their mission to train a reserve army for the nation. Illinois National Guard members emerged as powerful spokesmen for their organization, both at the state and the national level, in large part because of their financial needs.

Finally, a close social history of the various companies and regiments emphasizes the local nature of the Guard throughout this period, and would be lost in a study that did not focus clearly on a single, statewide organization. The local nature of the organization, and the myriad of ways that guardsmen and their companies were deeply embedded within their local communities, makes the National Guard movement important to any social history of the nineteenth-century United States. The broader histories that look at the Guard across the country necessarily lose emphasis on this strong tie, even where it is acknowledged, and this loss of emphasis has contributed, albeit unintentionally, to the popular notion of National Guardsmen of the era as faceless, corporate thugs, and not as varied and interesting men who devoted large amounts of time and money to an experience of manhood and citizenship that they valued. A close social history of the ING offers historians a vehicle for exploring the manifold concerns of American men at the turn of the last century.

The Illinois militia, functionally nonexistent in 1870, grew quickly to be among the largest in the nation by the 1880s. It appealed to men of widely different economic backgrounds, ethnicities, races, and regions around the state, successfully recruiting up to a third of its membership in any given year. As a result of the sudden and sustained growth, long-term members successfully lobbied to reshape the state laws governing the militia and to increase state, and eventually, federal budgets for the upkeep of the militia. The ING also served in more than two dozen strike interventions, allowing members to take the full measure of the consequences of this kind of service and ultimately deciding to find ways to minimize their politically untenable role in the maintenance of domestic order. Important as these lobbying and order maintenance duties were to ING members, however, the overwhelming bulk of an ING member's time was devoted to ceremonial, social, and competitive pursuits. These activities lay at the heart of their public persona within their local communities, and through them ING members created an organization that at once tested and confirmed their claims to manliness and citizenship.

To fully appreciate the fundamental newness of the organizations created after the Civil War, the history of the Illinois militia must be situated in the broader context of the history of militias in the United States up to the 1870s. What follows is a brief overview of the legal foundations of the militia, and then a brief summary of the multiple ways that communities and states met their legal obligations with regard to militia law from the colonial period until the post-Civil War era.

The legal foundations of the modern American militia lie in the Constitution, and as with all political and military authority in the United States, control is divided. The particularly complex and ambiguous position of the militia as established by the Constitution in 1789 has plagued the system to the present day. Congress has the power to organize, arm, and discipline the militia. The states have the power to appoint the officers and train the militia, according to the discipline established by Congress. When the militia is called into federal service, the president is its commander-in-chief. However, Congress must call the militia into federal service and can do so only to execute the laws of the Union, suppress insurrections, or to repel invasion. The rest of the time, the militia is under the command of the state governors and responsive to their calls to duty under conditions determined by their respective state constitutions.[11]

After ratification of the Constitution, the militia laws could be, but seldom were, altered by legislation. In 1792 Congress passed two acts concerning the militia that would not be superseded until 1903. The first provided that all free, white, able-bodied men between 18 and 45 owed military service to state and nation, and that they should provide themselves with the wherewithal to do so.[12] This act also stipulated that the states should all have similar organization tables, if it was convenient, and report on the condition of their militia once a year to the federal government.[13] The second act delegated to the president some of Congress's authority to call the militia under certain conditions. One purpose of these acts was more explicitly to create a body that could be considered and used as a national military reserve. The states all eventually followed the lead of the national government and established their own militia acts, similar in content to the federal statutes. In subsequent years, it rapidly became clear that supporting the militia was going to require a more serious commitment on the part of both the state and the national government. In 1808 Congress appropriated $200,000 annually to be apportioned out to the states to buy arms on the basis of the returns sent by the state adjutant generals to the secretary of war. Thereafter, despite repeated calls for reform, no more laws were passed at the federal level for the rest of the century.[14] The development of the militia from then until the twentieth century lay in the hands of the state governments.[15]

After the Spanish American War (1898–99), the federal government once again began to play a crucial role in the evolution of the National Guards as Congress passed reform legislation, backed with federal money, in 1903, 1908, and 1914. The result of this flurry of activity was what is now known as the federalization of the National Guards, that is, the ever-increasing integration of what were once independent state militias into the national defense structure, until, by the late twentieth century, the National Guards had become a virtually indistinguishable arm of the U.S. Army and its reserve systems. The federalization of the state National Guards in the early twentieth century naturally led to a decrease in the importance of state legislation concerning militias and to an uneasy sharing of authority over the National Guard system. All legislative action was at the state level between 1870 and 1903, and Illinois was a relative hotbed of experimentation and development; state law regarding the militias was revised or replaced no fewer than five times.[16] The experimentation and development of legislation at the state level during these years provides yet another rationale for looking closely at a single state.

A challenge for historians of the United States in addressing the militia lies in the confusion surrounding the use of the term, despite its legal basis, caused by different applications of it over time and space. "Militia," by definition, refers to the military service owed to the state (or community) by every able-bodied man in the area—and historically this definition meant exactly that, a duty owed only by males. In the American context, "militia" also refers to all the various permutations of systems for organizing civilian military obligations to the state that have developed over time. For example, owing to the precarious existence of the early settlements in the first phases of British colonization of North America, a rigorous training schedule was initiated for the entire militia complement—that is, all able-bodied men of the locale. As time passed, settlement increased, dangers faded, and general militia training fell to a few days a year. In order to maintain some defense force in the case of emergency, younger men were sometimes required to train together on a more regular basis. They became the militia company in the region, yet they were also the nucleus for the larger militia if the need arose. This pattern repeated itself over and over as the population expanded.[17]

The next phase of militia development began once frontier dangers faded away. Groups sprang up that voluntarily trained together more frequently and with more ceremony than did the larger militia pool. The general pool came to be referred to as the "common" or, if records were kept of available men, the "enrolled" militia, whereas the more active bands were called "volunteer" militia. The Minute Men, initially established in and around Boston in the mid-seventeenth century, are an example of the latter. After the Revolution, volunteer militia companies were highly visible in public celebrations and popular with many groups.

Companies were formed by wealthy young men, ethnic or immigrant men (particularly Irish), craftsmen, or clerks. Thus, a distinction between the volunteer militia and the common militia existed almost from the beginning of the colonial period and remained significant across time.[18]

After the Civil War, some understandings of militia faded, and more terms were added to differentiate various voluntary reserve systems from one another. Enrolling had gradually disappeared from practice during the antebellum period, and by the end of the Civil War, the old common militia had ceased to function. In the late 1870s, as new men re-energized the volunteer militias, the term National Guard came into wide use. It was adopted from the French term for the national enrolled militia, but in practice in the United States it referred to the active volunteer militia bands chartered or recognized by the various state governments. By the turn of the century, most state militias had formally adopted the name "National Guard."[19] Yet in 1916, the Army succeeded in establishing, in addition, a national reserve system, separate from that of the states and under its own control.[20] However, all these terms—Militia, Volunteer Militia, National Guard, Active Militia, Reserves—are often used interchangeably in primary sources, in histories devoted only to the civilian reserve structure, and in wider histories of the U.S. armed forces.[21]

The names are used interchangeably because distinctions among all these groups were easily blurred. Whenever situations demanded larger numbers than one or two volunteer bands could supply—as in periods of Indian fighting or the various more formal wars of the seventeenth, eighteenth, and nineteenth centuries—the common militia was called upon to make up the difference, but not indiscriminately; a call would be issued, and volunteers, draftees, or their substitutes would join the existing bands or create a new one. The whole agglomeration was, and is, referred to as the "militia." Thus, whenever large numbers of militia converged, the ranks could be filled with members of established volunteer bands, recent volunteers, and compulsory volunteers, but rarely, if ever, the entire available complement of the common or enrolled militia. Variations on these methods of supplying the necessary men have been used in nearly all wars of the United States.[22]

In the early nineteenth century, then, the older, general state militias withered across the eastern seaboard and in the settled regions of the northwest territories, until the last remnants became an object for mockery when they assembled for their increasingly desultory (and often drunken) annual training days.[23] The popular volunteer companies correspondingly became more visible and impressive. Initially, these volunteer companies owed little to state governments, but with the passing of the general militia's effectiveness in the 1840s and 1850s, many state legislatures began to recognize and support the volunteer companies as their active state militia, usually with some form of financial assistance. In return, the volunteers could be called out for riot duty, prisoner protection, and later, returning fugitive slaves. The relationship between state governments and volunteer militias varied from region to region; in contested frontier areas, the militias were distinctly more likely to be involved in military action. In 1856, for example, the Law and Order (pro-slavery) party in Missouri and the free-state party both formed territorial militias that spent four months during the summer fighting and raiding across the territory over the question of the political future of the state.[24] Despite the events in western areas however, the volunteer companies of the eastern seaboard and settled areas of the Old Northwest chiefly devoted their time to public displays.[25]

During the Civil War, the volunteer companies and territorial militias joined the Confederate or Union armies, and what remained of the militia became both the home guard, filled with boys and older men, and the recruiting structure for the volunteers who made up the bulk of both armies. After the war, the hundreds of thousands of men who were mustered into the Union and Confederate armies via their state militia systems, but were mustered out of state service and into federal service to serve during the war, were mustered out of the federal service without re-entering the services of their respective states. At the end of the process of mustering out and demobilizing state regiments, most states were left without any officially recognized, active state troops. The history of state military forces might well have ended there in 1865–66, with state regiments empty and no new military threat in sight to re-energize citizen interest in state militias. The South was the exception; militias were created in 1865–66 and were promptly filled by Confederate army veterans, right down to the worn uniforms. Congressional reconstruction eliminated those militias and allowed for the formation of African American militias. This action provoked further racial violence, as private "rifle companies" sprang up across the South to combat the perceived threat of armed African Americans. Eventually, the defeated southern states were denied the authority to establish militias at all until their constitutions received congressional approval. Once "redeemed" or returned to white democratic control, southern state militias followed trends already established in the Northeast and the Midwest.[26] Outside the South, most state governments were uninterested in funding any military structure at all, whether universal militia or volunteer, in the decade between 1865 and 1875.[27]

And yet, in the early 1870s, volunteer militias reemerged across the northern states. Some outfits retained the name of a volunteer company established before the war, though doing so was common mostly among the long-established volunteer units of the older seaboard cities. For the most part, the volunteer companies of the 1870s and 1880s were new organizations without prewar histories. Although at first the new companies modeled themselves after antebellum volunteer militias, members quickly discarded those models in favor of new organizational forms at both the state and the national levels. By the early 1880s, the state militias, or as they were increasingly called, the National Guards, had over 80,000 members across the country and organized lobbies seeking increases in both their state and federal funds. In 1898, the National Guards were the organizational framework for the volunteer troops raised to fight the Spanish American War, and by 1914 they constituted a federally supported reserve military force prepared to face overseas engagements. In 1916, the National Guards were mobilized for service on the Mexican border, and in the fall of 1917, the National Guards formed the nucleus of the American expeditionary force sent to Europe to aid the allies in concluding the First World War.[28]

The history of the militia in Illinois follows the national trends. After the Civil War, the antebellum frontier-state militia structure evaporated completely in Illinois. By 1870, the governor reported to the secretary of war that Illinois had no active militia at all. In 1872, seven small volunteer companies in Illinois can be identified, each with its own name in the antebellum tradition. In 1874, the adjutant general reported twenty-five companies with slightly over 1,500 members (though he expected four to be disbanded soon); each company chose its own name and also had a company and regiment number assigned by the state. In 1880, the total strength of the Illinois National Guard (ING) was 8,254 officers and men in numbered companies and regiments.[29] This dramatic growth spurred other equally dramatic changes in the organization and in the state laws that governed the militia, reflecting, and sometimes leading, the pace of development of state militias nationwide.

The Illinois volunteer militia was both familiar and flexible to Americans of the late nineteenth century, and as an institution it appealed to men of dramatically different backgrounds living widely disparate lives from the 1870s through the turn of the century. The militia certainly continued to appeal to men of the middle and upper classes, much as it had done for decades.[30] For example, in 1874 the adjutant general of Illinois noted that "at the present time there is being organized in Chicago a regiment composed of the elite of the city, which, from indications, will become a permanent organization."³¹ However, if indebtedness is one marker of less elite membership, then most companies were filled with common men. The Second Regiment, formed in Chicago by preexisting, predominately Irish companies at the end of 1875 and early 1876 (because they couldn't get into the new elite regiment), was $8,700.00 in debt by the end of 1876.³² One early Chicago company was so poor the members couldn't afford to rent an armory space large enough for the entire group and had to break into to smaller detachments for weekly drill.³³ Most of the new companies of 1875–76 were in small towns, and they also struggled to make ends meet. For example, the Mason City Guards raised sixty dollars by hosting two balls during their first ten weeks as an active organization and considered themselves off to a rousing start.³⁴ African American men in Illinois created military companies whenever and wherever they could find the numerical strength and community support to do so. In 1870–71, the Hannibal Guards formed in Chicago, and in the state capital the adjutant general commissioned the African American officers of Company C in 1869, and the Springfield Zouaves sometime between 1870 and 1872.³⁵ In 1872 the McLean County Guards (colored), formed by residents surrounding Bloomington, Illinois, joined the state militia.³⁶ The Sixteenth Battalion, made up of two Chicago African American companies, joined the ING in 1878. The ethnic and racial identification of companies, native-born Americans, Irish, Bohemian, Scottish, and African American, also show how broad the appeal could be.³⁷ When the statewide inspecting officers made any mention of members' occupations across the regiments in their annual reports during the 1870s and 1880s, it seems that the enlisted men at least were primarily clerks, farmers, skilled tradesmen, or small merchants. Even so, inspecting officers and enlistment rosters make it clear that professionals and laborers also found a place in the militias.³⁸

At the turn of the century, the picture of wide regional, ethnic, class, and racial background among Illinois militia members remained virtually unchanged. The socially prestigious First Regiment, ING, was still the home of men from relatively privileged backgrounds, particularly at the level of the commissioned officers. White-collar workers, especially in the job category "Clerk," represented almost half of the enlisted men as well. Of course, the rest of the enlisted men were primarily laborers or skilled tradesmen, so even in this most elite of regiments, a wide variety of men found a place.³⁹ (See appendix A.) In contrast, at the same time, Company A, Third Infantry, ING, of Dekalb, was almost entirely working-class in composition.⁴⁰ (See appendix B.) New professions also found a place in the National Guard. In 1916 the First Cavalry, ING, had so strong a component of journalists that when they served on the Mexican border that year they immediately set about publishing a weekly newspaper called *The Illinois Cavalryman* (using the presses of a local San Antonio paper), which started at eight full pages and grew to twelve by the end of their service thirteen weeks later.⁴¹ The African American Ninth Battalion joined the ING in 1894.⁴² These diverse patterns of company formation, rural and urban, rich and poor, ethnic, Anglo, and African American, continued through the call to active duty in 1917.

The benefits and rewards that kept such a large cross-section of men active in the Guard are striking because membership appears to have worked its transformation and confirmation of manhood and citizenship fairly quickly. The vast majority of enlisted men and officers stayed in the ING for three years or less.⁴³ In 1908, the adjutant general of Illinois estimated that over the preceding five years, the ING lost, on average, 20 percent of its almost 6,000 strong membership annually.⁴⁴ Thus, many years ING officers were successfully recruiting, on average, 1,200 new members. Their need for new recruits may also have helped contribute to their broad definition of soldiering, a definition that could attract and hold men of widely divergent backgrounds and tastes. That they were able to keep their reserve army at a steady membership while contending with rapid turnover in their troops reinforces the power of their representation of the ING as an important and meaningful experience in the lives of American men, as well as for the life of the nation. The fact that most men served only a single term of service also allowed the organizations' long-term leaders, those officers and enlisted men who served nine or more years, to shape the ING in their own vision of a reserve army.

The ING's active membership of roughly 5,000 to 8,000 men between 1876 and 1917 was supported by a combination of annual appropriations from the state treasury, appropriations that slowly increased over time, and extensive fund-raising activities in the various communities that supported individual guard companies.⁴⁵ These developments placed the ING near the top of guard organizations nationwide in terms of size and somewhat further down in terms of state funding, a position that the ING maintained through 1917.⁴⁶ (See appendix I.) Illinois had both large industrial and railroad centers—most notably, Chicago and East St. Louis—as well as a significant rural population and scores of coal mining operations located throughout the state. The ING was called to active duty during the nationwide strikes of 1877 and 1894 and also served during more than twenty coal strikes policing public order and protecting lives and property between 1877 and 1900, more than in any other state of the union.⁴⁷

Despite the profound importance and impact of strike policing on the development of the National Guards, especially in Illinois, strike policing was not the stimulant of National Guard growth. Membership in the Illinois militia surged in the year preceding July 4, 1876, and when paired with the reports of the adjutant general and histories of company formation, clearly roots the motivation for company formation in local patriotic and personal impulses. The great strikes of August 1877 arrived only after the Illinois volunteer militia was so large and so well organized that their lobbyists had already achieved the first of many militia reforms with the 1876 Illinois militia law overhaul. Guardsmen themselves claimed in later histories of the 1870s and 1880s that they were in training to be soldiers, to serve their nation as reserve troops to be committed in wartime to augmenting the small regular army. Although some Guard historians did argue that the presence of the Guard in turn had an effect on strikes and striking workers, this development was clearly a *result*, not the cause, of company formation. The Guard historians also claimed that the members were serving their communities and their nation by the act of military training, not just as potential soldiers, but also as molders of men and exemplars of manly responsibility and centennial patriotism. They applied the lessons of soldiering—self-discipline, obedience, healthy habits, and personal initiative for both self and group improvement—to the most desirable qualities of citizens and of masculinity.[48]

To state that policing capital-labor disputes was not the central aim or function of the National Guards is not, however, to deny the powerful connections between the role of state policing assigned to the Guards and their development as an institution. The history of strike-related active duty service on the part of the Illinois National Guard is a complex and fragmented record. Guardsmen could be nonpartisan or even prolabor in attitude and still ultimately contribute to the success of management in its contest with strikers.[49] This inescapable irony frames the history of strike interventions in Illinois from the standpoint of the Illinois National Guard from 1879 onward. It shaped aspects of the ING's identity in numerous and contradictory ways. It contributed to the cycle of growth in the ING over time. It led the ING to formulate specific tactics for dealing with strike interventions and for negotiating their relationships with local governing authorities during such service. After twenty years of experience in strike interventions, the ING successfully redefined their intrastate mission from policing "disorder" into policing "disaster," preferably natural but possibly social. This redefinition released the ING from responsibility for all but the most extreme cases of urban rioting and still allowed the ING to argue they were fulfilling their domestic responsibilities as outlined by the federal and state constitutions. This rhetorical and intellectual move allowed the ING to retain their claims to the intrastate service that continued to provide them with at least some of their rationale for their increasing requests for public funds. It also allowed them to direct the bulk of their resources, time, and public relations efforts to their self-identified primary mission to serve as a reserve army for the nation.

When a county sheriff or city mayor appealed to the governor for state troops, and only they had the authority to do so, to intervene in their county (or city) to restore an order that they were unable to maintain, implicit in that request was a confession of their inability to handle the strike situation themselves. In essence, it was an admission of weakness and incompetence. That one party to the issues surrounding the strike often considered this process to have been subverted by a different party illustrates the uncertain relationships between local and state authority. The history of Illinois strike interventions is fraught with tension between the local sheriffs and the ING commanders who arrived in their jurisdictions to take over the responsibility for order maintenance. The uneasy alliances and continual bickering about legitimate and illegitimate need for state aid surrounding the policing of disputes between capital and labor highlight far more issues of governing authority and responsibility in the late nineteenth century than they do the purpose of the ING. Illinois National Guard leaders could only hope and strive to escape the political fallout as unscathed as possible. On those occasions when Illinois governors did call the ING into state service, they ordered the militia to the scene of the strike to restore a public order that local authority was temporarily unable to sustain. Upon the restoration of order and the remanding of any captured criminal elements into local police hands, state troops returned to their homes, and the local authorities were expected to carry on themselves.

As their organization grew in size, active duty assignments, and funding, members of the ING also played an important role in the professional development of the National Guard movement. The ING developed summer camp programs, competitive exams for promotion, and prizes for marksmanship during the late 1870s and the 1880s. The ING developed specialized companies of artillery and cavalry as early as 1877 and continued to follow closely professional army innovations. The ING developed signal corps, bicycle corps, and medical corps in the 1890s and even predated the US Army in the innovative use of camp cooks during training rather than requiring each enlisted man to prepare his own food. Illinois National Guard officers were also key players in national organizations attempting to modify federal policy in the early 1880s and especially at the turn of the century. The ING had a diverse membership, made up of socially prestigious units, companies with strong ethnic associations, a steady procession of African American companies, and companies based in cities like Chicago to villages like Lincoln or Mason City. The ING was an organization rocked by the crises of its time, and yet it survived to prosper and grow into the role of reserve army in training at a time when it was far from obvious that this was the natural direction for development of state militia forces. Although no study of one state guard can claim to stand for all, a study of the ING that situates the organization firmly in their local context addresses all the significant issues surrounding the flourishing National Guard movement in the late nineteenth and early twentieth centuries.

This book begins with a close look at the decade of the 1870s and the revival of the volunteer militia in Illinois, a movement closely linked to the centennial celebrations of 1876, examining the early development of the Illinois National Guard as volunteers struggled to articulate their purposes and roles. It was in the 1870s that Illinois volunteers began to rely on language and images of manly men and responsible citizenship to explain and define their organization. Chapter 2 documents and explores the overwhelming importance of the social and public life of ING members to their identity as manly, patriotic citizens and to the survival of their organizations. The following chapter explores the way ING leaders and members responded to the task of policing strike-related violence between 1870 and 1890, tentatively embracing their role as stalwart protectors of public order even as they learned about the dangers of local political currents and racial violence. Chapter 4 focuses on the impact of the growing professionalization of ING training practices, and the resulting switch to marksmanship rather than drill as the preferred competitive sport, as the organization changed from focusing primarily on serving their communities as models and creators of manly citizenship to a much more individually focused form of self-improvement and national duty. Chapter 5 discusses the way ING members embraced service in the Spanish American War as both the test and the validation of their claims to be both patriotic, manly citizens and reliable soldiers. Chapter 6 returns to the subject of strike duty and the reasons that the ING leadership eventually turned firmly away from this sort of mission lest they be trapped forever by policing rather than soldiering as their primary identity. The final chapter contains a discussion of the political and financial position of the Guard, with particular emphasis on their lobbying efforts at both the state and federal levels, as guardsmen grew ever more nationalized in focus and professional in their approach to soldiering. The chapter also considers the potential implications of the growing federalization and accompanying pull away from the local communities on the Guards during the first decade-and-a-half of the twentieth century.

CHAPTER 1

Illinois Militia Revival in the 1870s

Be true to yourselves, be true to your country, be true to your God, be true to that old flag, and be true to the ladies of Springfield.[1]
—Governor John L. Beveridge

In 1875, Governor John L. Beveridge of Illinois challenged the members of a Springfield militia company to be true to themselves, to their country, to their God, to their flag, and to the ladies of Springfield. Beveridge left it to the company members to decide how to demonstrate that they were true men and true citizens, either to themselves or to the ladies. The members of the company might have found this a frustrating task because as the nineteenth century entered its final quarter, ideals of manly behavior and attributes of citizenship were changing rapidly. Literate Americans simultaneously held that American manhood, by which they generally meant the manhood of white, middle-class men, was increasingly under assault by their own civilization, and at the same time they were certain that the increasing power and importance of the United States was a direct result of the manliness of American men. Historians, particularly historians of women and of African Americans, have also made it abundantly clear that for all their concerns about the energy-sapping effects of modernity, white middle- and upper-class American men remained fully in charge of all they surveyed and brooked no challenges to their authority or autonomy.[2] In the midst of living through this period ripe with contradictions, paradox, and challenge, American men of all backgrounds struggled to find new ways to preserve, remake, and expand the numbers of American men who could be rated as manly.[3]

The governor's audience may have been spared some of the contemporary confusion over the content of manhood, however. Governor Beveridge was addressing a specific group of men, those who had volunteered their time and effort to their local militia company. The members of the Governor's Guard had turned voluntarily to the old American tradition of the militia in search of a way to express culturally approved manliness and responsible citizenship. The men the governor was talking to did have a rough idea of what it meant to be true. They were being true to their nation and their flag by volunteering to serve in their local militia company and training themselves to support and defend the nation at need. They showed the ladies of Springfield how true they were by donning the uniform and embracing their role as handsome and manly civic performers in parades and funerals and dances and drills. They demonstrated to themselves that they were true by making a promise to serve nation and community by volunteering for military training and responsibilities, and living out these promises in their militia membership.[4]

In the early 1870s, membership in the Illinois state militia jumped from just under 250 men in 1870 to over 1,500 members by 1874.[5] The new members, who ranged from Civil War veterans to young men just coming of age and who included both white and African American men, devoted their time and effort to the task of creating volunteer militia companies throughout the state. In doing so, they embraced a traditional way to put their manliness and their claims to citizenship on public display. Individually, the volunteers had reasons that were as diverse as the men themselves, ranging from an enthusiasm for military uniforms and weapons to Civil War memorializing. Together they found a single home in the Illinois militia, and once active companies demonstrated the rewards of militia membership to local audiences, more and more companies formed. The upcoming centennial celebrations also provided a tantalizing opportunity for a public display of responsible manhood. Men from all over Illinois seized the chance to be part of the celebrations as uniformed members of their local company.[6]

Manhood on Parade

In the early 1870s, militia volunteers paraded regularly and often as they worked to establish their claims to the history and social prestige of the elite bands of citizen-soldiers of the antebellum era. They liked parades, and parading in general, because it was such an excellent way to establish their credentials as responsible and attractive men in the eyes of their communities. As a result, volunteers pounced on those special occasions that allowed members to dramatically link themselves to the nation and its military history by participating in particularly important civic events. For example, on October 15, 1874, five Illinois militia companies marched in the procession leading U.S. President Ulysses S. Grant to the unveiling of a statue of Abraham Lincoln in the Oak Ridge Cemetery, Springfield, Illinois. By marching in this particular parade, company members visibly tied themselves to two U.S. presidents and to the Union general who won the war. The University Cadets, the militia company from the Industrial University at Champaign; the Sterling City Guards; the Governor's Guard, the veteran Sherman Guards; and the Springfield Zouaves were hardly alone in the parade. They joined several other military-style fraternal organizations in the two-mile–long procession, among them the national Union veteran officers' organization, the Army of the Tennessee; the Springfield Fire Department; the German Catholic Church Society; a number of bands; and many, many carriages of national, state, and city notables, all seeking to benefit by association with national heroes.[7]

The day of the parade began with rain, almost as though "nature was weeping over the memories of the past," but by midmorning the weather had cleared, and the members of the procession began gathering in the middle of the city.[8] Residents of Springfield had decorated almost every square inch of public space with flags, banners, flowers, and evergreens, and as the participants gathered, cannons set up at the cemetery began to fire at regular intervals. The procession finally headed out just after noon and wove its way through the city, up and down all the principal business streets and with a special leg that brought all past the Lincoln home, before ending up at the cemetery just outside of town. The march took about thirty minutes, but it was an hour before the entire procession was finally through the decorated gates of the cemetery. Crowds lined the parade route and filled the cemetery; by some estimates, as many as 40,000 people came to Springfield to participate in the ceremonies or watch them. So many people were pushing into the cemetery to gain a good view of the statue and the ceremonies to come that many militia members had been detailed directly to the cemetery and crowd control. The cannon continued firing even as the many bands that were part of the parade played marching music. The sounds ceased only once the last of the parade had entered the cemetery, when the cannon and the bands fell quiet, in a silence all the more imposing for the noise that preceded it. Each division of the march separated into the areas near the statue that had been set aside for them, and the speeches, anthems, and sermons began. Bishop Waymen, of the African Methodist Episcopal Church, opened the ceremonies with a prayer, and they concluded with a song.[9]

The militia members who marched in the Springfield parade and participated in the ceremonies were able to draw on a long tradition to secure the most important spots, those closest to the dignitaries, in the parade honoring Grant and Lincoln.[10] In the early nineteenth century, militia companies had begun appearing in public parades celebrating the United States, its holidays, and its heroes.[11] By marching in these parades, militia members helped to define a form of American patriotic manliness marked by uniforms, weapons, and martial music. Members used the orderliness of their processions to set themselves off clearly from the much rowdier crowds of banner-waving craftsmen or firemen also commonly found in antebellum parades. In particular, militia members used military funeral parades—both real and symbolic, both types fully under their control and authority—to cement their position as chief arbiters of the most solemn and impressive forms of patriotic behavior. Antebellum militia members successfully claimed a special and unique patriotic authority through the "precision of the march to the cemetery" while wearing fancy dress uniforms and accompanied by bands, gongs, and rifle salutes at graveside.[12] Militia members in 1874 were able to draw on both traditions in their quest to establish their new companies in the hearts and minds of their communities.

By 1874 these prewar conventions were so well understood that reporters in Springfield reviewed the procession to the monument dedication against this standard. They knew that what they saw was a civic pageant with widely understood meaning and roles. Reporters noted that the residents of the city had dressed the set with care, draping their city in bunting and flags and constructing six triumphal arches around the center of the city. Each of the five divisions marching in the parade provided the music of at least one band—marching, brass, or drum corps.[13] The local reporters particularly enjoyed the band that accompanied the African American Springfield Zouaves. The local audiences also judged the militias' efforts, seeking signs of seriousness and military bearing and style in both costumes and well-drilled marching. Local reporters reflected these conventions when they admired the nearly 300-strong University Cadets and "their neat, unpretending uniform." Reporters also noted that the Sherman Guards were "one of the great features of the processions . . . made up exclusively of veteran soldiers, commanded by old officers, [they] wore the uniform of 1861–5, and the manual of arms and drill in use during the war."[14]

The parade marked the first public appearance of the Governor's Guard, re-formed out of another defunct Springfield company only a month previously. The new Governor's Guard won the honor of directly escorting (preceding) President Grant, Vice President Wilson, Secretary of War Belknap, and other VIPs to the ceremony. One local reporter wrote, "Not withstanding its youthfulness, [the Governor's Guard] made a creditable and dashing appearance, with its seventy-six men in imposing uniforms, and gaily caparisoned staff and drum corps."[15] Altogether, the reporter from the *Daily State Journal* concluded, "The procession made a most imposing appearance. The military with their fine uniforms . . . together with the other societies, went to make up a picture worthy of the pencil of an artist."[16]

The reporters of 1874 were alert to the diversity of men—Irish, German, native-born, Civil War veterans, college students, and African Americans—who were members of the militia companies and military-style clubs in 1874, and they made much of the variety of ethnicities and ages. In many antebellum cities, socially prestigious militia organizations had sought to define patriotism beyond the reach of the masses when they paraded in expensive uniforms with expensive guns. In Springfield in 1874, the much wider range of men who marched used this same form to illustrate their own claims to patriotic leadership and meaningful citizenship. These men embraced this older strategy for claiming their space in the public pageant with uniforms, guns, and orderly performances because in the postwar years this option appeared readily available to any male group that could organize itself into a military-style company and join in the march. In 1874, university students seeking a connection with the all-important manhood experience of soldiering, reenacting veterans recalling their own wartime experiences, and African American men reinforcing the link between their service in the Union Army and their citizenship, all used the authority of brand-new, state-associated militia companies to publicly claim their identities as men and as citizens.[17]

Militiamen Become Gentlemen

Militia members used their membership in a militia company to link their existing patriotic authority to a new social and cultural authority. For example, in March 1875, as a fund-raising and publicity-raising event, the Governor's Guard of Springfield staged the play *Color Guard* in the Springfield Opera House. According to the advertisement that ran in the papers, the play abounded in "thrilling situations, beautiful

Tableaux, Striking Military Scenes, Drills, Marches, Exciting Battles, &c., and is the most perfect and life-like representation of army life during the great rebellion, ever written." The advertisement went on to boast that the play would be performed by "the best amateur cast ever put on the stage in the city of Springfield."[18]

A traveling theatrical manager, W. H. Gunn, and the "Dutch Comedian," Charles Collins, assisted the Governor's Guard with the production, and at several points in the play directed the entire company, some seventy members strong, to take the stage to perform drill revolutions. The play opened to encouraging reviews and, according to the papers, improved with each performance. The high point of the run was on the fourth night, when the female lead, Miss Emma Hickox, representing the "Ladies of the city," presented a U.S. flag to the company before the curtain rose, and Governor Beveridge, in attendance to accept the gift, offered thanks on behalf of "his" company.

In speaking on behalf of the community, Emma Hickox was a new figure on the American scene and a far cry from her antebellum sisters, who had appeared in public only as mute figures, dressed as Lady Liberty but rarely granted significant speech.[19] Hickox spoke not as a vague feminine symbol, but rather as the representative of the very specific women of Springfield. Hickox also claimed patriotic authority for herself, when she declared: "In the confident assurance that I entrust [this flag] to the keeping of brave men and true; that, should the 'long roll' ever hurry you from peaceful pursuits to form in earnest in the serried ranks of war, your record as soldiers will be as honorable as it now is as business men and citizens."[20] Having taken for herself the power to recognize respectable and honorable men and citizens, and to honor them with the gift of the flag, Hickox assured her listeners that she had made the right choice of recipients, and the flag itself was proof of her words. "In this unshaken faith and trust, in behalf of the ladies of the city of Springfield, as a testimonial of their respect for you as gentlemen, and their appreciation of your admirable proficiency and soldierly bearing as a military organization, I now have the honor and pleasure to present to you this flag."[21] With the flag, Hickox recognized and rewarded the admirable qualities and the gentlemanly status of the members of the Governor's Guard.

In his reply to Hickox, Governor Beveridge concluded his long and gracious thanks on behalf of "his" company with a warning about the seriousness of their endeavor, and an injunction to do their best with it. Drawing on his own identity as a Civil War veteran, Beveridge contrasted civilian training with the harsh realities of wartime service, "[w]hether in civil or military life; whether parading in your armory or in camp; whether marching in the streets of your city or upon the field of strife;

whether you are decked in your bright uniforms or are clothed in the nation's blue, all dirty, worn, tattered and torn; whether your bright muskets are resting in their racks, or, powder-burnt, are under your head for a pillow, as you lie down to dreams upon the battle-field, waiting for the coming of the bloody morrow." Despite the contrast between war and civilian life, Beveridge, like Hickox, assured his listeners that he fully expected them to shine under any circumstances, as long as they remembered to "be true to yourselves, be true to your country, be true to your God, be true to that old flag, and be true to the ladies of Springfield."[22]

Governor Beveridge and Miss Hickox together reiterated the antebellum linkage between gentle birth and certain types of public volunteer soldiering, but they reinterpreted it for the conditions of the 1870s. Rather than gentlemen claiming exclusive patriotic authority, as in antebellum communities, here in the Springfield of 1875, Governor Beveridge and Miss Hickox implied that patriotic military exhibition itself could establish an acceptable claim to the status of gentleman. They clearly believed that the volunteer soldier was by definition an admirable man, worthy of respect and deference.[23] Miss Hickox, representative of the ladies of Springfield, played a traditional role in placing a symbol of the nation (the flag) in the care of recognized defenders of the home and hearth. She also took it upon herself to grant all members of the troop clear manhood status and social rank as gentlemen.[24]

More interesting, Miss Hickox and Governor Beveridge also stressed the interchangeable qualities needed to perform well the roles of both soldier and citizen. Miss Hickox assured the militia members of her belief that their "record as soldiers will be as honorable as it now is as business men and citizens." She, and the ladies of Springfield, gave the flag as a testimony of "respect for you as gentlemen, and their appreciation of your admirable proficiency and soldierly bearing as a military organization." The governor urged his listeners to bring the same convictions to their soldierly activities that they would "in every circumstance in life," that they be true to their belief in themselves, their community, their faith, the nation, and "the ladies of Springfield." Miss Hickox and Governor Beveridge saw no contradiction or potential conflict in the roles of citizen and soldier. In their construction of the identity of the militiaman, they believed that citizen and soldier could coexist in harmony, each relying on the same attitudes and behaviors of self-discipline, honor, and personal integrity.[25]

The governor also used his status as an acclaimed veteran of the Civil War (he had commanded a cavalry unit at Gettysburg before being promoted to the rank of general) to speak to the younger men about the mysteries of warfare they had not as yet experienced for themselves. Even here, though, and following in the footsteps of fellow Illinoisan John Logan, the governor implied that those same values of civilian life would serve well on the battlefield.[26] The governor, the militiamen, the ladies of Springfield, and the theater crowd all drew on memories of war-torn Civil War battlegrounds as they listened to the governor's description of the dreams of the "coming of the bloody morrow." In this context, the audience and the militiamen appear to anticipate that the citizen will become the soldier in a distant geographic space, where the values of honor and personal integrity that serve him at home will also see him through the turmoil of war. The speeches, and the play itself—a Civil War drama—all served to present the community with a unified figure of the citizen soldier, honorable man at home, honorable warrior on the field. Illinois men, it turns out, could meet the governor's challenge to be true by donning the uniform and preparing, however awkwardly or theatrically, to be soldiers should the nation ever need to call on them.

New Companies Build on Antebellum Militia Traditions

The burst of growth in the Illinois Militia between 1870 and 1876 was dramatic and had far-reaching consequences for the Illinois militia and for the broader militia resurgence nationwide. At first, Illinois militia volunteers relied on antebellum models and practices as they rebuilt old companies or created entirely new ones. Gradually, the new militiamen discarded many of the older practices in favor of developing new forms that better suited their needs and concerns. They lived in a rapidly maturing urban and industrial society that demanded ever more sophisticated and professional structures for managing ever-larger enterprises, and they needed an organization that suited their times.

In 1870, five volunteer militia companies existed in Illinois.[27] These scattered companies represented tremendous effort and devotion on the part of their members. As companies were completely voluntary, first a man and his friends had to decide they wanted to try to form a company; then they had to canvass their community for the thirty or so members necessary for a minimum-strength organization.[28] Once gathered together, the new members chose a company name, elected their officers, located an armory, and then, if still together and if so desired by the majority, authorized their officers to apply to the state for membership in the organized militia. (Not all such companies, before or after the Civil War, desired or sought a spot in the organized militia.) "Membership" was, at best, a tenuous connection to the state in 1870. Under the Illinois state law of 1845, a company was recognized when the governor issued commissions to the officers. Noncommissioned officers and privates took no oath of office, there was no official mustering in of new companies, and only the members' own inclinations kept them active from one month to the next. As late as the early 1870s, the governor's recognition of a company could provide very little beyond the occasional loan of ordnance in the form of outdated weaponry. As a result of these conditions, the connections between state governments and military companies were so vague that in 1870, Illinois officials reported to the federal government that they currently recognized no active militia organizations, even though according to the state roster of 1874 there were at least five volunteer companies (then or later) affiliated with the state active at that time.[29]

As the 1870s progressed, an increasing number of determined citizen-soldiers braved the difficulties attendant on starting a local militia organization and maintaining state recognition. For example, in 1872, The Grand Army Zouaves, the Mulligan Zouaves, the Sheridan Guards, the Rantoul Guards, the First Battalion of Whiteside County Militia (made up of the Sterling City Guards and the Rock Falls Zouaves), the McLean County Guards (colored), and the reorganized Ellsworth Zouaves all joined the state militia.[30] These new companies represented 400 men, with an average company strength of fifty-three members. In 1875, the Chicago papers recognized the Clan-na-Gael Guards, the Alpine Hunters, the Irish Rifles, the Montgomery Light Guards, the Mulligan Zouaves, and the Hannibal Zouaves, along with six new companies in the Chicago First Regiment, for a total of twelve militia companies in Chicago alone.[31]

The popularity of Zouave companies highlights the persistence of antebellum practices common to many companies formed in the early 1870s. In 1859, Elmer Ellsworth of Chicago initiated the pre-Civil War Zouave craze with his company, the United States Zouave Cadets. He trained the Zouave Cadets in the gymnastic drill of the French-African Zouave regiments, which he had picked up from a veteran of those corps a few years earlier. Essentially, under Ellsworth's direction a Zouave unit was a drill team with an emphasis on athleticism and group precision in both marching and marksmanship. The flashy and distinctive Zouave uniform consisted of a red cap, short jacket, sash, and baggy trousers. Ellsworth drilled his company so well and was so encouraged by the result that in 1860 he took it on a successful twenty-city tour, and Zouave companies sprang up all over the country in his wake. There were many Zouave regiments during the early years of the Civil War, in both armies, but they never made headway with the professional officer corps and quickly disappeared.[32] In Illinois, however, the Zouave model retained its fascination and romance for militia volunteers even after the war.[33] The Springfield Zouaves, the African American company based in Springfield, marched in the parade honoring Presidents Grant and Lincoln in 1874. Highlighting the vagueness of "official" status until a new militia law came into effect in 1877, the Springfield papers accorded the Springfield Zouaves the same recognition as the other militia companies present that did have state-commissioned officers, even though the adjutant general listed the company as "disbanded" in 1872.[34] In Chicago as late as 1875, there were still at least two companies of Zouaves. The Zouave model remained popular long after other forms more closely tied to the U.S. Army became the norm among volunteer militia companies.[35]

Upcoming Centennial Pushes Company Formation, 1874–76

Thirty-five new companies entered into state service between October 1874 and December 1, 1875.[36] Momentum continued to steamroll through the first half of 1876, and thirty-eight more new companies were accepted into the Illinois militia and their officers commissioned between January and July.[37] The sheer size of the increase in membership, from under 900 members to more than 5,000, is remarkable, as was its wide geographical distribution throughout the state.[38] (See appendix J.) Despite the presence of new companies in thirty small towns around the state, the urban character of most guardsmen is also apparent. In 1876, twenty-one militia companies located in Chicago officially belonged to the Illinois State Guard, and several smaller cities, including Sycamore, Peoria, Pontiac, and Quincy boasted at least two active companies.[39]

The catalyst for this statewide burst of company formation was the upcoming centennial celebration.[40] Certainly the brand-new First Regiment of Chicago had high hopes for their participation in the July 1876 celebrations. "The drill of some of the companies, owing to careful handling, is really excellent, while in others it is not so good, but it is believed that the entire regiment can be so drilled between this and July, 1876, as to allow them to enter into a contest with the eastern regiments for supremacy." The best contests were far away, and therefore a "movement is . . . on boat, looking to the sending of the 1st regiment to Philadelphia, during the centennial next year. The state officials and centennial commissions have pledged to work for this end, and it is believed that some aid can be secured from the state to assist the movement." The reporter added, "[i]t is known that nearly all the states of the union will be represented by companies or regiments at Philadelphia, and the city of San Francisco has subscribed toward sending forward a regiment. It is estimated that 30,000 or 40,000 militia will be assembled in Philadelphia for a couple weeks during next year, and grounds for the purpose have been set apart."[41] To this reporter, the absence of the Chicago Regiment from these patriotic celebrations and competitions seemed a sad prospect indeed.

The leadership of the Illinois State Guard appeared to agree. In his third General Order of 1875, Brigadier General Ducat established a committee of senior officers to report any plans to participate in the National Jubilee in Philadelphia. Garrison equipment was to be furnished by the centennial commission for all military organizations visiting Philadelphia on or before July 4, 1876; but the various committees involved needed to be notified well in advance.[42]

No companies from Illinois actually made it to Philadelphia, but the Fourth of July, 1876, was the focus of their attentions nonetheless. The First Regiment, Illinois State Guard, was invited to Madison, Wisconsin, along with many other companies and regiments from the surrounding area. There they paraded through the city in the morning, and in the afternoon they performed on the drill ground, and companies competed for the drill "Championship of the Northwest" and money prizes. The Second Regiment, Illinois State Guard, which was identified as Irish and wore the uniform of the famous New York 69th (also Irish, and with great Civil War renown), had Chicago to themselves and provided a day-long schedule of activities in honor of the centennial. In the morning, they paraded in Chicago to the enthusiastic cheers of their many supporters, and in the afternoon and evening they performed drill revolutions at the Exposition building. The evening show was apparently the highlight of the day for this regiment.[43]

The celebrations of the centennial marked the peak of the 1874–76 growth of the Illinois State Guard. In his autumn 1876 inspection report on the First Regiment, H. B. Maxwell wrote, "[i]t appears to me, there is not as much interest taken in the organization as there was a year ago. The excitement about the presidential election may be the chief cause; many of the members holding position of officers in the torch light marching societies necessitates their giving much time to the latter at the sacrifice of the regiment."[44] The decline of interest in the new regiment, and the Illinois State Guard in general, after the centennial celebrations and in deference to the upcoming election is another measure of how strongly militia members felt the patriotic motivation for involvement in the local centennial celebrations in 1875 and 1876.

It is important to note that Maxwell did not link the new companies of 1875–76 to any particular political party, nor did he link the members to one or the other of the dominant parties in Illinois. The political connections of individual members or specific companies did not give the *statewide* militia a particular political identity. Chicago itself could hold the First Regiment, which self-consciously strove for social prestige; the Irish and working-class Second Regiment; and the Socialist-identified Bohemian Rifles.[45] Nonetheless, the general importance of membership in a militia company to political identity is highlighted by Maxwell's comment that many members were also leaders in active political organizations. The similarities between the methods of patriotic display adopted by militia members as they celebrated the centennial and the methods of late nineteenth-century political parties to garner and hold support also serve to illustrate a link between militia membership and the role of citizen.[46] Just as men demonstrated their political identification through party activities, they could demonstrate their patriotic and national identity through membership in a local militia company and participation in their public events.

The Creation of the First Chicago, and a New Model for Illinois Militias

In 1874 Adjutant General Higgins wrote, "the approach of our centennial anniversary is increasing the military spirit of our State. During the coming year a large number of militia companies will be organized, provided liberal provisions are made by the General Assembly . . . At the present time there is being organized in Chicago a regiment composed of the elite of the city, which, from indications, will become a permanent organization."[47] The story of this regiment's formation provides a glimpse of the individual and community effort and dedication needed to get a militia organization up and running in the early 1870s. These men's interest in militias was a response to a felt need for a new organization that would tie men to their community and their nation through the model of military service.[48]

The first organizational meeting for the proposed troop was held toward the end of August 1874. "We, the undersigned, desire to form a military organization to consist of at least 100 and not more than 1,000 persons, subject to such regulations as may hereafter be determined upon by a vote of the whole."[49] Organizers rapidly decided that there were enough interested recruits to justify organizing an entire regiment of eight to ten companies, rather than one or two companies, or even the four to six companies that would form a battalion. A prominent Chicago businessman and political figure, Guerdon S. Hubbard, Jr., made the lofts of his building on State Street available to the new regiment, free of charge.[50] On September 8, the first three companies of the new "First Regiment Illinois State Guard" were enrolled. Unlike any other companies then in the state militia, these three companies were assigned only letter designations A, B, and C, indicating the seriousness of their intentions to be a modern military organization. These companies continued the tradition of electing their officers, however, and the seniority of the three captains was determined by lot.[51] These first officers were commissioned by the state that same day.[52] When a fourth company, D, was enrolled, a "General" Frank T. Sherman was elected major by the entire battalion.[53]

According to Holdridge O. Collins, one of the founding members of this new regiment, Governor John L. Beveridge and various leading local citizens pledged to support the new regiment almost from its inception. There was some criticism in Chicago about this new regiment at the time, however, and the governor himself claimed to have looked on the early efforts of the regiment's founders with "indifference, not to say disfavor. But when he saw the young men who joined the organization persevered so untiringly, and seemed bound to make it a success, he felt his heart going out toward them and he resolved to exert his influence as an executive officer, and do his best for them."[54]

When news of potential public support and government supplies got around, several existing Chicago-based companies applied for membership in the new regiment. However, "[a]s their tenders of service were accompanied ... with the demands that they be accepted with their individual uniform, and take rank in the Regiment according to the date of their Captain's' commissions, etc., etc., it was not thought expedient to receive any old commissioned company."[55] Class and ethnic differences also had something to do with the reluctance of the founders of the new regiment to accept existing companies, several of which had strong Irish ethnic and working-class connections. The new regiment hoped to appeal to the city's elite for support, and judging by the following 1875 reports, they succeeded. A *Harper's Weekly* correspondent wrote, "[the Regiment] is to-day as great a favorite in Chicago as the 'Seventh' is in New York, for like the last-named Regiment, it is composed of men of high standing, whose great aim is to excel."[56] A reporter from *The Chicago Times* noted that the "only thing to be regretted concerning the display [a parade] was, that it occurred at a season of the year [July] when a large number of the members of the regiment are absent from the city, on their summer vacation, causing the number participating in the parade to be much smaller than it otherwise would."[57] The reporter claimed that almost 200 members (out of some 500) were absent that day. A rough count of membership lists suggests that almost 60 percent of this regiment were clerks and bookkeepers who, according to the *Chicago Tribune*, could not afford their own uniforms. An alternative explanation was that these members were at work, and unable or unwilling to take a day's vacation for the parade.[58]

With the October 1874 addition of eighty-four new members in two companies, E and F, the regiment began to drill, and the members decided that the issue of uniforms was crucial. As the regimental leaders did not intend for its members to outfit themselves, they relied on "assurances" that sufficient funds could be raised from Chicago residents through a subscription drive and the support of the *Chicago Tribune*. The Chicago Citizens' Association, an organization of business and community leaders devoted to civic improvements and good government, was called on to review the regiment and give its recommendation for support, which it did.[59]

The Citizens' Association judged the regiment against standards that reflect the contemporary understanding about the nature and function of militia companies. First, the members of the Citizens' Association were interested in the physical size and vitality of militia members. "From our observation and inspection, and from what we can gather in reply to our inquires, we do not hesitate to report that the materiel composing the First Regiment Illinois State Guard, is excellent, both physically and morally, in the military acceptation of that word."[60] This interest in size and appearance turns up again and again in commentaries on militia companies and reflects a broader concern with the physical condition of American men.[61] Along with judging the men, or "materiel," of the regiment against current measures of physical fitness, the committee members also looked for attitude and enthusiasm. They reported "that there is an evidence of quiet, determined ambition to excel as citizen soldiers, of willingness to undergo the ordeal of drill and discipline, that cannot fail, if proper encouragement be given them, to make them into a good and serviceable Regiment, worthy of the sympathy and support of our citizens, and we cordially recommend them to your favorable consideration and that of the Community at large."[62]

Judging by the language they used in their report, the committee members seem to have been looking for taller and broader men who would avoid the classic temptations of the soldier, including alcohol and rowdiness, and who showed a willingness to accept military discipline as a personal challenge. That these were the committee members' preferred qualities suggests that for them, the first role of a militia organization was to be a successful performance and social group in the context of the local community. The members needed to be attractive, and to be responsible about learning and playing their assigned roles.

With the recommendation of the Citizens' Association in hand, the captains of the six companies formed a committee to organize the canvassing of the city—"visiting all the more prominent citizens." By late December 1874, the *Chicago Tribune* reported that there were already six organized companies of 84 men each. In an editorial supporting the new organization and seeking public donations to assist them, the paper claimed that the "personnel of the regiment is excellent . . . all young men from 20 to 30 years of age, of respectable parentage, education, and of personal good habits and character." The editorial continued, "[t]o organize a regiment of soldiers is attended with considerable expense, and more so than these young men can reasonably be expected to bear. . . . It costs, on average, to uniform these men $50 each. The young men give their time and services without pay, but the tax for uniform is more than all can stand . . . there would be no lack of men to fill all the ten companies—each 100 strong—were it not that the purchase of a uniform is beyond the reach of those who will join it."[63] The *Chicago Tribune* editorial appealed to "those of our citizens who can afford to do so to contribute of their means; let each furnish a uniform for one, two, three or ten men, and thus get the six companies already organized into uniform." The editorial writer insisted that this "is not an appeal to public charity; it is an appeal to the self-interest of property-owners as well as to public spirit and pride . . . Can property-holders afford to refuse the necessary assistance and encouragement which this military organization requires?"[64] These efforts were so successful that "[a] sufficient fund was raised by the personal solicitation of members of the Regiment to warrant the renting of a permanent Armory and to purchase the uniform." Chicago residents eventually pledged $13,468.50 toward the equipment fund, and members of the Regiment contributed $2,349 to their own maintenance.[65]

At this point, it would seem that the organization was off to an excellent start. However, following in the long American militia tradition of electing officers from the ranks, the rules members of the First Regiment adopted in September of 1874 mandated that elections for all officers were to take place annually. Accordingly, the members held new elections on December 2, and eight of twenty offices changed hands. Stability of command would not mark the early years of this regiment at any level. A variety of reasons for the revolving nature of commissions is suggested in Collins's book, but the time conflict between the demands of career and regiment was most often put forward as the reason for resigning.

At the December 1874 meeting, the regiment also voted to break its own resolution and admitted the Ellsworth Zouaves to membership. The Ellsworth Zouaves in turn agreed to become Company G and don the gray uniform selected by the regiment. There are some indications that this company was composed of better-off men, which may have made them more acceptable to the First Regiment than were other, preexisting militia companies in Chicago and, of course, that more than rank was at stake in the initial decision to reject other extant Chicago companies.[66] In March 1875 an eighth company, H, joined, and the regiment had the minimum companies to elect a colonel. The last two companies, I and K, joined later in the year.[67]

The regiment first appeared on the Chicago streets in May of 1875, escorting the Grand Army of the Republic to its annual meeting. Their first formal parade was July 28, 1875, when Governor Beveridge; Lieutenant General Philip H. Sheridan, United States Army; and Brigadier General Arthur C. Ducat, Illinois State Guard, reviewed the troops. The parade excited so much local attention that it was written up in *Harper's Weekly* of August 21, 1875. "At its first parade, [the First Regiment, Illinois State Guard] was enthusiastically received by the citizens and distinguished visitors from abroad, and from Gen. Sheridan and other military men received high commendation."[68] The next day's headline in *The Chicago Times* read, "PLAYING SOLDIER. The Gallant First Marched to the Field for the First Time Yesterday. By the Aid of the Railroads the Warriors Reached It Very Comfortably."[69] The headline is a little mocking, but the general tenor of the article is more positive.

In his speech after reviewing the Regiment on July 28, Governor Beveridge spoke openly about his initial apprehensions about the formation of this Regiment. However, he pronounced them quite over, owing to the dedication and superior performance displayed during the inspection and revolutions. The governor then went on to compliment the "boys of the regiment on their splendid physique, their tasty uniform, the perfect order and neatness of each individual member, their efficiency in the school of the soldier, and the care and correctness with which they performed the most difficult evolutions in the battalion drill, and the success of the organization generally."[70] The governor's (or the reporter's) ordering of the fine qualities of the regiment begins by praising the individual members, laying stress on their physical vigor and attractiveness, their good taste in uniforms, and their discipline as soldiers. The governor praised the contribution of each to the performance of the whole only after noting the vitality and personal appearance of each member.

This ranking offers another reading on the popular conception of the personal rewards and benefits for a man, young or old, contemplating joining a militia organization. First, the body is improved. The reporter began by recognizing each individual for seizing the opportunity to attain a "splendid physique," which in the image of the day meant visibly muscular. This emphasis on physical vitality and strength was emerging as one of the most important aspects of what it meant to be a man in these years. During these decades of intense industrialization and urbanization, commentators and the public alike became consumed by worries that American men were losing their manhood. In response to that worry, in fits and starts, more and more men turned to shaping their outer bodies as a reflection of the man within. The militia proved to be one more place where men could acquire and display these outward signs of strength and vitality that were increasingly being connected to a healthy and strong manhood. The *Chicago Times* reporter (and the governor) next noted the neatness of the presentation and the "tasty uniforms," again an issue that was frequently addressed in advice books of the age when advice givers sought ways to encourage men, young and old, to present themselves as men before a skeptical world.[71] The militia, to these observers, was an excellent vehicle for demonstrating these visually desirable characteristics of manhood.

The physical skills of the soldiers, especially with regard to marching in complicated patterns and as part of a unified whole, attracted the reporter's praise. In this regard, the militia performance bears a close resemblance to the rise of team sports, both professional sports and the vast numbers of amateur leagues, in these years. In the case of the militia, alone or in competition against other companies, the whole "team" also served the community as a model for vigorous, manly comportment and loyal patriotic duty. All aspects of the military performance were graded and judged by an audience well aware of the categories and the standards for achievement. The linkage of manly vigor and patriotic authority certainly had its roots in the antebellum model, but it was in many ways ideal for the new concerns of a new era, including fears of failing physical vitality in an urban and sedentary environment, the lost sense of possibility for individual independence for every man, and at the same time the fears of social anarchy set loose by the anonymity of the city.[72]

Class, Ethnic, and Racial Diversity

Not every new organization had it so comparatively easy. Prokop Hudek was commissioned captain of the Bohemian Rifles, located in Chicago, on August 9, 1875. The story of this company is quite different from that of the First Regiment, which was comparatively wealthy and "appealed to prestige-seeking property-holders."[73] The adjutant general issued the company eighty Enfield rifles for drill purposes, but their available drill space was so small that they had been forced to break up into two detachments, headquartered in different buildings, for weekly drilling purposes. Company members had put great effort into these spaces, however, and built locked gun racks to hold state property. As the company was already fifty dollars in debt for the purchase of fatigue uniforms for the men (the cheapest blouse and cap combination) and rent for the armory spaces, these racks represented a considerable investment of time and care. In 1876, ING inspection officer Maxwell noted, "A monthly assessment of 25 cents is levied on each member of the company for the purpose of paying rent of armories, &c., but the assessment is too small for the purpose . . . The members are poor, and cannot stand a larger assessment than 25 cents per month. I am informed it is very difficult for many of the members to pay even this sum."[74]

At the time of the first general inspection of the Illinois militia in the fall of 1876, Captain Hudek informed the inspecting officer that the company had only lately re-formed. Presumably, the company collapsed between August 1875 and June 1876 owing to the difficulties attendant on maintaining an organization under such trying circumstances. The inspector was nevertheless pleased by the "good sized" men and their soldierly bearing, and wrote of the officers, "I was much pleased with [their] appearance . . . They are justly entitled to great credit for accomplishing so much in so short a time and without aid or assistance from any quarter." Without much else to praise in this impecunious company, Maxwell placed his emphasis on the size, appearance, and attentiveness of the men as qualities valued by the militia. Inspector Maxwell concluded his report on the company on an upbeat note. "I would respectfully state that I was agreeably disappointed at the condition in which I found [the company], and I would earnestly recommend that the organization be fostered and encouraged in every possible way." Maxwell went on to offer that, if "new uniforms could be provided for its members and small sum of money raised from some source to pay the rent of a proper armory, I am assured that the company could be quickly recruited to its maximum strength, and I believe that in a short time it would compare favorably in drill and discipline with any other in the city."[75] For Maxwell, at least, neither the poverty nor the ethnicity of this company stood between them and admirable service.

In the early 1870s, along with native-born men and recent immigrants, African American men created state militia companies. In histories of these companies, later members of Illinois African American regiments explained that African Americans created companies in the

1870s because a militia company was a tangible demonstration of independence and self-reliance.[76] As Eric Foner has argued, one freedom African Americans sought after the Civil War was the freedom to do the same kinds of things white people could.[77] And one thing white Illinois men were doing in the early 1870s was raising and sustaining militia companies.[78] By doing the same thing, African Americans demonstrated their belief that equality of military service could carry with it equal citizenship. With equal citizenship would come many rights, among them equal access to the public space. In public spaces, namely city streets, African American militiamen could perform in one common act of responsible citizenship and disciplined manhood—the formal military parade. African Americans actively serving in militia companies also provided a forceful reminder to Illinois residents, both black and white, of the importance of the role that African American troops played in the Civil War. Not only did African American troops tip the balance toward victory for the Union Army, but as Frederick Douglass put it, "Once let the black man get upon his person the brass letters, U.S.; let him get an eagle on his button, and a musket on his shoulder and bullets in his pocket, and there is no power on earth that can deny he has earned the right of citizenship."[79] Even if many whites remained skeptical of this argument, many African Americans put their faith in it. The connection that Douglass drew between the uniform, weapons, and citizenship highlights the importance of a recognized militia company for African American men in the 1870s.

The idea of citizenship itself was under great stress in the late nineteenth century. The Fourteenth and Fifteenth Amendments shattered the previous linkage of whiteness and citizenship. The continuing pressure of the women's movement challenged the necessary maleness of citizenship. Militia volunteers across Illinois saw their organizations as intimately involved with the issue of redefining citizenship in this new era, repeatedly stressing the ability of the militia to recognize, foster, and even create model citizens and manly men. Like Governor Beveridge, they believed that the role of the citizen-soldier in civic pageantry, especially parades, and the responsibilities of the citizen-soldier for national defense and maintaining order placed the militia squarely in the midst of the general debates about who was a citizen, what responsible citizenship was, and how a citizen might be made. By parading publicly as members of the state militia, African Americans secured their own place in the larger public dialogue about who was a representative, responsible citizen.

In 1870 and 1871, African Americans formed the Hannibal Guards in Chicago, though like many local companies in these early years their formal tie to the state militia forces remains ambiguous.[80] In the state capital, the adjutant general commissioned officers for the African American Springfield Zouaves sometime between 1870 and 1872. This company may have evolved from Company C, an African American company recognized by Governor Palmer in July of 1869.[81] In 1872, the McLean County Guards (colored), formed by residents surrounding Bloomington, joined the state militia.[82] On October 15, 1874, the Springfield Zouaves were among the five companies more or less associated with the state that marched in the procession leading U.S. President Ulysses S. Grant to the unveiling of the statue of Abraham Lincoln in the Oak Ridge Cemetery, in Springfield. The Springfield Zouaves were listed as disbanded by the state in 1872, but the company must have re-formed sometime before this occasion, though without seeking new commissions for its officers. Regardless, the Springfield papers accorded it the same recognition as the other companies with state-commissioned officers.[83]

In late February 1875, there were "riotous demonstrations . . . directed more especially against the treasury and building of the Relief and Aid Society" in Chicago.[84] Militia companies mobilized all across Chicago to protect the Relief and Aid Society from attacks by putative "communists." Among the militia companies were the Hannibal Zouaves, which were very likely the same as or a version of the Chicago-based Hannibal Guards.[85] In time the Hannibal Guards (or Zouaves) became known as the Cadets.[86] Like the Hannibal Guards, the Cadets never formally belonged to the state militia, though the newspaper reports do not make this distinction.

The brief, flickering existence of these ethnic and African American companies offers a testament to the interest and willingness on the part of their members to serve, and on the part of the state militia to accept their service. These brief histories also highlight the importance of money to the continuing existence of any state militia company.

Paying for an Expensive Hobby

The myriad needs of the average militia company—armories, uniforms, weapons, supplies, and special activities, like the 1875 Springfield play—had to be paid for. As the state had no funds to offer, the money could only come from the members' own pockets or from those of their neighbors. To raise the money to pay for their activities, militia members had to present a compelling case to their communities and, in time, to the state legislature, and they had to devote significant time and energy to these nearly constant fund-raising activities. They began with themselves. In 1874, Illinois companies required members to pay annual dues, ranging from a dollar twenty to twelve dollars. However, the amounts raised this way never came close to providing for a company's total expenses, which varied widely among the several militia companies recognized by the state. In 1874, expenses per company ranged from $285 to $2,075, depending on the size of the company, the cost of the uniforms, and the amount needed to rent the armory space. Each company selected its own uniforms, resulting in huge variations in taste and expense. For some, the uniform of the private was as simple as a blouse and a cap, which could be had for as little as five dollars per man. For one Chicago company, a *private's* uniform cost forty dollars in 1874,[87] and the First Regiment assumed a cost of fifty dollars per man.

The state provided no funds for its troops during these early years. Under the operative 1845 militia code with 1874 amendments, the annual military outlay was barely sufficient to cover the salary and expenses of the office of the adjutant general. The position of adjutant general, or AG, was that of chief administrator of the state military department. The AG's duties included overseeing the militia and forwarding all pension or disability requests from resident veterans of national service to the War Department in Washington, DC.[88] The only support the state offered to the individual companies was the loan of guns and a limited supply of ammunition. Many guns owned and loaned by the state were so obsolete that the adjutant generals regularly proposed selling them off at a public auction just to get them out of the way.[89] Even these small measures were unreliable, dependent as they were on Illinois' share of the annual federal militia appropriation of $200,000, established in 1808.

However, in the 1870s Illinois was receiving no money from the federal government. War Department accountants charged $163,674.40 to Illinois' portion of the annual distribution for supplies issued to state troops in 1863, 1864, and early 1865. From the 1860s through the 1870s, the $200,000 annual federal appropriation was apportioned based on the number of congressional representatives, and in 1872 Illinois was receiving only an $8,760.58 annual credit against its overdrawn account.[90] Because of this debt, Illinois was receiving no guns or other ordnance supplies from the federal government in the early 1870s. Between 1872 and 1874 the efforts of AGs Dilgar and Higgins were rewarded by the subtraction of $65,000 as "improperly charged," and AG Higgins claimed that with a further search in the records, the remaining $41,125.20 could also be removed, giving the state a positive balance of $60,000.[91] His calculations are difficult to follow and, in any case, were never performed. In 1878 Illinois was still listed as $98,674.40 overdrawn.[92] As a result of these problems, the companies of the state militia had to supply themselves with armories, uniforms, and weapons from their own pocket and/or raise the money required from the local community.

Financial issues were paramount to a company's success in these early years, and financial concerns drove a large portion of any company's daily and weekly calendars. The imperative to earn money for its own support, and to get whatever money it could from state and federal coffers, far more than any other single concern, affected the health of any company.[93] If the company could not pay its bills, it could not stay alive as an organization. As a result, the success of any individual company was entirely dependent on the enthusiasm of the members and the skill and leadership provided by their elected officers.[94] It should not come as a surprise that the half-life of most companies was little more than a year. In 1874, of the twenty-four companies listed on the rolls, four were disbanded; four more failed to report, leading the adjutant general to suspect they were disbanded in actuality if not formally; and one company had failed to complete organization, fizzling out before it ever got going. The oldest active company dated to 1869, and the most recent had been in existence barely two months. Adjutant General Higgins suspected that the state militia included only about 850 active volunteers.[95] Of those volunteers, Higgins remarked, "It would be difficult to find an equal number of men in the service of the State willing to donate their services without compensation, at a cost of over twenty dollars per man. The cause of four companies disbanding and four failing to report this year is plainly to be seen from this report."[96]

Most of the new companies of 1875 and 1876 were located in small towns, and some were created by ethnic groups—Irish, Bohemian, and African American. The militia was a sufficiently flexible institution that its appeal spoke to men of different backgrounds and living disparate lives. The militia connection between the individual and the state, both Illinois and the Union, carried across class and ethnic background the opportunity to participate in representative citizenship in highly personal and evocative ways. The inspector general reports filed during 1876 indicate a broad range of background and economic standing of the militia as a whole. Almost all rural companies had poor attendance at weekly drills. But they reported they had no trouble with attendance for parades or state occasions. As always during this time, inspectors noted the men's physical size and the general appearance of the uniforms and the men whenever they could. Where any indication is made of the members' occupations, it seems to be primarily as clerks, skilled tradesmen, or small merchants.[97] If indebtedness is one marker of less elite membership, then most companies were made up of common men. Many companies, especially those located in rural towns, had difficulty paying for all they felt they needed, from uniforms to armories. At the end of 1876, the new Second Regiment, formed in Chicago by primarily Irish ethnic companies at the end of 1875 and early 1876, was $8,700.00 in debt for uniforms and rent.[98]

A Larger Militia Leads to a New Militia Structure

By 1875, the Illinois militia was quickly growing beyond the ability of the governor and the adjutant general to oversee it on top of all their other duties. In 1874, an addition to the old militia code (1845) was approved, giving the governor power to appoint an unlimited number of major and brigadier generals. This new power had serious implications for patronage offices, but because the sitting governor was a cautiously serious supporter of the militia, in 1875 he chose to appoint only one brigadier general and delegated to him the authority to organize the rapidly growing state forces.[99] On June 8, 1875, Governor Beveridge commissioned Arthur C. Ducat brigadier general of the Illinois State Militia. Ducat, who achieved the rank of inspector general of the Army of the Cumberland during the Civil War, was an able officer and organizer. In August he issued his first general order to the state militia, creating one brigade and appointing his staff officers. By December the militia had grown from 895 members when Ducat took office to more than two thousand.[100] In December, General Order 4 reorganized and consolidated the then greatly expanded state forces. General Ducat also established the office of Inspector General of Illinois, and he received the first ever inspection reports of the ING in 1876. He announced that the regulation drill would be that of the U.S. Army, eliminating the Zouave drill from formal, but not informal, use by any recognized ING company. Governor Beveridge, who had publicly claimed a deep personal interest in the success of the state militia forces, also appointed a new adjutant general in 1875, Hiram Hilliard. Hilliard, like Ducat and Beveridge, was a Civil War veteran. The efforts of Generals Ducat and Hilliard represented the first implementation of any sort of organizational plan in Illinois that included not only rank charts and organizational tables, but actual systems of staff officers to track and teach the new companies and maintain and improve the old. This introduction of a new ethic of military professionalism learned during the Civil War marks a significant turning point in the development of the Illinois militia, away from the older antebellum volunteerism and toward the new forms of civic engagement emerging with a maturing industrial capitalism.[101]

Between 1870 and 1876 a new generation of men entered the Illinois Militia, slowly at first and then with gathering steam as the centennial drew nearer. This rush of new members gave the larger organization the clout it needed to seek out changes in current militia law, and to begin to organize their forces in new, modern ways. The pattern of growth in Illinois, clearly preceding the centennial celebrations of 1876, suggests that the dramatic growth of state militias in other midwestern states may have also been spurred by the centennial and not by the strikes of 1877 as has been long argued.[102]

The new Illinois militia members first replicated the small, antebellum militia companies, but they quickly began to dream of bigger, more organized, and more dynamic militias that would capture the imagination and the financial support of larger communities. Toward that end, these new militiamen crafted elaborate public performances to engage and teach their audiences that these new members embodied a national patriotism and manly attributes. The roots of the militia resurgence in Illinois in the 1870s are to be found in individuals who flocked to the revived militia and the communities that came to the support of their local companies.

CHAPTER 2

Manhood and Citizenship on Display

> The review on Illinois Day, in the presence of representatives from every civilized nation, was the largest and most imposing martial display during the Fair, and the troops elicited the highest commendation from military officers, the press, and the people for their discipline, precision of movement, and soldierly bearing.[1]
> —Alfred Orrendorf, Adjutant General of Illinois

Over the last quarter of the nineteenth century, the ING attracted tens of thousands of new members by offering men the opportunity to play dramatic civic roles while placing themselves at the center of community social life. As responsible citizen soldiers and public men, militia members claimed the right to parade and perform in patriotic ceremonies. These ceremonies proved powerful and effective popular vehicles for celebrating traditional manhood while also embracing a newfound modern, professional discipline. At the same time, militia members filled their communities' social calendars by hosting lectures, balls and dances, suppers, and amateur theatricals. Many companies also turned their armories into clubhouses for themselves and for members of the private associations that helped to support them financially, providing space for informal socializing of all varieties. In Illinois and across the nation, militias grew and prospered because they offered new members an opportunity to cast themselves as dashing and responsible men at the center of community social and patriotic life. Militia members and their organizations fit firmly into the panorama of late nineteenth-century responses to the challenges to identity and position, especially male identity and position, posed by the rapid pace of change by offering a clear, and powerfully attractive, vision of modern manhood.

National Guard members seized social occasions as prime opportunities to present themselves in the full panoply of military glamour, to each other, to potential recruits, and to their larger communities that offered them financial support. Fund-raising was inextricably linked with these performances of manly glamour, and it was in part the always pressing need for funds that drove the unending whirl of social activities. At social events, guardsmen buffed their image as handsome and manly soldiers and active and responsible citizens, while showing the community that their organization was worthy of the community's support by providing impressive and satisfying entertainment. Guardsmen also made a point of showing off in front of women. Women played crucial parts in crafting and hosting the myriad of events put on by the average company, not least, by dressing up in their best and dancing the night away in the arms of dashingly uniformed men. Although dining and dancing had their pleasures, they were not the only public venue for guardsmen to demonstrate their worth and importance. In addition to parties, parades, drill competitions, and drill displays, civic ceremonies and public funerals also offered guardsmen opportunities to impress on civilians and potential recruits that the Guard was the home of responsible citizens who honored their nation, their communities, and their brethren with solemn, patriotic ceremonies. These public performances, social and civic, were especially important to the African American companies of the Illinois National Guard. African American guardsmen struggled not only financially, but also against great social barriers as they secured and held their place as manly and responsible citizens through the medium of the ING, and their public events were an essential part of their strategy for success.

Self-Respecting Manliness

The occasion of dedicating a new armory was a special event in the life of an ING company before the turn of the century, especially if the organization had been lucky enough to have an entire building erected solely for its use. For ING companies, a new armory represented considerable fund-raising success in these years before state and federal funding caught up to militia needs, for members and their supporters paid for specialized armory construction out of their own pockets.

In 1890, the First Regiment of Chicago opened their new, privately funded armory, and in celebrating the building, they also celebrated the citizen-soldiers whom it would house.

> Let us, then, to-day dedicate this new armory to a ninety-nine years' struggle for supremacy in military efficiency: dedicate it as the home of the highest discipline; as the center and inspiration of a regiment which shall combine reliability with dash, conservatism with enterprise, culture with athleticism—a regiment whose gayety shall be but eddies in the current of devotion to duty—whose *bonhomie* and good comradeship shall be the foam lightening up the surface of its patriotism.[2]

The dedication speeches preserved in the *Souvenir Album and Sketch Book: First Infantry I.N.G. of Chicago* reflect the conscious attempt by members to capture the essence and the importance of their experiences in the ING. At the turn of the century, of Chicago's regiments the First appealed the most to the middle and upper classes, with almost 70 percent of the membership professionals, merchants, salesmen, clerks, or students. Even so, more than 330 members were skilled tradesmen, factory workers, or laborers.[3] (See appendix A.) Their commander, Lieutenant Colonel Henry L. Turner, drew no distinctions in his dedication between the men in his regiment. Turner continued in the tradition of the 1877 editor of the *National Guardsman*, who declared, "We believe in the advantages which a membership in the National Guard confers; and it is our purpose to set those advantages truthfully and clearly before the youth of the land, to the end that they may avail themselves of the privileges so conferred."[4]

In his dedication, Turner promoted the formal intent of ING members to achieve supremacy in military efficiency and to exhibit a serious and responsible patriotism by doing so. Turner's vision of masculinity was at once traditional—embracing reliability, conservatism, culture, and devotion to duty—and modern. Turner openly celebrated some of the more exciting and desirable newer benefits membership in an ING organization conferred on an average young man—dash, enterprise, athleticism, gayety, bonhomie, and good comradeship. Turner explicitly linked membership in the First Regiment with promoting his vision of manliness:

> Let us remember that vulgarity and bravado are fashioned out of infinitely cheaper material than manliness and courage, and that if we would enroll in our membership able men, cultivated men, men who will be an honor to us, we must give them manly, cultivated men for associates. Let us be athletic, reckless, wild—what you will—yet never drop below the level of self-respecting manliness.[5]

"Able men, cultivated men, men who will be an honor to us," men who could be "athletic, reckless, wild . . . yet never drop below the level of self-respecting manliness"; for Turner, this was the ideal guardsman. It was also an overtly romantic ideal. Turner believed that membership in the First, and by extension any ING company, could confer these traditional, romantic qualities on the willing, the dedicated, the loyal man in a state uniform. In this desire to model a manhood equally available to all men, the state militias bear a strong resemblance to the volunteer firemen of earlier decades, men who also espoused an ideal of civic manliness that had no class or ethnic divide.[6]

Once they demonstrated their ability, cultivation, dash, athleticism, and the rest, by joining up, ING members put it all on display for their public. Militia volunteers did so to prove to potential recruits, and to the communities that supported them financially, that they were who and what they claimed to be. They were, first and foremost, military organizations that trained young men in the rudiments of military skill, and most of their claims to responsible manhood rested on this patriotic duty. To provide military training, they needed money and willing recruits. Money they raised in an endless round of solicitation and fund-raising social events. They raised their recruits by offering young men an active, exciting, and fun vehicle for demonstrating their adulthood, their citizenship, their manhood, and their romantic and sexual appeal to the audiences that observed and applauded all of their parades and parties. Social events and parades were the heart and soul of most companies, most of the time, for without them, ING companies would have ceased to exist.

Social Events and Fund-raising

Militia and National Guard companies, in Illinois and around the nation, hosted an amazing array of social events, including parties, dances (often called "balls") both public and private, suppers, festivals, plays, "entertainments," banquets, amateur theatricals, lectures, picnics, and private dress parades. The range and variety of events attests to the importance of these activities in a militia company's yearly schedule, and to the importance of militias to their communities' social calendars. These social events were important for fostering an esprit de corps among the members of a company, and as companies lasted only as long as their members stayed interested, this interest was essential. The reputation for putting on good parties, like a winning competitive record, could also be good advertising for a company in the never-ending quest

Figure 1
First Infantry football team, 1897. Courtesy of the Chicago Historical Society. Photographer: Unknown. iCHi-39232.

for fresh recruits and for continued public and private financial support. Most companies charged admission for their various entertainments as a form of fund-raising, though doing so did not always net them very much money. These events did, however, make it possible for militia volunteers to create and foster the social ties necessary to asking for the large donations that their companies required to function.

Social events, from parties to dances to plays, also gave members opportunities to flaunt and enjoy their status as citizen-soldiers and freed them from the more serious work of training or active duty. Perhaps equally important, social events were a great deal of fun. In many ways, in their pursuit of the social side of life, ING members differed very little from any of the other wide variety of social, fraternal, and service organizations that flourished in the later nineteenth and early twentieth centuries and relied on social events to bond them together. Militia volunteers around the country devoted so much of their time and energy, easily far more time than they spent at drill practice, to maintaining a steady and full calendar of social events because it was in these situations that they nurtured the ties that bound them together and to the community that helped to pay their bills. As Wisconsin National Guard Colonel

Allen Caldwell put it, "Make your organizations the leader in social events and your citizens will patronize you and I venture to say the financial standing of the company will be rated A-1."[7]

It is impossible to extricate fund-raising from the social calendar of militia companies of the late nineteenth century. Throughout the last three decades of the nineteenth century, militia and National Guard companies in Illinois, as elsewhere in the nation, were constantly strapped for cash. Their home communities were the only funding source available to companies beyond the combination of the scanty federal and state appropriations and their own pockets. To maintain and increase community interest and financial support, militia members created opportunities for the kinds of public displays of patriotism and military skills provided by parades and competitions that brought them new members, and also set the stage for the personal informal interaction necessary to ask for money. Companies regularly charged admission to their events in order to raise funds, and smaller companies could produce a steady, if small, stream of revenue this way. For this strategy to work, however, company members had to put on events that many people would attend. To earn money from admission fees over the course of many years, companies had to create a reputation for themselves as skilled promoters and hosts of social events.

From the inception of a new company, the members needed to raise money, and to do that, they needed to create a positive reputation for the company. Social events were key to both activities. Take, for example, Company I, Seventh Infantry, ING, also known as the Mason City Guards, founded in September 1877. The company's minute book details their business meetings, during which the members managed their finances and planned and organized their social and fund-raising activities. Like the members of most companies just starting out, the new members of Company I spent their first business meetings electing officers, amending their constitution and by-laws, changing their drill night, and selecting uniforms. These activities occupied the first two months, and then at the November 11, 1877 meeting, Captain Amos Trout opened the discussion "to see if we can give an entertainment for the benefit of the company."[8] The company members decided to hold a general invitation ball on Thanksgiving, and charge $1.00 admittance to the public and $.50 for members. Six committees were set up to get ready for the ball: arrangement, printing, music, floor managers, doorkeepers, and tickets. At this time, the company did not yet even have a uniform. The members apparently considered the ball to be a success, for on November 30 the committees reported a net of $12.15, and two weeks later, on December 11, they decided to host a second ball, on Christmas

Eve.⁹ The total receipts of the Christmas ball were $71.70 and expenses were $24.00, leaving a net balance of $47.70.¹⁰ Together, the two balls raised over $60.00 for the Mason City Guards during their first ten weeks as an active organization.

The Mason City Guards, like all other ING companies at that time, needed to raise money to pay for facility rental and purchase uniforms, if nothing else. For their parties to pay—financially and socially—guardsmen had to earn a reputation for putting on successful entertainments, and so they devoted a tremendous amount of their time and energy to planning and hosting a wide variety of events. The Mason City Guards put on at least one entertainment of some sort almost every month during the four years they were together. Their third ball was held on January 17, 1878, and netted $42.15 for the company funds.¹¹ In February the company sponsored a lecture by a Mr. Josh Billings, which raised $84.20, $40.00 of which went to Billings as his lecture fee. Company members also contracted with a Mr. Viegard of Galesburg to produce a "military play," using the company as the cast, for a four-day run in mid-February.¹² Mr. Viegard was not available until March, so in the meantime, the company planned and held a "masked ball." The play, *The Dutch Recruit*, ran for four performances March 26–29, 1878, for a total gross of $158.43.¹³ By April, members were already planning to host a drill competition with several nearby companies on Memorial Day, and the company was drilling twice a week. Possibly as a result of the busy month of March and the upcoming competition, on April 24, the members decided to hold only an informal "social dance" after the next Wednesday's drill.¹⁴ On May 8 and May 18, members used their business meetings to make arrangements for their upcoming competition. At the meeting on May 8, the members divided the city into four quadrants so as to canvass the city for provisions for the competition and ball and, possibly, for board arrangements for all the visiting militia members. The members then created a committee to confer with city officials about the plans for Memorial Day. The members next decided to hold a "grand ball" on the evening of May 30, with music provided by the "Walker Brothers" for the entertainment of the visiting companies. The ball was to be public, with an admission price of $1.00 per couple, with no spectators admitted without paying, though members of the invited companies could attend for free. At least seventy-five couples attended the "grand ball" (the gross was $75.00) and the net for the company was $51.50.¹⁵ Earning over $200.00 in something like ten months, the company had what could only be called a successful debut season.

The money earned at social events that doubled as fund-raisers was vitally important in the life of a small-town company. In the 1870s, the state provided almost no monetary support for company maintenance. In the 1880s, state funds increased, but to go from nothing to something still did not go very far. Companies had to pay for rent of their armory space, for upkeep on their armory, and for uniforms, and they had to purchase whatever supplies they needed for training exercises and summer camp. For example, Company I, Seventh Infantry, paid twenty dollars a month for their armory space from 1878 to 1881, and $12.50 per uniform in 1878.[16] All of these expenses grew over time, for all ING companies. In the 1870s, the top floor of a livery stable or a merchant's warehouse could function as an armory with little or no improvement. Once he had modern breach-loading Springfield rifles to distribute, however, the Illinois adjutant general insisted that the weapons, accoutrements, and ammunition be stored in properly constructed and locked cabinets. Armory modifications became another company expense.[17] As the variety and amount of state property distributed to companies grew, so, too, did state regulations concerning proper storage facilities for such items as blankets, caps, overcoats, and eventually uniforms. With increased state property and money came increased demands from the state adjutant general for improved record keeping.[18] Companies gradually needed formal office space to maintain their records of enlistment and equipment, correspondence files, and financial reports.

In time, not just any big, empty indoor space would do as an armory without serious improvements in the form of offices and equipment storage facilities. Accordingly, the rent for specialized space went up, as did the cost of maintaining the armory. Some companies attempted to solve the problem by building a specialized armory of their own for their permanent use, but this was a very expensive proposition. Although some states, like New York, offered significant help to their state troops, the Illinois General Assembly offered no financial support for armory building until well after the turn of the century.[19] Instead, nineteenth-century Illinois companies that wished to have their own armory built had to turn to their communities for the funds.[20] This is just one example of the upward spiral of costs that constantly drove ING companies back to their communities in search of financial support.

Company I, or the Mason City Guards, kept up the steady flow of activity in their second year, which might be said to truly begin with their second annual Thanksgiving Day Ball.[21] In addition, they repeated their run of the *Dutch Recruit* early in November 1878.[22] The company sent out 250 printed invitations for another, quite formal, ball on Christmas Eve 1878, featuring two bands, including a string ensemble (the company also did not net very much, possibly because they decided to let members in for free).[23] Apparently quite bitten by the acting bug, members contracted with Viegard again and put on a second play, *The Spy of Shenandoah*, in February 1879, and hosted another public ball.[24] In March the company held a "club dance." By this time, the members had established an entertainment committee for each month, rather than creating new committees for each special event.[25] In March, the company also hosted another lecture, this one by a Mr. Burning. The company hosted a parade and "Jubilee Ball" on Memorial Day 1879, inviting the Havana Guards and the Delaware Guards to march with them, and held another ball on July 4, 1879.[26] In December, the company decided to hold a competitive rifle target practice and invited the Delaware Blues to meet with them on December 30 to shoot for a medal (not to exceed $5.00 in value) and afterwards to attend a New Year's Eve ball.[27] In February 1880, the company held another masked ball. Members with masks or in uniform were admitted free.[28] The company minutes stop naming each entertainment at this point, but continued listings of receipts and expenses suggest that they did not slow down their social calendar; it had merely become so integral to the company's life that a new secretary made no special mention of it in the minutes. One of the company's last entries, in February 1881, concerns the cancellation of an entertainment with a hired producer, something called "True Blue."[29] The Mason City Guards were unable to survive the resignation of their first captain, Amos Trout, in November 1880.[30] Company I, Seventh Infantry ING, was disbanded May 9, 1881.[31]

During its brief life, Company I must have been at the center of the social life of Mason, Illinois. Not all ING companies were as successful as the Mason City Guards in creating a steady flow of social activities, but the companies that survived over the course of years or decades were equally or more successful. Company histories and souvenir volumes stress the importance of the social schedule to the life of a company and of their communities. Newspaper accounts of picnics, armory dress parades, and the like reinforce the significance of these activities in the life of an average ING company.[32] The historian of the Governor's Guard of Springfield, Charles Headenburg, recalled that the "work of drilling and the social features which had heretofore formed the life of the 'Guard,' went forward as usual, as the records show no happening of unusual importance," placing drilling and social activities on an equal footing in his summary of the early 1880s.[33] Further, Headenburg chose to highlight only social events under one company administration, reinforcing the significance of this aspect of company life for the members and the community alike: "On December 21, 1886, John S. Hurt was elected Captain and H. M. Wolf First Lieutenant. During this administration the Company held its well established social and military position, playing a very important part in the social life of our city. The series of brilliant parties and receptions given by them are remembered still with pleasure by the participants."[34] That Headenburg included so many memories of parties and receptions of the Governor's Guard in his brief history emphasizes that these events, as much as or more so than the military goals of the company, created their identity within their community.

Headenburg was not alone in his choices. The historian of Company E, First Infantry, tells of an organization that "has always been noted for its weakness for the social amenities of life, [and in 1883] gave a reception to the governors of Illinois and Wisconsin during the encampment at Lake Geneva."[35] The historian of Company A, First Infantry, recorded in 1890 that, "its discipline, drill, athletic, and social records compare favorably with those of any other similar organization."[36] And from Horace Bolton, historian of the Second Infantry, ING:

> For nearly four years after its experience of active service in the stock yards district [1894] the Second led an almost uneventful existence, the social side of the organization being most in evidence, the only events worthy of note being this presence in 1896, at the inauguration of Governor John R. Tanner. During the annual encampment of that year General Merritt, commanding the Department of the Lakes, was the guest of General Wheeler, the Brigadier.[37]

All these historians of various companies at different times and from all over of the state of Illinois included a record of the social life of a company because social activities played such a critical role in sustaining a viable militia or national guard organization.

In the 1870s, some ambitious companies rolled several social events into one glorious event. In 1875, the *Chicago Inter Ocean* reported, "The Hannibal Zouaves (colored) Captain R.B. Moore, will give a grand military entertainment at Burlington Hall, on next Monday evening, August 2nd. The entertainment will consist of drills, speaking, sham battles, cotillions, etc. and a supper. The proceeds will go for buying arms for the company."[38] In 1877, Company I, Seventh Infantry, hosted a competition, a picnic, and a grand ball on a single day.[39] In 1879, "grand entertainment" was held "for the benefit of Co B, 16th Battalion ING," at the Exposition building in Chicago. "The Summer Guards of St. Louis were in the city on a visit, and of course, there was a great time generally among the colored population. After a competitive drill in which the Chicago company compared favorably with the St. Louis organization, there was a ball at which a large number of the ladies and gentlemen tarried well into the small retreating hours of the night."[40] Social events like these were both the lifeblood of companies and the reward for the labor and commitment of militia members. By the 1880s and later, events often grew too elaborate to manage more than one at a time.[41]

Female Appreciation and Admiration

Unlike many of the other social, fraternal, and service activities that drew people together in the late nineteenth century, most formal militia socializing was resolutely, powerfully heterosocial. Social events not only created a role for women in the life of a company, they demanded female participation—and appreciation. Women were vital contributors to most of the social events on the calendar. They served as bakers and cooks, hall decorators, dancing partners, and fellow actors in amateur theatricals. At particularly important ceremonial occasions, they served as central actors in the dramatization of the social and national importance and value of militia and National Guard companies, and of membership in those organizations. In all of these activities, women were perhaps most important because militiamen regarded and described, coyly to overtly, female recognition, appreciation, and desire as one of the ultimate confirmations of their dashing and manly selves. Guard historians imbued much of their writing of the social and public side of their organizations with a rosy glow of romantic conquest.

Women were the intended audience for much of a company's public display, and at the same time, women were solicited for help in provisioning, decorating, and organizing balls, picnics, and suppers.[42] In 1877, the secretary for Company D, Seventh Infantry, recorded in their minute book, "A committee of nine be appointed to assist the Ladies in getting of the festival."[43] And "the company attend[ed] the supper to be given by the Ladies of Peoria."[44] And a "committee of three [was appointed] to obtain six Ladies to solicit delicacies for festival and to wait upon Miss Kate Immel."[45] In 1884, Captain W. V. Jacobs, First Regiment Calvary, assured that his command's winter ball would be one "of the most successful combinations of camp and parlor ever made in the west" through his "personal solicitation" of "a great number of Chicago's representative society ladies" as patronesses, who in turn supervised the guest list and received a listing of their names in the *Chicago Tribune*.[46] At a "brilliant reception" in Aurora in 1894, hosted by Brigadier General "Andy" Welch for the officers of the Illinois National Guard, the Ladies Guild of Trinity Episcopal Church served 450 suppers.[47]

At key moments, women were also featured performers themselves. Women's speeches on the occasion of delivering a gift of colors (or flags) preserve for us contemporary images of the ING, and the roles they hoped to play in the lives of their members and their communities. Women, by virtue of being outside the membership, could speak as appreciative recipients while also noting the reciprocal relationship of a military and the larger society it aimed to preserve. In 1877, for example, Mrs. W.C. Rand presented a stand of colors to the Oakland Rifles at their first ball. She began with an apology for interrupting the festivities and then moved on to the purpose of this particular fund-raiser. "The truth is, sir, while we knew of the intention to devote the proceeds of the entertainment to the purchase of a stand of colors, we thought the opportunity so good a one for what you would doubtless term a flank movement, that we have been tempted to put it into execution."[48] Then she offered a testimony to the work of the company, noting all the hardships of training and service, and indicating that she was fully aware of the company's financial need.

> We desire your command should know that the devotion shown by them in attendance upon the exacting duties of drill, often at no little personal inconvenience and expense; their soldierly deportment; their perseverance in maintaining their organization in the face of grave obstacles; and especially their ready response to a recent call from the State to active duty, are fully recognized by the community in which they live.[49]

In conclusion, Mrs. Rand linked the company, the community, and the nation. "I have the pleasure of tendering to the Oakland Rifles, as a gift from the citizens of the delightful suburb in which all feel so just a pride, this stand of Regimental colors, and we are sure that these emblems are consigned to men who will gallantly guard and defend, under all circumstances, the National honor which they represent."[50] Mrs. Rand neatly toed all the traditional marks in this speech, distinguishing the company members as gentlemen, noting their devotion to duty and their patriotism, and recognizing their role as national defenders by gifting them their new flags.

The responsibility of women supporters of a company or regiment for supplying flags became so cemented over time that the following notice appeared in an 1890s souvenir of the First Infantry in Chicago. "The Souvenir wonders—and at every parade the wonder grows—that the ladies of Chicago do not see how ragged and forlorn our colors have become. We are proud of them, it is true, for the long service they represent, but some of these days we shall be literally drifting under bare poles unless some kind providence (feminine gender) comes to our relief."[51] This comment comes at the end of histories of the various companies of the regiment and of the regiment as a whole that boast of the regiment's fiscal strength and positive balance sheets. The regiment could have purchased new flags at any time. Flags obtained on the market however, clearly did not have the meaning and symbolism of flags made and given by women. Flags made (or paid for), presumably lovingly, by women supporters of the regiment and presented with proper pomp and circumstance clearly carried a weight and significance far beyond the fabric of the flags. By publicly recognizing and honoring the role of the militias and praising the men who made the militias their avocation, women also explicitly acknowledged and rewarded the adult manhood of all the volunteers.

Toward the end of his *Souvenir* history of the First Infantry, ING, Lieutenant Colonel Turner wrote:

> To that most important and most highly prized portion of the command which does not appear on parade, and whose names do not grace our roster—our wives and sweethearts—The Souvenir desires to make most ample acknowledgments. While it is true that the pronoun "our" is used purely in the editorial sense, and does not indicate possessory rights, yet The Souvenir appreciates fully the sacrifices which this unseen yet potent branch of the service is called upon to make. It will serve to even up matters in any sense, The Souvenir will make this agreement with you, Mesdames, Le Colonel, Le Majeur, Le Capitaine and ze Mesdames Lieutenant, Sergeant and Corporal; if you will allow these gentlemen to be colonels, majors, captains, sergeants, what not, down here at the armory, The Souvenir will accord you the right to wear the eagle, the bars and the chevrons at home.[52]

Despite the somewhat heavy-handed humor, Turner is also acknowledging the centrality of women to the affairs of any militia or National Guard organization. Women were vital members of the communities that supported and maintained guard companies.

In perhaps their most important task of all, women rewarded the dashing manliness of guardsmen by responding to their sexual and romantic allure. In 1889, Henry Barret Chamberlin, historian of Company C, Fourth Infantry, ING, wrote: "Interest in the Battalion has been maintained in many ways . . . the social features, when the armory became a ballroom, and the right arm of those new blouses were—never mind where."[53] Chamberlin's coyness only emphasized, as he no doubt intended, his perception of women's susceptibility to the sexual allure of men in uniform. In company history after company history, ING members boasted of their romantic conquests. At the same time, they delicately suggested that these same conquests were available to any man who would choose to put on the ING uniform. "It was on this occasion [a July 4 encampment in Lake Geneva, WI] that we fully came to understand the wonderful power of fascination exerted upon the fairer portion of our country cousins by a well-burnished row of brass buttons."[54] Or, "As a finale (breathe in not in————) the dainty stationery, bearing the Amboy postmark tells the story of the conquering march of the Oakland Rifles more eloquently than words can express."[55] This female fascination with the appeal of men in uniform was shared by eager guardsmen, who hosted ball after ball after ball, shamelessly exploiting every opportunity to put on their dress uniforms and dance the night away with all the pretty girls they could round up. The historian of Company C, First Infantry, recorded his organization's first "grand military ball" in glowing terms. This affair introduced "the fresh 'militia man' in all the glory of his new uniform to the admiration of the fair, and the envy of the sober citizen, a committee had elaborated a most select programme, and on the evening of May 13, 1875, the music of the orchestra and the delight of the dance fairly drowned the thought of forthcoming assessments."[56]

In the 1890s, Lieutenant Colonel Henry L. Turner of the First Infantry was famed for his skills as a host of glorious receptions and glittering balls, events where the "maneuvers last evening were directed by Cupid, who had dispensed with his quiver and wore the sword and other destructive implements of the Illinois Militia."[57] This particular ball, held during the dedication ceremonies of the Chicago World's Fair, was so glamorous that the *New York Times* carried a report of the festivities. "Fully 10,000 people thronged upon the floor of the armory of the First Infantry to-night in response to the invitations issued by Lieut. Col. Henry L. Turner of that regiment." The *Times* reported that the "armory was tastefully and elaborately decorated with flags and bunting . . . and when the festivities were at their height the great room, with the bright costumes of the ladies and the dark blue and gold of the military guests presented a handsome appearance."[58] From the multitude of uniforms and absence of civilian dress among the guests, the *Chicago Tribune* reporter concluded that it "was distinctively a military ball and the military men had the balance of power. The women who went there to see the military knew it, and the military was there to be seen."[59]

If uniformed National Guardsmen were observed to appeal to women before 1898, service during the Spanish American war only increased the impact, for women and reporters alike. On July 17, 1898, the *Illinois State Journal* published a large elaborate line drawing featuring a tall, handsome,

Figure 2
"Off with the Old Loves and On with the New," *Illinois State Journal*, July 17, 1898.

uniformed and mustached Guardsman dancing off with the belle of the ball, under the noses of a row of tuxedoed and wealthy gentlemen, all of whom clearly lack the Guardsman's handsome physique and sexual appeal.[60]

Dancing in uniform continued to excite the admiration of the fair, and perhaps envy among others, and ING histories steadily record balls and other elaborate entertainments up through well after the turn of the century.[61] Charles Headenburg, captain of Company C, Fifth Infantry, boasted, "The Company gave its annual 'military ball' on January 29, 1902. Many officers from other companies attended and the affair was a grand success. Former Captain M. F. O'Brien led the grand march. The hall was elaborately decorated with flags, Chinese and Japanese lanterns, bunting, festooning, military groups and pictures."[62] Captain Headenburg went on to note that the "organization is in good condition; but will be strengthened soon. Another military ball will be given by the members March 26, 1902."[63] In 1914, the Eighth Illinois finally received their own state-built armory in the Bronzeville section of Chicago, the heart of the African American Community.[64] The armory represented many things to African Americans in Chicago, not the least of which was state commitment to their formal equality and full citizenship, and they christened their new armory with a New Year's ball.[65] Guardsmen used military balls to put their best, most attractive side on display. Handsome, gallant, athletic men in formal military uniforms with rows of shiny buttons showed themselves and their institutions at their manly best, and the best reward was female appreciation.

If the admiration of women was a sweet reward, to be fought over by women was sweeter still, and John Skinner, historian of the Fourth Illinois USV, included in his history of his unit's experiences in the Spanish American War an exchange of poems between the girls of Savannah, Georgia and the girls of Matoon, Illinois. The series began when a 'Savannah, Georgia girl' issued a *Warning to Illinois Girls*.

> Listen young ladies of Illinois
> To a story I'll tell of your charming boys
> Who came to our city in '98
> To guard its citizens early and late.
>
> They guarded our town, and captured the hearts
> Of maids and matrons down in these parts
> By their pluck and zeal, and manly ways,
> And well the Fourth deserves the praise.
>
> How well they marched on the grand review,
> So well, indeed, that the president, too,
> Said to their colonel, standing near,
> 'Tis the best drilled regiment passed by here.
>
> And oh, how we cheered our boys that day;
> And oh, how we wept, when they sailed away,
> While since they are gone our girls are blue,
> And talk of going to Cuba, too.

The author went on to warn the women of Illinois that if they scolded the "boys" for flirting with the Savannah girls,

> We'll bring them back to our city fair,
> Then every day'll be "Thanksgiving" here;
> And we'll be so kind, and good and true,

They'll never go back again to you.

The author then offered praise of specific individuals.

Now think of the boys you'd make exiles,
Delightedly basking in southern smiles.
First Willie McKnight, a charming lad,
Next in the procession then comes Dad.

And after him comes trooping others,—
Rolla and Babe, and Kincade Brothers;
And right in line is our bonnie son Beam,
And all the men on the foot ball team.

There's many more I might mention yet,
Of the gallant Fourth, whom our girls have met;
Whom the girls all love, esteem and admire,
To sing their praises we never tire.

The poem concludes:

Don't threaten the lads with ire and wrath,
Lest Savannah girls may stand in your path,
To protect the Fourth with their lives they would,
The Fourth, so brave, so true and good.[66]

Once this poem was published in the *Matoon Gazette*, another poem appeared, this one "a northern girl's reply to a southern girl's poem." In this poem, the "northern girl" defends herself and her sisters as more beautiful, charming, caring, willing, and kind than the Savannah girls, concluding:

But the girl of the north-land,
The Illinois Fourth Land,
    Is queen of her own special throne,
And she'll keep not a part of,
But just the whole heart of
    Her hero in "Illinois' Own."[67]

In June, 1899 the "girl from Savannah" replied in defense of her sisters, proclaiming their true love for their own and praising one final time the character of the citizen-soldier.

> Tho' we frankly acknowledge your boys to be brave,
> Our hearts to our own boys, we long ago gave,
> Who are loyal and loving, brave, honest and true
> As the Fourth or any who wore Uncle Sam's blue.[68]

Guardsmen in Illinois, Skinner and other ING members suggested, could reasonably hope that by joining their local company, they would be recognized by the girls they admired as boys who were loyal and loving, brave, honest, and true.

Social events were central activities for ING companies. Social events supplied appreciative audiences, fund-raising opportunities, and the chance for members to enjoy their membership status beyond military training and patriotic parading. Social events established that members were participants in something special; their dress uniforms, speeches, colors, dances, and plays were the tangible rewards that made membership worth the expense of their time and their money. The importance of social events also makes plain that companies could not have survived without the support of women. The social calendars of guard companies, more than anything else they did, recognized the contributions and importance of women supporters. Balls, dances, dinners, plays, and opportunities to participate in the civic dramas that surrounded the existence of any guard company were aimed directly at the women in the community. Social events created and fostered not only esprit de corps within a company and for a company in its community, they welcomed, and even depended on, the active participation of women. Most of a company's social and ceremonial life would have been meaningless without women as symbols, as objects, as partners, as providers, and as the final guarantors of the sexual and romantic appeal of men in uniform.

Patriotic Performances and Public Parades

Militia companies paraded regularly in public throughout the United States, and throughout the nineteenth century. They paraded on patriotic holidays, during civic celebrations, for funerals, on their way to competitions, at summer camp, and for the entertainment of their friends and families. Companies paraded so often because parades put them most squarely in the public eye, and they were utterly dependent on the public for their survival. Companies needed members and money to continue from one year to the next, and from the 1870s until well after the turn of the century, both came primarily from their local communities.

Militia parades and the exhibition drills that often served to end short parades have a distinctive history of their own within this larger American public parade tradition, a history which contributed to the success militia members had in holding onto their place in the civic eye.[69] Early in the nineteenth century, volunteer companies and militia companies seized leadership in creating patriotic parades on significant national holidays, successfully linking patriotic celebration to the militia tradition and the role of the citizen-soldier.[70] A good portion of the authority of antebellum militia members to establish their dominance derived from their members' ability to embody the most respectable, most orderly and disciplined end of the spectrum of parade behavior at a time when other groups still embraced a much rowdier public tradition.[71] Militia members capitalized on the basic advantage drilled marching gave them to present an orderly, even flashy appearance during civic and patriotic events. They also used the long association of military marching to music to their advantage. As the century progressed, the vehicle of the volunteer militia, because of its public visibility, proved interesting to an ever-growing number of men hailing from an ever-wider array of social and cultural backgrounds. German and Irish immigrants sought out the militia forms to prove new-found American-ness, while nativist groups used their militia companies to defend a homegrown ideal of American manhood and citizenship. Poorer men used their connections with elite officers to further their own careers, and elite volunteers used ever more selective membership lists and ever more elegant and expensive branches of the military to illustrate their own status.[72] All these new militias enthusiastically embraced the parade traditions of the first volunteer organizations and for much the same reasons, because seizing a place in the parade also worked to solidify public claims to responsible and orderly citizenship and respectable manhood.

Following patterns developed in the late antebellum period, the postwar Illinois militia drew on a very broad base of men throughout the late nineteenth century. In the 1870s men from a variety of ethnic and racial groups, classes, and regions flowed into the ranks of the state militia. By 1880, the officer ranks of the Illinois militia were filled by men from every walk of life, from laborers and factory workers, through skilled tradesmen and professionals. Close to 80 percent of all officers were married and owned their own homes in 1880, a percentage that was nearly exactly reversed for enlisted personnel. In the early 1880s the state militia was home to companies made up entirely of African Americans, and heavily of Scottish, Irish, and German members, and many more men of various ethnicities were scattered throughout the ranks.[73] At the turn of the century, the strong diversity among members by race, class, and ethnicity remained fully in place. (See appendixes A and B.)

By the 1870s, state militias had become part of the official culture of patriotic memory, and civic authorities mobilized militias to mark the national events that helped to bind the nation together again after the Civil War. Community leaders who organized the most resplendent of parade spectacles were so eager to incorporate militias in 1876 to celebrate the centennial that scores of men created militia companies just to have one to march. Fourth of July parades, like many annual civic events, celebrated events in the nation's past, and these annual events were part of an ongoing negotiation about which events merited memorialization and how they ought to be commemorated. During the antebellum heyday of the urban parade, parades that took the whole community for their parade routes, the Fourth of July parade could encompass the entire urban population as both representative performers and as an enthusiastic and participatory audience.[74] As ethnicity increasingly came to be an organizing principle in urban social and political life, establishing a militia company was one more way for ethnic groups to indicate their desire to be political and cultural actors on the larger stage. As parades themselves splintered into smaller, more localized and somewhat rarer events, the militia splintered with them, managing in this way to maintain a military presence in almost every significant public ceremony.[75] Rather than diluting the power of the military in civic events, this splintering worked to increase the reach of the ING and other militias as men from a wider variety of communities adopted the form for themselves.

One of the most powerful ways National Guard and militia companies of postwar Illinois laid claim to public authority was through their participation in annual patriotic parades. July Fourth celebrations provided staple performance opportunities for ING companies. The following is a sampling of newspaper accounts of ING participation in July Fourth festivities in the 1880s and 1890s. In 1880 *The Chicago Tribune* reported "several companies of the Sixth Battalion [celebrated] the Fourth out of town, or have already done so. Companies A and D went to Wilmington with the Regimental Band and colors; Company C went to Joliet; and Company E to Sycamore."[76] In 1882 the Monmouth Guards, or Company M, ING, participated in the Monmouth Independence Day celebrations, while the Sublette Guards paraded in Dixon and Springfield had a military parade.[77] In 1883, four military companies staged a military parade and followed it up with competitive drills in Rock Island, Illinois, while Companies A and B of the Second Regiment of Chicago and their regimental band paraded with the Freeport militia company, held an exhibition drill and planned a sham battle (which was omitted because of the heat). The Freeport Company finished the day by hosting a ball. In Decatur, the ING company contributed the fireworks display.[78] On July 4, 1892, Company I, Sixth Infantry, paraded in Moline and Rock Island, and on July 4, 1894 the company marched in Sterling with several companies from neighboring towns.[79] This listing is hardly a complete record of the participation of ING companies in Fourth of July celebrations during these 14 years, but it does suggest the naturalness of militia participation in Independence Day celebrations by the mid-1880s.

Military parades and exhibition drills served to mark special occasions in the late nineteenth century because the militia's historic role in patriotic celebration had made them into valuable patriotic actors, a tie so strong that companies created just for the Centennial continued long afterwards. In 1885 the city fathers of Grand Rapids, Michigan, organized a parade to mark the erection of a new courthouse, a symbol of civic pride and of economic growth, and invited the militia company from Springfield, Illinois, to help commemorate the occasion. Their choice to invite to an outside militia company to honor the new building helped mark the importance and significance of the occasion. In choosing a militia company with a strong performance reputation, the ceremony organizers drew on the historical role of militia display to link the city, the courthouse, and the nation through the figure of the citizen soldier, who defended and maintained them all by force of arms. The celebration organizers' choice reinforced the ideal of civilian control over the military by asking a military company to honor, literally, the house of the law. A successful military parade also honored the community that sponsored it, or in this case, two communities—the home community of Springfield and the city of Grand Rapids—through a performance that celebrated shared values and patriotic ideals.

This particular parade ended with an exhibition drill designed to wow the crowd and earn their approval.

> Division street was cleared opposite the government lot, and the Springfield Company [Company C, Fifth Infantry, ING], with six sets of fours, made its appearance for an exhibition drill. The manual was gone through with, both with and without numbers, with good effect. When it came to marching, the Company moved off with a spring that showed wonderful drill, and all their alignments were made in such a way that the military men present broke into rapturous applause. Other features which were applauded were the marching to the rear, and the loading in ten motions. This last was, perhaps, their best exhibition of the manual, the snap of the closing of the breeches of the twenty-four Springfield rifles being like the

snap of one gun. The Company were heartily applauded at the close of the drill.[80]

The Grand Rapids audience judged Company C's performance of military skill against a familiar scale and rewarded their success with applause. Within the larger audience, the reporter identified "military men" as especially important observers whose approbation—expressed by "rapturous applause"—was particularly valuable. While the implication that these "military men" were Civil War veterans is hard to resist, it is important to remember that the professional military had yet to establish full control over rank and title. In the antebellum years and after, many men claimed military ranks and titles they had not earned, gave themselves in civilian life promotions that they felt mirrored their appropriate (or desired) rank in society, and generally behaved as if military titles were up for grabs.[81] Twenty years after the Civil War, "military men" could, and most likely did, also refer to other National Guardsmen, current or past, and veterans of military service at home or abroad in the years between the Mexican-American War and the 1880s.

Nonetheless, the idea that the audience held knowledgeable observers who approved of the performance was clearly important to the reporter. With such public applause, one group of men, veterans, recognized and approved the military skills of another, younger group of citizen-soldiers. In recognizing successful individual and group mastery of the drill revolutions, the members of the audience granted the members of the company the chance to share in their status as military men. Military men were, first and foremost, respected adult male members of their communities who actually or figuratively tied themselves to the nation through their service in arms, past, present, or potential (or even entirely fictive).[82]

For the Springfield ING company, the parade and exhibition were occasions for the members of the company to demonstrate mastery of a complex set of athletic skills, both marching in unison and handling their weaponry. Mastery of these traditional military skills indicated a seriousness of purpose and a high degree of discipline on the part of each member of the company. Mastery of parade drilling also broadcast the success of a company organization able to command the serious commitment of time necessary to the attainment of specialized parade drill forms, a reputation, in this case, good enough to garner an invitation to perform for a distant community. Militia members also embraced their history as they worked to live up to and build on the patriotic pageantry of the past in this kind of parade and exhibition. During a parade, each company member also enjoyed an opportunity to display the many desirable qualities associated with military men, including patriotism, manliness, and status as respected adult members of the polity. By earning applause, company members basked in otherwise difficult to obtain public recognition and praise.

When read as dramas of social power, these exhibition drills also provide a revealing glimpse of some of the ways the traditional military display could be adapted to the demands of modern society. The central tension in the drama of the drill manual is that of subordination to higher authority combined with the crucial component of extreme individual effort. While this deference to authority derives from much older traditions, it could be, and was, reconstituted in an industrializing world to meet new situations and new demands for obedience to commands. The success of a military performance depended on each player knowing his part perfectly and perfectly subordinating himself to the group for the attainment of a shared goal. The approval of the military men, and the larger crowd, demonstrated that in 1885, Company C reached that goal. Of course, ending the military demonstration with "the snap of the closing of the breeches of the twenty-four Springfield rifles being like the snap of one gun" vividly reminded the audience of the power of state authority backed by the instruments of war, and the vital role of citizen-soldiers in corralling and controlling that same power of the state.

Parading for Civic Legitimacy

Performing in a military parade legitimized a company in the public eye in a way few other events could match, and guardsmen made much of their parades for that very reason. Both early historians of the First Infantry ING cite the first two public parades of the Regiment, in May and July 1875, as foundational moments in the early history of their Regiment. In May 1875, the eight-month-old First Infantry escorted the Grand Army of the Republic to their annual meeting in Chicago. "The showing made was phenomenal," gloated regimental historian (and eventual colonel) Henry Turner. "Eight months previously there was not a man, a uniform or a gun on hand as a nucleus, but on this day the regiment turned out with ten companies fully organized, armed and equipped, and showing some five hundred and twenty muskets in line." In Turner's judgment, the best part was that "the effect on the citizens was in the nature of a genuine surprise party, and as a result the regiment sprang at a bound into the great popularity which it has ever since retained."[83] Charles Diehl remembered, "When the Regiment made its first public appearance, in its dress outfit, led by its drum corps, and its own band, the spectacle was so brilliant and unexpected, that even the caustic press surrendered. Every daily paper, without exception, printed a leader, declaring how proud the city was to claim so fine a command."[84] While the formal history of the regiment begins in September 1874, the history of the regiment as a successful organization began on May 15, 1875, with public approval of the First Infantry's demonstration of military bearing and parade skills as the First honored the veterans, the military men, of the last great war. In honoring, and being invited to honor, the Grand Army of the Republic, the young members of the First were also able to draw a direct connection between their service and that of the volunteers of 1861–64.

The First Infantry paraded again in July 1875, in a formal review for the governor of Illinois.[85] On this occasion, the First paraded, and then at the end of the march performed drills from the manuals of arms on the parade, or reviewing, ground in Hyde Park. Governor John L. Beveridge, himself a Union general in the Civil War; Lieutenant General Philip H. Sheridan, U.S. Army and military commander of the district headquartered in Chicago; and Brigadier General Arthur C. Ducat, ING, looked on from the viewing stand. The news of this parade even made *Harper's Weekly*. "At its first parade, [the First Regiment Illinois State Guards] was enthusiastically received by the citizens and distinguished visitors from abroad, and from Gen. Sheridan and other military men received high commendation."[86]

As with the news accounts of the 1885 parade in Grand Rapids, Michigan, this reporter also recorded the approval of military men, this time high-ranking officers with distinguished Civil War records. When General Sheridan, General Ducat, and Governor Beveridge acknowledged the members of the First Infantry as comrades in arms by receiving and publicly approving the military drill performance, they conferred their sanction on the First as a serious military organization. They also extended their reputations and their history in the Civil War to embrace the young volunteers of the First as members of the same tradition. They granted each of the volunteers recognition and status as fellow "military men," a status carrying connotations of bravery, discipline, honor, courage, loyalty, and patriotism that was simply unavailable in civilian life. Such status wasn't even necessarily available to all members of the professional branches of the U.S. military in these decades.[87] Both early historians of the First rely on these two parades to establish the basis for claims by the members of the First to patriotic authority, public honor, and social and political glamour as manly and upstanding citizen soldiers. Glamour was also very important to these historians, and parades like this one epitomized military glamour, with gleaming uniforms and arms and the power of cadres of men moving in unison, responsive to the beat of the drum and the commands of their officers, to the approval of genuine military heroes.

The 1902 *Souvenir History: Governors Guard: Company C, Fifth Infantry, Illinois National Guard* also uses parades as evidence for the success of the early organization from which the Governor's Guard traced their history. According to the *Souvenir History* the earlier company, then known as the Springfield Zouaves, marched in a procession to lay the cornerstone for the new state capitol building. Later, the *History* reports that the Springfield Zouaves traveled to Normal, Illinois to "assist in laying the corner stone of the Soldiers' Orphans' Home." In 1874 the company officially changed its name to the Governor's Guard and reorganized. Once reorganized, the company announced its new formation by marching in the parade to the unveiling of a statue of Abraham Lincoln in the Oak Ridge Cemetery on October 15, 1874. As the first parades of the First Infantry of Chicago would do the following year, the first parade of the new Governor's Guard marked the inception of their new public life and gained for them legitimacy and stature in a way no other public performance could. When the Governor's Guard escorted President Grant, Vice President Wilson, and the Secretary of War to honor President Lincoln, they, like the First, publicly linked themselves to the military history of the Civil War and to all its heroes, alive and dead. When they escorted the president and his party, members of the Governor's Guard also marked themselves as manly enough to lead and protect the leader of the nation.

The parade to Oak Ridge Cemetery was only one of ten parades in which the Governor's Guard marched during their first year under their new name.[88] The historian of the company boasted of their public parades that first year because parading marked the formal existence of a company and illustrated its status and respectability in the public arena, a need that did not fade with the age of the company. Later Governor's Guard parades significant enough to warrant a mention in the history of the company included an 1876 parade in Rockford to lay the cornerstone for a new county court house; an 1879 parade escorting President Hayes and General Sherman to the Illinois State Fair; and an 1880 parade escorting officers of the ING to a military convention in Springfield. In 1880 General Grant visited Springfield a second time, and the Governor's Guard once again performed escort duty. Also in 1880, the company traveled to Atlanta, Georgia, "to participate in the laying of the cornerstone of the armory of the 'Gate City Guards.'" In 1881 the company again escorted ING officers, this time to the inauguration of Governor Shelby Cullom, and on July 4, 1885, the company traveled to

Grand Rapids, Michigan, to participate in the cornerstone-laying ceremonies there.[89] This list includes only the most significant of the parades that Company C, the Governor's Guards, marched in during the ten years between 1874 and 1885. Escort duty to particularly notable public figures and Civil War veterans, and the honor of participating in the dedication of significant buildings, made the reputation of the Governor's Guard. Meanwhile, Company C spent only six days in active service, during the railroad strikes of 1877, less than a quarter of the time they spent traveling to parades and drill competitions during the same years.[90]

In a souvenir volume dedicated to the Eighth Regiment, ING (initially the independent Ninth Battalion), Harry McCard also called attention to parades as a vehicle for establishing the legitimacy of a company, or in this case battalion-strength, organization. The legitimacy and potency of the Eighth was particularly crucial, as it was the only African American organization in the ING during the 1890s. "The Ninth Battalion [their first number] was the Negroes' West Point. Nothing marked their Freshman, Sophomore and Junior years save many nights of hard drill, several brilliant parades, and now and then a solemn march when a comrade was borne to his final resting place."[91] The independent Ninth Battalion, struggling to survive until it secured a place in the ING, was especially in need of the public approval that could be won by putting on a good parade.

African American Men in the ING

On July 1, 1877, a new militia code became effective in Illinois, and among the provisions of this law was a section prohibiting any private companies from marching with weapons (meaning guns) without the express consent of the legislature. The following spring, African American men organized two Chicago-based companies, developing from the core of the older and unaffiliated Cadets. Their intention was to create an African American battalion within the framework of the new Illinois National Guard. The organizers reached their goal in the spring and summer of 1878, when the Sixteenth Battalion, ING, entered state service. The Sixteenth included companies A and B in Chicago, the Clark County Guards of Marshall, and in October the battalion gained the Cumberland County Guards of Greenup. The major, Theodore C. Hubbard, along with the battalion staff, was commissioned in September 1878.[92]

The Sixteenth Battalion, ING, remained active and on the state's rolls for three years, through 1882. Then, during the first months of

1882, a new adjutant general reorganized the state's militia, working to eliminate inefficient, undermanned, or virtually disbanded companies. At that time, the Sixteenth Battalion was mustered out of the state service.[93] The black community in Chicago, and in particular the members of the Sixteenth Battalion, were outraged at losing their place in the state forces. They held a number of meetings to express their dismay and sent a delegation to the Governor and to the adjutant general to plead for their place in the Illinois National Guard.[94] In response to their appeals, Alexander Brown was commissioned captain of a new African American company in Chicago on July 12, 1882, as was his first lieutenant.[95] Brown served previously with the Sixteenth Battalion. Brown's company is not listed on the register of state militia companies of 1882 or July 1883, but by December 1883 the company appears on the strength tables as the Chicago Light Infantry (Colored) with a total membership of 68 men and officers.[96] The Chicago Light Infantry, under Brown, lasted for almost five years, until May 2, 1887, when it, too, was mustered out of the state service. The historian of the future Eighth Illinois USV, W. T. Goode, wrote of this otherwise low moment for African American military organizations in Illinois that, nevertheless, "the colored men were undaunted. It was not their intention to be discarded."[97] So, in the early summer of 1890, African American men in Chicago gathered once again to start up a volunteer military organization.

On June 5, 1890, a group of determined organizers held a meeting to establish a new African American military organization. Their goal was to create several infantry companies and find them a place in the Illinois National Guard as a battalion-strength organization. Enthusiasm was high in the black community in Chicago in 1890, and a battalion-sized (from two to six companies) organization formed and applied to the state for membership in the Guard. Governor Joseph Fifer denied the application, apparently on the grounds of shortage of funds, though prejudice and politics both played a part.[98] Fifer made it clear that the only way blacks could serve in the Guard was as unattached companies or as a separate battalion or regiment-strength organization. Others were more supportive, especially in Chicago. In August 1890, the *Chicago Tribune* announced (somewhat prematurely) that the "Ninth Battalion, composed of young colored men of the South Side, became last night a permanent part of the militia of Chicago." The report, like so much newspaper coverage of the militia, noted approvingly that the members "are a lot of wide-chested, broad-shouldered young men who ought to make a good-sized regiment pretty tired."[99] Drill-master and editor of the *Illinois Guardsman* Henry Barrett Chamberlin supported the Ninth and worked as an instructor with the new companies, assisted and later succeeded by Lieutenant George W. Bristol of the First Infantry.[100]

Determined to gain a place for the Ninth in the ING, John C. Buckner, major of the still-private Ninth Battalion, ran for state representative for the Sixth District in 1894 and won. Born and educated in Illinois, Buckner completed two years of college at Northwestern College in Naperville before settling in Chicago, where he worked first for a foundry and later for a "well-known caterer, H. M. Kinsley." He joined the Ninth as a captain while it was still a private organization, and in time he rose to the rank of colonel.[101] Once a member of the General Assembly, Buckner framed and worked to pass a bill creating a vacancy in the militia and making an appropriation to fund it. The movement to find a space for the Ninth in the ING was undoubtedly assisted by Governor Altgeld's campaign promise to also find a place for the Chicago-based Hibernian Rifles, another organization seeking membership in the ING.[102] As the bill was moving through the legislature, Buckner approached Governor John Peter Altgeld, "who was impressed with and friendly to the scheme, [and] endorsed the movement, giving it his earnest efforts and support, and by orders emanating from his executive chamber, the Ninth Battalion of Chicago became the Ninth Battalion, I.N.G."[103] So, on November 4, 1895, four companies of the new Ninth Battalion, ING, were mustered into service, and on January 27, 1896, state representative John C. Buckner was commissioned major of the new Ninth Battalion, ING.[104] By September 1896, the Ninth Battalion boasted 18 commissioned officers and 407 enlisted men.[105]

That the battalion had managed to stay together for five years without any governmental support, money, loan of arms, or rent subsidies speaks volumes for the determination of the African American community in Chicago to make this battalion succeed. All financial support had to come from within the community, and all members had to sustain enthusiasm over the long haul without access to the shooting ranges or participation in summer camp that provided some of the main draws for ING membership in general.[106] The maintenance of the Ninth Battalion was all the more remarkable given the relatively tiny population of African Americans in Chicago to fill its ranks and pay its bills. In 1893, in a city with a population of over one million, there were just over 15,000 African Americans in residence in Chicago. A substantial proportion of the single young men between the ages of 18 and 30 were required to be active to keep the battalion going, and yet they managed. Fortunately for the Ninth, the African American population of the city was growing very quickly, and by 1900 there were 30,150 African Americans in the city.[107]

Figure 3
White and African American members of the First Division, ING, at Camp Lincoln, ca. 1895. Courtesy of the Chicago Historical Society. Photographer: D. H. Spencer. iCHi-26577.

Once accepted into the ING, the Ninth Battalion entered fully into the life of a state militia organization—the weekly training, the manual of arms, the parades, the whirl of social events, and the excitement of training camp during the summers of 1896 and 1897.[108] Although in the judgment of various inspecting officers the Ninth was in need of much work, they saw much promise in the battalion as well.[109] Some members of at least the First Regiment were willing to celebrate the success of the Ninth in entering the ING when they posed for some group "at ease" shots at summer camp in 1896.[110] Writing about the 1890 formation of the Ninth Battalion, Goode recalled, "The formation of such an organization, it was thought by many, would in time prove a beneficial and a social advantage to the colored residents of Illinois."[111] The benefits and social advantage that the African American community derived from supporting an African American military organization were several. A military organization publicly demonstrated the cohesion and determination of the entire community that created and supported it. Socially, a guard company fostered a situation in which African Americans were accorded respect that, in language if not in practice, was the same as that accorded to whites.¹¹² As the nineteenth century progressed, state militias, including the ING, and other fraternal organizations increasingly dominated formal civic ceremonies, especially the parades that marked important public holidays. African American guardsmen could capitalize on this tradition to make their own public claim to full membership in the civic body.¹¹³ An African American militia organization also confirmed and kept alive the Civil War military experience, which many—then and now—believed was an essential element toward securing the Fifteenth Amendment, the citizenship of African Americans.¹¹⁴ Emphasizing the connection to the Fifteenth Amendment and its guarantees for African American citizenship, Chicago-based African American companies held drills, parades, and balls to mark the anniversary of the adoption of the Fifteenth Amendment and the end of the Civil War.¹¹⁵ Just as the parades and participation in other important civic ceremonies confirmed the importance of the national guards, African American national guard companies could use their symbolic weight to add significance and luster to those civic commemorations that were particularly meaningful to the African American community.

Funeral Parades and Honorable Citizenship

Funeral parades were one of the most solemn and symbolically laden civic events in which militia companies participated. As the historian of the Ninth Battalion recorded, militia companies marched in funeral parades, to mark the passing of national leaders and for their own. The 1874 Springfield procession leading to the unveiling of a statue of Abraham Lincoln falls into this category of military parade. The military funeral procession, with or without the presence of the dead, was a particular form of public parade for antebellum and post-Civil War volunteer militias alike. Susan Davis notes that "precision of the march to the cemetery" accompanied by the sounds of bands, gongs, and rifle salutes at graveside was a particularly impressive and solemn way to demonstrate patriotic authority on the part of militia members.¹¹⁶ The 1874 Springfield funeral parade, elaborate as it was, paled before the opportunities for solemn ritual and patriotic authority National Guard members seized after the death of President James A. Garfield on Sept. 19, 1881. President Garfield died of complications from a wound received during an assassination attempt in July 1881. Like Mrs. Lincoln before her, Mrs. Garfield chose to have her husband buried at home, in Cleveland, Ohio. The funeral processions lasted for more than a week and began in Long Branch, New Jersey, where President Garfield died; continued to

Washington, D.C., where the funeral began; and finally traveled on to Cleveland, where the funeral was completed and Garfield was buried. National Guard companies took part in the processions in both cities, along the train route, and in many smaller cities around the country.

Along the route from Washington to Cleveland, companies of the Maryland and Pennsylvania National Guards gathered to observe and salute the passing funeral train.[117] In Cleveland, militia and National Guard companies from Ohio, Massachusetts, New York, Pennsylvania, and Illinois marched in the first division of the funeral procession.[118] The company from Illinois, Company A, Fifteenth Battalion, ING, from Alton, obtained a place in the Cleveland procession and so secured for the ING an important, national role.[119] Elsewhere in the East, companies of the New York and Pennsylvania National Guards participated in local mourning observations.[120] City officials in San Francisco, California also made plans for a grand funeral procession that would include both civic and military organizations.[121]

Small and large communities throughout Illinois also held local ceremonies to mark Garfield's funeral and to participate locally in an event of national importance. The ING in turn dominated many local civic ceremonies held to mark the funeral all over Illinois and in the surrounding states, claiming patriotic authority and leadership in a moment of national mourning. Illinois National Guard companies marched in funeral processions in Mount Vernon, Paris, Centralia, Decatur, Galesburg, Joliet, Rock Island, Paxton, and Morrison. Companies in the ING also marched in Indianapolis and Evansville, Indiana; in La Crome, Janesville, and Whitewater, Wisconsin; in Jackson, Coldwater, and Lansing, Michigan; and in Dubuque, Davenport, and Des Moines, Iowa.[122] President Garfield's funeral was the most solemn national civic event to take place since the funeral procession of Abraham Lincoln, and militia companies took the lead in many of the civic ceremonies marking the burial of the president in Cleveland.

In Chicago, civic leaders and militia officers put on a terrific display of solemn mourning that rivaled that in Cleveland itself, using the occasion to demonstrate the significance and wealth of their city, and the various Chicago ING organizations led the parade. The parade extended about one and a half miles, and some 15,000 men, in six divisions representing all of the military and civic organizations of the city, took part. The ING marched on the right of the line, and the veterans marched on the left. The First Cavalry marched dismounted (150 members turned out, more than they had horses) in five companies, preceded by their corps of buglers. The Second Infantry was next in line, led by a twelve-member drum corps, with ten companies and some 250 men. The Sixth

Infantry followed, with another 250 men in ten companies. Some companies of the Sixth Infantry were predominantly ethnic Scots and marched in a formal kilt-style uniform. Battery D, with eighty men and four field pieces and a Gatling gun—all five polished and draped with mourning crepe—marched ahead of the Sixteenth Battalion. The Sixteenth—the African American militia organization in the city at that time—turned out some eighty men in two companies headed by Major Samuel W. Scott, Quartermaster Williams, Captain Lloyd Wheeler and a Lieutenant Card. The Sixteenth's band and drum corps led off their section of the procession. The First Infantry concluded the militia portion of the procession, with 350 men marching with their regimental band and drum corps. Altogether, some 1,200 ING members took part in the Chicago funeral procession.[123]

Symbolizing national unity in a powerfully modern way, the procession was timed to begin at the same hour as the actual funeral cortege in Cleveland carrying the body of President Garfield from the ceremonies to the cemetery.[124] All along the parade route, Chicagoans had draped their buildings with crepe, hung mourning banners, and otherwise decorated as befitted the grand occasion. Many buildings sported portraits of President Garfield, President Lincoln, and President Washington—Garfield's shrouded in black, the other two in white. According to the papers, Chicago merchants sold some two million yards of black and white materials for decorative purposes. The Tribune Tower alone was hung with 9,000 yards of black muslin and 3,000 yards of paper decorations, at a cost of something close to $1,200.00.[125] Altogether, it is hard to question the *Tribune's* assessment that "[i]t was without doubt the most imposing parade which has ever taken place here, or perhaps elsewhere."[126]

Organizations reflecting all the major members of the community participated in the parade, following the old democratic parade traditions laid down in the early part of the nineteenth century. But where in antebellum parades the social and commercial elites led off the procession, indicating their superior status, in 1881 the military had taken that role for itself.[127] The military, veterans, and militia volunteers led the procession, veterans on the right of the line and current militia members on the left. Side by side, two generations of military men marched to honor their fallen leader. The Masons had the special privilege of escorting the catafalque that represented the presence of the body of the president. The rest of the panoply of civic, governmental, and ethnic associations were relegated to the back of the procession. The parade, fantastic spectacle that it was, followed closely in the footsteps of antebellum parades, where each unit of the polity had representative members (all male) in the procession, and the route was lined with an audience who understood the corporate symbolism on display. However, in 1881 the uniformed military in all its branches—active duty, veterans, and militia members—was rising to the top of the ceremonial heap in national commemoration and claiming rights of precedence for themselves. In a clear contrast to the class and ethnic organization of antebellum parades described by Mary Ryan, veterans' groups and the ING were both part of national organizations whose membership was not limited to men of a particular ethnicity—though individual companies or lodges might have a prevailing ethnic identification—the regular military and the National Guard were generally open to most white men.[128] The precedence given to veterans and the ING in Chicago, across the state, and beyond offered Illinois guardsmen the opportunity to stress again their identity as exemplary citizens of the United States who could be counted on to model the best kind of respectful, manly behavior for their communities and for the nation as a whole.

Memorial Day and the ING

Illinois National Guard members played in a visible role in another movement that became part of larger efforts to unite the nation—Memorial Day.[129] By embracing Memorial Day, ING members formally drew the Civil War into the annual ceremonial calendar of events dedicated to honoring the nation's past. For example, in 1880 the Mason City Guards held a ceremony to mark Memorial Day, and in 1883 ING companies participated in Memorial Day celebrations in Chicago, Ottawa, Rockford, Moline, and Monmouth, despite the steady rain.[130] In the 1890s, the entirety of the Chicago-based ING marched in several large-scale Memorial Day parades, sharing the glory with the grizzled members of the Grand Army of the Republic.[131] By the 1890s, ING companies were extending Memorial Day celebrations to include their own colleagues as well: "One of the sights which always stirs the patriotism in every breast may be seen on the last Sunday of May, in each year as it rolls around. The 'Veteran Corps,' [veterans of Company C] in connection with the 'Governor's Guard,' make their yearly pilgrimage to Oak Ridge, our 'City of the dead,' and cover with flowers the graves of those of the Guards who have 'crossed the bar' and gone over to the silent majority."[132] In extending Memorial Day celebrations to cover their own, militia members were able to legitimize and enhance their connection to veterans of the Civil War.

Militia and National Guard funeral processions were not limited to

Memorial Day observances, or to nationally important figures. Militia companies held military funerals to honor local leaders, veterans of the local company and most especially members of companies who died before finishing their terms of enlistment. Twice in 1887, Company C, Fourth Infantry and the Oakland Rifles marched in funeral processions that concluded with "Taps" at a graveside. They marched in June for Corporal E. G. Clark and in September 1887 for Sergeant Frank C. Byram. Both men drowned in summer accidents in the first year of the organization's existence.[133] Company C, Fifth Infantry, ING, the Governor's Guard, also marked the passing of members of their organization: "November 18, 1880, for the first time was the Company called upon to perform the sad duty of burying, with military honors, one of the active members, Harrison G. Fitzhugh, enlisted September 5, 1879, died November 16, 1880, of typhoid pneumonia."[134] With no major parades to report during the first three years of the companies' history, authors of souvenir historical sketches included these solemn moments as testimony to the serious purpose and intense commitment on the part of the members of the companies. These quieter funeral processions echoed the more dramatic processions to honor national figures even as they rendered the significance of membership for the public, in public ceremonies. During funeral performances for their own, Guard companies demonstrated to their communities the dignity and honor that Guard membership conferred was permanent. Companies also showed their communities that once a guardsman, a man always had a place with significance in the world; he would not be soon forgotten or his membership disregarded.

Parades, celebratory, solemn, national, or local, all helped to shape the public image about the militia and militia members. Militia parades drew on decades of traditions to solidify militia members' claim to stand as a link between individual, community, and nation. In their parades they presented themselves as selfless volunteers, willing to serve the nation with all the dedication and discipline at their command. Militia volunteers invested moments as diverse as dedication, national holidays, and private funerals with powerful images of patriotic sacrifice, national celebration, and the importance of individual subordination to the calls of community and nation. They also used these occasions to show themselves as attractive, athletic, manly men who represented the best their communities had to offer as responsible citizens and rightful inheritors of the valor and status of citizen-soldiers past.

Military parades not only established the legitimacy of a militia or National Guard company, they also confirmed National Guardsmen as key actors in the polity. By retaining and improving on the role established by volunteer militia companies in the antebellum era, the ING companies of the 1870s, 1880s, and 1890s solidified their claims to public authority on ceremonial and patriotic occasions. As parades in general diminished, militia parades emerged as significant simply by virtue of surviving into the new public ceremonial era of spectacle featuring elaborate performances by a few and for larger, largely passive audiences.[135]

The public territory claimed by the militias through parading and exhibitions bore fruit in both classic and new ways. First and most traditionally, as the militias paraded to establish legitimacy, they also secured a base for political action on behalf of their organization, and for themselves. Irish and African American organizations found the militia a particularly appealing vehicle to push forward their own claims to hold manly and respectable citizenship. Militia access to state funds increased as their representatives in Springfield and Washington, D.C. were able to point to these demonstrations as proof of the importance of and popular interest in a stable and orderly militia organization.[136] Militia members also were able to use parades to make a case for their new role as organizations that could model ideal forms of behavior for the public, and especially for young men aspiring to positions of adult respectability. Illinois National Guard parades were opportunities for members to demonstrate the outcome of the training process, to show that personal and individual commitment to the group and subordination to authority resulted in a visually and aurally powerful performance of disciplined manhood symbolically and practically linked to the power of the state.

Manly Citizens

A staple paradigm of U.S. history holds that the final decades of the nineteenth century were filled with turmoil, uncertainty, and social chaos. Most historians of the turn-of-the-century United States also broadly agree that Americans responded to the temper of their times by attempting to impose meaning and stability through institutions dedicated to determining appropriate social behavior for every particular circumstance. Many of these responses, formal and informal, have been the focus of excellent scholarship: professional associations, women's clubs, progressive reform associations, churches, families, fraternal organizations, and the working man's saloon, to name a few.[137] Not many historians of the era have counted the state militias among these types of social institutions, despite the central and highly visible role most militia organizations played in local public performances of civic order and discipline, or their function as popular social clubs—especially for younger men. These public, social roles have been largely missed, because militia actions in industrial conflict have received so much negative criticism and analysis, obscuring the day-to-day public life of these companies.[138] Despite the challenges and the occasionally negative press, the citizen-soldier held a powerful, and growing, allure for men of all ages and all across the nation over the last three decades of the nineteenth century.

Between 1870 and 1898, on top of whatever drilling they were doing, ING companies marched in numerous parades and performed exhibition drills, in all weathers, of all sizes, and on occasions from the most solemn to the most celebratory. Illinois National Guard members also hosted company dances, dinners, and picnics; produced amateur theatricals starring the company members; sponsored lectures and informal talks on a range of military topics; and generally enjoyed the social side of company life as thoroughly as they could. These public social events were so important to company members that in their company and regimental histories, they proudly recounted lists of parades, elegant dances, and glittering receptions for dignitaries of all stripes. They also preserved and shared treasured anecdotes of pranks and good times.[139] With these events, and the stories about them, ING members celebrated their manliness, their honor, and their embrace of civic responsibility.

Social events gave members the chance to show off their handsome and gallant uniformed manliness to adoring crowds—and as they frequently noted in their histories—particularly to crowds of attentive and responsive young women. Members of the ING were not only aware of their attractiveness to the opposite sex; they boasted of it, and they used it to entice new members to join in the fun. Social events could also be occasions for members to display their military honor and their good citizenship to potential recruits, and to the wider community that supported companies socially and financially. Militia organizations depended primarily on their local communities for financial support throughout the nineteenth and early twentieth centuries. Without the donations given freely by the local community, the admissions fees, the willingness to canvass for subscriptions or join the private associations that supported an active company, ING companies foundered and ultimately disbanded.

Social and ceremonial events, far more than the private training sessions, shaped the public face of the ING within their communities, and the public face is what earned the financial support and the new members that were essential for any ING organization's survival. Between parading on important occasions and providing a wide array of social events, guardsmen crafted a place for themselves as patriotic, responsible, and above all, dashing and manly citizens. As manly citizens they could command a steady flow of new members, and of private and public dollars. With members and money, they built their organizations from a handful of small, scattered companies in 1874, until, by 1897, the ING boasted some 7,000 members annually and had established for itself a strong base both in the state government and within their local communities.

CHAPTER 3

Confused Missions: The First Twenty Years of Strike Duty, 1870–90

> Next to serving the government there is no more patriotic manner of paying tribute to the flag than in that of serving the state faithfully and loyally under all circumstances.[1]
> —Rufus S. Bunzey, private, ING

In the last quarter of the nineteenth century, Illinois militia companies attracted new members and local support based on their presentation of manly men and responsible citizens. Guardsmen demonstrated their responsible citizenship largely through local performances of respectable patriotism and practice soldiering, performances that their local communities generally greeted with approval and applause and supported with community funds. However, in the later nineteenth century, the responsible citizenship of guardsmen also carried with it the potential call to riot and strike duty, and such duty turned out to be a controversial activity that earned the militia criticism and complaints rather than applause. In the early years of the militia revival in Illinois, some guardsmen embraced strike duty as a mission that was central and important to the militia and its future, and many more accepted the maintenance of order, if not the suppression of strikes, as an integral aspect of their civic responsibilities. Even then, though, enthusiastic supporters of strike duty were rare, and by the mid-1880s, guardsmen were expressing growing frustration with strike duty and its attendant difficulties.

Since Shays's Rebellion in 1786, state governors had deployed their active militia organizations to deal with civil unrest. Although few were completely happy about this, most citizens and militia members considered such service to be appropriate and useful.[2] At first glance, civil unrest triggered by strikes or labor disputes in the middle and later nineteenth century seemed to be the same sort of duty. By the end of the 1880s, however, most militia members in Illinois had come to see that policing strikes was quite different. For one thing, strike duty for the ING, and for most other state militias, could and usually did coincide with the failure of the strike. Many observers, focusing on this much-publicized activity, did form the idea that strike breaking was the primary function and purpose of the state National Guard. This idea left National Guardsmen in the difficult position of attempting to disprove what people believed they saw with their own eyes. It also left guardsmen struggling to satisfy competing constituencies. They had to respond to the state government that contributed—however insufficiently—to their upkeep and in exchange asked them to respond to moments of public unrest. Defending and maintaining public order was also an obvious act of responsible citizenship. At the same time, guardsmen in Illinois sought to avoid any service that rendered them little more than a private force for corporate ends, which would jeopardize their stance as responsible and representative citizens. Guardsmen needed to keep their reputation for military training and sociability focused on the positive rewards of admirable citizenship and on an honorable manliness, or they risked recruiting and fund-raising failures. Strike service inevitably placed these needs in direct conflict with each other.

Strikes and Strike Duty in Illinois

Striking was endemic in the late nineteenth century in the United States, and no industry or region of the country was without labor walkouts over the conditions or wages of work.[3] However, the overwhelming majority of strikes held in Illinois—and throughout the nation—were resolved at the local level, without appeal to the state government for aid or for intervention. In the 1870s, 1880s, and 1890s, twenty-six of forty-five state militias went into action in strike-affected regions, during moments of extreme crisis, during times when local authorities felt they did not have the power or the ability (or perhaps the willingness) to calm angry crowds and face down private security forces. Such service represented only a little more than a third of all state militia and National Guard instances of active duty, but strike duty was performed on a larger scale, and for a wider audience than almost any other single type of active duty. The ING, located in the heart of the central coal fields, had the greatest number of instances of strike service of any state militia between 1877 and 1900.[4] On the thirty-three occasions that ING members performed strike duty between 1870 and 1908, they found themselves grappling with situations that had already strained the ability and resources of local authorities. (See appendix C.) They also found themselves in situations for which they had no training and no real power, and in which it was difficult to determine fault and responsibility. To make matters even more frustrating for ING members, they often bore whatever political fallout could be pushed onto their shoulders—an outcome that was clear to them ten years before they figured out how to finesse the problem.

When Illinois governors did turn to the state militia to intervene in strikes, they sent the ING into service at the scene of a strike to restore a public order that local authority was temporarily unable to sustain. Guardsmen were ordered to restore order in whatever way they could, remand any captured "criminal elements" into local police hands, and then return to their homes. After that, state officials expected the local authorities to carry on themselves. It is in this simple, highly visible narrative that many, then and since, have read the interests of state authority in maintaining state military organizations to preserve public order and so have implied backwards that, therefore, this must be the reason why such organizations came into existence.[5] Critics of the assaults on organized labor have also tended to read in this narrative the clear relationship between industrial managers and the state governments that protected their investments.[6] Given the relative rarity of the call to the ING to police strike-related disorders, this reading has come much too quickly. Strikes that turned into community confrontations that led to state National Guard interventions were extraordinary moments and they do not, cannot, serve as a vehicle for understanding the history of strikes in general, the role of the state in labor/capital disputes, and these interventions definitely do not reveal much about the origins or purpose of National Guardsmen.[7]

The simplest narrative of state-supported strike-breakers also obscures the wicked undercurrents of local politics and disputed situations. The process of even acquiring state aid in a strike was complex. Local authorities—in the body of the county sheriff or city mayor—had to confess to the governor their inability to handle the strike situation and had to ask the state to intervene in their county (or city) to restore an order that they were unable to maintain. In essence, the request was itself an admission of weakness, if not of total incompetence. Even then, it was up to the governor to decide how to respond, and the governor did not have to send troops. In fact, Illinois governors often showed little inclination to rush troops into an unsettled local situation, learning over the course of the 1880s and 1890s that there was no political good to come from such involvement. Quite the contrary, it was often nothing but trouble, not to mention being quite expensive. Instead, Illinois governors could and often did choose to send a supply of state-owned weapons for deputy sheriffs, a personal observer, or some combination of the two rather than actual troops.[8] When governors did send troops, uncertain relationships between local and state authorities, illustrated by the frequent disagreements among the various parties concerned about when or even if disorder had taken or would take place, regularly complicated the situation on the ground even further.[9] The history of ING service in strike-related locales is fraught with tension between the local sheriffs and the ING commanders who arrived in their jurisdictions to assist in order restoration. Once on the ground, commanders regularly encountered uneasy local alliances and continual local bickering about the legitimacy of the need for state troops. Public opinion, local, statewide and national, was divided on how, or if, to police disputes between capital and labor.[10] Public sentiment was in a contentious and unsettled state about striking and strike policing, and about what role, if any, the state should play in those disputes. Nonetheless, ING officers found themselves in situations where, by default, they were expected to act clearly and decisively. Those who lived in strike-affected regions recognized, even agonized over, the problem that strikes were not a simple good vs. evil—labor vs. the state—situation. They also had a clear interest in limiting any disruption to their own daily lives. The simple narrative that casts ING strike service, and all state militia service in strikes, as tools of the emergent corporate class in their effort to squash labor organization is to miss both the political complexity of strike service, and, always, its relative rarity.[11]

Chicago Militias and the Relief and Aid Society, 1875: Hints of Future Troubles

Toward the end of February 1875, the Chicago newspapers were reporting that Socialists were threatening to march on the Chicago Relief and Aid Society to demand that the society change its policies to better respond to the desperate need created by the ongoing economic downturn.[12] Critics charged that the overseers of the Relief Society were mismanaging something between $300,000 and $1 million in resources and yet were denying relief to those who applied for help.[13] Some protestors even gave dramatic speeches about storming the society's building and seizing the funds. Many Chicagoans became convinced that civil war was going to break out over the dispute.[14] According to Holdridge Collins, writing some years later, "riotous demonstrations . . . directed more especially against the treasury and building of the Relief and Aid Society" posed a significant threat to local order and required a strong response.[15] Opponents of the so-called Communists mobilized all across Chicago.[16] The police stockpiled weapons in preparation for anticipated demonstrations in front of the society's building. The First Regiment, which then consisted of six companies, on its own initiative assembled at its armory to drill in preparation "to sally forth at a moment's notice," as Collins later described it. According to the *Chicago Times* reporter, Lieutenant Colonel McClurg of the new First Regiment did not "feel over confident that the troops under him [would] be called upon; nevertheless, he [had] felt it proper to make preparations for any emergency that may occur, and [was] determined to have the men in good condition for actual service, provided it [became] necessary to use them."[17]

Several other military companies located in Chicago also assembled at their armories to drill and otherwise gird themselves to defend the city from riot and war. The companies that readied for duty included the Clan-na-Gael Guards, the Alpine Hunters, the Irish Rifles, the Montgomery Light Guards, the Mulligan Zouaves, and the Hannibal Zouaves.[18] All these militia members took it upon themselves to prepare for action in defense of the Relief and Aid Society; there was no larger brigade or division organization in Illinois at that time. Individual companies reported directly to the adjutant general and the governor, and no orders issued from either of them about the situation in Chicago. It is not even clear if all the companies listed in the papers who were reported prepared for action were formally connected to the state, especially as an official connection in 1875 consisted of little more than a commission for a company's officers.

Although the existence of a formal connection between all the various mobilizing military companies and the state government is unclear, the daily newspapers in Chicago made no distinction between the organizations along those lines. It is unlikely that the general public was able to do any better. Nonetheless, the inability of the governor or his appointed generals to mobilize, demobilize, or control all of the military-style companies in Chicago that would have liked to participate in some sort of domestic order maintenance action in 1875 would not have shielded them from being held responsible by the majority of the general public for the outcome of whatever actions taken by these companies.

The vision of barely disciplined companies sallying forth with the "newest and best arms known to modern warfare" into a riot must have given Governor Beveridge a variety of nightmares. At the very least, when he had the opportunity later that spring to address the members of the First Regiment, he explicitly warned them against unauthorized activities in the name of the state. He announced that he was glad their "warlike" movements "meant nothing beyond display" until they were called to serve. But, in "time of peace," he desired them to "bear in mind, *they had no authority to act*, except by direction of the civil authorities— the mayor and the police officials [my emphasis]."[19] Beveridge touched here on tensions that were the result of the tenuous and semilegal ties of the militias to the state. There was nothing the governor could do to prevent the militias from acting as a *posse comitus* except revoke the commissions given to the officers and demand the return of state-owned armament. That the officers of the First Regiment were not equally concerned by the vagueness of their claim to act as soldiers of the state or their potential personal liability should the state disclaim them is clear from Collins's memories of these events. Collins wrote that his regiment's preparations "probably [sic] had a greater effect than any other cause in preventing an outbreak of the communistic element at that time."[20] The attitude of Collins and others like him lay at the root of Governor Beveridge's warning to the militias, the First Regiment in particular. It also marks the first of many differences in opinion, even among guardsmen and their friends and supporters, regarding the proper role and stance of militias toward intervention in domestic order issues.

The Great Strike of 1877 and the Illinois National Guard

Illinois militia members seized on the dramatic growth of the volunteer forces in 1875 and 1876 to revise the Illinois laws that governed the state forces. By the end of the 1876–77 session of the General Assembly, militia members had succeeded in securing the passage of a new bill, and the entire state militia was mustered out on July 1, 1877, in preparation for a complete reorganization of the state forces. National events intervened soon after, pushing all organizational concerns into the background. The Great Railroad Strikes of 1877 were about to begin. The economic downturn that began in 1873 and triggered the problems at the Chicago Relief and Aid Society in 1875 had deepened into a terrible depression by 1876 and early 1877. Railroads suffered particularly badly during these years and turned to massive rate cutting programs to keep business up, though many railroads failed despite this tactic. In order to continue paying dividends to shareholders of 2 to 8 percent, railroad managers repeatedly cut wages across the board by 10 or 20 percent. Railroad workers did not take these cuts passively. They struck often, and a series of strikes in December 1876 and early 1877 on eastern railroads had successfully pressured management to reinstate the most recent wage cuts. The successes of some railroad strikes was not shared across railroads or in other industries, and the strikes served ultimately to harden the position of industrial managers around the nation, on the theory that concessions had only yielded further trouble. Further, labor disputes had been anything but calm and orderly in the 1870s. The anthracite coal regions of Pennsylvania had been torn by spectacular violence for years. On June 10, 1877, several alleged members of the Molly Maguires, a suspected terrorist association with Irish nationalist overtones believed to be one of the most violent of the secret labor associations in the Pennsylvania coal fields, were hanged for labor violence.[21]

Beginning in June and July 1877, yet another 10 percent wage cut went into effect on a number of large eastern railroad lines. On July 16, workers on the Baltimore and Ohio Railroad struck in Baltimore to protest the further cut, with little immediate effect. However, down the line in Martinsburg, West Virginia, striking railroad employees were far more successful in stopping railroad traffic and tying up miles of freight trains.[22] By July 18, rail traffic was backed up two miles east and west of Martinsburg, and the strike had already begun to spread to other shipping trades and to other cities.[23] Strikes spread rapidly across Pennsylvania, and on the weekend of July 21, the worst riots to date erupted in Baltimore and Pittsburgh. State governors began calling up their militias. In Baltimore, a Maryland militia regiment marching toward the train station fired on the crowd and at least ten bystanders and onlookers were killed outright, and dozens more were wounded. Then on the night of July 22, a score or more people were killed in Pittsburgh by Philadelphia militiamen. The militia were vainly defending themselves from being burned out of the roundhouse where they had taken shelter for the night after being unable to find crews to run trains on newly opened tracks. Rioters torched oil carriers and ran them down the grade into the roundhouse itself, starting the fires, and at eight o'clock on Sunday morning the militia regiment was forced to abandon the shelter to the fire.[24]

The horrifying news spread rapidly across the country, and Illinois authorities watched the progress of the strikes with increasing apprehension. Chicago seemed a powder keg, and several unions with far more ambitious programs than those of the Brotherhood of Locomotive Engineers were attempting to gain control of the various labor activities and forge a general strike. The Workingmen's Party of the United States mobilized in Chicago in an attempt to provide leadership for what up to that point had been mostly independent strikes. The WPUS held a meeting on Sunday, July 22, as news from Baltimore and Pittsburgh reached Chicago, followed by a rally on Monday evening with some 6,000 in attendance. Albert Parsons, Philip Van Patten, and John McAuliffe led off the oratory. The leading speakers announced resolutions calling for the nationalization of the railroads and support for trade unionism. Railroad executives in the city professed calm, but tensions were seething throughout Chicago.[25] Describing the feeling several years later, Collins wrote: "Sunday and Monday, July 22d and 23d, were days of feverish uncertainty and repressed excitement at Chicago, Peoria, Galesburg and East St. Louis."[26] Late Monday night, a group of switchmen working for the Michigan Central line declared themselves on strike.[27]

On Tuesday, July 24, two days after the riots in Pittsburgh, Chicago workers began walking out. According to Holdridge Collins, "It was evident that unless the troubles were checked at this point, the Country would be thrown into a revolution. The time had come for the Militia to show whether it were capable of the stern duty and exacting discipline of the soldier."[28] Collins was apparently oblivious to the irony of his sentiments. Of the dozens killed and scores more wounded in the rioting up to July 22, rifle-toting militiamen were responsible for most of the deaths. Several of the riots were triggered by the appearance of militia troops on the streets. The Pittsburgh roundhouse was specifically targeted because the Philadelphia militia had taken shelter there. A militia regiment attempting to leave their (very poorly situated) armory and march to the railroad station provoked the killings in Baltimore. Eleven people killed by Pennsylvania militia in Reading were members of the crowd harassing militia progress toward the railroad station in that city. Although a few militia members were killed and dozens more wounded by rioters with guns and stones, the militia killed randomly, shooting into the crowds and hitting a variety of strikers, bystanders, and even a few policemen.[29] Only three or four men known to have been associated with the railroad strikers were killed by any militia troops, firing randomly into hostile crowds. There is no doubt that the crowds were quite hostile and would have liked to do more damage to the militia than they did. Militia troops fired in the belief that they were protecting their own lives, a belief that witnesses and militia officers did not see as unjustified. Nevertheless, their superiority of firepower gave them the killing advantage. At this late date, it is difficult to understand why Collins could not see the militia as potentially fanning the flames, but he, and many, many others like him, did not.

Worried that the situation in Chicago could explode at any moment, city and state officials moved to prepare for possible violence. On July 23, Illinois Adjutant General Hiram Hilliard summoned the brand-new Brigadier General of the Illinois State Guard, Alfred Ducat, back to Chicago from his vacation in Wisconsin. Ducat was in the city by 4:00 P.M. but was informed by Mayor Monroe Heath that the services of the militia were not wanted just yet. A Republican, Monroe Heath was then in his second term as mayor. Elected in 1876 after a series of election scandals and charges of corruption in the previous administration, Heath won his second term by campaigning on a pledge for honest government and reduced taxes.[30] According to Ducat, "His honor informed me that he was desirous of suppressing the disturbance without the aid of the military, if possible, and for the present he did not want a soldier seen on the streets, as he believed the military had much to do with exasperating the people of Pittsburgh, a few days before."[31] Given the events of the previous weekend in Maryland and Pennsylvania, Mayor Heath's observation was sound, though General Ducat did not share it. On the morning of July 24 Ducat telegraphed the governor, "I don't think the authorities here fully appreciate the gravity of the situation. Although the city was quiet last night and this morning, I believe trouble will occur here about tomorrow."[32] General Ducat grew increasingly concerned about the situation in the city as more and more shops were closed down on the 24th and 25th, but the mayor still refused to call the troops, and until he did so they could not act. Ducat did all he could by way of preparation. Revealing his own strong class and ethnic biases, he disarmed the two companies of Bohemian Guards, reporting later that "some of their officers [were] found in full sympathy with the riotous portion of the populace."[33] He made plans with the superintendent of police to have the bridges across the river opened, so when he had the use of his troops he could guard the approaches, and keep the crowd out of the central downtown districts. He ordered his Chicago-based troops to guard their armories in heavy rotations. He asked Governor Shelby M. Cullom to request the aid of six companies of U.S. Army Infantry who were currently in Rock Island, and Cullom did as Ducat requested.

After being assembled in their armories on the evening of the 24th, Ducat had his troops move across the city to better accommodations on the following evening, the predominately Irish American Second Regiment to the Michigan Southern Depot and the First Regiment to the Exposition building. During the day of the 25th, Ducat continued to ask Mayor Heath for permission to use the troops, which Heath continued to refuse, preferring instead to rely on the regular police, supplemented by "several hundred specials" paid for by a "prominent citizen."[34]

Given the events in Pennsylvania, Heath had every reason to fear the provocation for violence sending the Illinois Militia into the streets might prove to be. He also had good reason to distrust the reaction of the Illinois militia troops themselves, as the majority of the deaths in other states were the result of militia fire power. Ducat was clearly growing frustrated, and gangs of men continued to shut down the city, putting into effect a kind of general strike, and the railroad blockade continued to grow. Strikers in Galesburg took up the movement. By this time, some 600 Civil War veterans were drilling in Chicago with breechloaders, the police were breaking up crowds with clubs, and the militias continued to wait in their temporary armories. Police confrontations with the crowds grew more violent during the night, with more and more gunfire exchanged, though no reported casualties.[35]

As tensions mounted and sporadic violence erupted, on July 26 Mayor Heath replied to Ducat's latest request to use the militia: "You are hereby authorized to use whatever military you have in this city *subject to your command* to suppress the riots now in progress in different parts of this city, *subject to my orders* [sic]."[36] The same day that six companies of the Ninth Infantry, U.S. Army, arrived in the city from Rock Island, several citizen-organized, military-style companies were ready to render service, including an artillery battalion. Ducat had called up a volunteer militia cavalry company and posted the veterans' company around the city. The U.S. Army troops went to the stockyards to prevent any disturbances there, and they were then broken up by company and posted to various locations deemed important by Ducat (though the troops were not under his control, he suggested the placement to the U.S. Army officer in charge).[37] During the night, the Second Regiment, Illinois Militia was stationed on the Halstead St. viaduct and bridge near the stockyards. They fired two volleys, about an hour apart, over the heads of the crowds that were harassing them with stones and pistols. Although there were fears that the whole city would be burned (the 1871 fire was hardly a distant memory in 1877), nothing came of them. The following day, hundreds more police "specials" were sworn in, amounting by some reports to 5,000 men working as temporary law enforcers. The total forces stationed in the city smothered the protests by sheer numbers. The U.S. troops never even engaged the crowds and were used to guard industrial property.[38] By the end of July 27, "the Chicago riots melted away."[39] The price was high, however. At least eighteen men and boys, many onlookers, were killed by police or militia gunfire. Scores more were wounded, many brutally beaten, by club-wielding police.

Illinois was not past the crisis, however. The strikes spread throughout the state, just as they had in Pennsylvania. The governor himself handled militia operations in East St. Louis. The Second Brigade of the Illinois militia was called into action on July 27. The four regiments of the Second Brigade reported to Alton, and on the 28th, the brigade moved on to East St. Louis, where the governor was already in place. A crowd reported to be 10,000 strong was congregated at the Relay House, and so the militia headed right for the scene. They were able to disperse the crowd "without the loss of life or the shedding of blood."[40] Companies were stationed throughout the city, holding strategic points. Civil authorities, with detectives and police, arrested many perceived crowd leaders. On Sunday, the first attempt was made to get a mail train out of the city; it ended with the brutal beating of the engineer and fireman by the crowd. The second attempt went forward under heavy guard. A company escorted the engine to the roundhouse, where the train had been left by the switch engine. There a large crowd, "estimated at several thousand," announced a "determination to prevent this the first train, from moving out at any sacrifice" which "was openly and loudly proclaimed by a large majority, who were generally well armed and displayed their weapons." Five companies surrounded the train, and the rest of the command was ordered into line around the train yard. The militia kept the crowd away from the train until it was clear of the other trains, and "with sufficient open space for action," the train sped away. The troops previously surrounding the train turned at a signal and surrounded those who had been closest to the train, disarmed them and marched them away as prisoners. "The consternation of the crowd covering the cars, buildings, and lots in the vicinity was complete, and the panic which prevailed dispersed the crowd in all directions without even the slightest attempt to release the prisoners, who were safely delivered into the custody of the civil authorities." With constant patrol, the city returned to business, and the militia troops were dismissed to their homes on July 31.[41]

Meanwhile, General Ducat turned his attention to strikes and race riots in Braidwood and Joliet. Braidwood was a coal-mining town, and the striking miners there seized the opportunity presented by the general confusion to stage a race riot. The governor informed Ducat that the strikers had "driven the colored miners, with their families from the city, that the poor people had been violently treated and robbed, and were without food or shelter on the prairies and in the woods," and that the strikers "were about fifteen hundred strong, well organized, armed and desperate."[42] Worried that striking miners from Streator and Joliet might reinforce the Braidwood strikers, Ducat rushed to get to the scene with two regiments of militia. Arriving on the evening of the 28th, Ducat and some 700 militiamen faced about 500 rioters. Ducat ordered the mayor to tell them to disperse and return the arms stolen from the African

American mining families within twenty-five minutes. The crowd dispersed, but the guns were not returned. Ducat then marched in and established control of the city, instituting a search for the missing guns, which he found and gave to the mine superintendent. During the night some shots were fired at the pickets, and fire was returned, but as far as Ducat knew there were no casualties.

The next day, trains came into town with some 350 of the African American refugees. They were returned to their pillaged homes, and Ducat gave them a day's rations, "notifying the owners of the mines that hereafter they would have to provide for them."[43] The same day, the governor ordered Ducat to detail companies to Matoon and Galesburg to protect the black miners at those spots and to leave a company in Braidwood "to protect property until colored miners are allowed to work unmolested." The orders for forces from Ducat's command to go to Matoon and Galesburg were later rescinded, but a company from Peoria did serve, briefly, in Galesburg, quieting the crowds mostly by marching through the streets.[44] By July 30, order was sufficiently restored that, according to Ducat, all local authorities felt able to cope. All currently activated militia companies were then dispersed to their homes.[45]

Strike and riot duty proved chaotic and confusing, combining wildcat walkouts, race riots, and an organized general strike, and ING officers were not able to draw many shared conclusions to guide their future activities when they were called in to protect lives and property. In Chicago itself, riots resulted in the deaths of at least eighteen people, some from the rifle volleys fired by Illinois Militia members on the night of May 26, 1877. In East St. Louis, disciplined general strikers faced troops under the direct command of Governor Shelby M. Cullom, himself a Civil War veteran, and no rioting broke out. In Braidwood, miners turned the confusing situation into a race riot and terrorized and evicted all the African American miners and their families in the town, and the state militia restored the refugees to their homes. Ethnic and racial tensions also affected service in Chicago itself. In the midst of the crisis, General Ducat disbanded one company for their "sympathy" with the strikers, and he ignored the offers of service made by the African American Hannibal Guards, much to their displeasure. "This caused the members of our organization to feel somewhat 'miffed.'" . . . I can assure you . . . and all who may see this, that a good battalion of colored men could have been mustered together had it been necessary for them to bear arms against mobs in the protection of our citizens and our homes." The commander of the Hannibal Guards, R. E. Moore, came just shy of accusing ING leadership of overt racial discrimination when he concluded that "[f]eeling that recognition in time of peace is an assurance of recognition during time of war, and also feeling determined to discharge our duty as becomes all law-abiding citizens and soldiers, I sincerely hope this will satisfy the minds of many of our inquisitive friends."[46]

Moore was not the only critic of Ducat's handling of the 1877 crisis who skirted an open discussion of the ways racism impacted the unfolding events. Nearly two years later, in 1879, the *Chicago Tribune* was still recording the lingering effects of the controversy created by the governor and Adjutant General Hilliard's decision to send troops to Braidwood to protect the black miners there. "There as been considerable discussion, since the time of the riot, upon the subject of Braidwood, and the fact that a small army was moved down in front of that small city in order to terrify its inhabitants into an unconditional surrender." It seems that the critics felt that the white inhabitants did not deserve to be "terrorized," despite their attack on the black inhabitants of their town. The paper quoted "a trustworthy source" who claimed that generals Ducat and Joseph T. Torrence believed that a mere twenty-five ING troops would have sufficed to quell the disturbance.[47] When writing his own report at the end of 1877, General Duct did not sound like a man who thought less was more. He proposed a massive, ten-thousand-strong militia armed with Gatling guns to face down strikers.[48] He was soon replaced, suggesting that neither Governor Cullom nor the rest of the Illinois militia leadership thought that was a good idea, and certainly not an idea anyone appeared willing to pay for. In the end, no formal changes as a result of the 1877 strike service were made in the Illinois militia's structure, training, or public funding.

Types of Strikes in Illinois

Between 1877 and 1908, twenty-two of thirty-three strikes (or 67 percent) in which Illinois governors sent militia troops were strikes or walkouts called by bituminous coal miners in dispute with the operators of all the mines in a given region or across the state. Another nine strikes (or 27 percent) were related to railroad disputes. The remaining two incidents occurred in Chicago: the ING served briefly in the Union Stock Yards in 1886, and again in the Sanitation District in 1893.

Patrolling railway strikes presented specific challenges to the ING and to all state militia forces. In Illinois, railway strikes were usually focused in the two large rail hubs located in the two significant urban areas of the state, Chicago and East St. Louis. Strikes in these locations often quickly spread to related industries, and then to general trades in the urban environment, shutting down increasingly large areas of the affected cities. The combination of the excitement of the strike and the larger-than-usual numbers of people milling about on the streets had a frightening way of shifting gears and developing into an urban riot only tangentially related to the original intentions of the strikers and their unions. Rail strikes could also spread across the industry as members of the various brotherhoods struck in sympathy. Crowds would gather to block the tracks out of rail yards and to discourage, often violently, any man willing to run the trains past them. The ING's job in these situations was to break up these crowds to allow the trains to get through, and to guard the trains until they were safely out of the city. Making matters still more difficult for National Guardsmen, their presence in these urban strikes often acted as a goad to the crowds, turning previously nonviolent crowds into frightening mobs.[49] Urban crowds could outnumber the Guard companies by the hundreds and even the thousands. These crowds presented special challenges because the only real training guardsmen had for dealing with large, hostile forces was military—despite the name "riot duty"—and yet firing lethal weapons into the crowds was possible only as a last desperate resort, owing to the fear of killing unarmed participants by the score.

Despite getting most of the historical interest, the ING was called to rail strike duty only nine times. The ING was far more likely to find itself, during strike duty, in coal-mining country. In the twenty-two cases from 1877 to 1908 when county sheriffs turned to the governor to request state troops to intervene in coal mine strikes, they asked for assistance because of physical violence, ongoing or potential. Such violence was generally focused around striking miners attempting to shut down operations that were continuing to work and/or to prevent strikebreakers from either working or arriving to work. Illinois coal mines tended to be located in rural areas, usually on the outskirts of small towns, but sometimes near nothing at all but the railroad tracks laid to the mine itself. Thus, ING leadership generally focused their activities around the mines themselves, though general "order maintenance" duties could involve patrolling, eventually with the aid of something close to martial law, neighboring towns as well. Any actual confrontations in these localities tended to be limited to strikers, their supporters, the various private guards and strikebreakers hired by the coal operators, and the militia volunteers. Illinois National Guard officers quickly developed the practice, during mine strikes, of literally inserting their troops between the opposing parties and enforcing a cooling-off period, a practice that was largely useless in the larger, urban environments because the Guard itself was so likely to become one of the combatants.[50] In all twenty-two cases of mine strike duty, the state commanders on the ground and their superior officers in Springfield, including the governor, refused to sanction the use of troops as guards for private property or in aiding the direct importation of strike breakers, and did so only under the rarest of circumstances.[51]

In Illinois, the governor's staff of militia officers, as well as the individual officers who commanded each strike policing expedition and, as far as may be determined, the membership at large, together sought to preserve a formal neutrality on the issues of the strike when called upon to intervene in a locality stressed by strikes.[52] This was the only possible response to the varied conditions and issues that confronted the ING when they were called into service if they were to retain the ability to function effectively, both during the strike situation and afterwards as an institution that relied on community and public support for its own future maintenance. Each strike had its own history and each strike locality its own political and economic tensions that predated the strike itself. The challenges faced by the guardsmen in handling themselves in such a manner as to be regarded as neutral in intention if not result were extremely difficult to overcome, and the ING rarely managed to do so. Because ING leadership failed to overcome these difficulties directly, in time they moved to redefine those situations that required state militia involvement and simultaneously to more explicitly define the responsibilities and tactics available to local authorities when they were faced with "disorderly," as opposed to "violent," situations.

In many cases, the ING commanders on the ground were critical, indeed often scathing, in their judgment of the behavior of the county sheriff and his inability or unwillingness to handle the tensions himself, and they regarded state intervention as something that ought to have been unnecessary. And in fact, during the vast majority of strikes, even mining strikes, throughout Illinois during the forty years covered by this project as a whole, participants did not seek or require intervention by the state. For example, in early May of 1886 a wave of strikes peaked, and between May 1 and 3, 64,000 workers in Chicago went on strike. Despite the massive walkout, the ING was not called to strike duty in the city of Chicago in May 1886, and local authorities managed without militia intervention.[53] Illinois National Guard commanders came to resent being placed in situations that required delicate negotiation but not necessarily sizable military forces. They regarded the tendency of some county sheriffs to rely on the Guard to restore order, because doing so relieved them of the burden of making locally unpopular political choices, as a direct assault on the very premises on which the state militias were based. They also resented such service as an uncalled-for drain on limited ING finances. The active-duty pay, the supplies, and the transportation required to put and keep the state militia in the field while policing strike-related events all came out of the annual militia budget, and when expenses went over that sum, the Guard and their creditors often had to wait two or more years for the next session of the General Assembly to receive their payment. As a result, other items in the militia budget—like summer camps, new uniforms, and new armament and ordnance supplies—all had to be deferred as well.[54]

Madison and St. Clair Counties: 1883 Mine Strike

On the night of Wednesday, May 23, 1883, the striking bituminous coal miners of Madison and St. Clair counties, surrounding East St. Louis in southern Illinois, held a mass protest and strategy meeting. As the "machine miners" in the area remained unwilling to strike, those traditional miners who had walked out May 1 decided to close the "machine mines" by force. About two o'clock in the morning of May 24, some 400 strikers—marching to the music of fife and drum—surrounded the machine miners' boarding house at Abbey Mine No. 4, a few miles outside Collinsville, and demanded that they join the strike. When the 150 machine men refused, the strikers physically removed them from the boarding house and force-marched the machine men at gunpoint the twelve miles to East St. Louis. Any machine miners who objected to this proceeding were assaulted. The strikers further threatened to kill any men who returned to work. Throughout Thursday, strikers ranged throughout the area, forcing the rest of the Abbey machine mines to close. Early Friday morning, the strikers returned to the area to satisfy themselves that the Abbey miners had stayed away.[55] On Friday, May 25, the deputy sheriffs of Madison and St. Clair counties, the mayor of Collinsville, a justice of the peace, representatives of two coal mining operations, and a prominent local citizen wired to the governor:

> We the undersigned, testify that there are from 250 to 400 men armed with revolvers, clubs and stones, threatening the peace of this and adjoining towns. That they are preventing men employed in the mines here from pursuing their lawful business and threatening the public peace, and that further, in our opinions, the sheriff is not able to provide the necessary protection to life and property and the exigencies of the case demand the interference of the state militia.[56]

In the second half of the nineteenth century, bituminous (or soft) coal was mined throughout the state and shipped by rail to St. Louis or

Chicago and beyond. Coal mining districts throughout the nation were notorious for harsh conditions, frequent strikes, and strike-related violence. Illinois coal fields were no different, and 1883 was another bad year for management-miner relations in several mining operations surrounding Belleville, Collinsville, and Troy, all in Madison or St. Clair counties. There were two types of mining operations in the area surrounding East St. Louis. The majority were traditional coal mines, and the rest, a small number of newer mines, were known as "machine mines."[57] Owing to disagreements between the traditional miners and the operators of traditionally worked mines over wages and, more particularly, over the manner in which wages were assessed, some 2,000 coal diggers went out on strike on May 1.[58] The striking miners had already won a concession of a 1/2 cent increase in the piece rate per bushel, but they were unhappy with the manner in which the coal was weighed and wanted scales at each mine entrance rather than the single scale located at a midpoint between the mines and East St. Louis, as was then the case.[59] They also wanted to have a miner-selected scale checker to ensure the honesty of the coal companies.[60] The striking miners were determined to stick to their resolutions and to continue the strike until their demands were heeded.[61]

The counties had remained calm until May 23, when the striking traditional miners decided to force the issue with the nonstriking machine miners through a direct assault. Even then, the sheriff and his deputies declined to define the situation as disorderly, until it was clear that the striking miners would not allow the evicted machine men to return to work. It was only at this juncture that the deputy sheriffs turned to the state to request military aid in restoring the evicted miners to their jobs. In this particular case, order was related to the sheriff's ability (or willingness) to protect the lives of those machine miners who still desired to work in the face of the strike, and to protect the property of the machine mine owners. When leading local men became concerned that the sheriff was no longer able to adequately protect the interests of property owners and mine managers and to protect the lives of mine employees who were continuing to work in defiance of the strike, they requested outside assistance.

Colonel Barkley of the Fifth Regiment, ING reported to the governor that there were no further disturbances in Collinsville after the arrival of the militia on Friday night; and on Saturday, 110 machine miners returned from East St. Louis and started back to work. With the mines back at work and no "mobs" in evidence, Barkley "felt that the civil authorities should from this moment on, preserve order unaided by the militia."[62] Order, in this case, is synonymous with conditions prior to the specific events of May 23–24, and not conditions prior to the event of the strike itself. At least in this case, order was not the prestrike condition; rather, it was all conditions under which local authorities are able to prevent or punish harm to life or property on their own. So once the specific instance of the forcible closure of the Abbey machine mines had been rectified, order was once again under the jurisdiction of the local authorities, and the militia's duty had been performed.

When solicited by E. J. Crandall, president of the Crandall Mining Company located outside Collinsville, to keep the militia in the area, Governor Hamilton refused. Hamilton explained in his letter to Crandall that the "militia cannot be kept there to guard your mine indefinitely. Civil authorities must use the powers of the militia promptly if needed to disperse rioters and arrest them & turn them over to civil authorities for commitment to jail."[63] However, "[a]t the earnest solicitation of some of the mine operators and citizens . . . [Barkley—the commander on the ground] consented to remain till Sunday evening, as [he and his troops] could not have left East St. Louis before that time, at any rate."[64] Barkley had a strategy up his sleeve for determining if tensions had truly cooled enough for the ING to return home. He believed that the strikers were unlikely to cause any disturbances where the National Guard companies were in place. So Barkley loaded his men onto a special train Sunday night and pulled them out, letting the public assume they were going home. In reality, the train stopped at a switching station a few miles away. There, the militia companies waited out the night and then returned to the Abbey mines outside Collinsville early the following morning—where everything was quiet. The train passed machine mines at Confidence and Troy as well, and again, all was quiet and all the men at work, so the train went on to East St. Louis with all the militia aboard.[65] Because in the judgment of their commander the militia's responsibilities in this case had been fully discharged, he prepared to relieve the men of active duty and send them home. Order, or those conditions predating the specific outbreak of violence that compelled the local sheriffs to turn to the state for aid, was restored.

Events then took an unexpected turn for the worse Monday afternoon, May 28, just after Barkley and his three companies arrived in East St. Louis. While the men were waiting for trains to their home stations, Barkley received an urgent request for immediate help from Sheriff Ropiequet in Belleville, St. Clair County. "Cannot master mob at Reinecker Mine, No-1 on L. & N. R. R. There are about 300 men and fifty women that want to destroy pit. I just received telephone by L. & N. R. R. to ask you for militia & I hope that you will send a company immediately on special train to Birkner Station, about one mile from pit, or to pit itself if you can do so."⁶⁶ Barkley also received personal appeals from employees of both the Reinecker Mine and the L. & N. Railroad. The Reinecker employee told Barkley that the strikers had taken Reinecker himself prisoner and trapped his miners inside the mine, and were threatening to burn the shaft and "leave [the] work-men at the bottom to the mercy of the flames."⁶⁷ (The story in the *Chicago Tribune* claimed that an "Amazon Mob" had trapped Reinecker in his house and were threatening to tear it down around him.⁶⁸) Once he was apprised of the sheriff's request, the governor sent word to Barkley to take whatever speedy action he felt was advisable, but he added the proviso, "Sheriff must take command and capture as many as possible to be turned over to the civil authorities."⁶⁹

In Collinsville, the forcible, and potentially lasting, closure of a previously working mine prompted the county authorities to declare the situation disorderly without any actual confrontation between the local authorities and the strikers. In St. Clair County, by contrast, the Sheriff's request for state aid came in the midst of a large-scale attack on men and property that the county sheriffs did not have sufficient manpower or authority to handle alone. In particular, sheriff deputies used the presence of female strike supporters at the Reinecker mine attack to suggest a spectacular break with order, and as such, demanded an equally spectacular response on the part of local authority and state military aid. They clearly identified the disorder as ongoing violent actions and threats, in this case to the lives of trapped miners.

Spectacular was what they got. Because of a (deliberate?) misunderstanding, the engineer running the special train taking the ING troops to the Reinecker mine did not halt the train one mile away from the mine entrance and allow the troops to disembark and proceed on foot. Rather, he ran the train right up to the mine entrance and into the middle of the hostile crowd. While the troops were attempting to get off the still-moving train, shots were exchanged in the confusion, and one striker was killed and one was wounded by militia fire.⁷⁰ This action broke up the crowd, and the male strikers fled into the woods and down the tracks. Many of the women, however, refused to abandon their position at the mine entrance. "Deputy Anthony went up to the shaft and called on the women to disperse and go home. They refused to do so and he was obliged to take a club away from one of them who threatened him. He called on me [Barkley] for assistance; I went up to the shaft, where the women had possession; I spoke kindly to them asking them to disperse and go to their homes; which they finally did under protest, and taking their own time in with-drawing slowly."⁷¹ After the women left, the trapped miners were allowed to leave the mine, and the detained mine manager/owner was released. The crisis past, the county authorities were assumed able to resume sole responsibility for order, and the troops left the area shortly thereafter.[72]

Growing Frustration

The precipitating events in Madison and St. Clair counties in 1883 are the outside poles on the range of situations that prompted county authorities to request state militia intervention. (See appendix D.) In Madison County, deputy sheriffs and local leading men turned to the state for aid in reopening forcibly closed mining operations. Sheriff Ropiequet of St. Clair County begged state intervention to quell an attack in progress on miners and mine property that he was unable to disperse alone with the aid of his few deputy sheriffs. Because of this wide range of situations, there was often significant local disagreement on the moment when, or if, conditions warranted an appeal to the state for help. The variety of people who appealed to Illinois governors for aid is one reflection of these multiple perspectives on local strikes. For example, in the 1883 mine strike in Collinsville, one of the first people to urge the governor to intervene was George Parker, president of the St. Louis, Alton & Terre Haute Rail Road Company. Parker wrote to Governor Hamilton to complain that Sheriff Hotz of Madison County was failing to preserve order because Hotz was "either afraid to take action, or, what is more probable, is in sympathy with the strikers." Parker informed the governor that the strikers were attempting to close down the railroad lines, like his own, that were continuing to transport coal from machine mines into St. Louis, and that Sheriff Hotz had declined to interfere with these activities of the striking miners.[73]

Parker's 1883 letter did not lead Governor Hamilton to inquire directly of the sheriff of Madison County for an account of the local situation. Rather, Hamilton chose to send a militia colonel to personally inspect the local situation and report directly back to him.[74] Colonel Barkley, the man Hamilton sent into the area, did not arrive in Collinsville until after the strikers forcibly evicted the "machine men," and events pushed local leadership to act quickly. As a result, it is difficult to predict what Barkley's role might have been in the particular situation without such a provocative action on the part of the strikers. It is telling, however, to note that Barkley must have been involved with the decision to request state aid, though exactly what role he played will never be known.[75] Reports suggest that subsequent Illinois governors also used this method of information gathering (personal militia representatives), both to determine the seriousness of the situation and to prevent local leaders from turning too quickly to the state for military intervention. According to at least one adjutant general, and despite the 1883 case, the presence of ING officers as observers worked against local desires to turn to the state for militia aid in difficult situations and toward some "peaceful" settlement of the issues under contention.[76]

Back in 1883, however, Colonel Barkely criticized the local sheriff, George Hotz, in his report to the governor, saying that Hotz was "not able to provide the necessary protection to life and property."[77] Whether Sheriff Hotz was even party to the decision to ask for state intervention is unclear, though the absence of Hotz's name on the request for state aid is a meaningful omission in this context. At least one newspaper reporter noted that "the Sheriff and his posse early threw up the sponge, and the citizens, miners, and operators were placed in great bodily danger."[78] When Colonel Barkley wired Sheriff Hotz to ask for instructions once the request for state intervention had been made by Deputy Sheriff Lanham, Sheriff Hotz replied:

> I feel unable to come, Please consult with Deputy Lanham.
> George Hotz, Sheriff Madison County[79]

Hotz's apparent unwillingness to participate in any measures aimed at constraining the activities of the strikers in forwarding their cause reinforces the significance of his failure to personally request state aid.[80] Barkley wired him again to urge his speedy arrival. Hotz answered: "Will be down as soon as we can get there according to your order."[81] Barkley wired again to make it perfectly clear that he had no intention of letting Hotz off the hook, "Am here to act under *your orders* in assisting you to preserve the peace [my emphasis]."[82] Nevertheless, Hotz failed to arrive in Collinsville until well after the ING had established itself at the Abbey mine and the evicted miners were back at work.[83] Whatever role Hotz played locally, it was not in collaboration with the state troops sent to his county.

In several subsequent cases when the Illinois militia intervened in counties threatened by strike-related violence, the sheriffs did not actually request state intervention, either; what they requested was the loan of state arms for use by deputy sheriffs. The state did lend arms to county sheriffs on request until they no longer had arms to lend, at which point, if in the judgment of the adjutant general and the governor the situation warranted it, they ordered troops into the county.[84] On other occasions, the county sheriffs were in regular contact with the state authorities, apprising them of the situation from day to day and reserving judgment to themselves on when or if they needed state intervention in their jurisdictions.[85] On still other occasions, the sheriff repeatedly asked for assistance in dealing with mobs, but the ING officers on the scene felt that the sheriff was looking to get out of doing his job and rebuffed the requests for as long as they could.[86]

Disagreements over "if or when" state intervention was absolutely necessary could, and frequently did, extend from the local all the way to the state level. Community members and striking workers protested that militia troops were unneeded, and city authorities argued with county officials or corporate representatives over the need for troops.[87] Illinois National Guard officers frequently contested the legitimacy of intervention requests when in their judgment the county sheriff had not done all that he could have to prevent the outbreaks of violence that ultimately required militia presence. They also complained when they believed the sheriff exaggerated what threat there was in order to secure state aid in policing a situation for which he would rather not be held responsible.[88] Perhaps the most dramatic example of this belief in exaggeration came during the railroad strike in East St. Louis in 1886, when Sheriff Ropiequet of St. Claire County insisted for weeks that he could do nothing to stop the mob. Even the ING officers on the scene, up to and including Adjutant General J. M. Vance and Governor Richard J. Oglesby, were convinced that there was much more the sheriff could do to ensure the peace. They continued to feel that way, right up to the evening of April 8, when shooting broke out between strike breakers and strike supporters and poorly armed deputies, and seven people died.[89] Over time, ING officers grew more and more willing to argue that some sheriffs, like Ropiequet of St. Claire County, failed to exhaust their full resources in the task of order maintenance in their jurisdictions, and to place full responsibility squarely on the sheriffs' shoulders for what harm to persons or property subsequently occurred.

Despite the efforts of ING officers to shift blame for bad situations onto the heads of uncooperative county sheriffs, they could not escape all criticism. Feelings could run very deep about the conflicts during strikes. For example, after the events in Collinsville in 1883, J. D. Miner wrote a personal letter to the governor, in which he passionately declared that "it is now 20 years since we fought for freedom of the African Slavery which there was 1,000,000 men sacrificed there [sic] lives and we are as white Slaves in the hands of a few Capitalists which has crushed us to a starvation point these are the reasons for us standing out to try and better our condition."[90] Miner went on to call the working machine miners "scab," and to charge that "when [the militia] arrived here they seen there was no use for them so they went into the City of Collinsville and some pertook of Ice cream but most of a good Stomach full of Beer & Whiskey in which they have been keep over dozed with the Stimulant from Sunday 27th until Monday 28th ult [sic]. . . ."[91]

Miner was not the only critic to cast aspersions of alcohol abuse toward the ING. In 1882, Jas. Magie drew on a popular conception of the militia as heavy drinkers in his condemnation of the state militia when he wrote "It is very fortunate for these poor sick soldiers that, in addition to all other pay, that state pays their medicine bills. There are many soldiers who, when they meet each other, need some medicine. If they don't happen to have their bottle with them it makes no difference, Fleury or Weinberger keep bottles, and fill them with medicine when required, and the languid soldier after dress parade can have his drooping energies revived by the medicine which are thus furnished. Generous, noble state of Illinois!"[92] ING officers were obviously concerned about the issue of drinking and in their reports stressed that there was no drunkenness or "vice" among the men on active duty.[93]

To kill someone while policing strike-related disorders brought the most violent kinds of condemnation down on the heads of the ING and the governor as commander-in-chief. The death of miner Henderson at the Reinecker mine confrontation in 1883 was exactly the type of outcome that militia officers spent much time trying to avoid in subsequent years with their search for new tactics and strategies to calm confrontational scenes. When the worst came to pass and shooting did break out, the commander's first reaction was to stop the firing on the part of their troops. Once the firing was stopped, Colonel Barkley's next act was to assure himself that it had been no breach of discipline on the part of his men, but rather their proper response to a direct order from local authority. "The deputy sheriff, Anthony, then at my request, in the presence of General Reece, Col. Mills, Major Culver, Captain Ridgley, Captain Wilson, Captain Fahenstock, Captain Crooker and myself repeated the statement that he, Anthony, after calling on the mob to surrender in the name of the people, and being fired upon by the rioters, had returned their fire himself and ordered the men to fire upon them. I had this done in order to show clearly that the men had merely acted under the direction of the civil authorities."[94] These steps were dramatic in their formality, but fearing the likely consequences of the death of the striker, Barkely acted quickly before the deputy sheriff had time to reconsider the act of publicly and officially accepting responsibility for the striker's death.

Barkley's efforts notwithstanding, the death of the striking miner at the Reinecker Mine was the focal point for criticism that rained down on Governor Hamilton and the Illinois National Guards in the aftermath of the ING's 1883 strike-policing activities. In his letter to the governor, Miner blamed the alcohol, claiming that "in there [sic] Drunking [sic] state [the militiamen] fired on the strikers without orders and killed a young man woman & child."[95] Local residents held mass meetings to denounce Governor Hamilton and the Illinois National Guard for the killing and to demand that the company(s) responsible be discharged from the state militia. The resolutions at one such meeting contained the following points:

> Resolved, That we condemn the massacre of miners by the State Militia of Illinois, and declare it a lawless and mean crime and murder, committed on the orders of the coal monopolists, by which the Government of Illinois has proved itself the servant of capital.

Resolved, That we demand the discharge and punishment of the company of State Militia concerned.

Resolved, That we charge the coal miners not to give up a single point of their rights, and to organize themselves into groups, etc., for the purpose of opposing a solid front to such uniformed murderers in the future, and that we oblige ourselves, single as well as common, to avenge the brutal murder of our comrade Henderson.[96]

Barkley's attempt to clear the ING from all blame and get a public statement to the effect that the order to fire came from local authorities after receiving fire from the strikers themselves obviously failed to convince Miner that the ING had no political or economic agenda.

Conclusion

In the 1870s and 1880s, Illinois militia volunteers joined local companies and then sustained their membership with their own initiatives, by their own enthusiasm, and largely with their own money. They created and maintained their companies from a mixed set of personal goals; including a desire to acquire some military skills, to demonstrate their patriotism, to prove their manliness, and to show the world that they were admirable and responsible citizens. National Guardsmen chose to be citizen soldiers because they wanted their friends and neighbors to view them as manly men and as worthy citizens who would serve their nation with honor and distinction. Strike service complicated and destabilized this program.

During strikes, guardsmen found themselves in violent, unhappy situations in which they were cursed, kicked, and shot at. Rather than providing an opportunity to serve as model citizens defending order and community, strikes offered the ING chances to argue with local sheriffs, appear to be the tool of abusive corporations, and to be the killers of previously inoffensive fellow citizens. Much as individual guardsmen were frightened by civic unrest and violent riots, and believed that the state could and should use all the power at its command to prevent or quell such outbursts, the periods when guardsmen found themselves trying to bring about local order illustrated just how difficult a task this was. It was also not a task guardsmen were well equipped to handle, but it was not one they yet had a way to reject.

The history of the Illinois militia in the 1870s—explosive growth and development triggered by the centennial celebrations, followed almost immediately by deployment in a politically and emotionally charged strike—was to shape the evolution of the Illinois National Guard for the next thirty years. The Illinois militia grew and sustained itself prior to 1877 out of a combination of patriotic enthusiasm and growing worries about achieving and displaying honorable and true manliness in the modern world. Dramatic growth and the first legislative overhaul of the militia system in Illinois all happened prior to the riots of 1877. This fact should finally put to rest the limited notion that the National Guard was solely created through collusion between business and political interests aiming to smother rebellion out of the "Dangerous Classes."[97] Maintaining public order was an important concern of Illinois militia members and most other state forces and their governments, of course, but only *after* militia companies willed themselves into existence and sought opportunities to demonstrate their worth and importance. The roots of the militia resurgence in Illinois in the 1870s are to be found in individuals who flocked to the revived militia and the communities that came to the support of their local companies.

CHAPTER 4

New Training Practices, Drill Competitions, and the Rise of Sharpshooting

As the trained soldier is the real weapon of modern warfare, then see that you demand he receive the means to make him the best trained and most effective weapon that can be produced.[1]
—Lieutenant J. H. Parker

From 1870 onward, Illinois guardsmen held creating a body of knowledgeable and trained citizen-soldiers, ready to support their state or nation in time of need, as their formal objective.[2] Though their objective stayed the same, the ways in which guardsmen, in Illinois and around the nation, went about providing the necessary training to meet that objective changed dramatically between 1870 and 1916. In the 1870s and early 1880s, in Illinois and elsewhere, militia companies provided military training through unpaid, private, weekly drilling in their local armories and during sporadic summer training events. As the Illinois National Guard grew in size, financial health, and professional ambition in the late 1880s and the 1890s, officers added regular annual summer training encampments and increased access to shooting ranges to the training schedule. After the turn of the century, with another big increase in federal funds in hand and additional support from the regular Army, militia training in Illinois and across the nation grew still more professional and rigorous. Although the changes came slowly enough to feel incremental, the combined weight of change ultimately had a profound impact on the nature of the ING, on guardsmen themselves, and on their relationships with the communities that had supported them for so long. The ING joined with state National Guards around the country in its quest for greater military efficiency, guardsmen sought rewards that were more personal than public, and communities were gradually left behind through greater attention to national service and national goals.

The cumulative impact and significance of the changes in training practices are most visible in the changing nature of intraguard competitions. Throughout these decades, guardsmen competed against each other, testing themselves and their skills against absolute measures and against fellow guardsmen. From the 1870s through the 1890s, militia competitions in Illinois and around the country generally featured company members performing the various drill routines before a team of judges, and before large local audiences, for prizes ranging from inexpensive medals to purses worth hundreds of dollars. Beginning in the 1890s, marksmanship slowly gained ground as the central competitive sport for militia members, and by the early 1900s, inter- and intracompany competition was almost entirely focused on marksmanship, and company drill was reduced to an occasional public display.

The gradual rise of marksmanship as the central competitive event masked how profoundly different it was for guardsmen, in terms of their understanding of themselves and for their presentation to their communities. One change was spatial. Drill competitions regularly took place in central public spaces, squares, parks, or campgrounds serviced by public transportation. Marksmanship competitions took place in isolated, specialized spaces. Another change was in the reward structure. While the team prizes for both types of events ranged from simple ribbons to medals, trophies, and prize purses, marksmanship added the element of individual scores and individual ranking. This shift in focus from drilling to marksmanship, though seeming perfectly natural and rational as it occurred over the course of about fifteen years (1890–1905), in retrospect signaled a deep change in the nature of the ING and National Guards around the country. Over the course of twenty years, National Guards changed from organizations focused primarily on serving their communities as models and creators of manly citizenship to a much more individually focused form of self-improvement and national duty.

In the 1880s and 1890s, guardsmen in Illinois and elsewhere presented a compelling case that what they did was mold manly men and responsible citizens who served their communities as models of patriotism and defenders of local order. The political and economic difficulties attendant on strike duty that emerged in the 1870s and 1880s encouraged the ING, and other state militias, to embrace their national defense mission as their primary form of patriotic service and reduce their policing function as far as possible.³ At the same time, the expectations of what it meant to be manly in the complex urban and industrial world of the late nineteenth and early twentieth century began to drift away from responsible citizenship as a central attribute of manhood.⁴ In slowly shifting their attention from local and community concerns to individual and national ones, the members of the National Guards were not unique; rather, they were simply one of many groups whose members were grappling with how to align modernity with the values they held dear. These changes did not take place overnight, and guardsmen were able to accommodate and reflect them in their own training and competitive practices with both enthusiasm and satisfaction. They competed for local and national prizes throughout the period, and they continued to train once a week. But the guardsman of the early twentieth century was in many ways far removed from his 1870s predecessor in terms of his understanding of who he was and what he was supposed to be doing, and nowhere is this more clearly marked than in the change from drill competitions to marksmanship as the central skill that emerged from guard training.

The Evolution of Military Training

In the early 1870s, militia companies in Illinois and elsewhere generally tried to meet once a week for what they called "drill." Drill was derived from books like *The Manual of Instruction for the Volunteers and Militia of the United States: With Numerous Illustrations*, by Major William Gilham, first published in 1861. This particular manual covered everything from the structure of the military to the basic responsibilities of the soldier—from marching through care and maintenance of his arms.⁵ By the early 1880s the most basic drills had been reduced to a series of instructions that could be printed on small cards for ease of reference, like those printed by the New Hampshire National Guard.⁶ How much of "the manual"—as most militia members referred to it—a company worked through at any one time is hard to say; limitations of space, supplies, materials, and weapons existed for nearly all companies and varied by company as well. Inspecting officers also regularly noted that poor attendance at weekly drills remained a challenging problem for company cohesion and skill acquisition through the 1890s at least.⁷ In the 1870s and 1880s, most militia companies functioned on a financial shoestring with little to no aid or support from state or federal agencies, mostly because the agencies that might have helped them did not yet exist. The

ING and the officers of other state militias had little power to compel drill attendance or discipline infractions, either. So to survive, ING officers could not alienate their members with too much discipline or lose the support of their communities by avoiding their public functions. Drill time was further limited in the 1870s and 1880s because company members also had to use the time they gave to their companies to raise money for armory rents; to make whatever modifications those spaces required; to uniform themselves; to supply themselves with modern arms and equipment if they were unhappy with the old and broken equipment that was the best the state could supply; even to purchase their own copies of the *Manual of Instruction*.[8]

Tensions gradually appeared around and within the ING and other Guards because all the parades, competitions, and social events so common in the 1880s and 1890s were the direct result of the conflicting interests and needs of Guard companies. Parades played a key role in the history of Guard companies because it was during parades that they were able to make the most convincing case for their importance and usefulness to the largest possible audiences. The need to make that case persuasively kept most guard members focused on parade drills during their training, despite the torrents of criticism that rained down on them from professional observers as a result.[9] Competitions allowed participants to explore both the military training they received by measuring themselves against each other and the possibilities of violent display for themselves and for larger audiences. Drill competitions also celebrated military pomp and circumstance, and the balls that often concluded competition days rewarded everyone present with an evening of military glamour and excitement. However, the need to parade and to compete kept Guard companies focused on marching and group weapon handling. It constrained the ability of guards to adopt more modern training practices and manifestly did not encourage officers to take the military side of their administrative responsibilities with much seriousness, especially at the battalion or regimental level. Social events took up an incredible amount of time and effort that might otherwise have gone into a wider variety of training programs. To the irritation or consternation, or both, of senior ING officers and U.S. Army officers who foresaw a need for a well-trained reserve military force in the future, the demands of the various nontraining activities were often given primacy in the life of many companies, even the best companies, because without these events, companies could not have raised the money to keep themselves in operation. Once more money did become available to the ING and other national guards after the turn of the century, their training and competitive practices did begin to change.

It should not be surprising that the training that took place as a result of the interest and rewards for preparing for the competitive summer season was inconsistent and varied, not just across companies, but during the year within companies. Although inspection reports are not able to record regular drill practices, inspectors did record in their semiannual evaluations how well the various companies measured up to the standards set by the *Manual of Instruction*. In the late 1870s and early 1880s, inspectors from the Illinois adjutant general's office were consistently underwhelmed with the performance of most companies, suggesting that training was just as erratic and inconsistent as one would suspect, considering the conditions under which the ING had to function.[10]

Beginning in the 1870s, an important cadre of professionally minded National Guard officers began working to promote and develop their institution as a serious military organization, ready for federal or state duty whenever called. These activist officers generally did not seek to create a full-time militia. They remained committed to the ideal of citizen-soldiers who voluntarily trained together outside the obligations of their jobs and their families in order to be available to answer a call from state or federal authorities in the case of emergencies. These dedicated militia officers usually stood in opposition to those men who sought commissions in the state militias for more personal political, social, or sporting reasons.[11] Officers who viewed the Guard as an opportunity for socializing or for advancing personal political carriers via contacts cultivated through the militia, or increasingly as an organization through which to compete nationally for marksmanship trophies, were rarely among this dedicated cadre. Sometimes, too, they were one and the same. National Guard promoters were not limited to those men who made the ING a lifetime avocation and chose to serve in the National Guard for years or decades at a time. Officers with shorter tenures could also be committed to and promote the guard's interests as a military body, as opposed to only a social or sporting club. What marked these militia officers as a group was their dedication to military-style missions and training. They were committed to becoming as much like the regulars as possible, despite the repeated calls on the state militias to function primarily as a state police force with a domestic order maintenance mission.[12] These officers were remarkable for their dedication to following as closely as possible at the state level the development of a modern army in form and function, occasionally even leading the regular U.S. Army in adopting new innovations pioneered by other national armies, even as they pushed for more formal recognition and larger public support for their mission.[13]

From the early nineteenth century forward, military reformers, militia enthusiasts, and professional military officers had been urging Congress to pass legislation more firmly organizing a reserve army out of the militia system and to completely overhaul the 1792 militia act, an act whose detailed provisions for arms and equipment were outdated within twenty years of its passage.[14] While this movement initially had few interested followers, much less active members, in time more and more military enthusiasts took an interest in the federal system of organization for the state militias. Militia officers committed to the idea of state militias as formal military organizations were active from the beginning of the militia revival in Illinois and elsewhere in the country in the early and mid-1870s. These officers undoubtedly had a range of reasons for their commitment to this ideal, but one common factor among the earliest state militia officers in Illinois in this study was the high number of Union Army veterans of the Civil War.[15] In 1890 an historian of the First Infantry, ING recorded of his regiment that their "present commander, like all his predecessors, has been chosen from the ranks of our old soldiers."[16]

In the 1870s, veterans of the Civil War strove to put the new First Regiment of Chicago on as strictly military a basis as possible from the inception of the organization. From the birth of the First in 1874 on, the men in charge insisted that they would form a regiment with companies identified by letter as in the Union army, as opposed to a conglomeration of imaginatively titled, company-strength organizations that was then the prevailing norm among the Illinois state militia companies. They selected a uniform for the entire regiment modeled after the West Point Cadet uniform, expressly and visibly linking themselves to the federal military establishment.[17] Beyond the First Regiment, key figures at the state level throughout the 1870s, including Governor John L. Beveridge, Brigadier General Arthur Ducat, and Adjutant General Hiram Hilliard, all served in the Union Army. General Ducat, a particularly able officer and organizer, propelled himself up the ranks of the Union Army to Inspector General of the Army of the Cumberland during the Civil War. As Brigadier General of the Illinois State Guards, Ducat was responsible for reorganizing and consolidating the state forces from 1875 to 1876. He established the office of Inspector General of Illinois and received the first-ever inspection reports of the Illinois State Guard in 1876. The efforts of Generals Ducat and Hilliard represented the first implementation of any sort of organizational plan in Illinois that included not only rank equivalency charts with the federal forces, but also organizational tables and systems of instruction and inspection.[18] In the 1870s, these and other veteran Union Army officers in the Illinois state militia created a formal military organization modeled on the

Union Army and worked to ensure that militia practices followed those of the regular army as closely as was possible or practical in their situation. Working in the winter of 1876–77, Ducat and Hilliard established a system that assumed the Illinois militia was, first and foremost, a military body, and one with a reserve army mission.[19]

Throughout the 1880s and 1890s, with the difficulty of effecting change at the federal level overwhelmingly apparent, National Guard enthusiasts turned their focus inward to build on the development of their various state organizations as established by the Civil War veterans in the 1870s. In these decades, National Guard officers shepherded through a number of crucial developments at the state level around the country. More and more states adopted the regulations and protocols of the regular army for training and inspecting their troops. Summer training encampments became a standard feature of most state organizations, with more and more state legislatures purchasing a camp specifically for the purpose of holding summer exercises for their state militias.[20] Illinois acquired a state campground, christened Camp Lincoln, in 1885. Throughout the 1880s and 1890s, state governments were also gradually induced to lease, build, or purchase one or more rifle ranges for the use of their National Guards in practice and competition. Camp Lincoln, which opened in 1886, was constructed with a modern rifle range, and in 1888 the Illinois General Assembly purchased ground and approved the construction of a rifle range outside Chicago for the use of the various regiments based in and around the metropolitan area.[21] Many rural companies established makeshift rifle ranges near their communities as well.[22] Increasing numbers of states mandated a standard uniform, more or less matching the standard uniforms of the U.S. Army. Illinois did so in 1884. Finally, state appropriations for National Guards significantly increased over the twenty years between 1877 and 1897, to around $3 million a year from the states alone at the end of this period.[23] In 1897 the Illinois General Assembly appropriated $314,547.01 for the use of the ING over the next biennium.[24]

While identifying the committed volunteers who supported and pushed for these developments is difficult, it is possible to seek out all those men who stayed in the ING for longer than the basic three-year commitment expected of all members. Out of 3,668 officer slots available in the ING between 1874 and 1904, only 932 officers had held their current rank for more than three years. Men who found in the ING an avocation occupied every rank, from second lieutenant through general, and many who held higher ranks had spent several years moving up from private to commissioned status. Many of these committed volunteers also spent time as staff officers at the regimental, brigade, or divisional level.

It was these men who held the institutional memory of the ING and who shaped its identity and its future.[25] (See appendix F.) Although it is impossible to attribute the same motivations to all these men, those who became active at the state and national level were committed to the reserve army mission.

The regular Army had ignored state militias as much as they could over the decades, and when they did notice them, they had nothing particularly nice to say about them and much to criticize.[26] However, in 1885, the traditional judges of the efficiency and success of ING training practices—the state inspection officers and other National Guard companies against whom they competed in drill—were joined by regular Army officers. Beginning in the 1880s, and in 1885 in Illinois, the regular Army began to take a more active role in creating closer ties to the state militias, prodded along by requests for their services from state governors. At the governors' requests, the War Department detailed supernumerary and retired officers as inspectors and advisors to state adjutant generals on a fulltime basis to observe and report on the readiness of the state militias. These inspectors attended regular drills and inspections and also attended summer training camps. In time the Army also arranged for joint militia–regular training maneuvers and made courses at some of the specialized schools—artillery in particular, but also engineers and medical and signal corps—available to National Guard officers under certain conditions.[27] The role state militias played in policing strikes in 1877 and afterward also had some effect on the Army's somewhat begrudging interest in the National Guards. Another factor was the growing size of the National Guards and their increasing clout in their various state legislatures. Further, some senior Army officers, for example, Generals William T. Sherman and Philip Sheridan, recognizing in the Guard the men who would fight in any future war, actively sought ways to support and encourage the state forces.[28]

Enthusiastic and ambitious militia members created a national lobby in 1879, and in 1887 the National Guard Association secured the doubling of the annual federal appropriation ($200,000 annually to $400,000) for the state militias.[29] As long as the National Guard existed and had access to federal funds under the terms of the 1792 militia law and the 1887 increase, Congress was unlikely to abandon the National Guards in favor of an entirely federal reserve force—especially in the face of a growing interest in militias and their upkeep across the country—no matter how much the War Department might have preferred to substitute some force more fully under their control. So, as the National Guards grew and established themselves ever more firmly in their states, communities, and families, the War Department and the U.S. Army had to find a way to accommodate itself to the existence of the National Guard. They did so by detailing invited inspecting officers to observe and teach; later, by sending officers to three- and four-year terms of duty with various state militias; supporting the NGA and their lobbying efforts in Congress; and welcoming, after 1885, National Guard officers into the Military Service Institution of the United States.[30] Once regular Army officers began to engage with the state militias, they introduced where they could far more ambitious training exercises, including extended details that involved long marches and temporary camps, and invitations to attend joint schools for specialized skills.

The U.S. Army had very different expectations and standards for judgment than any of the other audiences the National Guards were used to. Not only were regular Army observers inclined to be highly critical, but their standard for judgment was the same ideal that they held up for the performance of the regular military establishment. Army officers, retired or unassigned, and detailed to the state National Guards, looked for a professional approach to military training, and this was their primary measure for National Guard performances. The regular officers were not impressed by a great parade, an honorary salute, a play, or a picnic. The views of these regular Army inspectors became important because through them, the regular Army became the guarantor of acceptable practices in the National Guard in the eyes of the congressional committees responsible for crafting the military budget bills. They wanted to see evidence of serious training by the rules established by them for their own services. The ING faced their first inspections by regular Army officers in 1885 and 1886.[31] By 1908, regular Army inspectors were both judge and jury for assessing the national value of the National Guards.[32]

Inspectors from the regular Army shared the gloomy assessments of the state inspectors regarding the regularity and quality of weekly training when they began inspecting ING regiments and companies after 1885.[33]

> The 3rd and 4th regiments showed the most want of instruction, but when it is remembered that the companies are largely made up of recruits and were never assembled for battalion exercises except at the annual encampments one wonders that they do not blunder more seriously and frequently. . . . That skirmish drill forms an important, in fact indispensable, part of military instruction did not seem to be fully recognized. . . . The manner in which men and officers performed guard duty, zealous as they doubtless were and commendable though their progress certainly was, left much to be desired. In the

matter of salutes the performance of the sentinels was especially faulty.[34]

Despite their concerns, most inspectors, like Colonel Theodore Schwan, U.S. Army, took great pains to include positive comments about the efforts, dedication, and abilities of the militia volunteers with whom they came into contact. Such inspectors were always painfully aware that the voluntary nature of the institution precluded unremittingly harsh criticism lest it drive away volunteers and local support.

Tensions on Parade in the 1890s

By the mid-1880s, ING members—and other National Guardsmen around the nation—had begun to model themselves much more explicitly on the regular Army, even as that organization was striving to modernize along new professional and technological models.[35] By 1886, shooting ranges became more widely available and marksmanship rankings became increasingly important to companies as a measure of their successes in training, in recruitment, and in popularity. All of this more rigorous and specialized training began to divert ING members' attention from their traditional bread and butter activities of regular parades, competitions, and social events. Parades had not yet, however, lost their significance as moments to secure public approval and support, or to demonstrate to friends and family, as well as to the members themselves, that what they were up to was important and significant, and tensions began to rise as a result. Two ING parades that marked special occasions in the 1890s illustrate militia members' continuing faith in the public benefits of parade performances to establish legitimate claims on the public good and the public purse coming into direct conflict with their role as a subordinate national military force.

In late October 1892, a large and elaborate three-day ceremony was held in Chicago to dedicate the partially completed grounds for the upcoming Columbian Exhibition, and Illinois Guardsmen were eager to take part in an event with national importance. The leadership of the ING wanted very much to use this occasion to parade the entire ING command all together and in public for the citizens of the state to see and appreciate.[36] However, for reasons of his own, the often-irritable General Nelson A. Miles, chief marshal of the dedication exercises, decided that the military exercises would take place inside the fenced Exhibition grounds. He decreed that the military would parade from Jackson to Washington Parks along the Midway Pleasance, according to the *Chicago Tribune*, on the grounds that "the military [were there] to do honor to the national and State dignitaries, and in no way to contribute to the pleasure of the people."[37] Miles was even unwilling to let the entire ING join in the military parade and demonstration and requested that two, and later three, regiments be detained for "police duty" outside the fence. The ensuing negotiations showed no official—either military or as part of the Columbian Exhibition authority—in his best light. The conflict even made the pages of *The New York Times*.[38]

In the end, through stratagems of dubious honor, the entire ING did parade as a whole in front of the national dignitaries present, proving to itself that it was as important as it hoped to be. Brigadier General Charles Fitzsimons of the First Brigade, ING resorted to the position of never receiving any formal order from Miles *after* receiving his own orders from the adjutant general of Illinois officially placing him in command of the ING for the purposes of parading the whole ING at the dedicatory exercises. As Fitzsimons never did receive any orders asking for his troops to be stationed elsewhere, he got them all to the parade ground on time. Once they were there, confusion continued to reign. The parade was disorganized; no one appeared to Fitzsimons to be in charge of indicating in what order all the various military organizations would march; and then, in an affront to military dignity that irritated Fitzsimons beyond politeness, commands where given out of order and for the wrong steps.

> The lines were not presented to the reviewing officer, orders to pass by the President *en masse* were given *en route* instead of taking wheeling distance and were disobeyed by some of the regiments, and properly disobeyed by the Illinois, the colonels well knowing that a review *en masse* defeats the object, which is to "review" or see the troops. In column of masses only the right of each company is en-review, and there is no warrant in General Miles or any other officer to mar or change a ceremony so clearly laid down in regulation.[39]

Fitzsimons's distress with the resulting parade was still fresh a week later. "I regret to say that the review was a dismal failure in a military sense, and was only redeemed from utter absurdity by the intelligence of the commanding officers of regiments and the "get there" spirit of western soldiers."[40] Fitzsimons also sought to deflect the criticism he and his command received in the press following the disastrous parade.[41] The acting commissary, E. A. Potter, summing up the fray, recorded his opinion that "the atmosphere surrounding the higher military officials (in the 'stars') seems to be rather lurid."[42] Despite the fray at the top, there were members of the ING who remembered the 1892 parade fondly, and in the end the *Chicago Tribune* approved wholeheartedly of the entire spectacle.[43]

Fortunately the parades held in 1893 were much smoother affairs, "culminating on Illinois Day [August 24], at which time the Governor and his staff and the entire organized military force of the State participated in a parade through the streets of the magic White City."[44] This parade, which included only the ING, was handled completely by the state, without any recourse to federal military authority, or for that matter, General Fitzsimons, who was by then replaced by a General H. A. Wheeler.[45] "The review on Illinois Day, in the presence of representatives from every civilized nation, was the largest and most imposing martial display during the Fair, and the troops elicited the highest commendation from military officers, the press, and the people for their discipline, precision of movement, and soldierly bearing."[46]

The ING continued to participate in ceremonial and dedicatory parades after the World's Fair ended, both at home and away. In 1895, for example, the First Regiment participated in the dedication exercises of a monument erected at Oakwood Cemetery to the Confederate soldiers who died in prisoner of war camps, which led in November that year to a trip to Georgia. The First Regiment served as a military escort for the Chicago & Southern States Association on a visit to the Cotton States and International Exposition. The regiment received some criticism for these activities, but members insisted that they were part of the continuing process of memorializing all the soldiers of the war as part of national reconciliation efforts. Members also crowed about the smashing success of their parade as a symbol of all that was excellent about Chicago, their regiment, and their service.[47]

Increasing Rigor and Professionalism after 1898

National Guard officers in the Interstate National Guard Association (INGA) used National Guard service in the Spanish American War to make their case for the primacy of the reserve function of the National Guards. Congress and public more or less accepted this claim, and agreed to foot the bills for a dramatic refurbishment of the National Guards. After passage of the Dick Act of 1903, Congress, through the Army, provided millions more dollars in cash and military goods than the National Guards, especially the ING, could ever have raised from their states or their local communities. By the early twentieth century, the ING, and National Guards across the country, were shaping many of their performances to satisfy the expectations of the professional military establishment, and through them, Congress. National Guardsmen were willing to make the necessary changes in their daily activities required by the new standards because they seemed to mark the fruition of their own long-term goal to become the first-line reserve army for the United States. That they ultimately weakened the bonds between the ING, and more broadly the bonds of National Guards in general, to their states, their municipalities, and their local communities was a gradual, little-noticed, and seldom-mourned consequence.

With the critical focus of the Army squarely on their performance after 1898, National Guards began to change their practices and their performances to better meet the requirements and expectations of this new audience based in Washington, D.C. Training in general became more regularized, and more in line with professional army practices. Parade marching was out, and skirmish and extended order drills were in during weekly training sessions. Expectations for military discipline regulating militia behavior went up, and tolerance for the more casual relations of the past went down. The ING refined the practice of examination for advancement in ranks, so that only men who had passed the examination for the office could stand for election to that office. Summer camp became a time for more serious training than was previously the case, as each camp had regular Army observers, inspectors, and training advisers. With increasing frequency, the Army even offered selected National Guard regiments the chance to participate in joint maneuvers with regular Army regiments. ING officers were given the opportunities to hone their increasing professional skills at the camps for specialized skills—artillery, medical, signal corps, officer school—offered by the regular army. These camps or schools were most commonly joint operations; that is, both regular Army and National Guard officers took part. These schools also emphasized the increasing specialization within the guards, with medical corps, signal corps, engineering corps, and naval brigades as well as the traditional infantry, cavalry, and artillery companies. This specialization mirrored changes in the regular Army. The regular Army observed it all, as they had been from 1885 onward, observing, critiquing, teaching, and sometimes praising all of these activities.[48]

Summer Camp

One solution to the problem of a lack of modern, professional training in the 1870s was summer training camps. The militias and National Guard of Massachusetts first established summer training programs before the Civil War, and the practice gradually spread to the militia organizations of other states.[49] Summer camp was designed as a training exercise, the better to mimic the conditions of active military duty. Summer camp gave both men and officers the opportunity to practice the full range of military skills that constituted the daily regimen of military service—from setting up and policing a camp to following the routine of camp life, with responses to bugle commands and working out-of-doors in both small and large groups, from detail to brigade, with various schools for officers at all grades and for various specialized branches.[50] Summer camp provided members of the guard the opportunity to learn and practice new military skills. It afforded both state and federal inspection officers the chance to see and assess the discipline and training of the various companies of the ING.

Summer camp also offered daily dress parades, constant opportunities for guard companies to measure their performance against each other, huge audiences, sham battles, and a nearly endless round of socializing, dinner giving, and general entertainment for ING members and the public alike. As seriously as much of the ING membership undertook their training at camp, the chief reward for most participants resided in the opportunities to cement the social, ceremonial, and political ties created by parading, competing, and community-based socializing—an issue commented on with increasing concern by many critics as the century drew to a close.[51]

Between 1875 and 1900, Illinois did not offer ING members summer camp every year, though some wealthier companies managed to hold them on their own in the years the adjutant general could not offer it to the entire militia. As state financing improved, summer camp became a more reliable feature of the ING calendar. The years 1885 and 1886 marked a success for the activist officers, when the state acquired a permanent campground for use during the summer training sessions. Christened Camp Lincoln, it was (and still is) located directly northwest of the capital city of Springfield. The first sessions were held there in 1886, and camp was held almost annually thereafter until the 1920s.[52]

The central object of summer camp, of course, was military training. A typical week of camp during the 1880s and 1890s consisted of three to seven days in camp for each regiment or, occasionally, brigade (made up of two or three regiments during most of this time). Each day followed a strict routine laid down in general orders and more or less following standard U.S. military practice. The mornings were broken into half-hour segments for a variety of official business from reveille at 5:00 A.M. through breakfast, sick call, morning drills, and assemblies, to dinner at noon. The afternoon was generally an unscheduled block of time from around 1:00 to around 4:30 and was reserved for a variety of larger drills, sham battles, field exercises and maneuvers, various specialized schools for the officers, or time on the rifle range. Generally, after supper there was a dress parade and then taps between 10:00 and 11:00 P.M. ING members guarded the camp throughout the week, seizing the opportunity to practice those skills as well. Because for many of the smaller downstate companies this was the only time in the course of a year that they drilled in formations larger than that of a company—in the view of some more cynical inspection officers, it was the only time some drilled the relevant military skills at all—while for the Chicago-based regiments it could be a chance to try new techniques and more exciting, warlike training exercises, the results from a training standpoint were generally something of a mixed bag.[53]

On the whole, the various inspecting officers adopted a tone of moderately hopeful despair, even with the real improvements that they acknowledged came over the years and with increased practice and standards of company discipline. Federal and state inspectors consistently recognized and applauded individual and company enthusiasm for military drill and practice while bemoaning the shortness of the time, the lack of preparation for the more advanced work of camp and the problems caused by the steady turnover of junior officers, both commissioned and noncommissioned, on whom so much depended. In the early 1890s inspectors were still noting that "every year, after the companies are assembled in camp for regimental drills, it is found necessary to devote much of the valuable time to company training in discipline and guard duties, and in teaching the company officers the close-order battalion formations." As a result, "very little more can be done, and several of the colonels told me that if their regiments reached the point where they left off the year before, they felt that under the circumstances they ought to be satisfied."[54] Nevertheless, most inspection reports concluded on a hopeful note. For example "The spirit with which [the men] received instruction showed them ambitious to reach a higher standard, and their zeal proves them worthy of the great State that has done so much for her 'citizen soldiery.'"[55] And over the years ever more ambitious training maneuvers and field exercises were attempted, and with slowly increasing success.[56] By the early twentieth century, boredom with the routines demanded by the relatively small space available at Camp Lincoln led ING officials and their regular Army advisers to plan ever more challenging field exercises. In 1908, 1909, and again in 1913, either together or by regiment, ING troops set off on marches across parts of the state for their summer training rather than stay put in Springfield.[57] Federal inspection officers continued to note many problems during these ING training events, but they attributed most to lack of practice that could not be obtained in armory training anyway (setting up tents, for example) and generally concluded that the men and officers were able and would, if needed, serve admirably.[58]

Socializing at Summer Camp

The increasing professionalization and specialization of skills fostered by camp training should not, however, overshadow the continuing emphasis on socializing and community celebration that Guard companies featured as they appealed to membership and the greater public alike for continued financial and emotional support. Summer camp featured banquets, balls, and elegant entertainments at, if anything, a greater rate than the rest of the annual calendar. The daily dress parade alone was a regular and enduring feature of camp life, albeit one whose military utility was somewhat obscure. As one federal inspector noted of ING encampments in 1896, "The field work was merely an incident of camp routine and did not interfere with drills and ceremonies on the same day."[59] Of that same year the historian of the second regiment ING, who normally never mentioned summer encampments at all, included the information that General Merritt, commander of the U.S. Department of the Lakes, was the guest of Brigadier General Harris A. Wheeler at that year's summer encampment.[60] An important dinner guest counted as a memory-worthy moment while on the whole, training exercises did not. In fact, most nineteenth-century historians of ING companies are as silent on the subject of summer camp as they are of all training practices, except when they are able to record the unusual social coup or the humorous story of schemes and pranks.

Along with such notable military figures, other guests of the ING companies at camp included such statewide important figures as the governor and his staff, who attended camp quite regularly in the 1890s, often bringing with them large crowds of wives and other female guests. Not only did the governor make official visits, but he and his wife also responded to social invitations extended by officers during their stay in camp. For example, in 1897 the officers of the First Illinois Cavalry gave a tea for the state's first lady, Mrs. John R. Tanner, and her friends. The event featured a dress parade followed by tea and a band concert. A photograph of the event pictures almost two dozen of Springfield's eligible young women and Mrs. Tanner decked out in lovely summer dress in the company of several officers in front of a tent.[61] Local dignitaries from both Springfield and the home communities were regular guests at dinner on Sundays.[62] And finally, whoever wanted to see the sights of the

Figure 4
Members of the Third Infantry, playing cards at Camp Lincoln, 1903. Courtesy of the Abraham Lincoln Presidential Library. Photographer: Guy Mathis, Guy Mathis Collection.

Figure 5
Ladies visiting the Third Infantry at Camp Lincoln, 1903. Courtesy of the Abraham Lincoln Presidential Library. Photographer: Guy Mathis, Guy Mathis Collection.

Figure 6
ING members in costume (many in ladies' undergarments) at Camp Lincoln, 1904. Courtesy of the Abraham Lincoln Presidential Library. Photographer: Guy Mathis, Guy Mathis Collection.

encampment also visited regularly. Daily visitors could add up to a quite significant figure. According to a newspaper report of a single day in 1896, "People kept coming and going during the entire day and evening, and on the whole the attendance amounted into the thousands."[63] Sundays were particularly busy days, as both out-of-town visitors and Springfield residents went to the camp to see the sights.[64]

One traditional feature of military practice that encampments especially seemed to encourage well into the twentieth century was the burlesques on military conventions. Melon thefts, baseball games, and dinner parties were also common highlights of summer camp memories and were recorded more often than the specific training exercises in company and personal memoirs.[65] Aside from notable dinner guests, the historian of Company I, Sixth regiment ING, provided only one other mention of camp activities—a long anecdote about stealing watermelons from a nearby field when returning from camp on the train.[66] Mock drills and mock court-martials were considered good fun and even made the local papers. Guardsmen and reporters alike found mock parades to be particularly hilarious events.[67] Guardsmen regularly posed for photographs while playing cards, boxing, lounging around, and goofing off.

Figure 7
Captain Clarke's Midway Squad, Company E, First Regiment, Camp Lincoln, ca. 1895. Courtesy of the Chicago Historical Society. Photographer: Unknown. iCHi-39236.

They also posed for pictures in oddly costumed "Pony Clubs," in skirts and while wearing ladies' undergarments.[68]

Summer camp fit seamlessly into the annual rounds of training, parading, competitions, and socializing for most of the Guard membership. Indeed, summer camp was for many members one of the main attractions and rewards of guard membership. In 1896, an astute reporter wrote that "the 'boys' came down to do their duty, of course, but to have a good time. To many it has been their vacation—the one week away from unpoetical business during the year. They left their workshops, their counters, and their desks to be the guests of the State for seven whole long summer days. . . . In his military trappings and flanked by his fellows the most ordinary man carries with him an inspiration."[69] ING historian Rufus S. Bunzey wrote:

> Camp week is looked forward to, for months. It is the one incentive, urging the men to extra work, in preparing themselves to appear before the public as soldier. It is the only break in an otherwise monotonous, un-remunerative, voluntary service and is very beneficial to the troops, bringing the officers and men of the regiment in contact with each other, where discipline and obedience are not only expected, but demanded, teaching the men that a soldier's life is

based upon those two principles, also teaching them the duties of a soldier in many ways. The knowledge thus gained being invaluable, and attainable in no other manner.[70]

Cary T. Ray, of the First Infantry, recalled going "to camp at Springfield that year [1895], with all that such Tours of Duty meant to us. Two weeks, or about that time, of outdoor life, Camp Cooking, etc. meant much to the Boys from Offices, Stores and shops." Ray's fond recollections of camp life included the daily dress parade, which was a "colorful occasion, and one looked forward to by most of the personnel of the Regiment," and holding camp fires down along the Sangamon River, with sandwiches and beer. "All Company Officers were there. Also the 'Glee Club' and how that good old Song—'Tenting Tonight' rang through the woods!" Ray also remembered visiting the sites of Springfield with passes to the city, including the former home of President Lincoln, and the monument dedicated in 1874.[71] Scores of photographs taken at Camp Lincoln in the 1890s and 1900s capture images of men at camp, formally posed or relaxing in hammocks, playing cards, drinking beer, standing in the mud, marching through the woods, and goofing off in casual dress and in elaborate costumed performances, particularly while dressed in drag.[72]

Bunzey, of the Sixth Regiment, went on to stress that at camp, companies appeared "before the people of the state, and the Governor, their commander-in-chief," audiences that were "ever ready to criticize, reflecting on the fitness of this or that officer for the position he holds."[73] Certainly, throughout the late 1890s and first decade of the 1900s, Springfield photographer Guy Mathis recorded a steady stream of visitors to Camp Lincoln, families and dignitaries alike.[74] Audiences for public performances, training related or simply to justify or sustain the importance of continued military reserve training, ultimately decided on the long-term viability of the ING and national guards in general. If the people of the state and the nation decided that the national guards were not performing up to standard, they would stop paying for them, and that would end the movement. Guardsmen had to continue to impress their audiences with their importance, their seriousness and their martial abilities, or their institution would not have survived.

Competitive Life of ING Companies

One of the most dramatic changes in the practice of the national guards after 1900 was the virtual elimination of drill-marching training and competitions in favor of marksmanship competitions and training. Traditional drill-marching competitions continued into the early twentieth century in the limited form of specialized drill teams, but competitive shooting events grew increasingly popular within the ING—and National Guards more generally—throughout the 1890s.[75] In the years after 1900, drill team displays were reduced to occasional parade or performance attractions. The focus of intra- and intercompany competition became marksmanship scores. In marksmanship competitions, individual skill took precedence over shared group skills featured in drill-marching competitions. Even in those events that were considered team competitions, final scores were compiled from individual scores to determine the winning "team."

Competitions were very popular with militia members and the public alike, and they had been for a very long time. Like parades, intercompany competitions were an antebellum tradition of the volunteer companies that gained in popularity after the militia re-emergence in the 1870s and 1880s. Like parades, competitive events provided militia companies with opportunities for the display of military skills, the physical discipline of the skills on display, the vigor and athleticism of the individual members, and military rituals of formality and deference, all surrounded by the glow of military glamour and the sweat of competition. Companies earned respect and admiration from their audiences and from each other for their military bearing and physical skills when they entered into a competition. Competitions also celebrated military prowess and explicitly explored the possibilities of disciplined military violence; the aura of risk, bravery, and sacrifice were never far from a generation raised in the long shadow of the Civil War. Competitions brought to the forefront of public attention the basic purpose of the militias, to prepare for an actual combative encounter.

Elliot Gorn and Warren Goldstein claim that the rise of vigorous, rugged sports in the post-Civil War period was a reaction to the increasingly stifling restrictions of Victorian propriety and industrial Capitalism. They suggest that the field of sport was both a release from the strictures of industrial labor and the moral equivalent of war, a war in which the participants contested not only the outcome of the game, but also each participant's sense of personal dignity and manhood. At particular stake for many participants was manhood or manliness, as they sought a strenuous life dedicated to the opposite of the corrupting feminine qualities of commercial life and material consumption.[76] Militia competitions, as much as any other, embodied the popular notion of sport as a battlefield; after all, the object of the competition was to determine which groups most closely adhered to the rigorous demands of preparing for an actual field of battle. At the center of the military training was absolute obedience to commands, an obedience that not only depended on understanding the order, but also required absolute faith that fellow company members would do their part. It was this knowledge and this dependence that was tested in the competitive drill.

The ritual of staging a competition began when one company decided among themselves to host a competitive event and so invited one, or more, other companies to meet them on the field. Once the host company set a date, usually in the summer months as the competitions were held out-of-doors, they sent formal invitations to those companies they decided would provide the best level of competition. Once the opponent companies accepted the invitation and agreed to participate, the host company went into a flurry of planning for the great day. Once the day of the competition dawned, and the weather was fair, the invited companies began to appear, usually by train. The host company would have designated locations on the "parade ground" for the invited companies to set up a "camp" of more or less permanence, and the visiting companies would be escorted to their "home base" for the day.[77]

Meanwhile, crowds would gather around the parade ground, ready to be entertained and ready to judge.[78] The competitions could begin in the morning or the afternoon, depending on the number of companies competing and on the range of events. In the 1870s and 1880s, and even into the 1890s, the central competitive event was to go through a variety of drill maneuvers to determine the most proficient.[79] The drill was broken into three parts, the school of the soldier (1) with and (2) without arms, and (3) the school of the company. The following list of exercises is taken from a competition in 1875:

> *The School of the Soldier (without arms)*
> Forms squad in column of files—single file.
> Side step to the right and left.
> Rest and attention.
> Wheel from a halt to the right and left—halting and aligning after each movement.
> Face to the right, left, and about, resuming the front.
> March in line to the front.
> Change step during march.
> Change into column of files, and again form in line—halt and align.
> March by the flank, and change direction of column.
> Marching in column, change direction by the left flank.
> In line, march oblique to the right and left to the front—halt and align.[80]

The competition concluded with "Fire by company, file, obliquely and kneeling."[81]

Sometimes the competition portion of the day might be followed by an exhibition drill by those companies that still kept up the Zouave drill, which involved both running an obstacle course and trick target shooting, as well as more conventional marching and rifle handling.[82] Often the day began or ended with a formal dress parade by all the attending companies. In the later 1880s, and especially in the 1890s, marksmanship and other target shooting events began to be added to the "revolutions of the manual" as competitive events.[83]

The drill competition was formally judged and scored by a committee selected before the competition began.[84] Informally, the audience also judged the event. Late nineteenth-century audiences were familiar with the manual drills performed by the militia and guard companies both from experience and because the newspapers would sometimes publish descriptions of the various maneuvers. Audiences looked for the same qualities that the formal judges did. They expected precision in the drill formations, unison in the various movements, an appearance of youth and vigor on the part of each member of the company, athleticism and strength in performing the physical moves, and an appealing and attractive presentation overall.[85] Audiences judged the competitors not only on their adherence to the prescribed physical forms, but on their costumes and their practice of elaborate military formalities as well. The prize given at the end of the day could vary from a simple certificate of the win, to a trophy of more or less elegance and size, to officers' swords engraved with the date, to prize purses for the top finishers.[86]

Competitions, like parades, could be held to mark days set aside for patriotic celebration. For example: Company I, Seventh Infantry, ING, or the Mason City Guards invited the Havana Guards, the Beardstown Guards, the Virginia Guards, and the Harris Guards to a competition on May 30, 1878, Memorial, or Decoration (meaning to decorate soldiers' graves), Day.[87] On July 4, 1883, militia companies from Muscatine, Moline, Ottawa, and Rock Island participated in a competitive drill in Rock Island. The Muscatine Company won the first prize purse of two hundred dollars, the home company taking the second prize of seventy-five dollars, "losing the first by nine-tenths of one point."[88] On July 4, 1878, Companies A, C, H, and G of the First Infantry, ING, competed for prizes in Terre Haute, Indiana; Company C won, Company H took second, and Company G placed third.[89] Competitions held on patriotic holidays were a natural extension of the drill exhibitions that often ended military parades. If more than one company was marching and drilling, the urge to compare the performances easily bled over into overt competition. Once prizes were established, from blue ribbons to silver cups to prize purses, the competitive drive was impossible to ignore.

Intercompany drill competitions were held all summer long, but many of the most prestigious drill competitions were in September, timed to come at the end of the summer drill season. In September 1878, the Company C, First Infantry, ING, won first prize and $750.00 in prize money. In September 1887, Company A, First Infantry, ING, won the second prize of $500.00 in gold at the Inter-State Competitive Drill at Evansville, Indiana.[90] As the prize purses increased in value, so did the seriousness of the competition. In the 1880s, ambitious companies created smaller drill squads or teams for competition and sent these teams all over the state and even the country to compete for cash prizes and prestigious awards.[91] One Texas company, the Houston Light Guard, took home almost $30,000 in prize purses and trophies valued at $10,000 over about ten years of competition in the late 1880s and early 1890s.[92]

During drill competitions, militia members from different companies gathered to share their enthusiasm for their military avocations, to judge each other's proficiency at military drill, and to create a community beyond their armory walls. Competitions fostered and reinforced shared militia and National Guard values of athleticism, vitality, discipline, physical strength, military rituals, and gentlemanly gallantry and honor. It was during competitions that the tensions between the social rewards and the professional aspirations for military prowess were most buried, and robust performances of a vigorous civic manhood were most fully on display. Competitions celebrated the outcome of the training process in ways that satisfied most observers and apparently virtually all of the participants. After the competition was completed, the day often ended with a picnic or even a military ball, a celebratory reward for the military skill on display earlier in the day.

The Rise of Sharpshooting

Accuracy with a rifle was difficult for most American soldiers, full- or part-time, to acquire through the middle years of the nineteenth century for a variety of technical reasons, including the difficulty of producing rifles in the large quantities armies demanded; the slow development of breech loading and repeating fire mechanisms; and the unwieldy size and weight of the military rifle. But, as the nineteenth century progressed and industrial developments made it possible for large numbers of soldiers to be armed with modern rifles for a relatively low cost, officers responsible for military training brought the scientific practices of observation and measurement to bear on the old art of rifle shooting.[93] At this point, rifle marksmanship was not only a desirable skill in soldiers; it was also something that could be fostered on a large scale. Of course, for military authorities to truly encourage marksmanship among soldiers and National Guardsmen, they had to provide each soldier with a modern rifle, plenty of ammunition, quality instruction, and sufficient practice time on a modern rifle range.[94] These requirements were not forthcoming in Illinois during the early years of the ING. In a very lengthy *Chicago Tribune* article in the summer of 1887, the author argued for the absolute necessity of training guardsmen in the use of their weapons and insisted that Congress should foot the bill for doing so. The author charged that while "plenty of energy [was] manifested in the discharge of other portions of the education of a soldier; prizes are offered by citizens for superiority in manipulation of the piece—seldom for execution with it." He continued: "Company commanders study hard and drill assiduously in order to win these trophies. The rivalry between companies and individuals is for manipulation of the piece . . . the popular companies are those possessing the ability to act in concert. Emulation is based on preeminence in motions and movements. Little or no effort has been made to excel in marksmanship." As further testament to the inadequate attention that marksmanship was receiving from ING members, the author pointed to the wholly inadequate shooting galleries of the First and Second Regiments, one relegated to the attic and too small for more than two shooters, the other in an unused hallway accessible only by a trapdoor.[95] A later ING historian recalled:

> Very little attention was given to target practice for several years. The cause for the lack of enthusiasm in this respect was accounted for in the difficulty in securing the necessary ammunition and ordnance supplies with which to carry on a successful shoot, saying nothing of the expense connected with the building of rifle butts, etc., for which the men were compelled to secure funds without expense to the State. The officers higher in command of the troops evidently took but little interest in this matter which today [1902], is considered a very essential feature in determining the efficiency of the National Guard.[96]

National Guardsmen hosted marksmanship competitions as early as the late 1880s, and the first Illinois State Rifle team was created in 1890.[97] Nonetheless, these early marksmanship competitions did not completely replace the drill competitions until after the Spanish American War, which suggests that marksmanship came to dominate intercompany competition for a variety of causes, only some of which were technological or financial. The social and cultural impact of marksmanship on the ING was that it rewarded emphasis on individual skill at the expense of certain group skills. This distinction between the individually honed skills required for successful rifle shooting by all members of a company as opposed to the drill-marching group skills is central to the timing of the shift in performance paradigms favored by the ING.

Marksmanship gradually became a crucial component of the ING's program to impress their new federal audiences after the 1885–86 arrival of federal inspectors. Marksmanship was valuable to the ING, and to National Guards in general, because it had a prima facie quality when it came to notions of professional military training. It was just so obvious that soldiers should be well trained in the use of their weapons that no one could argue that marksmanship practice was a waste of time or resources. Quite the opposite, in fact, most officers concerned with training both professional soldiers and the National Guards insisted that marksmanship was a vital component of any training regimen.[98] A focus on marksmanship was useful to the ING in winning continued and increased state and federal financial support because it was such an easy matter to demonstrate continued improvement through the hard, statistical evidence of marksmanship rankings and seasonal scores. The adjutant general of Illinois began reporting marksmanship scores on a biennial basis in 1882, and by 1904 the adjutant general was devoting the bulk of the biennial report to rifle practice returns and military inspections.[99] Guardsmen could use these scores to demonstrate the measurable improvement of the National Guard from one fiscal cycle to the next. Improving scores showed that National Guardsmen were more accurate with their weapons and demonstrated their seriousness and dedication to the school of the soldier.

National Guardsmen also discovered that they could continue to accommodate their traditional urge to compete between companies and among individual members while meeting new demands for increased professionalism through marksmanship competitions. Competitions were a basic component of ING activities prior to 1898–99 for a variety of reasons, but especially because they helped companies create a reputation as a desirable company to join and to support. So, turning rifle shooting into a game with medals, prizes, and published rankings for both individuals and companies successfully accommodated the expectations of many of the audiences important to the continued existence of the ING.[100]

Manly Sport

During the late nineteenth century, ING officers made a series of claims about the desirable moral and civic characteristics fostered by National Guard membership, alongside the admirable physical skills acquired through military training. They claimed that membership in the ING would not only improve the physical qualities of National Guard recruits, but also mark their coming of age as republican citizens and manly men. They expected that, in the midst of all their other activities, ING members would "not . . . lose sight of those other duties and obligations which rest upon us as citizens . . . to maintain the liberty and equality of citizenship under law."[101] ING officers argued that their training created men out of boys. Thus, as marksmanship absorbed ever more time and interest among National Guardsmen, ING officers either had to find a way to show how marksmanship demonstrated the traditional qualities associated with National Guard membership or find new desirable qualities for National Guardsmen to have that marksmanship could demonstrate to interested audiences.

This task was difficult for a host of reasons, but certainly among the most dramatic was the difference in press coverage between parades, drill competitions, and marksmanship contests. Newspapers rarely reviewed shooting meets as they once did parades and drill-marching competitions; rather, they reported the range scores and ratings in much the same way that professional and college sports were reported. All descriptions of the men, the uniforms, the athleticism, and the style, disappeared in favor of the hard statistics of marksmanship scoring. For example, see this early report of a shooting competition:

> Scores at all ranges for two days of shooting:
> Jackson   464
> Fenton   458
> Browne   451
> Warren   447
> John Rigby   444
> Laired   441
> Joynt   438
> Fisher   424[102]

The team affiliation of the men is not even included in the brief report excerpted above. If the reader was not already familiar with both the composition of the teams and the intricacies of marksmanship scoring, this report is pretty meaningless. The reporting even moved to the sports

Figure 8
Soldiers firing with "Texas grip" at Camp Logan, Winthrop Harbor, Illinois, 1899. Lt. Cary T. Ray, standing; five men of the Second Infantry, firing. Courtesy of the Chicago Historical Society. Photographer: Unknown. iCHi-39219.

columns in many papers, and away from the front of the paper and "news." In contrast to the style of coverage of other National Guard events like parades or drill competitions, National Guardsmen were not described in careful detail as individual actors, and then as members of a specific group performing drills for a large and knowledgeable audience. Under the regime of marksmanship reporting, National Guardsmen were reduced to little more than the sum of their marksmanship scores for the year. Anonymity was hard for some to accept, of course, and as late as 1906, President Theodore Roosevelt scolded National Guard officers for continuing to waste time on traditional drilling and parades at summer camp. Roosevelt wanted guardsmen to concentrate on marksmanship and rifle shooting.[103]

National Guard officers needed to establish tangible rewards for behaviors they valued, and this was one of the prime forces behind the development of the medals and published rankings of sharpshooting for all members of the National Guard. The critical importance of these rewards for dedication to the acquisition of difficult technical skills is reflected in the letter books of ING companies in the first decade of the twentieth century. Captains from "shooting companies," those companies with reputations for excellent sharpshooting scores, and captains from companies that ranked near the bottom of the ING in terms of marksmanship all devoted a significant amount of their correspondence with regimental and division headquarters to marksmanship issues, target practices, target frames, practice supplies, scoring problems, and most important of all, the published rankings and delivery of medals and awards.[104]

Between the lack of audiences for actual shooting events, held at isolated and noisy rifle ranges and not in central public spaces, and the dramatic change in coverage of ING activities, National Guardsmen could no longer easily demonstrate the desirable qualities of personal character that they had previously put on display during parades and drill competitions. In parades and drill competitions, they had shown off their patriotism, manliness, athleticism, vigor, and gentlemanly gallantry and honor. With marksmanship, National Guardsmen celebrated qualities that could be indicated with rifle scores—qualities like self-discipline, dedication, and deadly accuracy with long-range weapons. Even the increasing anonymity of National Guard members within their communities could be made to work for the National Guard once ING officers, and National Guard officers across the country, established a system of rankings that valued and rewarded individual skill, professional dedication, and a commitment to the nation. By 1912, Walter Merriam Pratt could write, "The National Guard is an organization wherein its members learn self-control, get self-confidence, improve their bodies and develop their minds." He continued, "It is one means by which can be shown your patriotism to your country, your loyalty to its institutions, and by which you can repay in a measure what you owe for its protection and the liberty you enjoy."[105] The National Guard provided these rewards by offering "a vast amount of healthy, honest sport which will improve the mind as well as the body. Unlimited opportunity is given for target shooting (the cleanest and best sport in the world), and a companionship exists among soldiers such as can be found nowhere else."[106]

Of course, with new activities came new opportunities for abuse. Where the National Guards had once put up with complaints that they were nothing but overdressed drunks playing at a serious game with no talent and no skill, they now were accused of harboring men who joined the National Guard only to have access to the premier shooting competitions in the nation.[107] These new rifle hobbyists did find a home in some National Guard companies despite their refusal to attend weekly training sessions or summer camp because of the traditional competitiveness within the National Guard. Where National Guard companies had once used their reputations as successful drill teams as a recruiting tool, they now used their rifle teams' performance to draw new members into their orbit. These abuses, real as they were, received less criticism than the drill-marching competition did for all the reasons that rifle practice was considered to be good for military training in general.[108]

Modern Guardsmen

The Guardsman of the early twentieth century no longer found his definition of manhood and citizenship in performances for the local community, such as in parades and drill competitions. Rather, the Guardsman of the early twentieth century saw himself as a soldier. He no longer considered his primary duty to be a protector of public order and a leader in patriotic display; he was a soldier who served at the pleasure of the nation. Continuing deficiencies in training and financial support notwithstanding, Guardsmen increasingly saw themselves as more than dashing and patriotic men; they knew themselves to be professional soldiers in training, and they could point with pride to their marksmanship scores to prove it. In a December 1898 speech to the Interstate National Guard Association, Lieutenant H. P. Parker declared, "[A]s the trained soldier is the real weapon of modern warfare, then see that you demand he receive the means to make him the best trained and most effective weapon that can be produced."[109] The modern National Guardsman knew himself to be a weapon in the hands of a great nation.

CHAPTER 5

Death, Manhood, and Service in the Spanish American War

> We have taken up "The White Man's Burden." We have done with "Childish Days." We go to face new problems in lands beyond the seas. In the first rank stands the Regular, but behind him is the Volunteer, the bulwark of "Old Glory" in time of sorest need.[1]
> —Dedication by the Illinois National Guard

When the U.S. Congress declared war on Spain on April 25, 1898, National Guardsmen eagerly seized the opportunity to demonstrate to themselves, their supporters, their communities, the nation, and most of all the professional Army that they were well-trained soldiers ready and willing to do their duty.[2] After President McKinley's decision to accept some 200,000 volunteers via the existing National Guard regiments, guardsmen rushed to prove the seriousness of their claims to the titles and history of the citizen-soldier. That the record achieved by the National Guards while in federal service was uneven at best—some state regiments or companies received high praise, others nothing but the most serious condemnation for their gaps in training, supply, and discipline—was ultimately less important for the National Guards than the experience of national service itself. The lessons guardsmen learned during the war, from the day-to-day realities of camp living to the politics of command and the complexities of logistics, served to forge a stronger identity for the National Guard as the nation's reserve army, distinct from the burdens of state policing and the joys of public spectacle that previously constituted their most public face. The opportunity for large numbers of guardsmen from many different states to gather and undergo shared privation and tribulations, hardship and glory led them to conclude that the wartime experience was the vital turning point for the National Guards as an institution, as well as for themselves as individuals.

The Illinois regiments in the United States Volunteers experienced the full range of the opportunities and challenges facing National Guards in 1898. Two Illinois companies actually saw combat, and briefly at that, in Puerto Rico. After the two days of major combat had passed, eight out of eleven regiments from Illinois served in Cuba and Puerto Rico for varying lengths of time. Illinois volunteers endured the terrible conditions in the large southern training camps early in the war, thousands suffered from illness and hundreds died, some mutinied, and more served to honor and distinction during garrison duty in Cuba and Puerto Rico.

One of the more impressive successes for the National Guards in general, and for the ING in particular, was the highly praised performance of the African American Eighth Illinois United States Volunteers (USV). When Governor John M. Tanner persuaded President McKinley and the U.S. Army to recognize and commission the African American officers of the Eighth Illinois Infantry on the same terms as the rest of the regiments of the ING, he put the honor and manliness of the entire ING on the line.[3] The War Department rose to the challenge and ordered the Eighth to Cuba in August 1898. In time their colonel was made governor of the province of San Luis and commander of the post, eventually becoming the senior officer of the Twenty-Third Kansas USV and Ninth "Immunes" USV as well.[4] The members of the Eighth met and mastered the challenges of their assignment and left Cuba after nine months of duty, with the praise of the inspector general of the U.S. Army, among others, ringing in their ears. The Eighth's achievement was all the more notable in that observers at home and abroad described it as a path-breaking experiment. The Eighth Illinois United States Volunteers was one of the first regiments in the history of the U.S. Army to be commanded entirely by African American men. Their colonel, John Marshall, was among the first African American colonels ever in federal service. African American men had struggled since the close of the Civil War to retain and build on the symbolic and practical importance of soldiering for the Union. The Spanish American War gave African American men their first real chance to do so in the public eye. They did so via the National Guard. As a result of all these circumstances, the war and the Eighth's role in it was of especial importance not only to the African American community in Illinois, but to the broader National Guard movement as well.

Illinois sent nine infantry regiments and one cavalry regiment into the United States Volunteers. When the members of these regiments looked back on their war experiences, they read them as significant benchmarks in the life of the companies and regiments to which they belonged. Where they had been untested boys, they were now men; where their organization had been dismissed as youthful play-acting, they now had combat scars to prove their seriousness. Illinois guardsmen pointed proudly to their war service to downplay the messy business of police work during strikes, and to celebrate their role as citizen-soldiers and honorable men, voluntarily taking up the serious and honorable business of training in peace for war. Many guardsmen even drew somewhat strained analogies to the experience of Civil War veterans, so eager were they to prove their own manhood on the field of battle. With service in the Spanish American War behind them, Illinois guardsmen were able to solidify the National Guards' position as the nation's reserve by taking leading roles in the national association lobbying for stronger and newer militia legislation. This association and its members were also able to lay the groundwork for the centralization and intensified training of the state militias that would prove essential for their service in World War I.[5]

When they returned home from Cuba, Puerto Rico, the Philippines, and bases scattered across the southern United States, veterans of the United States Volunteers told stories of manly valor and heroism, of dedication and purpose, of desperate illness and logistical confusion, of ultimate triumph and dramatic patriotism. These stories reflected the ways in which these patriotic and professionally minded members of the National Guards wished to understand and share their experiences. These men generally understood their wartime service as a rite of passage, one that marked a distinction between youth and manhood for the institution of the National Guards as it moved the soldiers themselves from boy to man. In doing so, they deliberately echoed one the most common popular understandings of the role the Civil War played for its veterans.[6] They also seized on the popular language about the war that cast the United States in the role of the manly savior of a passively beautiful and helpless female Cuba.[7] Had the war been only short and easy, their attempts might have fallen utterly flat, and as it was they were largely hyperbolic. Nevertheless confusion, privation, sickness, and death stalked the early days of the United States Volunteer Armies of 1898. The chaos and resulting morbidity of the early days of mobilization lent solemnity, grief, and righteous anger to the tale of federal service that otherwise might have suffered from the same jingoism that propelled men to volunteer by the hundreds of thousands in the spring of 1898.[8] From these experiences, ambitious and committed guardsmen were able to craft and tell stories that ignored their reputation as strike police and instead constructed a persuasive history of a trial by fire that tempered and strengthened the institution and its members, proving beyond question their manhood and their citizenship, and secured their place as the reserve army of the United States.

Preparing and Mobilizing for War

In a paper delivered before the officers' convention of the National Guard of Missouri in 1897, Brigadier General Milton Moore, National Guard of Missouri, observed that in "any future conflict in which the United States may become involved the National Guard will form part of the 'first line.' This statement requires no argument. Volunteers entirely untrained, un-uniformed, and unarmed could not be gotten ready for the field in less than six months." He pointed out that under "modern conditions a campaign might well be decided in that length of time. Any enemy that may confront us will be one with a large force of trained soldiers and its movements will be rapid." To him, the consequences of these observations seemed clear. "Our government will be compelled to meet it with the best trained troops at its command which will be the regulars and National Guard."[9] General Moore was stating the obvious. In 1897, in comparison to European armies, the 28,000 regular soldiers of the United States "did not represent an army in any operational sense of the word," and General Moore's assessment of the military readiness of the United States was widely shared. In the late nineteenth century, professional military strategists and unofficial military watchers alike recognized that if the United States should enter into war, any war, with any opponent, the only partially trained reserve available to the United States existed in the body of the state militias.[10]

Events in 1898 proved General Moore's words prophetic. The United States went to war with Spain over events in Cuba, and the president and Congress called the state National Guards into service as the best-trained reserve troops at their command. The leadership of the state National Guards, ING leaders among them, seized this opportunity to prove that they had indeed created the body of well-trained reserve troops they had been claiming all along. The war also gave the ING, and the rest of the state troops, the opportunity to demonstrate that the citizen-soldier could still function well in a modern war, and to prove the critics in the regular Army wrong. ING members also embraced wartime service because it provided them with the occasion to put their ideals of responsible citizenship into action, to show that citizen-soldiers would indeed take the plunge, leave their businesses and farms and employers, and come when the nation called; and to show that well-trained citizens would become soldiers at need. Nearly all Illinois guardsmen valued this opportunity to demonstrate their active citizenship to a skeptical world, and African American ING members were extremely dogged as they sought to use their peacetime training and wartime service to reaffirm their own citizenship. Finally, ING members saw in their service proof not only of their organization's utility and value, and of their citizenship, but also of their own manhood—at last the equal of the generation that fought the Civil War.

Illinois guardsmen had been seeking just such an opportunity for years. In the winter of 1892, for example, when tensions with Chile seemed close to breaking out into open conflict, many guardsmen eagerly sought the war: "'Hurrah for the war! Let's wade right in and punch the impudence out of Chile!'" screamed the newspaper leaders. General Fitzsimons and his officers in the First Brigade boasted that the state could provide 4,000 well-drilled and well-equipped men on forty-eight hours' notice. According to one reporter, the members of the still-independent Ninth Battalion, all African American, were "fairly wild with enthusiasm. They want to go down to Chile at once."[11] All of the men were eager to go into action to prove wrong the charge that "boys who enlisted in the National Guard did it for the social advantages it offered and that they [were] neither fit nor anxious to go into actual service." On the contrary, said Fitzsimons, they did it "for the love of things military, and not for things social." What all Illinois militiamen, and militiamen across the country, so desperately needed was a chance to prove their claims.

On February 15, 1898, the U.S.S. Maine—in Cuba as part of the McKinley administration's policy of attempting to encourage the Spanish government to find some way of negotiating peace with the Cuban revolutionaries—exploded and sank in Havana harbor, taking with it 266 American sailors. The most sensational American papers immediately blamed the disaster on a Spanish mine or torpedo.[12] From all over the United States, popular expectations of war with Spain burst forth directly after the tragedy of the Maine, undoubtedly primed by the preceding three years' worth of press coverage of atrocities on the island that heavily favored the Cuban revolutionaries over the Spanish Army. In Illinois, Governor John Tanner sent a message to the General Assembly on February 17, 1898, requesting that before they ended their session the state legislature authorize him to offer the president "whatever moral and material support may be necessary in this emergency to maintain the honor of the American flag and prevent or punish any attempt at hostile invasion of our common country."[13] Both houses of the General Assembly granted the authority without delay. As Jasper Reece, adjutant general of Illinois, wrote in his biennial report to the Governor for 1897–98, "[t]he thunders of a nation's resentment filled the air, while millions demanded that full punishment should be meted out to those guilty of this wholesale murder."[14] These sentiments and preparations were not isolated or unique to Illinois or to members of state militias or state legislatures. Newspapers were filled with stories detailing the preparations of the Army and Navy, supplemented by careful comparisons of the Spanish and the American military establishments.[15] However, all the indignation and the preparations were tempered by the sentiment expressed in Governor Tanner's request to the General Assembly. Tanner asked to be able to help the president to "prevent or punish an attempt at hostile invasions of our common country." In no minds but those of the most rabid expansionists was Cuba a common country of the United States. All in all, public sentiment may be summed up in the words of Chicago's *Daily Inter-Ocean*: "Spain can't whip us on this side of the Atlantic, that's sure: we shall not fight on the other side."[16]

With the generally perceived public hesitation to openly attack Spain without clear provocation in mind, as well as other considerations of domestic politics and foreign interests, the McKinley administration proposed a course seeking a diplomatic solution to the crisis precipitated by the *Maine* tragedy. Nevertheless, war was welcomed and even sought by a rough coalition of expansionists and supporters of Cuban independence during weeks of frenzied press speculation and accusations and wild rumor mongering. The one issue holding the public in check seemed to be the wait for the publication of the reports of the Spanish and American boards investigating the sinking of the *Maine*. Once the American report was made public, with its—unstated but implicit—conclusion that the *Maine* sank as the result of the detonation of an underwater mine, public demands for war reached a fever pitch, and conflict was only weeks away.[17]

National Guard officers across the country welcomed the opportunities presented by the war and the unpreparedness of the U.S. Army to fight it.[18] The total strength of the regular army in 1898 was set at 30,000 men and officers, but the army rarely had more than 28,000 total members. Until 1897, the regular army had been scattered across the nation in more than two hundred small posts, and none had more than a single regiment in residence. This small frontier constabulary was not in a strong position to take on the much larger, if hard-pressed, army of Spain. It was obvious to most officers in the National Guards that their organization was the only body capable of providing the men that the nation now required.

On April 25, 1898, Secretary of War Russell A. Alger notified governors around the country of the number and type of regiments that each state would be responsible for raising. Graham Cosmas argues that the "powerful" National Guard lobby—possibly the Interstate National Guard Association (INGA), but most likely the National Guard Association of the United States (NGAUS)—was instrumental in arranging for the format of the volunteer army in such a way that almost all the existing National Guard regiments across the country would be accepted into federal service intact, up through the regimental officers.[19] It must be noted that at least some governors did not choose to deploy their existing state troops and instead chose to raise new regiments specifically for the war with Spain.[20] Nonetheless, the number of Illinois units requested by Alger matched the number of National Guard regiments that Illinois maintained. Alger cabled that it was "the wish of the President that the regiments of the National Guard or State Militia shall be used as far as their numbers will permit, for the reason that they are armed, equipped and drilled." Alger's telegram informed Governor Tanner that Illinois would be responsible for providing seven infantry regiments and one cavalry regiment.[21]

It rapidly developed that all their best intentions and hopes aside, the claims of the National Guard officers about the war readiness of the National Guards were unequal to the emergency. Alger's assumption, fostered by National Guard officers in Illinois and across the nation, that the militias were "armed, equipped and drilled," was overly optimistic at best, profoundly misleading at worst. Weapons were all too often the outdated single-shot Springfield rifle, for which no state had an adequate supply of munitions or complete "kits"—bayonet, cartridge boxes and belts, cleaning supplies, and so forth. Artillery companies made do, for the most part, with muzzle-loading weapons rather than modern steel breech-loading pieces. National Guards across the country were uniformed in the sense that uniforms had been purchased at various times by the states or the units themselves and at some moment handed out to their members, but by 1898 those uniforms often turned out to be worn out, improperly cared for, and incomplete. Few states had included overcoats as part of their uniform requirements, and none issued knapsacks as standard equipment. State purchases rarely included boots of sufficient quality to survive much serious use, and at any rate, few, if any, had re-shod their entire guards recently. Certainly, Illinois had not. Tents, camp equipment, and transport wagons were discovered be in an equal state of undersupply and poor repair. Few state guards had ever made provisions for mess kits or other individual cooking supplies or trained their men in the use of such implements. (Illinois was typical in this case; many, if not most, companies messed together at camp on food often prepared for them by hired professional cooks—a development not yet standard in the regular Army.[22]) On top of all their material inadequacies, few National Guard companies or regiments were recruited to their full strength when the *Maine* sank, with the result that the units that actually served were often half or more filled with new, entirely untrained men. Enthusiasm for the war was incredibly high, and after President McKinley issued his call for 125,000 state volunteers on April 23 for $13.00-a-month pay, more than a million men presented themselves to the various militia recruitment officers around the country.[23] Between old members who failed the physical exam for federal enlistment and members freshly accepted to complete regimental rosters, probably half or more of the men in the National Guards/United States Volunteers were little more than raw recruits. Illinois was no exception.

The War Department initially mustered into federal service each regiment as soon as it was ready—meaning uniformed and equipped—to take the field. For this reason, Alger urged state adjutant generals around the country to work on supplying their regiments one by one. All seven of the ING infantry regiments and the cavalry regiment arrived in Springfield by noon on April 27, two days after Governor Tanner received Secretary Alger's orders. Even as he ordered the various colonels to bring their regiments to Springfield, Illinois Adjutant General Jasper N. Reece telephoned "wholesale grocers, bakers and butchers, urging them to increase their working forces so that subsistence stores of all kinds could be at the State Fair Grounds by noon Wednesday."[24] Over the next four weeks, until the last of the eight regiments responding to the first call for troops were mustered into federal service, Reece and his staff worked feverishly to equip the ING regiments for the war and supply them while in camp. Reece "telegraphed every supply house in the country from Boston to Omaha, and purchased everything on hand in lots from a dozen hats to two hundred leggings and three hundred blouses, and upwards, that could be found . . . [and] took options so far as [could be gotten], to be delivered in ten days, perhaps sufficient to supply the seven regiments."[25] And by "sending agents to Chicago and St. Louis, [Reece and the ING] picked up enough hats, leggings, shoes, ponchos, and blankets, to not only relieve the most pressing needs of the troops, but to fit them out fairly well for practical field service."[26] Reece also struggled to get enough blankets for the troops "in the raw and inclement weather," and "although the limited number of blankets in the [open retail] market [had] nearly all been purchased by agents of the Government," he was successful in acquiring several thousand.[27] The problem Reece faced over blankets—competition with the War Department for supplies—appeared in almost every category of supply and equipage that Reece struggled to secure for the ING. "It must be remembered that the United States, and every State in the union, were buying clothing and equipments for their troops; that the amount of these articles that were on hand had been purchased at the first intimation of war, and that now it was conceded to be almost an accommodation on the part of the manufacturer to listen to proposals of any kind."[28]

Illinois Troops Enter Federal Service

On May 7, 1898, the Third and the Fifth ING—the first two Illinois regiments with minimum-strength organizations and completely outfitted with uniforms, weapons, and camp equipage—were mustered into federal service after all their members passed the physical examination. They were followed relatively quickly by the Sixth (May 11), Battery A (May 12), the First (May 13), the Second (May 16), the Seventh (May 18), the Fourth (May 20), and finally the First Cavalry on May 21. The Fifth and the Third not only had the honor of taking the federal oath ahead of all their ING colleagues; on May 13 they were also the first regiments to leave Illinois for Camp Thomas in Chickamauga, Georgia. Thereafter, the various regiments were sent to one or another of the several training camps in the South, including Chickamauga, Camp Alger outside Washington, D.C., Camp Cuba Libre outside Jacksonville, Florida, and the main embarkation point in Tampa, Florida.[29]

From the moment Illinois regiments entered the federal service, the race was on to see which would get actual front-line service. The honor and privilege of being ordered to Cuba or Puerto Rico was one that regiments schemed and fought to attain. Reece reflected popular views about the desirability of front-line service when he wrote of ING Battery B's unsuccessful attempts to be mustered into the Volunteers: "officers and men . . . persistently pursued every honorable method within their reach or power to be included in the volunteers from this State, and that it was only as the result of the peremptory refusal on the part of the National Government to accept additional troops, that they did not go to the front with their more fortunate comrades."[30] Reece wrote these words even after the terrible conditions of the camps and the tremendous number of men who had fallen victim to disease were public knowledge.

Illinois regiments that made it as far as one of the large camps were desperate to take the next step. When the Fifth Illinois USV's place in the Puerto Rico expedition was given to a regiment from another state, the third time they had lost a chance to leave Chickamauga, the officers sent the following telegram to Governor Tanner from Chickamauga Park, GA, on July 30, 1898.

> We thank you in behalf of the 1,300 men we command for your prompt expression of confidence in the Fifth and denial of sensational lies of an irresponsible reporter. The regiment is the same loyal, obedient and disciplined regiment it has ever been. NO orders have been disobeyed, every duty has been performed promptly and cheerfully. Colonel Culver has our loyal obedience, confidence and respect. Men and officers are disheartened and discouraged at treatment they can not understand and the responsibility for which they can not place; but they are soldiers and aside from the charge of taking about twenty dollars' worth from hucksters by stragglers on the march, there is not even a shadow of foundation for the sensational lies sent to the press from here. We want you to use every effort to put us back in our just place in the Porto Rican expedition.[31]

Colonel Culver himself wired Tanner with a personal "plea for justice" for the Fifth and their moment in the sun, and the Springfield papers followed the travails of their unit with passionate interest.[32]

Tanner wrote to the War Department about the Fifth and in reply received a telegram from U.S. Adjutant General H. C. Corbin—according to most historians of the war, the real force in the War Department in managing the American military during 1898 and 1899—explaining the reasons for the Fifth's loss.

> Replying to your telegram asking that the Fifth Illinois Volunteer Infantry be sent to Porto Rico you are informed that it was no fault of the regiment, or anyone connected with it, that it was not sent. The facts are that the First, Third and Sixth regiments of Illinois volunteers were ordered to active service when it was noted by the Department that other states had none, notably your neighbor, Indiana. In view of this fact the commanding general at Chickamauga was ordered to substitute an Indiana for an Illinois regiment, and in the exercise of this discretion he selected the Fifth. This may be and doubtless is a hardship for the regiment. It had to be done, however, to give scant justice to the State of Indiana, and you will say it is but fair.[33]

The only infantry volunteers from Illinois who saw service outside the United States before hostilities ended were two companies of the Sixth Illinois USV, who took part in the Puerto Rican campaign. The Sixth Illinois was part of the Fifth Army Corps that sailed for Cuba on July 5 and arrived around July 15. On July 21 at least two companies of the Sixth, I and E, were part of the expedition that sailed for Puerto Rico. The invasion force put ashore in Guánica on July 25. Early on July 26, the companies were involved in a brief skirmish with some Spanish troops, with no reported casualties on either side. On the 28th, the men from Illinois marched fifteen miles east and participated in the capture of Ponce. On August 9, General Miles, commanding the Puerto Rican expedition, who had previously arranged his troops into four columns, ordered them to break camp and begin their assault on the Spanish forces concentrated in San Juan on the northern side of the island. The two Illinois companies were part of the column sent through the interior across the mountains on a newly discovered trail that led from Guánica to Arecibo. An armistice ended the fighting on August 12, and the companies E and I stopped in Utuado, were they stayed until the 25th, when they received orders to return to Ponce and await orders to head for New York. The orders arrived on September 6.[34]

The rest of the Illinois regiments served between July 1898 and May 1899 in a variety of postings at home and abroad.[35] In brief, the First Illinois just missed seeing combat in Cuba and served in a garrison there from July 9 until August 29, when, burdened by illness, they were relieved by the Eighth Illinois. The Second Illinois went to Cuba in December of 1898, after spending six months at camps in Jacksonville, Florida, and Savannah, Georgia. They stayed through April 3, 1899. The Third Illinois was in Puerto Rico from July 31 through November 9. The Fourth Illinois had the distinction of having spent the longest amount of time in federal service, almost a full year, from May 20, 1898, to May 2, 1899. The Fourth Illinois arrived in Cuba in January of 1899 for garrison duty and left on April 5. The Fifth and the Seventh Illinois, along with the First Cavalry, never left the United States. The Eighth served in Cuba from August 16, 1898 to March 15, 1899. The Sixth also served briefly in Puerto Rico, July 25 through September 13, as did Battery A.[36] (See appendix G.) The two most dramatic wartime experiences, however, belonged to the First and the Eighth. The First limped home almost decimated by disease, and in their place, the Eighth earned high praise for the behavior of their officers and men.

Tragedy for the First Regiment

The First Regiment, ING, of Chicago paid the highest price for active service in 1898. The First was sworn into federal service as the First Illinois United States Volunteers on May 13, 1898, at Camp Tanner. Three days later, the First left Springfield for Chickamauga Park, GA and arrived on May 19. For the next two weeks, the First endured firsthand the disarray created by the sudden mobilization. Thirty-five thousand volunteers had arrived in Chickamauga by May 21. The ordnance and commissary bureaus of the War Department almost collapsed under the strain of attempting to supply and feed such a large number of men. Although the War Department eventually sorted out its supply problems, it would not be until almost the end of June that logistics were running smoothly. In the meantime, the First was moved several times, unfortunately from one bad situation to another, especially from a medical point of view. The Army, in general, was unprepared to cope with large troops of men ignorant of the most basic health and sanitary precautions, and some general officers were unprepared for the number and seriousness of the infractions. From a medical perspective, Chickamauga and Tampa were two of the unhealthiest camps, and the members of the First began to fall ill even before they left for Cuba.[37] On June 4 the First arrived in Tampa, and on June 8 relieved a regular infantry regiment stationed on Picnic Island, Port Tampa.

On June 30, the First embarked for Santiago, Cuba, and arrived on July 10. Once in Cuba, the regiment spent a week in the trenches surrounding Santiago, then it moved into the San Juan Hills and began guarding Spanish prisoners on July 22. During their two months of service in Cuba, members of the First were increasingly vulnerable to the true killers of the Spanish American War, diseases—mostly malaria and dysentery, with increasing incidence of yellow fever, though all forms of illness related to bad water and unsanitary conditions were rampant. By early August, men were dying in every company, and the sick lists were growing.[38] As Cosmas wrote, "disease wrecked the Fifth Corps at Santiago almost before General Shafter could consolidate his victory over the Spaniards."[39] Out of twenty thousand U.S. troops in Cuba on July 27, four thousand were in the hospitals. By August 1, the Fifth Corps was dying at the rate of fifteen men a day. Thousands of men died of yellow fever, and thousands more suffered through malaria. Malaria rarely killed the soldiers who contracted it; it only left them weak and feverish, unable to digest their food. Often found in combination with dysentery, malaria left its victims emaciated and hollow eyed as well. Most of the sufferers from malaria and related illnesses never reported sick; they just stumbled through their duties as best they could.[40]

Figure 9
Fourth Infantry leaving Savannah, Georgia, for Cuba, January 3, 1899. Courtesy of the Abraham Lincoln Presidential Library. Photographer: Unknown.

The First was harder hit than any Illinois regiment in Cuba, and before their service with the USV Infantry was over, eighty-seven men out of 1,300 had died of disease or injury (see appendix H).[41] At one point, only forty-four of some 320 men of the First detailed to Siboney were able to answer at roll call.[42] The commander of the First appealed to Governor Tanner and to the War Department to release his men from constant exposure to diseases and death. United States Adjutant General Corbin himself wrote to Governor Tanner that the "main trouble with our troops now in Cuba is that they are suffering from exhaustion and exposure incident to one of the most trying campaigns to which soldiers have ever been subjected."[43] The War Department offered Illinois the chance to replace the First with another regiment if one was willing to go immediately to Cuba to take the place of the First.[44] Even then, some members of the First, like Pvt. Cary T. Ray, remained frustrated by their "missing out" on more impressive duty: "Held back on the way to Tampa, by circumstances beyond our Control, and POSSIBLY jealousy on someone's part . . . we did NOT have the opportunity given another or two Volunteer Infantry Regiments." And, "don't forget this: THE FIRST ILLINOIS VOLUNTEER INFANTRY, did everything it was ALLOWED TO DO, in the Campaign."[45]

Figure 10
First Infantry troops entering their Armory, returning from the Spanish American War, September 10, 1898. Courtesy of the Chicago Historical Society. Photographer: E. Hergt. iCHi-39625.

Triumph for the Eighth Illinois

The tragedy of the First Illinois provided the Eighth Illinois with its golden opportunity. If the declaration of war with Spain presented welcome challenges to National Guardsmen in general, it presented far greater opportunities to the African American companies of the National Guards. Laboring under the handicaps of prejudice, oppression, and disinterest, African Americans nevertheless had managed to hold volunteer companies together in almost all states for longer or shorter periods of time, and many of these companies managed to secure a place in their respective state's militia organizations.[46] African American men in Illinois maintained an almost steady military presence for the thirty years from 1870 to 1900, both within and outside of the state militia structure. By 1898, African Americans were supporting a four-company ING battalion located in Chicago.

When the first call for Illinois National Guard troops for service in the federal army issued in April of 1898 did not include the Ninth

Battalion, many in the African American community feared that between prejudice, racism, and the recent, highly politicized court martial of their Colonel John Buckner, the Ninth would be left out of the spoils of war.[47] A committee headed by Captain John R. Marshall, Co A, Ninth Battalion ING, approached Governor Tanner, and was somewhat reassured when Tanner explained that the War Department had requested seven regiments from Illinois for service in the United States Volunteer Army, and as the ING had seven full regiments already, there was no place for an unattached battalion. Tanner nevertheless promised that if there should be a second call for troops from Illinois, he would allow the Ninth to recruit a full regiment, and he would call that regiment first.[48]

The president issued a second call for more troops on May 25, and Tanner kept his word to the Ninth and summoned them to Springfield. Unofficial recruitment had been going on for some weeks, but now it began in earnest. On July 1, 1898, the new Eighth Regiment, ING arrived at Camp Tanner, outside Springfield, and commenced the final, frenzied efforts to bring the new regiment up to full strength. Goode noted in his history of the Eighth that the full regiment could have been recruited out of Chicago, but the adjutant general decided that six companies would come from Chicago, and six from various locations downstate. John Marshall was acting colonel of the Eighth Infantry, ING, but after the regiment was sworn into U.S. service, there was a period of concern about who the final staff officers would be. Marshall, born and raised in Virginia and trained as a stonemason, moved to Chicago in 1880, where he worked for many years for a large contractor. He joined the Ninth Battalion early on and believed he had been instrumental in securing their place in the USV, and he very much wanted the top job.[49] There were a number of other African American aspirants for the position of colonel of the new Eighth Illinois USV as well, including recently suspended John Buckner and Charles G. Young of Ohio—one of the early African American graduates of West Point. There were also white men who sought commissions with the Eighth in the hopes of going to the front sooner, and with an important commission, "but, believing that this race should have the opportunity to show the country at large whether or not its members possessed the ability to govern themselves, and in a spirit of 'fair play' [Governor Tanner] determined, and carried into effect [his] idea the Negroes could, and in this case should, be commanded by Negroes."[50] Ending all further speculation, on July 23, 1898, John R. Marshall was sworn in as a colonel in the United States Army along with his staff, all African American men.[51]

The commissioning of Marshall was a truly significant departure from previous practice and was recognized as such by all concerned. The adjutant general of Illinois wrote that the "Eighth Infantry organization is composed of men of the Afro-American race throughout, from the Colonel to the last name on the roster of Company M."[52] The newspapers hailed the remarkable step, as did the governor himself. Tanner addressed the Eighth after the regiment had joined the USV forces, telling them, "even from the very doors of the White House have I received letters asking and advising me not to officer this regiment with colored men, but I promised to do so, and I have done it."[53] Even the "men who raised provisional regiments in Chicago" and who were desperate to join the war effort conceded "that the colored troops should have preference" when the second call for troops came.[54] Not all Illinoisans were quite so supportive, and the editor of the *Illinois State Journal* chastised critics of the Eighth for their treasonable instincts and their "outrageous and wholly unjustifiable attacks" on the "character and conduct of the volunteers who have enlisted in the colored regiment now at Camp Tanner."[55] Now all that the Eighth needed was a trial by arms to prove that faith in African American officers had not been misplaced.

When the news of the ailing First reached Illinois, it was the moment the Eighth had been waiting for. Colonel Marshall immediately tendered the services of the Eighth to replace the First, and the War Department promptly accepted the offer. "The Secretary of War appreciates very much the offer of the Eighth Illinois Volunteer Infantry for duty in Santiago, and has directed that the regiment be sent there by steamer Yale, leaving New York next Tuesday."[56] So on August 9, 1898, the Eighth regiment received orders directing them to Cuba. Meanwhile, the First was moved back from the front lines, and on August 25 the regiment boarded a boat for home, arriving back in Chicago on September 10, 1898. In the end, eighty-seven men of the First Illinois Volunteer Infantry died of illness acquired while in the federal service.[57]

One reason that the offer of the Eighth Illinois was accepted was the popular (and quite false) notion that certain types of people, in particular African Americans, would be less susceptible to the kind of illness rampant in Cuba because of their supposed acclimation to the sun and heat and their general physical hardiness.[58] As it was, the Eighth Illinois indeed stayed quite healthy, especially in comparison to other Illinois units that saw service in Cuba or Puerto Rico.[59] The health of Marshall's command was the result of a happy confluence of events. The Eighth Illinois never spent any time in the large southern training camps established for the volunteer forces that became epicenters for spreading all types of camp diseases. They arrived in Cuba after the logistics of supplying an occupying army had been worked out by the War Department, and exposure to the various tropical diseases had given army doctors time to acquire much-needed experience in treating them. Finally, Marshall demanded an extremely high standard of camp sanitation, which worked to keep his men alive during their stay in Cuba.[60]

The Eighth arrived at Guantánamo Bay on the morning of August 14, 1898, and the regiment disembarked in Santiago the following afternoon. On the 17th of August, the First Battalion of the Eighth Illinois USV left for San Luis to take charge of the Spanish prisoners there, and the rest of the regiment followed a few days later. Once there, Colonel John Marshall was appointed governor of the province of San Luis and commander of the post.[61] Later, a detachment under Major Robert Jackson, made up of two companies, was sent to Palma Soriano, a largish town some 20 miles into the hills from San Luis, to keep the peace there between the Spanish and the Cubans. The two companies performed garrison duty in Palma Soriano until February 1899, though Major Jackson returned to the main body of the regiment after a few weeks.[62]

Meanwhile, in San Luis, Colonel Marshall moved the regiment into the old Spanish barracks in town and began to institute the policies of the American occupation, including sanitation and Capitalism American-style. McCard and Turnley wrote that as payday for the troops was regular and large amounts were spent among the local merchants, soon "listlessness and stagnation gave way to activity and life. The storekeepers commenced to put on their shelves delicacies and foods that would tickle only an American's palate. American beer was soon to be had on every hand."[63] Eight members of the Eighth married Cuban women (though at least two left their wives behind when they returned to the States).[64] At least two officers' wives, Mrs. John Marshall and Mrs. Robert Jackson, joined their husbands in Cuba, along with at least one of their children.[65]

It was never far from the minds of the soldiers of the Eighth that they were constantly being judged as representatives of their race, and as the test case for the honor and merit of their African American officers. Dr. Curtis, first lieutenant and company surgeon, wrote home: "The statement heretofore made that colored officers could not command colored soldiers will never be made again. If it is, our only reply will be to point to the Eighth, and to examine her records as kept in the imperishable archives of the War Department ... We realize the fact that we are making history for our race, and we are willing to make the sacrifice."[66]

Thus it was all the more distressing for members of the Eighth when a disturbance caused by members of the Ninth Immunes USV, an African

American volunteer regiment raised from four southern states and commanded by white officers, was laid at their door. The Twenty-third Kansas USV, an African American battalion that also had African American officers except for its colonel and lieutenant colonel, and the Ninth Immunes were stationed at San Luis with the Eighth Illinois. The Eighth was billeted in the town of San Luis proper, and the Twenty-third Kansas and the Ninth Immunes were encamped nearby. Some enlisted personnel of the Ninth Immunes got into a shooting fight with a few Cuban policemen, and Colonel Marshall was the officer who intervened and put a stop to further conflict. The situation was "thoroughly investigated" by Major General Henry W. Lawton, who reported to Lieutenant General Henry C. Corbin that there was "no foundation whatever for [the] report" of disorder in the Eighth Illinois at San Luis.[67] For his good judgment and prompt action, Colonel Marshall's position as provisional governor was extended to make him commander of the post, or the senior officer to the colonel of the Ninth Immunes, as well. The result of this action was to have word go out that at Colonel Marshall's post, soldiers were disorderly and undisciplined.[68] Another result was a new policy that placed all United States soldiers in camp some three miles from San Luis proper.[69] Nevertheless, despite having at least one senior army officer in Cuba whom Goode believed was disposed to find the Eighth always problematic, Colonel Marshall retained the confidence of his immediate superiors and kept his offices until the Eighth left Cuba.[70]

The Eighth uniformly impressed all the visitors who made an effort to see them. A correspondent from a New York paper quoted by Goode witnessed a dress parade held one evening for the benefit of a visiting English officer and reported that "the men presented a splendid appearance. They have mastered the intricacies of the drill. Their even military movement is a thing of beauty."[71] On the subject of African American officers, the reporter noted, "[t]he man who thinks the Negro will not obey officers of his race has but to visit the camps of the Eighth Illinois."[72] The reporter suggested that one reason for the success of the command was that there was "no prejudice here on account of a man's color, the Negro soldier is treated the same as other soldiers are."[73] The reporter also had praise for Colonel Marshall: "I found him an affable, pleasing military gentleman, unaffected by the grave responsibilities resting upon him and void of the arrogance assumed by the average white officer."[74]

On the occasion of their last inspection by the Inspector General in Cuba, the Eighth outdid themselves. General Breckenridge, U.S. Inspector General, and Brigadier General E. P. Ewers inspected the

Eighth on March 6, 1899. When the inspection was complete, "General Breckenridge said to our Colonel, 'It is a shame to muster out of service such a regiment. It is as fine a volunteer regiment as was ever mustered into the service.'"[75] General Ewers said that the planning of the camp outside San Luis was among the finest in Cuba, and the medical inspector complimented the surgeons on the sanitary conditions prevalent in their wards.[76]

Manhood and Wartime Service

After the men from Illinois were mustered out of federal service, many turned their attention toward recording the history of their wartime duty before the passage of time faded their memories. Several of the regiments or companies published one or more books or articles containing their service histories, and others produced individual memoirs of their experiences. One of the most common images that are shared by many of these memoirists and writers is their vision of Spanish American War service as marking the border between youth and adulthood, for themselves and also for the Illinois National Guard as an institution. Chaplain H. W. Bolton, in his history of the Second regiment, boasted, "[T]he old warriors of the Civil War were constrained to acknowledge that their experience could recall no examples of loftier enthusiasm, more vigorous manhood, more complete forgetfulness of self than were shown by the boys of '98."[77] By exhibiting their "vigorous manhood" as they marched to war, the boys of the Second showed themselves on the cusp of adulthood even as their forgetfulness of self demonstrated their grasp of the essentials of republican citizenship. In the same vein, Chaplain John R. Skinner of the Fourth regiment wrote that the "composite of this regiment is of the young blood and sturdy manhood of central Illinois, coming from the fields of her thrifty farmers, the shops, stores, and officers of her provident towns."[78] These writers celebrate images of youth and manhood, united in ING guardsmen on the cusp of war, a war that would turn them into men.

Many Illinois guardsmen firmly believed that the war, especially the hardships and death, turned Illinois boys into men the equal of the Civil War generation. A somber collection of photographs published by the First Regiment of Chicago in 1899, all taken by Claron S. Wagar, a member of the regiment who died during his term of service, show increasingly rough and lean soldiers who have fully made the transformation from youthful jauntiness to hardened adult veterans during their painful term of service.[79] The collection of images stands as mute testimony to the hard-won experiences of wartime. John F. Kendrick, himself a victim of yellow fever while in Cuba, wrote a long memoir entitled "The Midsummer Picnic of '98," offering a "slap at those who don't understand that a short campaign in a short war can be deadly."[80] Lieutenant J. H. Parker, also of the First Infantry, offered the following praise to his fellows at a banquet in December 1898, just a few months after they returned from Cuba, calling them "men who are sweet to see again with the realizing sense that having quitted themselves like men and soldiers they are now returned to the bosoms of their families and to the enjoyment of the laurels they have so justly won." He went on, "we were comrades, and we are bound by the dearest ties of mature manhood—ties that were formed on the field of battle where we faced together all the dangers of that awful time of sickness and suffering in the siege of Santiago."[81] The dangers, the sickness, the suffering, and the death of the Spanish American War turned the youthful males of Illinois into mature men.

Extending the metaphor of growing up from the soldiers to their organization, Skinner described the "childhood and youth of [his] military organization" prior to their embarkation for southern training camps, and the service that would mark its passage into adulthood.[82] R. S. Bunzey echoed Skinner when he referred to the "infancy" of the Illinois National Guard during the 1870s and 1880s, especially in comparison to its status after returning home from wartime service.[83] The historians of these Illinois companies and regiments all concluded that wartime service had ultimately made their organizations stronger. In writing of their wartime service, these guardsmen historians seized the opportunity to make the case for the respect and praise they believed their organizations had justly earned through their service to their state and their nation during wartime. Bolton included admiring press reports of the Second that echoed his sentiments. From the *Chicago Evening Post*, the members of Second Regiment "have shown themselves to be well-disciplined and true soldiers."[84] The maturing effects of wartime service proved enduring. Writing two years after returning home, Bunzey of the Sixth Regiment noted approvingly the way "the military spirit which had enveloped and swayed our people from one end of the country to the other during the late war, had left its effects on the youths through the land and they were anxious to become connected with the State troops."[85] These youths wanted the connection to the mature men who had returned, and the organization they served with, because it could make men of them, too.

If white guardsmen felt their identity as men and citizens was at stake in their participation in the United States Volunteers, for African

American guardsmen the situation was far more acute. They believed that war service would not only test their manhood, it would display it for the world in a way that they hoped it could never be questioned again. W. T. Goode opens his history of the Eighth Illinois U.S. Volunteers, "Far back in the early seventies the desire for military organization first began to inspire the hearts of the leading colored men of the state of Illinois. . . . As early as 1870 this military spirit and feeling bubbled up in the hearts of the colored men in Illinois, and like the subterranean activity of a passive volcano, kept constantly bubbling, burning and boiling up until it reached the crater of their ambition. The lava of aspiration, overflowing the open apex of the mountain of 'Success,' crept down its steep slopes until its warmth had animated the ambition of the entire colored population of the commonwealth."[86] These images dramatically capture the powerful feelings harnessed to military symbols and membership by late nineteenth-century Americans in general, and by African American men in particular. For African American men, the symbolism of military service was especially evocative because of the heritage of the African American troops who fought in the Civil War, for the Union Army and for their own freedom from the stifling confines of slavery.

Tanner's actions on their behalf were not forgotten by the men of the Eighth, and he received much praise from them for his decision to insist the U.S. government take African American officers along with their men into the federal service. "To his Excellency, John R. Tanner, the able and fearless executive of the great State of Illinois, who believes and who has the courage of his convictions, that it is the heart, the brain, the soul, not the skin, that go to determine manhood; who acting upon this belief and upon the fundamental principle of this government that 'taxation without representation is tyranny,' had the manhood to appoint colored officers to command a Colored Regiment, this book is affectionately dedicated."[87] Harry McCard and Henry Turnley presented the experience of the Eighth Illinois USV during the Spanish American War as the final and unanswerable argument that African American males had manhood the equal of their white comrades in arms, up to and especially including the ability to command themselves and the obedience of others. Honorable wartime service was regarded as the final proof of African American manhood, to which there was no possible rational or serious reply. The linkage of the ability to command obedience, the expectation of being treated equally and fairly under the law, and service in war expressed by McCard and Turnley in the dedication of their memorial souvenir volume about the exploits of the Eighth Illinois indicates the complexity of the ideas and feelings that surrounded military service in general and the citizen-soldier in particular. This complex of ideas expressed by McCard and Turnley suggests that what was at stake was not manhood as the opposite of womanhood, but manhood as the opposite of childhood. Adult men voted, paid taxes, and served in the nation's armed forces, all on an equal basis. As African American men voted and paid taxes, it seemed only just that the third of this basic litany of the responsibilities of citizenship should be open to African American men. To be allowed to serve only as enlisted personal was an obvious stigma that symbolically and practically limited the citizenship extended to African American men to that of dependents, children unfit to make decisions or command authority. To serve as officers, therefore, would symbolically extend full citizenship to a group long denied recognition as fully adult members of society.

McCard and Turnley elaborated on the challenges faced by African American men within the armed forces to achieve recognition for accomplishments as leaders as well as followers of men. Although it had been assumed since the Revolution, and proven decisively in the Civil War, that African American men made ideal private soldiers, theirs "heretofore, was to obey, not to command. They were always to be led, never to lead. Though his shoulders were broad, they were too narrow to bear the gilded shoulder straps. Though his hands were strong, they were too brawny to wield the commander's glittering sword."[88] But with the commissioning of Marshall and his staff, Governor Tanner forced the U.S. Army to indulge in an unprecedented experiment. The only remaining question was whether or not the Eighth would ever have the opportunity to serve the nation outside its borders, or whether members of the regiment would be condemned to languish in camp for the duration of their service and with no opportunity to demonstrate that the faith in them had not been misplaced.

The consequences of the historic events surrounding the Eighth Illinois were profound on both the personal level and the institutional level. On a personal level, Marshall himself was able to parlay his experiences to an appointment as a deputy sheriff of Cook County. Several of the junior officers of the Eighth were so keen on their military experiences that they accepted lieutenants' commissions in the regular army and joined the fighting in the Philippines with the African American regiments there, and several enlisted men also joined the regular army. Institutionally, the Eighth secured a permanent home in the ING that was never challenged again, and the Army itself, though slowly and with much foot dragging, began to commission African American men as officers on a more regular basis.

The efforts of the volunteers to make true soldiers of themselves were not always applauded during the Spanish American War, but as their service lengthened, guardsmen were able to make an ever-stronger case for the importance of their prior training to the well-being of the nation's military system. Even if their term of service was not all that they hoped for, or close to equaling the experiences of the Civil War veterans, guardsmen were firm in their conviction that they had proven their mettle as men and soldiers. The guardsmen themselves saw their story as one of coming of age, of a time when they proved themselves men and soldiers, citizens and warriors. In the words of Colonel Francis A. Riddle:

> A hero, loving his kind, scorning outrage and defying despotism, stood beneath our victorious banner in the plain of Mars. Born in the new world, educated in her common schools, he grasped the standard of our blood-bought republic, and with no purpose but to set the stranger free, he had carried it with added lustre upon a mission as sacred as any in which men of high courage and exalted sentiment ever enlisted.[89]

From their wartime service, guardsmen were at last able to earn the institution of the National Guards the long sought official recognition for their efforts to become citizen-soldiers.

Passing the Test of War

After the end of Reconstruction in 1877, the U.S. Congress, despite repeated calls to develop a new military structure for the nation, returned to antebellum traditions of maintaining a very small standing army while simultaneously ignoring calls for any serious reform of the militia system. Professional strategists, regular military officers, and unofficial observers had been complaining about the state militia system for decades, to little avail. They had developed dozens if not hundreds of schemes to improve the militia system to better meet the need for effective and efficient training. As a result, there was a variety of proposals for what the state militias could and should be floating around Washington, D.C. and various state capitals. These plans ranged from a completely federalized reserve army in training; to temporary troops to hold the line until volunteers could be raised, supplied, and trained; to a coastal defense league consisting primarily of heavy artillery battalions.[90] Some in the military had also proposed altogether new federal reserve systems as alternatives to the state militias.[91] But no one reform proposal gained momentum, and after 1899 these and other alternative missions and their attendant political positions and recruitment strategies fell by the wayside, and the National Guards emerged as the nation's active reserve army.

National Guardsmen emerged from the Spanish American War heady with triumph that they had produced the first-line reserve forces for the nation. They believed that they had demonstrated to the world that they could perform, more or less, as advertised—and certainly as well as the regular army itself. By the late 1890s, National Guardsmen, particularly in western states like Illinois, Indiana, Ohio, and Michigan, had been calling for public and private support and new members for more than two decades, on the grounds that they were training the boys who would be the men who would serve the nation in need. They had managed to achieve incremental growth of state and federal militia budgets, and forge ever-closer ties to the federal army via inspectors and instructors. The money and the training had produced visible results in increasing professionalization and standardization among the National Guards. Pointing to their real achievements, dedicated National Guardsmen around the country insisted that they had indeed become a reserve army even before the war with Spain.[92] The most potent challenge to their claim was the charge that they were little more than play soldiers, boys who knew nothing of real war.[93] The Spanish American War offered National Guardsmen the opportunity they had been seeking to prove that they, and their institution, were indeed the reserve army they believed themselves to be.

CHAPTER 6

Lessons Learned: The ING and Strike Duty, 1894–1916

> As to the general situation . . . it appeared that the local authorities had made no effort to control the situation.[1]
> —Captain C. C. Craig, Artillery Battalion, Battery B, ING

From 1877 onward, members of the Illinois militia accepted strike duty as a normal component of their civic obligations and a reasonable exchange for the support they were given by their communities. Nonetheless, in 1900 the Illinois adjutant general proposed mechanisms to remove the Illinois National Guard from strike duty in the future. A number of different developments combined to lead Illinois guardsmen to the conclusion that strike duty was best avoided. In part, guardsmen pulled away from strike service because of the ongoing professionalization of their training practices. Beginning in the 1870s, guardsmen celebrated their role as a reserve army in training, with explicit training for war the center of their weekly regimen. As their training practices grew more professional and rigorous throughout the 1880s and 1890s, so did their focus on themselves as members of a reserve army.[2] Strike duty became a distraction, miring guard units in messy local political situations for which their training was mostly useless and in which they could not hope to shine. Further complicating matters, in Illinois, guardsmen recruited and raised money based on their presentation of themselves as dashing and patriotic citizens, and not as uniformed strike breakers, home invaders, or, on rare occasions, killers; these were thankless tasks that fell their way during strike duty in the 1880s and later, tasks that compromised their presentation as worthy and honorable men. Finally, strikes themselves also changed, growing more charged, more acrimonious, organized, and bitter, and in some cases far more violent than anything guardsmen had encountered in the 1870s.[3]

Strike service in 1894, from 1898 to 1899, and again from 1904 to 1905, dramatically illustrated the unbridgeable gulf between what guardsmen wanted to be doing and the messy realities of strike duty. Illinois National Guard officers began actively questioning their part in strike service during the mine strikes of 1894, which overlapped with the strikes that radiated outward from the infamous events in Pullman and led to a banner year for ING active duty. Their stance hardened further after service during particularly bitter coal strikes in Pana and Virden in the period from 1898 to 1899, and in Ziegler from 1904 to 1905. Based on these experiences, ING leaders developed the firm conviction that in many instances of strike service, they were being used to cover for cowardly local politicians, feckless county sheriffs, and craven mine operators who had failed to do their jobs, and they resented the cost to themselves in terms of reputation and money. After the events in Ziegler in 1904 to 1905, Illinois National Guard officers managed to evade being called out for strike duty through 1916, while still professing their devotion to protecting public order.

Growing Criticism of Strike Duty

Over the two decades between 1877 and 1898, ING officers grew more willing to critique county sheriffs or other local law enforcement officials, namely, U.S. marshals, for their behavior prior to and following the request for state military intervention. Illinois National Guard officers began to argue that militia presence more often than not indicated an unacceptable breakdown of local law and order maintenance through the willful abdication of authority by local officials. When they made this argument, ING officers had a long list of strikes to point to as examples. (See appendixes C and D.) Collectively, ING officers had more experience with strike duty than those of any other state militia in these years, mostly owing to the many labor struggles in the coalfields of central Illinois, and their attitude reflected that experience.[4] Before 1893, ING officials never expressed an official judgment on the job the sheriff did or failed to do in handling the events in his jurisdiction himself, though the officers did find cause to criticize. Even then, ING officers recorded their frustration with the way in which some sheriffs requested aid and then declined to even show up to provide the formal leadership by civil authorities that the ING sought in their early experiences policing strike-related disorders.[5] After 1894 ING officers never hesitated to critique sheriffs if they felt it was warranted.

Beginning with the calls to police mine-strike–related turbulence in 1894, ING officers grew much bolder in expressing their opinions about the poor jobs sheriffs had made of handling strike-related events prior to issuing a call for state aid. In the twelve strikes dating from 1894 where they offered judgments in the biennial reports, officers praised sheriffs for fully exhausting their resources before turning to the state for military intervention only four times. In six cases, officers stated that the sheriff had failed to act promptly or with enough force to prevent outbreaks of violence, and in two cases, ING officers did not endorse either position but expressed doubt about the sheriff's actions prior to the appeal for state aid. By 1905, with nearly three decades of experience policing strike-related disorders behind them, ING officers reached the conclusion that most calls for their aid in strike situations ought to have been unnecessary and were reflections on the poor ability or failure of will on the part of local authorities to act to prevent disorder within their jurisdictions. To be sure, such a conclusion was self-serving. It blamed others for problems that the ING was not well equipped to solve and suggested that they should not get involved in these difficult situations in the first place. It shifted responsibility from the state down to the county or city and removed the ING from the question of the proper role of the state in responding to contentious labor disputes.

The officers in charge of these strike-related periods of active duty may have shared increasingly critical attitudes about strikes and local sheriffs in their official reports, but they did not question the role of the state in responding to what they did view as dangerously volatile situations. In 1892, Colonel William S. Brackett, inspector general for the ING, published a paper entitled "The Rising Menace Against the Peace of American Society," in which he insisted that the National Guards stood between "ignorant and unguided men" and the safety of American society.[6] Brackett went on to argue that "the National Guard, as the preserver of peace and public order, has proved itself to be the 'security of a free state.' The state troops of New York, of Pennsylvania, of Illinois, and of Wisconsin, have again and again, and yet again, enforced the mandate of the sovereign power that there *must and shall be peace* [sic]."[7] Brackett concluded, "There are thousands of ignorant and misguided men in a great city like Chicago, who fondly believe they could establish their propaganda of revolution if they could but once thoroughly 'down the police' and the First and Second regiments of the city. Little do they dream what the military power of the United States is."[8] Like most other commentators of the time, Brackett drew careful distinctions between struggling but honest men and the minority of immigrant radicals who would lead them astray, and he roundly condemned the "game of grab" that motivated the nation's corporate elite.[9] Nonetheless, he placed the highest possible value on orderly means to resolve difficulties, and he staunchly defended the possible role of the military, both regular and state troops, in keeping the peace.

The most that can be said of officers' views of strikers is that they were complex. The attitudes of enlisted men are more difficult to determine, but some, at least, had no need to appear gentle with regard to strikers. Some embraced strike duty as a central part of state-soldiering. In 1883, after the shooting at the mine in Belleville, Thomas J. Morton, sergeant, Company F, Fifth Regiment, was featured in the following news story.

> [Morton] states that he and another Sergeant were on the platform of one of the cars as the shooting began. His Captain, Fahenstock, was on the lower step, getting down, and just at that moment Morton saw a man fire deliberately with a revolver at the Captain. The bullet sped high, and Morton says both he and the other Sergeant felt or heard the sharp whistle as it passed over their heads. Morton immediately raised his gun and fired at the man, but missed him. The man ran off a little distance and turning, fired again, and then ran for the bluff. Morton, having slipped another cartridge in his gun, took deliberate aim at the fellow and fired again. The man dropped dead. Morton says other shots were fired at the same time, and he does not know that he killed the man, but he does know that he shot at him, and would do it again under the same circumstances.[10]

Like Thomas Morton of the Fifth Regiment, historian of the Second Regiment Horace Bolton believed that strikers and rioters were interchangeable, and that they deserved what ever they got. Bolton made his own sympathies plain when he wrote of the 1894 Pullman Strike: "the aid of the all-powerful American Railway Union was invoked, with the result that in a short space of time the entire railroad system was tied up, a reign of terror had been established, and the utmost efforts of the civil authorities to establish order were fruitless."[11] For his fellow members of the Second, Bolton had nothing but praise. "In fact it is difficult to determine which merited the greater approbation, the steadiness, coolness and self-possession of the Guardsmen while the commands of their Captain held them in check, or the dash and resolution with which they took the offensive when their commander decided that bloodshed could no longer be avoided."[12] Of his service with the First Regiment during the 1894 strikes, in Pana and then later that summer in Pullman, Cary T. Ray wrote that it was "an attempt to stop all traffic, and something President Grover Cleveland could not tolerate. He said—THE MAIL MUST GO [sic]. And then U.S. and National Guard troops were ordered into action."[13]

On another occasion, in 1898, during strike service in Virden, the engineer assigned to the train that was to carry the first troops to the scene of the firefight refused to drive the train, out of sympathy with the strikers. The ING officer in charge quickly discovered that he had among his membership a former engineer who was willing to take over the running of the train to get the troops to the scene. Although there is no other information about the ING member, it is certainly suggestive of general ING member attitudes that he no longer felt any obligation to the striking miners, if he ever had, or at least, not enough to override his commitment to the ING.[14] On the other hand, Ray of the First Regiment recorded that at the start of his company's service in Pullman, their second lieutenant, W. G. Adkins, resigned, having "decided not to continue in the Service."[15] Ray doesn't offer more than this explanation, but the timing is certainly interesting.

Of course, much as some of the ING members who wrote about their experiences during strike duty praised their own efforts, disparaged the strikers, and saw their service as "impress[ing] upon the rioters that the community would and could be protected against their lawless attempts to overthrow the safeguards thrown around it by the strong arm of law and justice," they performed strike duty because they had to, not because they sought it out.[16] Bunzey, the historian of the Sixth Regiment, dignified strike duty with only the story of a slain pig—and of the panicked young man who feared briefly that he had murdered someone. Bolton of the Second Regiment did manage to include a much longer complaint that forty-nine cents a day was not enough to convince men with "good positions, commanding good salaries, to stand guard and perform other irksome duties during riots or other disturbances for the pay of the regular army man."[17] On the issue of pay, Bolton reported with some satisfaction that in 1886 the legislature raised the per diem strike duty pay to two dollars a day per man.[18] Concluding his tale of service in 1894, Ray wrote that "aside from all frivolity, 'foreign service' is preferable to Strike Duty—if prolonged, and rough."[19]

Conclusions from these scattered personal impressions are hardly definitive. Another measure of the impact of strike-related duty on the attitudes of enlisted men might be the changes in enlistment figures over time. However, there is no correlation between strike-related active duty and the variation in membership over time. (See appendix E.) The lack of correlation suggests that strike service played little or no role in individual decisions about whether or not to volunteer or to stay active over time. The few dramatic changes in the size of the ING were legislatively mandated (as happened in the early 1880s), and, later, the result of the 1900 reorganization of the ING following their participation in the Spanish American War from 1898 to 1899. Taken together, then, ING officers and enlisted men appear to have viewed strike duty as an obligation at best, a thankless duty at worst, and, with some exceptions, they did not embrace it as a central part of their purpose or their identity.

1894: Turning Point

By 1894, Illinoisans were beginning to suffer from the recession-related cutbacks of the early 1890s, and unionized miners walked out in the central Illinois coalfields as early as mid-April.[20] Around the state, more and more miners rapidly joined in, and before the end of the strike, 25,207 out of 25,817 coal miners in Illinois walked out. Illinois was not the only state affected by the coal mine strike, which was truly national, with 180,000 miners out across the country in June of 1894. Along with the ING, state troops from Colorado, Indiana, Iowa, Maryland, Michigan, Ohio, and West Virginia served in mining areas in response to violence or potential violence.[21] With this many men out of work and participating in organized protest marches and rallies even as mine operators sought to bring in scab labor to keep the coal moving, tensions escalated rapidly across Illinois. On May 24, 1894, the sheriff of LaSalle County telegraphed Governor John P. Altgeld for help. Initially Altgeld refused, but later that same day he relented after learning of threats to storm the jail to release men arrested after an earlier strike meeting ended in a brawl. Illinois National Guard companies arrived late that night and stayed in LaSalle for seven days. The same day Illinois troops also went to Centralia, and stayed for three days. The next few weeks were very busy for Illinois guardsmen. Illinois National Guard troops went to Pana on May 26 for two days because the sheriff there reported rumors of a threatened "invasion" of miners from Indiana planning to close four working mines—an invasion that did not occur. On May 27 the ING went to Minonk for three days after reports of a train seized by strikers who blockaded the tracks. On June 5, the ING went to Carterville for

Figure 11
Company I, First Infantry, at Calumet during railroad strikes, 1894. Courtesy of the Chicago Historical Society. Photographer: Unknown. iCHi-39229.

three days after strikers prevented strike breakers from working. After direct conflict between sheriffs and strikers that resulted in one death and a "destroyed" mine, the ING was called to Pekin on June 7 and stayed for seven days. On June 8, the ING went back to Pana for another three days because the sheriff was once again worried about an "invasion" of strikers (appendix D).[22]

Guardsmen felt unwelcome in most of these cities, and more so in June than in May. Pana, in particular, became the center of very ugly confrontations between strikers and imported strike breakers, confrontations that eventually put everyone there on edge. Crowds in Pana responded to the militia's second appearance in June by yelling abuse at them, and guardsmen responded to the provocations by searching and arresting protestors "for being 'strangers,' 'insulting the troops,' 'hostile movements,' and 'jeering at the soldiers.'" One Frank Bardowsky, arrested by the militia in Pana during their June service there, "urged the crowd to attack the militia" in retaliation for his arrest, even as his wife ran alongside the arresting party, pleading for his release.[23] Tensions between guardsmen and residents were worse by July, and selected companies spent nine days in Spring Valley that month before the authorities were satisfied that conditions allowed them to be sent home. Illinois National Guard officers had not disputed the need for their services in the coal fields at the end of May, but by June they were beginning to resent being called into situations that they claimed should have been quelled by local authorities. This frustration may have made things more difficult, and by July in Spring Valley, a place the ING commander did not think initially needed them, troops began forcing their way into miners' homes looking for weapons and stolen property, and generally terrorizing the residents. At least three people were killed during these weeks, but it is not entirely clear if the ING was responsible or if it was regular Army troops riding on trains being cleared from Chicago.[24]

The Pullman strike of 1894 soon upstaged even this unprecedented level of service. The Pullman strike remains among the most infamous railroad strikes in Illinois, or the nation, between 1878 and 1916, though Illinois and the ING were hardly alone in suffering the effects of the strike. State troops from twelve different states were sent to quell violence stemming from the Pullman strikes as they radiated out across the nation.[25] In Illinois both federal and state troops were called to Chicago and to various locations downstate. The Pullman affiliate of the American Railway Union (ARU) struck on May 11 after the corporation refused to negotiate about the union's grievances with regard to rents, prices, and pay in Pullman proper. Initially public sympathy lay squarely with the strikers at Pullman, but the corporation stood firm in their refusal to negotiate. In response, in late June the national body of the ARU declared a boycott of all railroads using Pullman sleeping cars, bringing traffic between Chicago and the West Coast nearly to a standstill by July 1. On July 2 a federal court handed down an injunction declaring the strike illegal, and on July 3 President Cleveland ordered federal troops into Chicago.[26] The mayor of Chicago, the sheriff of Cook County, and the governor of Illinois all believed this action was unwarranted and protested it vigorously on the grounds that it would lead to violence rather than prevent it, but to no avail.

The fears of Illinois officials were realized when rioting subsequently erupted in Chicago. The governor, his military staff, and the mayor of Chicago were quick to point out that the city of Chicago was calm until after the arrival of federal troops on July 3, 1894, at which point, they said, the crowds reacted violently to the appearance of the U.S. Army troops on the streets, and serious rioting and property damage ensued. Mayor John P. Hopkins of Chicago finally requested state intervention on July 6, 1894, after it was clear to him that the federal marshals and regular troops were not going to be able to either restore order to the city or lift the blockade on the mail trains. The governor immediately sent the ING into the streets of Chicago. According to Illinois Adjutant General Alfred Orrendorff, Illinois guardsmen were able to restore order within a day or so of their arrival in Chicago.[27] The delay in calling out the ING to Chicago allowed Altgeld and ING leadership to blame the federal troops for all that went wrong and to take for themselves all praise for restoring order (a position regular Army officials did not accept and the press did not respect, blaming Altgeld instead for the violence).[28] The ING stayed on duty in Chicago for thirty-three days (decades later, Cary Ray remembered it as sixty days), mostly serving in Pullman itself, though smaller detachments were regularly sent out with the trains.[29]

Mayor Hopkins of Chicago did not want troops, but as the effects of the Pullman boycott spread outward through the state and nation at the end of June, some downstate officials did seek state aid. On July 1, 500 rail passengers trapped at Decatur because of the strike telegraphed the governor seeking help in moving out, and the general counsel of the Chicago and Eastern Illinois Railroad Company notified the governor that no mail trains had moved out of Danville for forty-eight hours.[30] Altgeld, like Illinois governors before him, did not act without official local requests despite having the authority to do so, and he telegraphed the respective county sheriffs and asked them about their respective local situations. The sheriff of Macon County (Decatur) replied that he had been able to preserve order to date, but he now felt he needed troops. The sheriff of Vermilion County (Danville) replied that if the state could send him 100 rifles and ammunition, he would "try to protect the C. & E. I. R. R. Company's men and property."[31]

After assuring himself that troops were wanted or needed, Governor Altgeld sent the ING to intervene in Decatur and Danville. Altgeld sent three infantry companies and one cavalry troop to Decatur, where they moved the trains and dispersed "several mobs."[32] The Decatur ING Company (Company H, Fifth Regiment) itself was called up early in the morning of July 2 and served until three outside companies—from Delavan, Lincoln, and Peoria—arrived at 10:00 A.M. Once the new companies arrived, the commanding officer relieved the Decatur Company from duty in their hometown and sent them on to duty in Danville that evening, along with the Decatur cavalry troop. On July 5, two of the companies in Decatur were sent home after three days of service, and a fresh company arrived on the 6th and left on the 7th, leaving the last company to ensure that the trains continued to run freely until the 13th, when that company, too, was ordered home.[33] In Danville, five infantry companies under the command of Colonel J.S. Culver and the cavalry troop arrived on the evening of the 2nd and repeated the process of clearing the tracks of stopped freight and passenger cars and guarding the trains once strikebreaking engineers could be found to run them out of the city. On July 5 Colonel Culver left Danville with two companies and the cavalry troop and headed for Springfield, where more trouble seemed to be brewing—however, that came to nothing, and the troops were relieved and dismissed before they arrived. The remaining three companies stayed on in Danville until July 16, when they, too, were relieved of duty.[34]

Troops, state or federal, were never universally welcome. Union members and other strikers regularly objected to the appearance of state troops in the 1880s and 1890s, for no matter the intention or cause, the arrival of troops nearly always resulted in the end of the strike on terms unfavorable to the union, mostly because once troops were on the scene, strikebreakers could go to work. Once strikebreakers were on the job, the strike, for all practical purposes, was over.[35] Local and state-level officials also objected when they believed that troops were thrust upon them, making a bad situation worse. In 1894 the mayor of Chicago, the sheriff of Cook County, and the governor of Illinois all strenuously objected to the arrival of federal troops in Pullman and Chicago. They complained vociferously about the way in which railroad management inveigled President Cleveland into ordering federal troops into Chicago without prior consultation with state authorities of any kind.[36] Outside of Chicago, authorities also complained that they did not need state troops, and like Mayor Hopkins and Governor Altgeld, they blamed the unwanted soldiers for sparking the violence that came hard on their heels.[37] Federal troops riding the train cars after July 3 drew popular anger outside of Chicago as well as in it.[38]

Along with the disagreements between the governor and the president, and between county sheriffs and the governor, strike service in 1894 also served to remind ING leaders that when strikers or bystanders died, they were always to blame, regardless of cause. They were blamed for the men who were killed by soldiers riding the trains, they were blamed for the deaths during a riot in Chicago before their arrival, and they were blamed when an artillery piece blew up in Chicago, killing three members of the ING.[39] When ING officers and troops were sent into strike situations and ordered to protect property and lives, they entered highly contentious and potentially explosive situations in which there were no clear rules of engagement. They had to grapple with local disputes about whether or not they were even welcome, they had to meet their obligations to the state government that contributed to their upkeep, and they had to do so in a way that did as little damage as possible to their long-term survival or to their ability to attract members and private funds. After 1894, most ING officers seemed convinced that the best strategy was for the ING to stay as far away from such situations as possible.

New Tactics for Strike Service

The stated purpose of the militia while called out for strike duty hardly wavered over the years. In 1877 the state militia was ordered to Chicago to "protect the lives and property of the people."[40] In 1904 two companies of the ING were sent to Ziegler "to protect life and property of the citizens of that county."[41] Despite the similarity of mission, the conditions the militia faced and the options open to them in carrying out their mission were quite different in 1877 and in 1904. In 1877 the Illinois militia was in the midst of a complete reorganization of command structure and had a wide variety of arms and accouterments, uniforms, and drill proficiencies; had no real experience in civil order maintenance duties and none in strike-related situations; and was, in fact, at that particular moment entirely demobilized. By 1904 the Illinois National Guard had a formal command hierarchy backed with examinations for promotion, uniform training, weapons, and command procedures, and had the results of experience from nearly thirty years and thirty different strike-policing actions, more than any other state militia, combined with their wartime experiences of 1898–99, on which to draw in "protecting life and property."[42] In 1877 the militia was thrown into a variety of entirely new situations, ranging from infant general strikes to race riots, amid general fears of class warfare. By the 1890s, the strikes in which the state was asked to intervene were called by formal unions with specific grievances against specific corporate managers, who often worked diligently to oppose the interests of the strikers at the local, state, and federal levels. These later strikes generally took place in environments where there was a little to a lot of local sympathy for the plight of laborers and their families, alongside much concern about threats to persons and property and/or convenience.[43] Within these changing circumstances, the militias always tried to position themselves so as to "protect life and property" in as nonpartisan a manner as possible, if only to ensure their own future funding from the state legislature.

Illinois National Guard officers struggled to develop new tactics for use while policing strike-related disorder; doing so would help them to achieve both their stated aims and their private purposes, which likewise evolved over time and in response both to their growing experience and to changing outside conditions. Illinois National Guard officers grappled first with the problem of how to protect private property threatened by the confrontations between strikers and management without giving the impression that the ING were merely lackeys for company interests. They began by refusing to be in the position of guarding property without the presence of a real, immediate threat, and they wanted to be the ones to determine when and what threat was serious enough to warrant their presence. In the 1883 call to police a mine-strike–related situation, Governor Hamilton resisted all efforts to reduce the militia to mere mine guards, despite the fact that the militia outside Collinsville was actually camping in a boarding house owned by the Abbey Mine. In response to a request from the sheriff of St. Clair County for one hundred men to be detailed to his command, the governor notified the ING officer present: "Sheriff Ropiequet, St. Clair, has heretofore reported his entire ability to keep the peace in that county, and has not called on me for assistance. When you have restored the peace and dispersed the mob in Madison County withdraw troops as ordered to-day."[44] And Governor Hamilton wired Sheriff Ropiequet of St. Clair County, "I cannot furnish troops to guard property. Troops will be supplied to put down and disperse rioters where it is demonstrated that civil authorities cannot control them. Troops will be held in Madison County and [missing word] until tomorrow."[45] And to E. J. Crandall, president of the Crandall Mining Company located outside Collinsville, Hamilton sent a wire explaining that the "[m]ilitia cannot be kept there to guard your mine indefinitely. Civil authorities must use the powers of the militia promptly if needed to disperse rioters and arrest them & turn them over to civil authorities for commitment to jail," and that the colonel present, he stressed, was "ordered to use his discretion about withdrawing."[46]

Eleven years and six strike-policing actions later, on May 26, 1894, General Order No. 8 was issued to the entire ING, stating that "it is not the business of soldiers to act as custodians or guards of private property. The law authorizes them simply to assist the civil authorities in preserving the peace, quelling riots and executing the law. Whenever troops are ordered, and an owner of property feels it necessary to have it guarded, he must do so at his own expense, and in such case troops should be stationed near enough to promptly quell any disturbance, if one should occur."[47] The adjutant general at the time noted that "[t]his order met with the universal approval of the National Guard, who, under it, could no longer be used as mere private watchmen."[48] Troops still occasionally set up camp on mine property, but after this time they mostly selected baseball fields, city parks, or open land near the city or between the affected properties for their encampments.[49] In 1898 Governor Tanner insisted that troops were sent to preserve order, and not sent to protect mine property.⁵⁰ By 1899 the Colonel commanding a strike-policing action in Carterville had to wire the governor to receive special permission to move the ING camp onto mine property.⁵¹

Along with the issue of where to pitch camp without jeopardizing their nonpartisan stance, the militia had to develop new tactics for dealing with large crowds without causing injury or harm. Doing so presented a serious challenge because the only weapons the bulk of the militia was armed with were rifles, and the only tactics they knew were designed for the battlefield. As a result, what tactical theory there was for strike policing was based on weapon use or nonuse. For those who recommended weapons, artillery fire was often suggested as a way of clearing the streets—it was also never used that way in the United States. Tactics not involving weapon use tended to focus on early crowd psychology theories and recommended highly visible massed forces, or increasingly, the use of mounted cavalry for dispersing crowds. Ironically for the ING, all of this prescriptive literature was aimed at the large-scale, largely urban general strike. The central assumption in all of these published tactical theories was that the strikes the guards faced would be located in the central cities and accompanied by large crowds of onlookers, supporters, and general passers-by.⁵² The vast majority of the strikes for which the ING mobilized were located not just in small towns, but often outside these towns, at the mines themselves.

Fortunately for the ING, the presence of guardsmen in a strike-torn region was often all that was needed to convince crowds to disperse without resorting to physical confrontations, though troops did sometimes find it hard to endure the "blackguarding" and other verbal harassments that came their way.⁵³ When marching into town alone was not enough of a display of force to encourage strikers to back down and disperse their crowds, ING officers followed the primary tactical advice of the day and turned to their bayonets as the weapon of choice for poking and prodding people to move along. Also, when setting up and manning guard positions and walking patrols, ING officers recommended that their troops make quite a display of their rifles and bayonets for the purposes of intimidation. For the same reason, artillery battalions were instructed to haul their Gatling guns with them while policing strike-related situations.⁵⁴

One innovative ING commander, Colonel J. S. Culver of the Fifth Regiment, ordered his dismounted cavalry to wade into an angry crowd and start using the flat of their blades to "spank" strikers and other bystanders, and so encourage them to head for home. During the railroad strike policing action in Decatur in 1894, Colonel Culver asked the county sheriff to "present my compliments [to the crowd gathered] and say, 'That I would be over in an hour and spank them until they would eat their hash standing for the next week.'" In his official report, Culver concluded that "the sheriff had delivered my message, and as many of the miners and toughs at Tilton had been in the reception committee I met at Danville Junction on the morning of the 3rd, they lost interest in the movement of the troops and went home before my arrival at Tilton."[55] Culver considered this a tremendous advancement over the bayonet as a crowd-dispersing tool. This tactic caught the interest of a number of ING officers because it was potentially effective and yet inflicted very little serious damage. Illinois National Guard officers developed these approaches as alternatives to actual firing of their rifles, which was only a last resort, but there is no evidence that their innovations were widely adopted in Illinois or outside of it.

Illinois National Guard officers sought out alternatives to rifle fire because whenever guardsmen fired into masses of people they were quite certain to injure and usually kill outright some member(s) of the crowd. In 1883 militia fire killed at least one person, and at least six more were killed by on-duty guardsmen in 1894.[56] The question of the legitimacy of rifle fire as a viable tactic while policing strike-related events did have its defenders in Illinois. In the aftermath of the 1877 strike involvement, Arthur Ducat, the senior officer of the ING at that time, recommended a guard 10,000 strong and the use of Gatling guns, after fair warning, to clear the streets.[57] In 1883, at least two infantry men involved in the shooting that resulted in the killing of the striking miner told a news reporter that they had fired deliberately into the crowd and that this act was justified because they were fired upon.[58] In the 1894 shooting episodes, including those where people were injured or even killed, guardsmen again insisted that they fired only because they believed themselves to be in danger, and that their use of firearms was justified.[59]

Illinois National Guard officers' attempt to deflect blame and defend their choices at the same time was an artfully chosen course of action, a course selected to protect the integrity and the future of the ING. Governors and their military staffs wanted to respond quickly to situations that threatened to develop into large-scale social unrest, and they did not want the troops to kill anyone. In later years, when weapon fire was exchanged between strikers and the state militias, the adjutant general expected a full explanation, and in 1889 and again in 1894 there were formal inquiries into the causes and outcomes of such exchanges.[60] Gunfire was the one tactic no ING officer wanted to be held responsible for, and yet it was always their responsibility in last resort. In 1898, in Virden, Captain Craig of Battery B promised, "I hope I shall not have to use my Gatlings, but if I do there will be nobody left in the vicinity but us."[61]

Strike Service Goes Long-Term: Pana, Virden, and Ziegler

Members of the ING reached the point of total frustration with county sheriffs despite, or perhaps because of, the violence that could accompany confrontations between strikers and their opponents. Their frustration led them to usurp more and more local control and authority, until they had no one to turn the situation back over to so they could leave. One unintended result was that the length of time the ING spent on individual strikes skyrocketed. In 1898, 1899, and again in 1904, ING companies patrolled some locations for as many as five months at a time. These much longer terms of service fundamentally changed the nature of the task the ING was facing. Whereas in the earlier strike situations the ING functioned as quick responders, rushing in to corral violent offenders and remove them from the scene as they, too, exited, now the ING put itself in the position of guaranteeing a public order that, by their own observation, local officials were incapable of maintaining.

In 1898 and 1899, the coal fields that had been the site of so many bitter strikes in 1894 were again the location of strike service. Miners in central Illinois struck again in late 1897 and early 1898, once again largely stemming from disputes about the rates they were being paid. The miners were unionized and disciplined, and they succeeded in closing or rendering nearly useless many mines across the central part of the state. They sought out the new arbitration offered by the state government, but the operators refused to reopen the closed mines at the price set by the board of arbitration.[62] In Pana, by July the sheriff and his deputies were providing "around the clock" protection for the few nonunion miners who were willing to work, and they had arrested at least ten union men who had attempted to block the way for nonunion miners headed for the shafts.[63] The managers of several mine operations, among them the Pana Coal Company, the Penwell Coal Company, and the Springside Coal Company, decided, rather than to accept the price set by the arbitration board, to try and break the 1898 strike by importing African American miners, previously almost completely excluded from the region, up from the mines in Alabama. By mid-August, striking miners and their families were actively harassing the few local men still willing to work, and strikers and the imported strikebreakers were exchanging gun fire.[64] After these events, the mine operators began locking out the union men. The mine companies built stockades around their shafts, enclosing the mines and boarding houses for the new miners. In protest over the arrival of the African American miners, several local businessmen refused to serve as deputies when called for service and were arrested.[65] Over the next few weeks, the new African American miners took to parading in the streets while visibly armed, drawing the ire, and gunfire, of furious residents.[66] On September 28, tensions crested, and the strikebreaking African Americans lined up on the streets of Pana facing union miners, both sides armed with pistols and rifles, and firing commenced.[67] After this incident, the sheriff of Christian County requested aid from the governor, who ordered Battery B and two new provisional companies of the ING to Pana, where they stayed for the next four months.[68] Once in Pana, ING troops concentrated their efforts on assisting sheriff's deputies in keeping the approaches to the mines safe for the miners who were working, keeping the strikers from converging on the strikebreakers when they were off mine property, and policing neighboring communities. Guardsmen patrolled both inside and outside of the stockade built by the managers of the Pana Coal Company. Guardsmen also assisted in the enforcement of temporary or permanent bans on public carrying of weapons and on alcohol sales, and in the arrest of violators.[69]

In nearby Virden, to keep the new African American miners and the mine itself safe from the depredations of angry strikers, Chicago-Virden Coal Company managers, like those at Penwell and Springside, enclosed the mine and fifteen acres holding the mine-operated dormitories with a wooden stockade, complete with sentry boxes and topped with barbed wire.[70] To protect the new African American miners from assault, the managers then hired about seventy private detectives from St. Louis and laid in a supply of arms and ammunition and prepared to bring in more trainloads of African American strikebreakers.[71] The train carrying African American miners arrived on September 25, but at least sixty of the one hundred new arrivals decided to return to Alabama after hearing appeals from the local United Mine Workers officers.[72] To prevent the importation of still more strikebreakers, striking miners and their supporters (up to 3,000 by some estimates) from neighboring districts assembled outside the stockade over the next few weeks. When a heavily guarded train carrying another two cars of strikebreakers reached the outskirts of Virden on October 12, 1898, firing broke out between the private train guards and the strikers and continued for the last mile of the trip to the stockade entrance. During this exchange, two occupants of the train were killed and several were wounded, including the engineer, and the local newspapers put the total at ten fatalities and twenty-five injured.[73] Once the train arrived outside the stockade, the private guards inside joined the firefight, and one private guard died and six or seven were injured. Outside the stockade, thirteen strikers and strike supporters were killed outright

Figure 12
Pana-Virden strikes, ING members escorting a train, 1898. Courtesy of the Abraham Lincoln Presidential Library. Photographer: Unknown.

and twenty-eight wounded, four of whom later died of their injuries. The strikebreakers refused to leave the train, and only a few private guards made it inside the walls. The engineer finally started the train and took it on to Springfield.

On October 13, 1898, the ING arrived in Virden in response to the local sherrif's plea concerning this sudden escalation in the ongoing confrontation between striking miners and mine operators. The militia arrived on the scene well after dark on the evening of the 13th, creeping slowly down the track from Springfield, with skirmishers out front and Gatling guns ready on a flatbed car. When they reached the stockade at Virden, the militia hailed the men inside and got them to open the gates. They learned there that if the leader of the private guards had not just then been killed by a stray shot, he had intended to order his men to fire on the ING, thinking that the hail was a ruse on the part of the attacking strikers.[74]

Figure 13
ING members patrolling the stockade at Virden, 1898. Courtesy of the Abraham Lincoln Presidential Library. Photographer: Unknown.

Captain Charles C. Craig of Battery B, the artillery battalion that went to Virden, included scathing commentary on the sheriff's execution of his responsibilities in his report to the adjutant general.

> As to the general situation at Virden and the causes, which made the presence of troops finally necessary, it appeared that the local authorities had made no effort whatever to control the situation. When we arrived the sheriff was not there and did not appear until two days afterward. It was said that he was sick. There was but one legally appointed deputy in the town that we could find. Two hundred rifles and the ammunition sent to Virden by the State authorities on requisition of the sheriff had not been used and the boxes in which they had been shipped had not even been opened as we found when we came to take possession of them. General Reece with but one hun-

dred and twenty-eight men, all strangers to the locality, the people and the general conditions prevailing, took the town from the possession of the mob and restored order in a few hours. In a county of the size and population of Macoupin it ought to have been an easy matter to have enrolled twice that number of deputies to enforce the law. We were informed by Col. McKnight of the Governor's staff, who lives in the neighboring village of Giraud, and who met us on our arrival, and by other reputable citizens, that a posse could easily have been organized to preserve the peace.[75]

The company managers had a different version of what took place in Virden. Managers held Governor John Tanner and the ING responsible for the violence because they had repeatedly requested state troops to guard the importation of black miners—something Tanner explicitly refused to do in a public speech and in private communication with the mine owners in the days preceding the catastrophe in Virden. Fred W. Lukins, manager of the mine and spokesman for the absentee owner, held that Tanner invited the lawlessness when he refused to support mine owners and managers in their move to import labor from the South. Lukins swore at the inquest that neither he nor any of the hired guards fired first, and that the guard who was shot just before the ING entered the mine stockade—an ex-police lieutenant from Chicago—was cut down by militia fire after opening the gates. "The blood of every man shed here is on the Governor's head. He is absolutely outside the law and has no justification whatever in refusing to send troops. If this train had come before the interview with the Governor was printed there would have been no bloodshed."[76]

Republican Governor John Tanner followed the model of his predecessors in office when he refused in no uncertain terms to allow the ING to serve the interests of owners and managers in labor disputes. He forcefully and repeatedly argued that the deaths and injuries in Virden were all on the heads of the mine management, who disregarded his warnings and acted recklessly to endanger not only their own employees, but the unfortunate strikebreakers who had not been given any idea of the dangerous situation into which they were being shipped. "I, therefore, charge the owners and managers of this company as being lawbreakers and morally and criminally responsible for the bloodshed and disgrace to our State, and I further charge every man in their employ as detective or guard in the stockade or on the train who participated in this fiendish outrage as guilty of murder, who should and I believe will be indicted by the grand jury of Macoupin County and tried for murder." He went on to defend his decision not to send troops in earlier because had he "done so

I would have been using the State as an agent to further the interest of the mine owners, as the moment the troops had been landed they would have dispersed the idle miners, and of course the avaricious mine owners could have landed their imported labor without difficulty, thus accomplishing their end."[77]

Tanner stumbled into another controversial issue when he initially categorized the African American miners as "drawn largely, if not entirely, from the criminal class, ex-convicts who learned their trade while doing terms in the penitentiaries of Alabama."[78] This description later turned out to be an inaccurate picture of the miners and the families who accompanied them to Illinois, but it did accurately reflect long-standing prejudices among white miners in Illinois.[79] Tanner later gave several statements to the effect that African American workers and their families were welcome in the state at any time if they came freely looking for work at competitive wages; it was only when they, or any other class of laborers, were shipped in by the locked carload that he objected.[80]

The ING stayed on duty in Virden for twenty days, and as in Pana, the guardsmen imposed something close to martial law as they worked to keep the peace. Once the ING was in place in Pana and Virden, as in Homestead, Pennsylvania in 1892, operators were able to import more strikebreakers, who went to work and reopened the mines. Local tensions did not ease quickly in Pana, however, and though the ING troops finally left in February 1899, they were back in place by April 10 because of the resumption of sporadic nighttime gunfire, and the Guard stayed on another five months. The ING was also called out to Carterville over a miners strike in 1899, but troops were able to leave after only thirty-three days.

The ING avoided strike duty altogether for the next five years, but in late 1904 they were summoned again. The situation in Ziegler was eerily similar to that in and around Virden and Pana in late 1898. Faced with a long-term strike, the mine owner, Joseph Leiter, built a stockade around his mine and began to import willing workers. Unionized strikers gathered outside the stockade and on the edges of the corporate town to discourage strikebreakers from either starting or continuing to work. By late November, tensions had reached the point that residents were reporting nightly gunfire, and on November 26, at the request of the sheriff of Franklin County after a shooting incident at a local church, Governor Richard Yates sent Company F, Fourth Regiment, to Ziegler, followed two days later by a second company.[81] On December 2, the sheriff insisted that he "was absolutely unable to preserve order," and so Governor Yates complied and left the two companies in place.[82] With the troops in place, by late December Leiter was able to import as many as sixty new miners at a time. More troubling to the ING officers in Ziegler were the daily discoveries of dynamite in and around the mine itself. "That it is not the work of the men on the outside is admitted . . . it has become so common Guardsmen fear it is the work of men imported into the mine."[83] The two companies stayed in Ziegler until February 8, 1905, at which point things were calm enough that they were sent home.[84]

The duration of mine strike policing actions stayed relatively flat from 1877 to 1890, at less than ten days, and averaging about four and one-half days. The first sign that change was coming was a five-week stint in East St. Louis in 1886 during the railroad strikes and immediately following a fight that left six people dead.[85] By 1898 and 1899, organized national unions were locked in conflict with corporations for their right to negotiate for their members, even as the courts were beginning to acknowledge the legitimacy of union organization.[86] In the coal fields of central Illinois, tensions reached new heights as miners and owners of nearly worked-out mines fought over wage scales, and miners and their neighbors rioted over the continuing stream of African American strikebreakers. John M. Tanner, the Republican governor of Illinois, sought to make a clear and strong comparison between his administration and that of the previous, Democratic, and labor-friendly governor John Altgeld, but the added element of racial antagonism brought him closer to the support of unionized miners. Ironically enough, as a result Tanner followed Altgeld closely in his struggle to limit the use of the ING for strike-policing purposes. Tanner repeatedly denounced the mine operators during the 1898–99 strikes.[87] Like Altgeld, Tanner attempted to deny militia protection to mining interests desirous of importing strikebreakers, at one point even accusing mine operators of attempting to "degrade the citizenship of Illinois for selfish purposes" in importing African Americans from Alabama to take the jobs of already resident, and white, miners.[88] Even more dramatically than Altgeld, Tanner was willing to use the ING to arrest managers and their private guards as well as striking workers.

The role of race in the Pana and Virden confrontations cannot be underestimated. The strikebreakers who attracted such violent opposition were African American. The deputies whose weapons the guardsmen confiscated with such rigor were deputized African American strikebreakers, and the men arrested before the ING arrived were white men who refused to serve as deputies to protect the African American miners. Once on the scene, Illinois guardsmen went out of their way to patronize the shops of merchants who were supporting the strikers and who were opposed to the arrival of African American strikebreakers, a small gesture of their solidarity with the white strikers.[89] More broadly, according to Eric Arnesen, African American strikebreakers raised fears of an "industrial race war," and white ING members were torn between doing their duty and standing with the white strikers whose jobs were vanishing under the watchful eye of white guardsmen.[90] Before the full-scale outbreak of violence at Virden, acting governor William Northcott explained to a United Mine Workers representative that "the men who made the trouble at Pana had played directly into the hands of the operators. By inciting a riot they had made the presence of troops in the town necessary and now the operators were able to take advantage of the presence of the soldiers and ship in all the alien labor they wanted." Northcott went on to suggest that as long as the strikers "could demonstrate that there was no necessity for sending troops to Virden" by keeping order, the troops would stay away, and the strikers could continue to prosecute their cause.[91] At least in Virden and Pana, white Guardsmen sympathized with the white striking workers and did not bring blind loyalty to corporate desires to their strike service.

Simultaneously, the ING itself paved the way for Governor Tanner to allow the ING to stay on duty for such extended periods of time. Not only did they assume full control of their activities while policing strike-related disorders, they also began to redefine what constituted a threat to life and property, focusing in particular on the job of disarming strikers and strikebreakers alike in the name of ensuring security for residents and laborers. Once they took this job onto their own shoulders, ING officers ended up with the unenviable task of ensuring that when they left, the situation would remain orderly and the combatants would remain disarmed. The only way to do that, it turned out, was to stay for a very long time.

Rejection of Local Authority and the Rise of "Martial Law"

In order to minimize any possible violent confrontations between militia and strikers, ING officers initially opted to try to work solely under the direction of local authorities in their early rounds of strike service. In 1883 both Colonel Barkley and Governor Hamilton were very careful to ensure that the militia never acted without the full knowledge and direction of locally elected or appointed civil authorities. They stressed this point repeatedly throughout the duration of active duty that year. No move was made without consultation with the sheriffs or their deputies. This scrupulousness was not explicitly mandated by law, but it was the manner chosen by ING officers, under the authority of the governor, to protect their own interest in neutrality in the face of antagonistic relationships between labor and owners of mines or railroads.[92] However, this stance was difficult to maintain given the ING officers' other frustrations with so many of the sheriffs who requested their presence, and mayors, in turn, who were frustrated by their sheriffs.[93] In 1894, ING officers discovered the limits to how far they could force an unwilling sheriff to go in assuming responsibility for his jurisdiction. In some cases, ING officers were able to continue with their old strategy of close cooperation with the sheriff and other local authorities. In other cases, particularly where the ING believed that the sheriff and his deputies were so involved in the local strike politics as to be virtual combatants themselves, ING officers in charge imposed conditions that the press called martial law. In Virden in 1898, ING officers treated the sheriff and his deputies exactly the same way they treated the strikers. They denied them the opportunity to harass or threaten strikers as well as noncombatants and confiscated their weapons with the same rigor with which they confiscated whatever armament the strikers had managed to amass. In both Pana (1898) and Ziegler (1904), grand juries also handed down indictments against the mine owners and managers for carrying weapons.[94] During the later instances of strike duty, ING officers in charge expected all current residents of a locality, regardless of status, to obey the imposed curfews, temporary "dry" restrictions, rules forbidding the bearing of arms, and edicts about formation of crowds, all imposed under the formal authority of the county sheriff.[95] In 1898 and 1899 in Virden and Pana, reporters were quick to deduce from these regulations that "martial law" was in effect, a natural conclusion given statements like the following from Captain Craig in 1898: "In a sense I am in charge of the town and martial law is in force. We will disarm every man suspected or known to have a weapon."[96]

There was no state of martial law in these places—as the governor's spokesmen were quick to point out.[97] Colonel Theodore Ewert, assistant adjutant general, explained that he "did not know what arrangement has been made at Pana, but I suppose that Captain Craig and the sheriff of Christian county, together with the mayor of the city, have entered into some agreement by which Captain Craig's men are to patrol to the town and maintain law and order." Ewert insisted that until or unless "the governor declares martial law, the responsibility of the sheriff to maintain the peace and to keep order, does not cease, no matter how many soldiers he may have called for."[98] Again in 1904, there was much fevered speculation that the governor would impose a state of martial law, but Governor Yates issued a firm statement that "[t]here has been no proclamation of martial law."[99]

The officers may also have been drawing on lessons of occupation learned during the Spanish American War, 1898–99. The regular Army imposed and then struggled to maintain domestic order in Cuba and the Philippines during the Spanish American War and the military occupations that followed, and at least one recent study argues that the experience of the Colorado National Guardsmen during their service in the Philippines was a significant contributing factor in the Ludlow Massacre of 1914.[100] Likewise, ING service from 1898 to 1899 during the Spanish American War may have contributed to their changing perceptions and choices about the ability of military forces to serve as peacekeepers during times of civic and social crises. For example, Battery B, the unit that served in Virden in 1898, was unable to join the United States Volunteers, and the members were quite aware of their lack of federal service in comparison to their luckier brethren in Battery A. The fighting in Cuba and Puerto Rico was over quite quickly, and the U.S. army of occupation turned its attention to peacekeeping and the restoration of law and order and American-style commerce in the districts ravaged by the most recent three years of guerrilla combat.[101] In both Cuba and Puerto Rico, this transition moved relatively smoothly and on the whole, the military had reason to be pleased with its record as model governors and agents of social uplift. By late September of 1898, between news reports and the first trickling home of fellow servicemen, Illinois guardsmen were well aware of what their fellow ING members were doing while in federal service.

In the years immediately following 1877, ING leaders defined the threat to life and property as disorder, and once order was restored, the ING could leave the scene of the intervention with full confidence that local authorities would handle whatever might occur. However, by the late 1890s, not only had ING officers come to disparage the abilities of many local sheriffs to act decisively to protect life and property, they had also redefined the threat to "violence," and the cessation of the threat to "the restoration of law and order."[102] The combination of the loss of respect for the abilities of some county sheriffs and the assumption of judgment to themselves as to what constituted conditions for violence and the restoration of law and order, created situations in which the ING found themselves policing strike-affected localities far longer that they had ever previously contemplated. In fact, the "restoration of law and order" in these late strike situations turned out to mean the end of the strike itself.[103]

The only way out of the linguistic and strategic trap the ING thus laid for itself of essentially becoming world-class mine guards and corporate thugs was to repeatedly stress the importance of local law enforcement handling strike-related confrontations themselves. In addition, ING officers began to imply that a call to the ING for intervention was to advertise a total breakdown in local control. In 1883, despite Colonel Barkley's frustrations with Sheriff Hotz, neither he nor his senior officers argued that the initial failure was Hotz's and that the militia should not have been necessary. By 1900, ING officers, up to and including the adjutant general, were so frustrated by the behavior of some county sheriffs that Adjutant General Jasper N. Reece proposed a significant shift in fiscal responsibility for militia service during strike-related duty. "If, by legislative enactment, counties would have to pay the cost of the strikes occurring in their border, sheriffs would endeavor through force of public demand to restore peace and harmony themselves, and would call for military assistance only when they themselves had become, in fact, powerless."[104] Reece never detailed more specific goals, but the basic thrust of his plan seems obvious enough. Reece wanted the counties to pay for the services of the Illinois National Guard if they served in their jurisdictions during strike-related tensions. He made this suggestion because he thought the high cost would serve as a deterrent to requests for state troops, and the cost could be quite high. For example, in 1894 the ING racked up $360,091.51 in expenses during the strikes that year.[105] General Reece clearly wanted the ING to be able to avoid future strike duty if they possibly could.

Ultimately, ING officers solved their dilemma by redefining the proper request to the ING from unspecified "aid to civil authorities" whenever local officials should request it, to a rapid response to a domestic crisis in which case civil authorities could not be expected to cope without outside intervention. In light of the controversies, frustrations, and sheer length and expense of service spawned by events like those in Virden, Pana, or Ziegler, it is not difficult to understand why the adjutant general of Illinois sought ways to force local authorities, particularly the sheriffs, to take full responsibility for preventing such violence in communities under their jurisdiction.

Strikes and ING Controversy

In terms of their behavior toward the strikers while policing strike-related events, ING officers always attempted to remain neutral on the issues of the strike and to suppress riots, break up mobs, and protect mine property from destruction at the hands of the miners. These two aims were not always complementary. The ING almost never broke up meetings of strikers (the only instance where they did while policing a mine strike situation was immediately after their arrival in Virden in 1898, when some seventeen people had already died that day). In 1898 the

ING even attempted to prevent the arrival of new, African American strikebreakers on the scene. In many cases, the ING officers present worked to reach some compromise, not on the issues of the strike, but on the issue of the behavior and practices to which both sides (or multiple sides if the local law enforcement officials had become virtual combatants as well) would adhere for the duration of the strike.

In their reports, pamphlets, histories, and memoirs, ING members were quite careful to distinguish between crowds of strikers, bystanders, and "mobs"; they assigned the latter label only to crowds during actively hostile encounters. Members also carefully noted ethnic and racial distinctions among the strikers and strikebreakers, indicating that they were aware of the manner in which corporate managers attempted to use these differences to divide their laboring forces, and that these tactics usually worked. When ING members claimed that a "mob" was present, they commonly reported that it contained very few strikers, or that the strikers were being urged on by "toughs" or "outside, professional agitators." Interestingly, one signal that always indicated to ING members that a "mob" was in formation was the presence of female strike supporters, especially because of their presumed mastery of the verbal attack. As soon as the ING dispersed the "mob"—including the women—officers reverted to their previous characterizations of strikers, or sympathizers, or bystanders, or strikebreakers, or even curious crowds. Accurate or not, the way members attempted to draw clear distinctions is another measure of how much they strove to understand themselves as neutral supporters of order. "Mob" was a temporal and flexible description of events and conditions that could change quickly as a result of outside stimuli.[106]

Despite these efforts on the part of ING officers to ensure that all parties recognized their valiant attempts to remain neutral peacemakers, they did not always succeed. Their failure to convince all participants of their neutral intentions was partially related to the intensity of emotions on both sides of the capital-labor contest, and among the various residents of a strike-affected community. Feelings could run very deep about the conflicts between company managers, strikers, and strikebreakers. In 1898 and 1899, the mine managers were furious that the governor did not respond to their pleas to intervene sooner, and they roundly blamed Tanner for all subsequent violence. At the same time, the strikers and the unions initially praised Governor Tanner for his staunch refusal to send troops to protect the mine owners in their plans to import large numbers of African American strikebreakers. The county sheriffs waffled between asking for help and refusing it, and they proved unreliable partners once the ING arrived on the scene. Once the troops did arrive, mine managers were able to reopen their mines, sheriffs were able to hand responsibility off to the ING commander, and strikers took what compensation they could from the personal sympathy of the troops stationed in their communities. In 1904 in Ziegler, a similar story unfolded, with local residents supporting the strikers and opposing imported strikebreakers, until several men were killed in nighttime clashes, at which point the troops were welcomed even as they allowed more and more strikebreakers to enter the mines. From the perspective of ING members, there was nothing they could do in regard to a strike that would not anger someone.

Finding a Way Out

Strike duty was one of the ING's most visible activities between 1877 and 1916, and it certainly draws the most criticism of their activities during these years. However, though strikes in general were complicated events for all concerned, the overwhelming number of strikes, in Illinois and nationally, passed without intervention from the state level. When the state was asked to intervene, it was because local authorities, in their own judgment, could no longer maintain order alone. That order was variously defined and complicated the issue for the ING because it left them with different, short-term goals when called to police various strike situations, and it left them at the mercy of local officials' judgment. Illinois National Guard officers in time came to seriously question the judgment of local officials in these matters. They developed strategies that would encourage local law enforcement officials to act decisively and without state aid to prevent violence rather than calling in the state militia after violent confrontations had already produced significant property damage or, worse, loss of life. These strategies were twofold. First, ING officers began openly criticizing local law enforcement when they felt it warranted, making the personal and political costs of the action quite high for local officials. Second, militia members expanded the definition of their duty while simultaneously raising the level of crisis under which they should be called out. In the end, what ING officers managed to do was unify their definitions of order to the prestrike conditions of each locality, and to insist on staying until those conditions were met in any strike intervention, whether it was rail, coal, or some other issue altogether. The unified ING equation of order to the preconfrontation conditions prevailing locally grew out of the ING officers' need to assume both a noncontroversial role and at the same time make it a very tough decision for local authority to ask for their help. Throughout these decades, ING members regarded strike duty as an unpleasant but necessary function. However, as the political and financial costs of that service grew over time, ING officers also, and without embarrassment, sought ways to avoid the assignment and to focus their time and energy on preparing to serve in a truly military emergency.

CHAPTER 7

The Pursuit of State and Federal Support

> What should the government do for the National Guard of the states in order that we may maintain this unsurpassed fighting force at its maximum state of practical efficiency?[1]
> —Jasper N. Reece, adjutant general of Illinois and president of the Interstate National Guard Association

Nowhere is the ING transition from a local, community-based organization to one element of national reserve army more clearly observed than in their aggressive pursuit of state and federal funding. Guardsmen built their organization on the twinned notions of military training and manhood training, and as long as the latter relied on the former, they had to pursue military training with as much rigor and seriousness as they possibly could. To pursue serious military training in the later nineteenth and early twentieth centuries required an ever-increasing expenditure of funds for an ever-growing array of supplies and equipment. In the early 1870s, Illinois militia companies relied primarily on their own financial resources plus whatever funds they could raise locally, making them aggressive fund-raisers and providers of local attractions. Militia members quickly discovered that these resources were not enough to outfit and equip a true statewide reserve training force, and so they turned to the only possible source to make up the difference, the coffers of the state and federal governments. To become a tax-supported organization, guardsmen in Illinois and across the nation learned to create effective local, statewide, and eventually national lobbies that worked together to turn what was essentially a private organization into a permanent and fully integrated part of the bureaucratic machinery of the state.[2] The logic of soldiering drove militia volunteers to broaden and deepen their relationships with the state and, especially, the federal government until by 1916, they had begun the final, irrevocable turn away from their local communities as they established a new, national identity as the dedicated core of the national reserve army.

Seeking State Funds in the 1870s

Illinois National Guard officers dedicated to a reserve army role for the ING and all state militia forces faced their greatest challenges in securing the militia's financial base. Volunteer companies, in Illinois as elsewhere, traditionally were supported primarily by their members' private contributions and whatever largesse their local communities could spare. Because their local communities couldn't spare as much as militia volunteers believed they needed to outfit and arm themselves with modern rifles and equipment, as early as 1874 Illinois militia officers went to the Illinois General Assembly to ask for an increase in the tax dollar support awarded to the state militia.[3] They did not get an increase in 1874. However, most local communities could not supply the amount of money required to supply and train a modern reserve army, and communities certainly could not do so equally across the state and over time. Complete reliance on local funding sources, even in a community that generously supported its militia companies, could produce wildly uneven results. For example, in 1875 the Committee on Ways and Means of the First Regiment of Chicago reported that citizens had subscribed $13,468.50 and members of the regiment had given $2,349.50 to the regimental coffers, for a total budget of $15,818.00.[4] Just a little over a year later, the Second Regiment, also entirely made up of Chicago-based companies, was $8,700.00 in debt, with no immediate relief in sight.[5] These awkward and unfortunate results of too great a dependence on local financial sources drove Illinois militia members to their state representatives again and again in ever more organized lobbying efforts, seeking increased militia budgets.

The dramatic upsurge in membership during the period 1874–76 gave renewed impetus to the perennial attempts to get a new militia code passed through the Illinois General Assembly. In 1875 Brigadier General Alfred Ducat traveled the state and personally visited many militia companies. According to Holdridge Collins of the First Regiment, Ducat was met everywhere with desire for a new and better militia code. So Ducat established a committee and set a date for its meeting in Chicago.

Unfortunately, enthusiasm for a new law was not yet at such a pitch as to induce members from outside the city to attend the meeting. The militias were still creations of local communities, and their members did not yet see the benefits of working together at the state level. In this respect, Illinois militiamen continued to reflect national norms.[6]

It fell to Ducat and his volunteer staff to come up with a bill. The general staff gathered copies of militia codes from other states as well as a "large mass of statistics" to use in creating their own bill and in lobbying for its passage. Ducat also sent out a circular to all militia companies stressing the importance of a united front and steady pressure upon their own state representatives. The major features of the new code centered around a yearly appropriation to "meet the expenses for rent of armories, ordnance stores, camp equipage and transportation of all battalions for at least one yearly muster, and for ammunition and a Rifle Range for practice, with an allowance *per diem* for every man who shall turn out upon order," and "with such provisions for the perfection of discipline as may secure an effective and creditable soldiery."[7] The bill was drawn up and distributed to all interested and necessary parties.

The Illinois General Assembly met every two years during the late nineteenth century, and 1877 was a session year. Outgoing Governor Albert Beveridge and incoming Governor Shelby S. Cullom addressed the thirtieth session of the General Assembly on the subject of the militia. The governors' remarks are particularly interesting for what they reveal about contemporary concerns about the link between citizen and soldier and the role of citizen-soldiers in society.

Beveridge concluded his remarks on the incredible growth, and real problems, of the militia with the following recommendations for a new militia code: "The Militia Law of the State is very crude and imperfect, and needs revision. In my opinion, the state should provide for the organization and discipline of a limited number of Regiments, and for the encouragement of such organization and the preservation of its own property, should provide, at least, suitable armories." He went on to address any concerns about the presence of these regiments might raise, assuring his listeners that a "well-organized Militia, composed of our own citizens, will not endanger the liberties of the people, but on the contrary, give greater security to life, property and liberty."[8]

Governor Cullom seconded Beveridge's sentiments in his own remarks, saying, "I desire to add one suggestion in reference to the affairs of our own State, by calling your attention to the Militia Law. I believe a more perfect law should be enacted, which will secure a more thorough organization of the State Militia." He continued, "The spirit of our institutions, and the temper of our people, are hostile to a standing army; and

I am opposed to any policy, State or National, looking to governing the people by the bayonet. Yet, in the most highly-civilized communities, a trained Militia, recruited from the intelligent and industrious classes, is an almost indispensable auxiliary to the civil power, in the interests of peace and good order."[9] Beveridge and Cullom both took care to point out that they did not advocate use of the militia as an extension of the policing function of the state. However, with the unacknowledged but powerful underlying subtext of the events concerning the Chicago "commune" of 1874–75, they both also acknowledged that domestic order maintenance was a potential function of the militia. They argued that the best way to ensure that the police function did not become oppressive was to draw militia members from the citizenry. They believed that the citizen-soldier by his very nature would act as both a brake on and an indispensable support to police power. Cullom even went so far as to link citizen-soldiers with civilization itself, implying that citizens can best police themselves, and the government, through the tool of the citizen-militia.

To advance the growth of such an institution, both governors drew attention to the two most frequently cited problems and solutions for the better development of the militia. First, the state should pay for the absolute essentials, that is construction of or rent for armory space and its upkeep. Second, the law should set a specific term of enlistment (three to five years) and give militia officers the necessary authority not only to establish order, but also to enforce discipline. This was not all Ducat had proposed in his new bill, but it was the obvious minimum.

At this point a possible roadblock loomed, in the form of Adjutant General Hiram Hilliard. Hilliard was dissatisfied with the proposed code for a number of reasons, most centering around the rank and responsibilities of his office. As a result, Hilliard apparently was not willing to lobby for the bill or to act in any way to help secure its passage. This was a real blow because Hilliard was the only one with rank and authority located in Springfield. Ducat lived and was headquartered in Chicago. Just when it seemed as though yet another militia bill was going to die in committee, Ducat undertook leading the lobbying effort himself. He used personal contacts with the Cook County representatives and also sent two of his officers down to Springfield to present their position to a joint committee hearing finally arranged by Hilliard. The bill was finally accepted by the House in 1877, but not without some difficulty. There was a substantial minority staunchly opposed to the bill, and this minority attempted to derail it with a number of mockingly obstructionist amendments, for example, raising the number of musicians per company from two to 250.[10] The bill was then shepherded through the Senate by Martin A. Delany, state senator from Cook County, sixth district, chairman of the militia committee and supporter of the bill. The bill was passed May 14, Governor Cullom signed it on the 18th, and it became law. The new militia code went into effect July 1, 1877.[11]

The bill was not without its flaws, but most everyone concerned agreed that it was a good start and that they would try again during the next session to address the remaining problems. One of the problems that most irked formalists was that after heavily amending the first half of the bill and, among other things, changing ranks and organizations, the House had passed the remainder without consideration for any inconsistencies. The rank charts of the original bill, modeled after the New York militia, were all one grade higher than in the regular Army. The House had cut all the division ranks down to regular Army equivalents, but left Brigade and Regimental ranks alone, so that technically majors were ruling on lieutenant colonels. The Senate passed the House bill without much debate and no attention to this issue. The tax was limited to one-twentieth of a mil, enough to build on, according to AG Hilliard, though not really sufficient to meet all proposed obligations, and far more disappointing, it represented a one-time-only dispersal of funds.[12]

The new act carried with it no permanent funding clause; under it, all funds awarded to the militia had to be renegotiated in the general state appropriations bill every two years.[13] So in 1876 the General Assembly appropriated approximately $20,000 annually for the next two years for the support of the entire Illinois state militia. This money was still not a permanently reliable income.[14] Further, the mobilization of the infant Illinois state militia for strike duty in 1877 and 1878 left the state government with unpaid bills for militia service and supplies totaling $82,060.27, a debt that could not be paid until the Illinois General Assembly appropriated the funds to do so.[15]

Militia supporters continued to work hard for a new law, one with a permanent funding provision, and they were largely successful with the Militia Act of 1879.[16] By 1882 the annual tax levy, as provided for by the Militia Act of 1879, had grown to $70,000, and in 1888 the adjutant general requested an annual appropriation of $120,000.[17] The state of Illinois paid close to $400,000 to support the ING from 1895 to 1896, and in 1896 the AG asked for an annual appropriation increase to $210,000.[18] A decade and a half later, during the period 1911–12, the ING was costing the taxpayers of Illinois $890,553.36.[19] These figures dramatically illustrate not only the increasing legislative savvy of the ING leadership, but more significantly, their successful establishment of the ING as a part of and the responsibility of the state government. The increases in state funds for the militia followed a steady, upward course, never once diminishing over the years, even in periods when the ING itself shrank. The chief lobbyist for the militia during these years was inevitably the adjutant general, appointed by the governor and responsible for paying the bills rung up by the militia. As a result of this executive branch responsibility, the growth in militia appropriations does not appear to be strongly linked with the political party in power, either in the General Assembly or in the statehouse.[20] The funding increases for the ING, no matter how gradual over the decades, were not without detractors. Even such generally supportive voices as the *Chicago Tribune*'s raised questions and objections to the steady growth of the state's military budget throughout the 1880s.[21] A minor 1883 investigation into what the paper called "outrageous charges" accumulated during a court-martial had grown by 1887 into a chauvinistic assault on the excessive militia budget that could have been shrunk if only a northern camp site, near the city of Chicago, had been selected over Camp Lincoln down near the state capitol.[22] In 1889 the *Tribune* was producing exposés on the extravagances of such Camp Lincoln expenses as swimming pool maintenance and the inflated price of camp rations.[23] Despite the negative press coverage, the steady biennial budget increases continued.

Changes in the adjutant generals' biennial reports over the years from 1876 to 1912 are another sign of the success of ING leadership's legislative and social agenda to convince the taxpayers of Illinois, and through them the General Assembly, and vice versa, that the ING warranted this significant outlay of state moneys. In 1876, in his first biennial report to the governor who appointed him head of the state forces, adjutant general Hiram Hilliard laid out his case for government support of the militia. His lengthy argument began with a reminder of the various constitutional provisions organizing militias for "the defense of the country and the maintenance of public order."[24] It was the latter that Hilliard chose to elaborate on for the state legislature, concluding:

> If Illinois intends to keep pace with the other States in the march of improvement, and if a militia organization is to be maintained, let such legislation be had as will not reduce our volunteers to the level of a rabble, and when you place the power to commission officers in the hands of the Governor, give him and the officers he commissions the power to enforce discipline.
>
> Taking into consideration that there will always be dangerous men in society, who, when once aroused, may inflict losses of millions upon quiet and unoffending citizens, it is not well for a great State, like Illinois, to allow its militia to fall below a proper standard of excellence.

Their skill and efficiency must in great measure take the place of the discipline of regular troops; the greater their proficiency in drill and marksmanship, the less we shall have to fear from riots and lawlessness.[25]

In stressing the public order functions of a militia, Hilliard was reacting, in part, to events in Chicago over the previous few years, from the rioting following the Chicago fire to the events surrounding the Chicago Relief and Aid society in 1874 and 1875.[26] However, the bill applied to the whole of the ING, and the money would be spent throughout the state, as the number of militia companies statewide was growing quickly in 1875 and 1876. (See appendix J.) To achieve a drilled and disciplined militia, Hilliard made several recommendations. He argued that giving the volunteers of the state militia "good arms of the latest pattern, and plenty of ammunition for target practice" would "fill the ranks with the best young men of the State" and encourage them in "habits of coolness, discipline and temperance, which in turn will command universal approbation."[27] Hilliard then went on to warn that if the state did not fulfill this minimum for the militia, not only would the "rabble" have free rein, but also, this veteran of the Civil War pointed out, the "reverses that befell the Union armies in the early part of the recent war" would be repeated again and again in the face of similar national crises.[28] With this conclusion of his argument for a better-supported state militia organization, the adjutant general devoted the next several paragraphs of his report to a summary of the key points of a bill prepared by General Ducat and modeled after the militia codes of other large states, tacitly offering his support to this bill.[29] In 1876, the adjutant general of Illinois clearly believed that he had an important role to play in aiding the lobbying efforts of militia supporters. In 1878 Hilliard—still adjutant general—devoted more than half of his report to making the case for the importance of the militia to the state on the same themes. He made still more detailed recommendations for changes in the current law and an expansion of the current budget to $200,000 annually.[30] Hilliard got less than 10 percent of his funding request, but he was able to win a steady, if small, permanent appropriation.

I. H. Elliot, Hilliard's immediate successor, also argued for increased state support for the state militia, but his arguments shifted away from Hilliard's focus on internal order maintenance and toward a broader understanding of the role of the National Guard in the life of the nation. Elliot chose to quote two "distinguished" and "eminent" observers who remarked on the bulwark the state militias created for the United States.

> I cannot forbear to quote a sentence from a letter on this subject from one of our most distinguished citizens: 'A nation of fifty millions ruling a continent bounded only by the great oceans, upholding and pledged before God and man to defend a form of civil government adverse in its fundamental principles to every other power on earth, ought in some way to be a military people;' and also the remark of an eminent Englishman upon witnessing the maneuvers of one of our State Regiments; 'A country that possesses such a citizen soldiery as that, has no need of a regular army.'[31]

Here Elliot chose to emphasize not domestic order, but rather the role of the militia as a national force in a potentially hostile world. Perhaps the most telling distinction between Hilliard's 1878 report and Elliot's in 1882 is a single sentence: "If [our State troops] are worthy of being sustained at all, they should be well sustained and given a fair chance to make favorable comparison with the best State Soldiery."[32] The difference between this argument and Hilliard's long and elaborate debate points indicates the progress that militia leadership had made in becoming a regularly supported state agency. The line suggests that Elliot was sure that the General Assembly already viewed the ING was an integral part of the responsibilities of state. Elliot actually devoted the bulk of his report to an argument for increasing the militia appropriation, a case he made by pointing out that the requirements established by the 1879 Militia Act could not be met under the terms of the current appropriation.[33]

By 1888, Adjutant General Joseph Vance limited himself to reminding the governor and the General Assembly not to forget the National Guard in peaceful years, attributing the peace itself to the "existence of an organized body of citizen soldiers, which have proven equal to any emergency in the past, known to be equipped for any active service . . . doubtless contributed in moral effect to this state of tranquility."[34] After this opening, Vance kept his argument simple:

> In a moment when no clouds obscure our peaceful horizon, will our General Assembly forget that a few thousand dollars expended in maintenance of this institution may save the lives of hundreds of citizens and the value of millions in property? Will they preserve this institution, which has been so wisely and substantially builded [sic]? Or, influenced by false considerations of economy, will they withhold the sustenance that gives it life and strength?[35]

In 1896, Adjutant General Charles Hilton felt no need to make any particular plea about the necessity or importance of the ING to the state or the nation in his biennial report. Instead, he concentrated his efforts on a lengthy and thorough report on the state of the ING at his command.[36] In 1898, the adjutant general of Illinois boasted that his troops had achieved "a high and commendable state of discipline and efficiency."[37] The adjutant general credited Governor John R. Tanner for fostering the institution, but he also recognized that it was mostly owing to "the great personal interest and sacrificing devotion to duty of all commanders . . . reinforced by the eager desire to learn, the intelligent absorption of lessons and instruction, the unstinted donation of time and energy by officers and enlisted men alike." It was these men who "placed the active National Guard on a high pedestal of usefulness and reliability."[38]

By the eve of the Spanish American War, the ING was firmly established as a state institution, with a large and active membership committed to preparing the organization for a role as the nation's reserve Army. Seizing on the Spanish American War as a chance to demonstrate that their long years of preparation had paid off, Illinois guardsmen mobilized ten full regiments and one artillery battalion for service in the United States Volunteers for periods of a few months up to a year, a record of service ING members were able to point to with pride forever after.

In the years after the Spanish American War, ING advocates were able at last to convince the Illinois General Assembly to begin a building campaign to house the National Guard, in Chicago and across the state, in state-owned and state-operated armories, and to see their state budgets grow substantially. With the new money, ING members were able to increase the rigor and professionalism of their training and acquire the ever more sophisticated technology they needed to keep pace with international military developments. And each year, some twelve hundred new young men from a wide range of backgrounds continued to find the ING an appealing organization that allowed them to take leading roles in patriotic celebrations, participate in competitive shooting events, and stake their claim to both citizenship and manliness while having a good time.[39]

Partisanship, Politics, and Intraguard Tensions

Politics and the state militias have a long, complex history, from the way individuals used militia rank as a stepping stone to political office, through parades as statements of civic engagement, to securing the right to the franchise, to the basics of gaining and holding a berth in the militia.[40] Holdridge Collins's lengthy account of the effort to secure satisfactory new militia legislation in the 1870s is a primer for the ways politics, money, and political egos affected the Illinois militia, and the ways long-established hostility between downstate politicians and those from Chicago continued to shape the development of the ING.[41] The back-and-forth between Hilliard and Ducat, and between politicians from Chicago and from downstate, was at once supremely political and intimately personal. And during the very next session of the General Assembly, Martin Delany, supporter of the 1877 legislation, protested violently against further modification of the militia code, and especially against the permanent budget that was part of the 1879 bill.[42] Over the years other personal and political grudges would continue to affect ING leadership, from the resignation of Brigadier General Joseph T. Torrence of the First Brigade in 1882 to the long, involved drama over Colonel John C. Buckner of the Ninth Battalion in 1897 and 1898.[43] Political alliances for the ING were not necessarily stable or long lasting.

The politics of the ongoing struggles to gain a berth in the ING reflect similar tensions. In March 1893, the *Chicago Inter Ocean* reported that then-Governor John P. Altgeld was going to accept a private regiment, the Hibernian Rifles, as the new Seventh Regiment, ING. According to the paper, the "Hibernian Rifles have strong Clan-na-Gael affiliations, and have long been recognized by Chicago Irishmen as belonging to the anti-Cronin faction . . . In light of these facts it would seem that Governor Altgeld's object in admitting this regiment into the State service is to show his recognition of this element with the hope of attaching to himself no inconsiderable part of the Irish vote." The article goes on to record the objections of several current ING officers to the scheme, all of whom found a military reason (the companies had too few members) to object, as well as their complaint that this was an overtly political move on the part of a struggling governor.[44] The *Chicago Tribune* was less hostile than the anticorruption *Inter Ocean* in its coverage of the story, noting that the previous objections to the Hibernian Rifles' attempts to gain an ING berth was that "the State did not want class organization in the Guard," and that they succeeded because of their contributions to Altgeld's election the previous fall.[45] Despite the objections, the Seventh joined the state ranks.

The African American Ninth Battalion had an even tougher time than the Seventh. African American voters in Chicago had come to wield enough influence that they were courted by some factions of the Chicago Republican party as well as Chicago Democrats, and so they were by necessity pulled into the fray of Illinois party politics, gaining at least a little leverage to achieve some of their goals.[46] Willard Gatewood unraveled the major threads of the story in his 1975 article on the Eighth Illinois in the Spanish American War, and "complicated" only begins to suggest the twists and turns of this tale. John Buckner, major of the private Ninth Battalion, though an active Republican politician, was not a member of the same Republican faction as John Tanner, governor from 1896 to 1900. In 1895, during the Altgeld administration with its strong ties to Republicans, including Buckner, in the city of Chicago, Buckner was a political asset to his regiment. Elected to the General Assembly in 1894, during the Altgeld administration, Buckner was able to secure a place for the Ninth Battalion in the ING. In 1897 during the Tanner administration, Buckner had significantly reduced political pull with the new Republican administration, which came close to destroying his organization on the eve of the Spanish American War.[47]

Major Buckner faced two courts-martial in 1897.[48] At the center of both was a disagreement concerning rail travel to and from summer camp in 1897. Major Buckner claimed that the train cars provided for his troops were dirty and unfit for service and refused to use them, eventually making arrangements on another line. The representative from the adjutant general's office disagreed, and the first court-martial on two charges of refusing an order was the eventual result of the face-off. Governor Tanner disallowed the "not guilty" findings of the first court-martial, and he sent the case back to the ING. At the second court-martial, Major Buckner was also charged with leaving the route of a parade early, so as not to pass in review before Tanner, and disrupting the procession as a result. He was found guilty of all three charges, and in November of 1897 Buckner was suspended from his command for six months, much to the disgust of the editors of the Springfield *Illinois Record*. The editors, Charles E. Hall and James H. Porter, were avid supporters of Buckner and vitriolic opponents of Tanner, staunch though they were in their loyalty to the Republican Party.[49]

The "Buckner affair" highlights the political role of the militia within the African American community and on the larger Illinois political stage. The political role shouldered by the members of the Ninth Battalion operated on several levels. The affair was overtly political in the sense that Buckner belonged to a faction of the Illinois Republican Party that was competing with Governor Tanner. Some critics suspected Tanner of attempting to use the Guard to build a statewide political machine, in which case forcing Buckner out of the Ninth in order to replace him with someone from Tanner's own faction makes some sense.[50] The affair was also political in the sense of the ongoing struggle for African American civil rights. Buckner's original offense was to refuse transportation that he felt would not have been offered to white regiments. "We were furnished cars for that trip that were unfit for use. Some of them had been used in picnic excursion trains and had stood several days without cleaning. They were actually filthy, and so dusty you could write your name with your finger anywhere inside them." Some of the other cars provided for his men had not "apparently been used in years, and were not safe to travel in. Before we had covered the one and one-half miles from Camp Lincoln to Springfield an air brake broke on one car and another got out of order so the train had to be stopped."[51] He protested what he felt was overt discrimination against African American guardsmen, and when he did not receive satisfaction, he refused to use what he felt were demeaning accommodations and arranged for new transport, presumably some that treated his organization with more dignity and respect than they received before. In fact, it is possible that as much as Tanner's irritation with Buckner derived from his loyalty to the wrong Republican faction, it was also exacerbated by Buckner's uncomfortable challenge to overt racial discrimination.

As a final note on the intensity of the political and personal battles fought over the regiment, Tanner's choice for colonel of the new Eighth Regiment in 1898, John Marshall, infuriated the editors of the *Illinois Record*, who remained steadfastly loyal to Buckner and their faction of the Illinois Republican Party.[52] The editors took issue with everything the Chicago-based leadership of the battalion (soon-to-be regiment) did once Buckner had been suspended.[53] Regarding Marshall as a traitor to Buckner, they castigated him for recruiting problems, for being chosen over Buckner as colonel, and for being a traitor to his race.[54] Later, they would gleefully publish a series of inflammatory letters from disaffected soldiers, in particular a Corporal George J. Beard (also a former employee of the *Illinois Record*), in Cuba who blamed all their hardships on Marshall.[55] The vitriolic correspondents of the *Illinois Record* complained about food, discipline, the heat, and having to stay in camp. They also continued to slam Marshall, claiming that Marshall had had an affair in Cuba, and then complaining later that when the several officers' wives arrived, all the extra tents and bedding were requisitioned for them rather than renting quarters for them three and half miles away in town.[56] Despite the criticism, Marshall remained colonel of the Eighth Regiment until 1913, and he was able to use the position to gain political appointments, including deputy sheriff of Cook County and a position as a state game warden.[57]

Over the next decade, the Eighth Illinois continued to operate as a full member of the Illinois National Guard. The members shared in the benefits of the gradual expansion of both state and federal budgets, including the expansion of training opportunities, and they generally impressed their federal inspectors.[58] However, in these years of increas-

Figure 14
African American Officers of the Eighth Infantry, Camp Lincoln, 1903. From left to right, top row: Edward S. Miller, unidentified man, James S. Nelson. Bottom row: Major Allen A. Wesley, Colonel John R. Marshall, James H. Johnson. Courtesy of the Abraham Lincoln Presidential Library. Photographer: Guy Mathis, Guy Mathis Collection.

ing racial tension and the rise of Jim Crow in the South, the members of the Eighth Illinois faced more overt discrimination and racial violence than they had before the turn of the century. On July 6, 1908, the *Daily Inter Ocean* of Chicago reported that members of the Eighth Illinois had attacked "obnoxious motorists" who disturbed a parade. Making matters still tenser, on August 14, 1908, Springfield erupted into one of the most horrific race riots in Illinois history, with whites turning on blacks and destroying lives, homes, and property. Before it was over, the majority of the ING was called into service, with over 3,500 men and officers arriving in Springfield to help restore order.[59] Only two regiments and a few scattered companies were not called into service. Neither the Sixth Infantry from northwestern Illinois, nor the African American Eighth Infantry, not even the company stationed in Springfield, were called.[60] In 1913, a federal inspector acknowledged, in a confidential report to the chief of the militia bureau, that the Eighth would never be called for domestic service, as the "regiment is always spoken of as a political regiment in that it is believed that it would be criminal to order it out for local duty, i.e., for strike or similar duty here in the state, as it would be almost certain to precipitate a race war."[61] Giving force to his observation, the summer following the Springfield race riot, on July 18, 1909, the *Daily Inter Ocean* carried reports of worries about possible violence in Springfield while the Eighth Illinois was there for summer camp. On April 8, 1911, the *Chicago Defender* shared the story of Colonel Marshall being snubbed at an officer's school training in San Antonio. The 1913 federal inspection report tells of a brick being thrown through the windows of a train car carrying the Eighth Illinois to camp.[62] On August 11, 1915, the *Chicago Defender* reported that a race "melee" erupted after a white man slashed a member of the Eighth Illinois in Springfield.

It is impossible to divorce politics from the story of the Eighth Regiment—or from the history of the ING—but these stories also illustrate why the statewide organization never explicitly articulated a preference for any one political party. Politics within militia organizations could be vitriolic and nasty, and each unit could have its own political identity and alliances. Despite the internal feuds, the greatest criticism ING officers leveled at governors over the years was that governors were attempting to turn the state forces into a "machine" for their particular party.[63] To prevent that from happening, and to lobby for their own interests as an organization, ING members created the private "Illinois National Guard Association" in 1882.[64] Their purpose was the "promotion of the interests of the State Guard and mutual improvement in military matters."[65] By 1887 the association had 227 members who gathered annually to listen to papers on military affairs and to prepare amendments for the improvement of the laws governing the state forces.[66] By the 1890s, the association had settled into a permanent role as an advocate for professionalization and increased public funding. The statewide organization could not embrace any one political faction or party without alienating a significant portion of its own membership, not to mention the always-important legislatures, and even destabilizing the republic itself. In the words of *The National Guardsman*, "The spectacle of a militia composed exclusively of democrats or republicans, or Roman Catholics or Presbyterians for instance, would not only be a singular one, but one involving the elements of danger and sedition; a menace to all government and law, and to be suppressed with the same methods as would be employed in destroying a band of guerrillas or a gang of pirates."[67]

Costs Grow Faster than State Support

The ever-growing state budget for the militia in Illinois brought with it increasing state oversight and multiplying regulations for the state militia. Each militia law had more sections than the last, detailing matters as diverse as the formation of companies, the election and examination of officers, the regulations for court-martial, and riot control provisions.[68] Each new law also carried with it increased disciplinary powers for all ING officers to enforce compliance with the increasingly detailed and demanding regulations. Each new adjutant general imposed further restrictions on the freedom of militia officers to structure their own company's time, either at weekly drills or in their annual calendar of events.[69] In 1884, the adjutant general imposed a standard fatigue uniform for the ING. In 1885, the General Assembly appropriated the funds to purchase Camp Lincoln, a permanent campground for the ING, so that every company could spend four to seven days encamped each summer for training purposes.[70] The adjutant general began to mandate the types of equipment and equipment storage that every armory would have available to house state property in the mid-1880s. The adjutant general imposed record-keeping forms and ledgers to unify record keeping throughout the ING about the same time.[71] The office of the inspector general, created in 1876, was responsible for seeing that all these new codes, regulations, and practices were followed by each company, and as such, the office grew in power and importance with each new increase in state funds and expansion of state policies. State money was, naturally, the stick as well as the carrot. If the inspecting officer wrote a negative report, a company could find itself pushed out of the ING in favor of one of the long list of new companies awaiting a place in the Guard.[72]

Whatever the price for the funds, however, money from the state never matched the needs ING members felt they had. For example, the adjutant general purchased only fatigue uniforms for the ING's enlisted men, and not every year. Officers' uniforms of all types and parade uniforms and accouterments for everyone had to be paid for privately. Any expedition to another city or state had to be privately paid for. Cavalrymen who owned or rented their own horses paid for these things out of pocket.[73] As a result, fund-raising continued to be an important and central activity for most ING companies until well after the turn of the century. Companies held balls, lectures, amateur theatricals, drill performances, and parades, all in quest of money. They printed up beautiful, glossy souvenir books full of photographs and unit and individual histories as a means of selling advertising to raise funds. They also worked all the individual and group connections they had in order to ask for the big sums of money necessary to keep ambitious organizations afloat.[74]

One of the most expensive items that drove companies or regiments to their communities for support was armory costs. Armory rent subsidies from the state barely covered the upkeep of the average leased facility, and they definitely could not cover the construction of a new armory; private fund-raising was the only way to achieve that. Illinois moved quite slowly to state-subsidized armory construction for an otherwise large and relatively well-supported state militia system. A number of states had started building or subsidizing armory construction as early as the 1870s, including New York, Maryland, Pennsylvania, and Connecticut.[75] As late as 1901, the state of Illinois still owned no armories for the use by state troops. All armories used by ING companies and regiments were rented for a combined annual cost to the state of $50,000, with the rare exception of privately constructed armories for particularly well-financed companies or regiments. Throughout the 1880s and 1890s, adjutant generals requested in increasingly desperate tones a large arsenal in Springfield to house the adjutant general's operations and the Springfield-based ING regiment, and for a new lakefront armory in Chicago.[76] In 1896, Adjutant General Charles Hilton described the Chicago situation:

> The amount expended in Chicago is not sufficient, and in many cases the deficiency has to be made good by private contributions. Even with this aid, the armory facilities are entirely inadequate. Thanks to the great interest taken in this matter by General H. A. Wheeler, commanding the 1st Brigade, the city of Chicago has given to the State troops 20 acres on the Lake Front, provided it be used for armories and drill ground. I strongly recommend that the next General Assembly be asked to make the necessary appropriations to utilize this gift. The housing of all the troops in Chicago in adequate armories on this ground, would be economical in that it would diminish the annual fixed charges; would do much to encourage them; and would make them independent of private or extraneous aid, desirable for many reasons.[77]

In 1897, the General Assembly did appropriate $10,000 to contribute to the costs of armory construction in Chicago, but that sum represented only a fraction of the cost of the proposed armory, and two years later it remained unbuilt.[78] In fact, ten years later, in 1906, Adjutant General Thomas W. Scott penned an appeal to the General Assembly that strongly echoes that of Hilton from the previous decade. "Armory conditions in the city of Chicago are such at this time that, with impunity, it might be said that an emergency exists, and I recommend to Your Excellency the great importance of steps being taken at an early date to provide permanent armory buildings for the several commands in that city." [79]

It was only after the successes of the ING during the Spanish American War that the state of Illinois began to build as well as rent armories for the ING. The long-dreamed-of and oft-requested new State Arsenal and Armory in Springfield was completed in the period from 1901 to 1902, though not without problems. AG Scott mentioned in his 1906 report that it was "imperative that the electric system in this building be attended to, as the wiring in its present condition has been a pronounced a menace to life."[80] Finally, in 1907, the General Assembly appropriated $185,000 for the first armory purchases and constructions outside of the state capital.[81] AG Scott remarked that "this marks an era in the history of the Illinois National Guard and lends great encouragement to the officers and men who have for years devoted their time and money to maintaining the high standard of our guard."[82]

Of course, once the General Assembly opened the door to armory construction, they were bombarded with pleas for assistance by the many, many companies and regiments that had been making do in horrible, rented quarters. In 1908, the Chicago-based First Cavalry published an extensive report to present to the General Assembly, documenting the truly awful conditions in their armory and stables, complete with an album of photographs illustrating the dangerous condition of their facility.[83] These appeals and others like them had a clear effect, and in 1911 the General Assembly appropriated $395,000 for an armory for the First Cavalry.[84] Two years later, the General Assembly approved a new armory for the African American Eighth Regiment headquartered on the South Side of Chicago. The Eighth Regiment Armory opened in the winter of 1914–15.[85]

In the meantime, the vast majority of companies and regiments across the state made do with rented facilities. Troops outside Chicago were "usually quartered in make-shift buildings, sometimes unsuitable, usually too small, and nearly all in crowded portions of the town, where no ground is available for drill out of doors."[86] A historian of Company I, Sixth Regiment, provides this list of armories that served the company in Morrison from 1877 to 1898.

> For an armory and drill room, the basement of the old frame building which stood on the lot now occupied by the Hub Clothing Store was secured, remaining here but a short time, the company removed

to the City Council room, and shortly afterward to the second floor of Hollar Smith's blacksmith shop on east Main street. At that time the members considered themselves extremely fortunate in being so snugly located. From there they 'trekked' to Milne's opera house, and later to the old skating rink on Grove Street where they were at home at the outbreak of the Spanish American War.[87]

In Springfield, Company C, known as the Governor's Guard, made do with the top floors of livery stables.[88]

In Chicago in 1881, the Second Infantry moved into two rented upper floors on Randolph Street, the lower devoted to a drill hall, which was "handsomely papered," with silvered pillars, an ebony-framed mirror and a "very elaborate chandelier," and the upper held the "cosy" company rooms.[89] That same year, Battery D arranged to build a simple, one-story brick building on city-owned land that was also used for a circus ground. When pressed that this might inconvenience the circus, Mayor Carter Harrison responded, "No, sir . . . It gives them a little less room for side-shows, but they still have room enough."[90] As the first appropriations for state-financed construction in 1907 were specifically for regiments located in Chicago (the Second and the Seventh), the situation in Morrison, Springfield, and elsewhere throughout the state was not significantly altered for a very long time to come. In the meantime, elsewhere as in Chicago, private contributions had to make up the shortfall between state rent subsidies and the armory needs of each regiment or company.

Sometimes, private money could be enough. The First Regiment of Chicago—the wealthiest and best-connected, politically and socially, regiment in the state—was able to secure custom armory space early on. The First started out on the top floor of a warehouse when they organized in 1874, and then in 1875 they moved to a midsize facility built for their use and then leased to them on Jackson Street. When the fifteen-year-lease was up in 1890, the owner declined to renew, and the regiment, feeling the space was too small, moved to a larger, grander armory built by donated funds on a piece of Michigan Avenue property owned and donated, via a no-payment ninety-nine year lease, by Marshall Field.[91] The large, new First Regiment armory in Chicago, designed by the well-known architects Burnham and Root, was completed and dedicated in 1890. Unfortunately, the armory was destroyed by fire less than three years later, and it was completely rebuilt in 1894.[92] The First Infantry Association, the private association to which members of the regiment also belonged, owned both armories. All the amenities—desks, tables, chairs, pianos, locker rooms, basketball courts, kitchens, and dining rooms—were privately funded and owned. The inspector general noted in 1902 that the "company's quarters are superior to the field and staff officers' and have been furnished by the company officers and enlisted men, at their own expense." He went on to share his opinion that "these company quarters are as well fitted as many of the first-class clubs of the city and [are] conducive to the enlistment of the very best of our citizens. Books on military affairs and the best literature and music are provided in each of the company quarters . . . which reflects great credit on the members of the several companies for their zeal and liberality in making their respective quarters most attractive and unsurpassed."[93] The "Dandy First," as they were christened in local papers, was, of course, the most unusual of regiments, and their amenities merely served to highlight just how substandard the accommodations for the rest of the ING were until well after the turn of the century.

The First Regiment was not the only ING organization that was able to build privately. Capitalizing on their record of wartime service, the new Captain of Company I, Sixth Regiment in Morrison, was able to secure a new armory for his organization. This was a tremendous undertaking for a single company and required much "time . . . expended in formulating plans and securing the assistance, financially, of interested citizens. . . . [T]he armory was practically completed by January first, 1901."[94] Like the members of the First, the historian of Company I was very proud of the company's home.

> The building is constructed of brick and is the full depth of the lot. The drill room is on the first floor and is large and well proportioned. The wardrobe room is also located on the first floor. The front of the building is two stories in height, the ground floor being occupied as a store room. The second floor is given to a suite of rooms for the use of the "Morrison Military Club," an organization founded by the members of company I. On the east side of the upper floor is the bathroom, which is equipped with both tub and shower bathing apparatus, also toilet rooms. Joining this is the captains [sic] office which opens into the main room or clubroom proper. This room is large and fitted up for the convenience of the club members, and is a very pleasant resort for both the old and young men of the town as well as all citizens are eligible to membership upon payment of the regularly established quarterly dues. A janitor is in attendance both day and evening.[95]

This comparatively luxurious and dedicated facility was built and maintained by private funds, raised locally and from the membership dues assessed by the Morrison Military Club, and not with state funds. The existence of this facility serves as a strong reminder of the incredible importance of local fund-raising for ING companies.

Some of the more massive armories constructed privately or by state funds in the 1880s and 1890s were built, among other purposes, to protect the contents (equipment and people) from the putative danger of rampaging urban mobs. Of the First Regiment's second (1894) armory, Inspector General Walter Fieldhouse noted that it was "built in the normal style of architecture, having massive walls and is practically impregnable against riot or civil insurrection. . . . The main entrance has massive doors situated in a Norman archway and cannot be entered excepting by and with the aid and consent of those in charge of the armory. . . . The turret and battlement of this armory are conveniently placed to repel attack. The windows and firing ports are well arranged about 30 feet above the street to protect the entire armory."[96] Historian Robert Fogelson has dubbed this "normal style of architecture" the "castellated style," and the First Regiment armory in Chicago is one of his examples of the form. Fogelson goes on to argue that these armories can be read as true statements about fears of the mob and of civil insurrection rather than as symbolic statements of wealth and power, as some contemporary critics dismissed them. He points to the realities of the heavy construction, and to the language the architects and their clients used about their buildings, language that was heavily laced with issues of defensibility, impregnability, and the like.[97] The fears may have been real, and the massiveness of the construction certainly was. Exactly how these castellated armories would have stood up to the test of an attacking civilian mob is unknown, however, as none were ever so attacked. Castellated armories were also extremely rare among the many, many makeshift, rented facilitates that stored state arms and equipment for most companies and regiments in Chicago and around Illinois. The new armory the Morrison company built in 1900 certainly didn't have battlements or rifle slits, and their storeroom was on the main floor, right by the main door. The powerful need for defensibility appears to have only come into play when the regiment (and all castellated armories that Fogelson discusses were built for regiments, as opposed to single companies or battalion-sized organizations) had plenty of money to spend.

The realities of stone work, masonry, rifle slits, and battlements that were invested in these large, elaborate armories served chiefly to mark them as armories in the urban space. They also spoke to fears and situations, both real and imagined, that the companies they housed might face. In the final summation, however, it must be noted that the castellated armories, like the First Regiment armory, mostly functioned as

Figure 15
New Eighth Infantry Armory, 1915. Courtesy of the Chicago Historical Society.
Photographer: Chicago Daily News. Glass negative DN-0064686.

elaborate clubhouses for members and as a tantalizing vision to potential recruits, and contemporary critics understood this concept. The state of Illinois, at least, did not feel called upon to provide its state troops with any state-financed armories until well after the turn of the century, after the demise of the castellated style.[98] Certainly, as of 1901 the other organizations in Chicago (the Second Regiment, the Seventh Regiment, the First Cavalry, the Illinois Naval Militia, and the Eighth Regiment) did not have large, impregnable castellated armories for their use or to protect themselves and their equipment in riotous situations. The Illinois Naval Militia, to cite a particularly whimsical example of nondefensible architecture, used a brick building built to mimic a ship for the Columbian Exhibition of 1893 for their armory.[99] Regardless of what the members of the First may have felt about the defensibility of their large, castle-style armory, the members of the General Assembly, and guardsmen in general, didn't appear to think it necessary to provide any organization in the state with such a space. A photograph of the new Eighth Infantry Armory built in 1914 reveals that it was a simple two story building with big windows and a standard door. More than anything else, it strongly resembles school buildings of the era.[100]

Armory construction in Illinois was not only the most expensive hurdle for militia companies; it also was up to them to make up whatever shortfall there was between state appropriations and their needs for uniforms, equipment, weapons, and supplies. So ING members relied on extensive fund-raising within their communities to subsidize their aspirations. Throughout the three decades from 1870 to 1900, most militia companies in Illinois spent much of their time on fund-raising efforts, hosting a bewildering array of entertainments—from balls to lectures to drill performances—to raise the money they needed to raise and maintain their organizations.

After the Spanish American War, the ING continued both to be quite politically active by lobbying on their own behalf and to avoid particular party alliances, positioning itself in the long tradition of the regular Army as a nonpartisan organization that stayed above the fray for all but their own interests.[101] As one testament to their success, the Springfield papers carried pictures throughout the late 1890s and early 1900s of summer camp festivities showing a succession of governors and their wives and daughters visiting officers for picnics and parades.[102] Despite their constant efforts, most National Guardsmen were not able to raise enough money from their communities to make up the difference between their needs and the state subsidies, except in the rarest of situations. So National Guard officers also lobbied their state representatives throughout the late nineteenth century to increase the state allotment of funds. Periodically throughout the 1880s and 1890s, and more persistently after the Spanish American War, they also turned to the federal government to supply the difference between state appropriations and militia desires.

Creation of a National Lobby for Federal Support for State Troops

Flushed with their early successes in gaining increased support from state governments in the wake of the events of 1877, National Guard activists in Illinois and in other states began to think in grander terms. In 1878 in Virginia, and in January 1879 in New York, militia activists from around the country held meetings to establish the National Guard Association of the United States (NGAUS), which had its first formal convention in St. Louis in September 1879. The officers who established this association were, for the most part, the kind of long-term members who would come to dominance in the various National Guards around the country during and after the Spanish American War. The officers who gathered in St. Louis in 1879 did not focus on domestic order. Rather, they articulated a belief that the volunteer associations of the National Guards constituted the best possible defense of the nation. National Guardsmen from Illinois who shared these sentiments were active in the organization from the beginning, sending representatives to the first National Guard Association convention in St. Louis in 1879, and again in 1881 when Colonel E. D. Swain and Colonel J. H. Shaffer represented Illinois at the annual convention.[103]

These militia activists from Illinois and other states held as their goal nothing less than a complete overhaul of the state militia system nationwide, with the explicit aim of turning the militias into a serious reserve army.[104] In the published minutes of the 1879 St. Louis convention, the secretary proclaimed, "the wars of this country have all been fought by citizen soldiers." The implication that the entire gathering appears to have drawn from this statement was that all future wars would have to be fought with the same type of volunteer, and that such volunteers should receive serious training with this end in mind. After decrying the "expensive standing army . . . [which was] always increasing in costliness" from $1.5 million in 1799 to over $40 million a year in 1879, the secretary went on to suggest the models of Great Britain and Canada in organizing large, efficient volunteer home armies or militias. Such militias, according to him, allowed these countries to "dispense with all regular troops," and "have convinced our people that our own citizen soldiery can be soon placed in an efficient condition of organization, equipment and discipline."[105] Of course, militias like those of these other countries were paid for by the national government, which was not the case in the United States. In 1881, Colonel Swain of Illinois spoke for many when he described the cavalry and artillery organizations of the ING. "Our cavalry was not equipped by the State. It belongs, however, to the National Guard . . . Of course, both branches of the service under discussion labor under the same difficulties that they do in other localities, in the men not owning the horses."[106] Later, talking of the importance of summer camp, Swain noted that Illinois set aside about $25,000 annually for camp and garrison equipment and to pay for the entire ING to encamp for four days training, though the state did not yet own a single campground. He concluded a long report of the most recent camp experience of the First Infantry with "I do not think there can be any question as to the advantage of encampments. They are the most efficient schools that we can have, and more can be done in a week's encampment, I think, to instruct the National Guards in the duties of the soldier, than it is possible to do in armories or by the companies at home and alone during the year."[107] But to achieve this training, the states needed to supply still more money.

The suggestion some officers made during the 1879 convention, that it might be possible to do away with the regulars altogether, turned out to be a more of a debate point than a serious alternative military structure, and the notion of abandoning the standing army was quickly dropped by the National Guard Association. In any case, the association spent the next several years defending itself from charges ranging from trying to establish state forces designed to challenge the federal government to a strategy to create a 150,000-man standing army under the sole authority of the president.[108] Wild accusations aside, General Wingate of New York explained in 1881 that the "really great obstacle which we have to contend against is, the apathy of Congress. Few who have no actual experience can imagine the difficulty of procuring the passage of any law by that body which involves no personal or political interest, and particularly on a subject like this, upon which the average Congressman knows nothing, and cares less."[109] Despite the apathy of Congress, concerted efforts by the association over eight years of lobbying did result in a modest gain in federal funding—from $200,000 annually to $400,000, secured in 1887. However, after several years of such hard work with so little accomplished toward the original goal of a new militia law, the association volunteers lost their energy, and the association dwindled to a shadow of its former self.

In 1897 a new national lobbying organization was formed by a new group of activist officers. The Interstate National Guard Association (INGA)—created initially by representatives of western states—hoped to achieve much more modest formal gains at the federal level than the earlier association. Chiefly, they hoped to secure a significant increase in the federal appropriation—from $400,000 to $1 million—for the state militias, and they did not seek any dramatic changes to the standing militia laws.[110] However, their vision of the purpose of the National Guards was nearly identical to that held by National Guard Association (NGAUS) members twenty years previously. In 1897, General Bell, adjutant general of Missouri, reminded INGA convention delegates that "[w]e should realize that the safety of American firesides, in the event of war with foreign powers, will depend largely upon the standard of our National Guard."[111] Officers once again cited the models of Great Britain and Canada as worthy of study and emulation.[112]

Officers from Illinois played a much more significant role in this second National Guard Association than they had in the first. Then adjutant general of Illinois, Jasper N. Reece, served on the first executive committee, followed by two terms as president of the association from 1898 to 1900. The ING sent by far the largest number of delegates to the INGA conventions in 1897 (ten delegates), 1898 (twenty delegates), and

1900 (sixteen delegates), and the 1898 convention was held in Chicago, hosted by the ING. General Reece was personally instrumental in the negotiations that eventually merged the older association (NGAUS) and the newer (INGA) into one national association.[113] Illinois officers were quite active in the new organization, perhaps because although it ranked third among the state militia organizations by size of membership, the ING ranked only twenty-seventh among the forty-nine state militias in terms of funding per man. (See appendix I.) Other states with smaller appropriations managed to make them go further by limiting the size of their militia organizations or, like Ohio, which had nearly the same size organization, managed to provide three and a half times the state funds. The National Guardsmen from Illinois made no attempt to explain why they elected to arrange for such a comparatively large National Guard organization without being able to provide for it as generously as most of their peer organizations. In strict cash terms, the state ranked ninth in terms of state funding. By cutting the size of their organization in half to bring their membership size in line with their budget, ING officers could have effectively doubled the amount of money available to support each company, as, in fact, they did do in the early 1880s. However, very soon after, they allowed the ING to grow again.

The ING leadership chose instead to turn aggressively to the federal government to address the shortfall. They were eloquent on the subject of national defense and the role played by the National Guards in serving the nation. In his opening address to the third INGA convention, Jasper Reece, adjutant general of Illinois and president of the INGA, thundered:

> What does the national government owe the states who furnished the President with such magnificent fighting material on a single day's notice? What have we, the instructors and teachers, a right to expect from Congress in the way of fair and reasonable appropriations—in arms, clothing, and equipments—to enable us to again prepare for unlooked-for emergencies, when the brawn, brain, and muscle of the volunteer may again be demanded for immediate and dangerous service? What should the government do for the National Guard of the states in order that we may maintain this unsurpassed fighting force at its maximum state of practical efficiency? . . . [W]e do care to have the national government assume a fair share of the burden and responsibility in fitting out the soldiers that will some day be required at our hands to fight national battles; we do care to see the patriotism and valor of our militia boys adequately recognized by Congress, and we will have this recognition.[114]

In 1900, following the third annual convention, Congress answered Reece and raised the annual federal militia appropriation from $400,000 to $1,000,000. The ING's claim that the state of readiness of the National Guard reserve forces was a national responsibility ultimately carried the day. The power of this argument drew on the experiences provided by the mobilization of the National Guards for the Spanish American War, but the members of the INGA claimed complete responsibility for their triumph in Washington. At the opening of the fourth annual convention in 1902, the chair summarized the results of the previous convention for the delegates by asserting that "the result of that meeting was the increased appropriation which has enabled the National Guard to equip an organized militia as never equipped before . . . I want to congratulate the organization on the splendid work they did."[115] The vigorous debate at this fourth INGA convention concerned the proposed bill to revise the long-outdated militia law of 1792. This effort, too, was ultimately successful.

Wartime service from 1898 to 1899 gave representatives of the INGA the clout they needed to secure long-sought changes in federal militia law and dramatic increases in federal funding, changes and increases modeled on those they had already managed to achieve in their own states. In 1903 Congress passed the first new federal militia law since 1789, and Congress elaborated on the 1903 legislation in 1908. These new laws recognized the National Guard as the Nation's reserve Army and provided significant federal funds and support for that mission. Over the next decade, this federalization of the National Guards increased the professionalism and level of training and preparedness among the National Guardsmen and slowly decreased their reliance on the relationships with communities and states they forged in the final quarter of the nineteenth century.[116]

In 1903, as part of a wider series of military reforms at the organizational level, Secretary of War Elihu Root pushed through Congress the Militia Act of 1903, or the "Dick Act," as it came to be called in honor of the Ohio National Guard officer and member of Congress, General Charles Dick, who shepherded the bill through the House of Representatives. The Dick Act contained many of the provisions debated and selected by the INGA convention in 1902. The Dick Act recognized the National Guards as the organized militia of the United States. In exchange for organizing units and uniforming themselves according to regular Army regulations, drilling a specified number of times per year, attending summer camps, submitting to annual War Department inspections, and generally complying with Army regulations on all subjects, the National Guards of the various states received arms and equipment from the War Department and federal funds to pay for attendance at summer camp and at occasional joint maneuvers with the Army. This last funding was not even drawn from the militia appropriations, but rather from the regular military budget. The Dick Act also mandated that volunteer forces raised for wartime service would be organized according to the legislation for raising the state troops for the Spanish American War. Five years later, in 1908, National Guard officers believed that militia reform had attained all their goals when Congress passed a series of amendments to the 1903 act. The 1908 amendments permitted the president to use National Guard troops outside the boundaries of the United States and removed the nine-month time limit on active service imposed by the 1903 act. The 1908 amendments also explicitly required the president to call the organized militia (i.e., the National Guard as recognized in the 1903 act) in advance of any other volunteers, which put firmly into law what had only been implied before.[117]

In many ways, the 1903 legislation was the natural outgrowth of the previous twenty-five years of development. Militia members across the country had spent two decades lobbying their communities, their state governments, their congressmen, and the U.S. Army itself for increased financial and professional support for their organizations in pursuit of their ambition to create a modern, professional reserve military force. As a result, by the turn of the century, National Guard enthusiasts were experienced lobbyists with a number of important successes under their belts. They had also spent twenty-five years or more as the beneficiaries of full-time agencies of their state governments, and fifteen years receiving regular Army inspections and advice. These experiences only encouraged National Guard enthusiasts to work harder for new federal legislation, finally securing the strong federal relationship they wanted in the first decades of the twentieth century. National Guard officers may not have predicted exactly how their relationships with the various levels of government would change as a result of the 1903 federal reforms, but they certainly knew that they would. National Guard officers embraced the accelerating pace of change as the twentieth century progressed.[118]

An important aspect of the successful lobbying efforts on the part of the National Guard activists in the INGA, and previous efforts by Illinois guardsmen with the Illinois General Assembly, is that they were careful not to tie the success of their movement to a particular political party. The INGA proceedings from these years are full of tips on lobbying legislators and getting press support to influence local congressmen, but never is there a word breathed about the importance of one political party over another. The presence of a Spanish American War volunteer in the White House, Theodore Roosevelt, must have interested the 1902–3 lobbyists, but the INGA members never mentioned him or his party by name. Their focus remained squarely on their cause.[119]

Consequences of Federalization

The ING actively and aggressively sought tax dollar support at the state and the federal levels from the 1870s onward. Illinois National Guard officers and National Guard Association members were not interested only in the money, however much they needed it. They also wanted government identification and the seal of approval that could be given only by the military professionals of the U.S. Army. That seal of approval was available only if the National Guard worked hard to meet the minimum standards established by the U.S. Army. The equipment, time, and training they needed to meet that standard were expensive, ultimately more expensive than most communities could afford to raise on their own to support their local company, and so available only from the federal government.

With government money came government oversight. In the years between 1903 and 1916, correspondence between National Guardsmen and the secretary of war (from 1903 to 1908) and the chief of the Bureau of Militia Affairs (after 1908) grew exponentially as both sides struggled to adjust to their new relationship. National Guard officers barraged federal officials with questions about funding, uniforms, procedures, and property management. Federal inspection officers exhorted the National Guard to improve its discipline and military skills. The new, closer ties between National Guardsmen and War Department officials also created new tensions. Several troubling disagreements arose about issues ranging from pay for National Guardsmen to the exact role the Guards would play should the United States be drawn into war with a foreign state. Many guardsmen also experienced intense frustration with increased War Department oversight and regulation of militia affairs, which had previously been very much in their own hands.[120] In the middle of the adjustment, the men themselves sometimes got left behind. Cary T. Ray of the First Regiment, ING, ended up resigning his commission, without ever making his goal of the captaincy of Company D, over problems with property returns from the previous captain. Ray had signed a receipt for the supplies on the promise that the resigning man would make good the deficiencies, which he never did. Ray got caught in the ensuing property accounting and left the ING.[121] In another ironic turn, by 1914 federal inspecting officers were complaining that guardsmen were giving so much time to rifle and target practice while in camp that "proper field instruction could not have been given, and it may be stated that it is not the intention that rifle instruction, important as it is, shall displace the other forms of field instruction to the extent done" at camp in 1913.[122]

As they reconfigured themselves to meet the professional standard laid out by the War Department and recognized by Congress, the Illinois General Assembly, and the general public, guardsmen significantly altered their practices. Drill marching was out, and marksmanship was in. Much that could be demonstrated with drill marching, qualities that they had traditionally relied on to convince their local communities that they were worthy of emotional and financial support, could not be so easily demonstrated with marksmanship scores. The very identity that the National Guards had established to secure community support and a steady stream of new recruits was challenged by the new realities of federal funds and federal alliances. For the most part, the members of the ING appear to have been very happy with the change, and the ING continued to grow in the early years of the twentieth century, attracting much the same kind of young man it had for decades. The chance to make a serious claim on the identity of the modern soldier, trained for the modern battlefield while ensconced in the comfort of a modern, state-built armory, seemed to satisfy the needs of ING members to convince themselves that by 1915 they had attained the realization of their goals.

Realization of the Federal Future: Mexican Border Service and the National Guards

In June of 1916, U.S. troops under the command of Brigadier General John J. Pershing, chasing the Mexican rebel commander "Pancho" Villa and his army across northern Mexico, clashed severely with Mexican government troops in Carrizal. In response to the subsequent diplomatic crisis, President Woodrow Wilson called 75,000 National Guard troops into federal service to police the Mexican-U.S. border.[123] The members of the ING, like their counterparts in most states, were thrilled that they had the opportunity to gain experience in a large-scale military mobilization and that their organization was the tool to achieve mobilization in a national emergency. Many Illinois guardsmen saw the expedition as a giant training exercise, aimed not so much at containing Pancho Villa as preparing the U.S. Army and its National Guard reserve troops for their much-anticipated joining of the ongoing war in Europe.[124] Once on the border for their three-month tour of duty, Illinois cavalrymen had little reason to change their minds about the importance of their activities; in fact, high-ranking Army officers supported this version of events. In the second weekly issue of the *Illinois Cavalryman*—a paper published by members of the First Illinois Cavalry during their thirteen weeks of service on the Mexican border—the front page featured an interview with the general in command of the portion of the border under the control of the Illinois troops. The headline reads, "PLAN FOR HUGE ARMY REVEALED—General Parker Declares Border Mobilization Big Training School—Preparedness Step."[125] From the point of view of many military men, the Mexican problem was clearly secondary, an excuse to train for large plans and larger wars.

Illinois guardsmen regularly measured the daily routines of training and leisure, movement followed by stasis, that they experienced while on border duty against the horrible conditions troops fighting in Europe in 1916 were enduring day after day in the trenches. These guardsmen attempted to seize in their border service the chance to ready themselves as much as possible for the trials they were convinced awaited them on the Continent. The writers and reporters of the *Illinois Cavalryman* filled its pages with a variety of advice columns devoted to encouraging the interested soldier to pursue and further develop and refine his professional skills. Articles discussed everything from camp sanitation to marksmanship and offered a primer in basic Spanish so soldiers could converse with any potential prisoners of war. Of course, the paper also covered sporting events—boxing, polo, horse racing, basketball—and social news for the entertainment of the men marching around the dry mudflats of the late-summer border region.[126]

Those thirteen weeks on the border turned out to be the merest shadow of the work that lay ahead of what would become the nucleus of U.S. troops in France. On April 6, 1917, the United States declared war on Germany, and by the end of 1917, the first of the U.S. troops, including divisions made up of National Guardsmen, were training for war outside Paris. General Pershing was again in command, and knowing just how much his troops had to learn about conducting themselves in modern warfare, he devised a ten-month-long training period to prepare them for battle. The experiences on the border the previous summer had taught regular soldiers and National Guardsmen alike how much more they needed to know if they hoped to survive to return home. Those who participated in the border experience also learned the importance of organized leisure-time activities and distractions for bored troops. If guardsmen made one small contribution to the preparations of the United States, it may have been their long experience with providing popular entertainments and competitive events for their members.

Guardsmen training in late 1917 for war in France were exactly where ambitious National Guard officers for the previous forty years had hoped to see them—on the front lines as a full partner to the regular U.S. Army. The National Guards had won their battles—with their communities, their state governments, and the federal government—to prove that with sufficient time and money, American men could effectively train themselves as the elements of a reserve army from the secure position of a civilian life. That the reality always fell short of the dream was less important than the fact that the National Guards had some training, whereas raw recruits had none.

The reserve army mission was paramount to the volunteers who filled the ING, and National Guards across the country, because it was through this role that they elaborated their shared language for identifying themselves as men and as citizens of the republic. Having committed to the power of the word and the image evoked by "soldier" to bring diverse men together in one common bond, the men who volunteered their time and money to the ING had to give soldiering their serious attention. Although change had been almost imperceptibly slow throughout the 1870s and 1880s, by the 1890s it was clear that a commitment to soldiering that was founded on shared social needs would take on a life of its own and would in time claim the entire National Guard movement for the reserve army mission.

As National Guardsmen left their local communities further and further behind—as the locus of their funding, activities, and identity shifted ever further toward the center—issues of manhood and citizenship were recast to fit the new realities. The mobilization for World War I and the creation of a whole new crop of "real" veterans of wartime service once again helped to draw a dramatic line between the soldier and the civilian, the boy and the man. This new crop of veterans would be the ones to shape the National Guard in their own image over the next decades. They did not identify with their civic fathers who were striving to mend the union as had a much earlier generation of militia companies, or the Spanish American War veterans out to turn still amateur soldiers into true reservists, but with their fellow soldiers and officers from an overseas combat experience. Citizenship did not seem to be at stake in this new war (despite the overt and demeaning segregation of the African American troops), so for the National Guardsmen its only message may have been one of the deadly rituals of combat.

The National Guard of the late nineteenth century was an organization of civic participation, of manly citizenship, and of patriotic service.

The Spanish American War was an exciting opportunity for National Guardsmen to prove that they had been serious all along, an experience turned sour by lack of preparation and training. The National Guardsmen who emerged from that contest were finally successful in prying money, time, modern equipment, and training from the state and federal governments as their skills and image seemed to reflect on the possibilities of the rising world power. The Great War was an entirely different event. The United States was a late and relatively lightly harmed participant in a grim slaughter. How this experience would shape the next generation of leadership in the National Guard is an untold story, but it is a tempting place to look for the fall in popularity and public approbation that the National Guard suffered, particularly in the late 1920s and throughout the Depression years, a time when a sense of civic leadership and identification with responsible manhood might have allowed the National Guard to shape a different, more traditional future.

Appendix A

Occupations Named by Members of the First Infantry, ING, 1890–1903

Occupation	No.	Occupation	No.	Occupation	No.	Occupation	No.
Accountant	1	Dentist	6	Medical student	8	Solicitor	2
Actor	1	Designer	3	Merchant	8	Stage worker	1
Advertiser	3	Doctor	2	Metal worker	1	Steam fitter	3
Agent	4	Draughtsman	8	Meter setter	1	Stencil maker	1
AK keeper	1	Driver	5	Milk dealer	3	Stenographer	10
Architect	1	Drug clerk	3	Milkman	1	Stock yards	1
Artist	4	Druggist	6	Mine operator	1	Stockman	1
Assembler	1	Editor	2	Musician	35	Stone cutter	3
Attorney	2	Electrician	26	Music dealer	1	Student	64
Baker	2	Elevator conductor	3	Music student	1	Superintendent	1
Banker	1	Enameller	1	Newspaper man	1	Supv.	1
Barber	3	Engineer	5	Nickel plate	1	Surveyor	2
Bicycle maker	2	Engraver	3	Office manager	1	Tailor	1
Blacksmith	1	Farming	1	Operator	3	Tally man	1
Bookbinder	1	File setter	1	Optician	2	Tavernman	1
Bookkeeper	58	Fireman	3	Orderly C.C.H.	1	Taxi dispatcher	1
Brass finisher	1	Florist	2	P.O. clerk	1	Telegraph operator	2
Brick layer	1	Foreman	5	Packer	1	Telescoper	1
Broker	5	Forester	1	Painter	15	Teller	1
Butcher	8	Furniture builder	1	Paper hanger	2	Timekeeper	2
Butler	2	Gardener	1	Paper ruler	1	Tinner	3
Buyer	2	Gen. manager	1	Pass. agt.	1	Train Dis.	1
Carpenter	17	Glove maker	1	Pharmacist	1	Trainman	1
Carriage driver	1	Grain Inspector	3	Photographer	11	Treasurer	1
Carriage maker	1	Grocer	4	Physician	2	Undertaker	1
Cashier	6	Horse-Shoer	2	Plasterer	1	Upholsterer	1
Caterer	1	Hotel employee	1	Plumber	8	Usher	1
Chemist	2	Iceman	2	Porter	1	Vocalist	1
Cigar dealer	1	Illustrator	1	Post office Clerk	1	Wagon maker	1
City buyer	1	Inspector	7	Postal employee	1	Waiter	1
Civil engineer	5	Insurance	9	Pressman	1	Wireworker	2
Clergyman	1	Interior decorator	1	Print sec.	1	Unclear	54
Clerk	598	Jeweler	1	Printer	27	No occupation given	44
Cloak cutter	1	Joiner	1	Publisher	4		
Coachman	1	Laborer	2	R. P. clerk	2		
Collector	15	Laundryman	2	Railroad man	1		
Com. merchant	1	Law student	2	Real estate agent	1		
Composer	1	Lawyer	28	Receiving clerk	1		
Compositor	2	Letter carrier	1	Reporter	5		
Conductor	8	Librarian	1	Rubber worker	1		
Confectioner	2	Life insurance solicitor	1	Sailor	1		
Construct fire proof	1	Lineman	1	Salesman	104		
Contractor	3	Lithographer	1	Seaman	1		
Cornice maker	2	Lumber dealer	1	Secretary	2		
Court clerk	1	Machinist	30	Shipping clerk	1		
Credit man	1	Manager	9	Sign maker	1		
Cutter	4	Manf.	3	Sign writer	1		
Cycle mfr.	1	Mechanic	6	Silversmith	1		
Total occupations 1484							

Source: Compiled from Descriptive List, Illinois National Guard, First Infantry, 1880–1904, Miscellaneous, RS 301.96, Illinois State Archives.

Appendix B

Occupations Named by Members of Company A, Third Infantry, ING, 1899–1908

Occupation	No. of Men	Occupation	No. of Men
Unknown	8	Molder	3
Baker	2	Nail maker	7
Barbed wire maker	2	Operator	1
Barber	6	Painter	6
Blacksmith	2	Penman	1
Bookkeeper	1	Photographer	2
Butcher	4	Piano maker	2
Cable maker	1	Piano stringer	1
Cement worker	2	Piano tuner	1
Clerk	12	Plumber	1
Cooper	1	Porter	2
Die maker	2	RR signal operator	1
Drayman	1	Restaurant	1
Druggist	1	Salesman	2
Electrician	1	Shoemaker	32
Factory hand	2	Spooler	1
Farmer	25	Student	20
Fence maker	39	Switchman	1
Fireman	1	Teacher	1
Galvanizer	2	Teamster	4
Glove maker	2	Telegraph operator	1
Laborer	35	Telephone service	3
Other	1	Tobacco dealer	1
Landscape gardener	1	Watchmaker	1
Lather	3	Well driller	1
Laundryman	1	Wire drawer/maker	8
Machinist	10	Wood worker	2
Mason	3		
Mechanic	2		
Miller	1		

Source: "Descriptive Book, Co. 'A,' 3rd Infantry, ING." Regional History Center, Northern Illinois University.

Appendix C

Incidents of Strike-Related Active Duty on the Part of the ING, 1877–1904

Railroad Strikes	Chicago	15 days service	7/27–8/11/1877
	East St. Louis	15 days	7/27/1877
Coal Strike/Race Riot	Braidwood	2 days	8/9/1877
Coal Miners' Strike	Pike County	?	1878
	La Salle County	?	1878
Railway Strike	East St. Louis	?	1878
Coal Miners' Strike	Madison	5 days	5/25–29/1883
	St. Clair	5 days	5/25–29/1883
Coal Miners' Strike	Joliet	?	5/1/1885
	Lemont	?	5/4/1885
Railroad Strikes	East St. Louis	5 weeks	4/9/1886
Coal Miners' Strike	Braidwood	5 days	5/27/1889
	Spring Valley	6 days	6/1/1889
Coal Miners' Strike	LaSalle	7 days	5/24/1894
	Centralia	3 days	5/24/1894
	Minonk/Winona	3 days	5/27/1894
	Carterville	3 days	6/5/1894
	Pekin	7 days	6/7/1894
	Pana	3 days	6/8/1894
	Mt. Olive	2 days	6/18/1894
Miners' Strike	Spring Valley	9 days	7/8/1894
Railway Strike	Danville	15 days	7/2/1894
	Decatur	13 days	7/1/1894
	Springfield	3 days	7/5/1894
	Mounds	17 days	7/3/1894
Railway Strike	Chicago (Pullman)	33 days	7/6/1894
Miners' Strike	Virden	20 days	9/29/1898
	Pana	4 months and 23 days	9/30/1898
Miners' Strike	Pana	5 months and 1 day	4/10/1899
Miners' Strike	Carterville	33 days	9/17/1899
Miners' Strike	Ziegler	78 days	11/26/1904

Source: "Report Prepared by the Bureau of National Guards for the War College,"1908, Document #3135, Box 57, Bureau of Militia Affairs, RG 168.7, National Archives; *Biennial Report . . . 1877 and 1878*; *Biennial Report . . . 1889 and 1890*; *Biennial Report . . . 1893 and 1894*; *Biennial Report . . . 1897 and 1898*; *Biennial Report . . . 1899 and 1900*; *Biennial Report . . . 1903 and 1904*.

Appendix D

Precipitating Event for Request for State Intervention in Coal Strikes, 1877–1908

Location	Date	Event
Braidwood	8/9/1877	Colored miners and their families evicted from their homes by striking miners
Pike County	1878	
La Salle County	1878	
Madison County	5/25/1883	Nonstrikers from Abbey "Machine Mine" evicted by strikers, threats to life and property
St. Clair	5/29/1883	Ongoing confrontation between county sheriffs, strikers, and nonstrikers at Reinecker mine shaft
Joliet	5/1/1885	
Lemont	5/4/1885	
Braidwood	5/27/1889	Direct confrontation at county line between sheriff and strikers; sheriff satisfied that threat was beyond his means to control with 25 deputies
Springvalley	6/1/1889	Attack on sheriff and deputies while protecting miners at work by striking miners
LaSalle	5/24/1894	Sheriff attacked by rioters
Centralia	5/25/1894	Sheriff with 200 armed deputies could not guard 75 miners arrested after destroying a local mine and protect 4 more local mines from destruction
Pana	5/26/1894	Sheriff worried about threatened "invasion" of miners from Indiana planning to close four working mines—invasion did not occur
Minonk and Winona	5/28/1894	Train seized by strikers who blockaded the tracks. Sheriff asked for guns or troops—state sent troops
Carterville	6/5/1894	Strikers prevented laborers from loading slack—deputies present, not sheriff, could not stop the attack
Pekin/Peoria	6/7/1894	Direct conflict between sheriffs and strikers; one fatality; mine destroyed. Sheriff asked for state arms—troops sent
Pana	6/8/1894	Sheriff worried that presence of some 300 strikers threatened four working mines—no direct confrontation
Mount Olive	6/18/1894	U.S. Marshall requested aid in making arrests
Spring Valley	7/8/1894	Two coal-company-owned stores looted; striker invasions threatened
Virden	9/29/1898	Ongoing confrontation between strikers and private mine guards/strikebreakers. Twenty-one fatalities before militia arrived; almost forty injured in fighting
Pana	9/30/1898	Confrontations between strikers and imported strikebreakers
Pana	4/10/1899	
Carterville	6/17/1899	Confrontations between strikers and mine operators
Ziegler	11/26/1904	Sheriff needed aid to protect life and property

Source: *Biennial Report* . . . *1877 and 1878*; *Biennial Report* . . . *1889 and 1890*; *Biennial Report* . . . *1893 and 1894*; *Biennial Report* . . . *1897 and 1898*; *Biennial Report* . . . *1899 and 1900*; *Biennial Report* . . . *1903 and 1904*.

Appendix E

ING Membership vs. Days of Strike Policing, 1874–1911

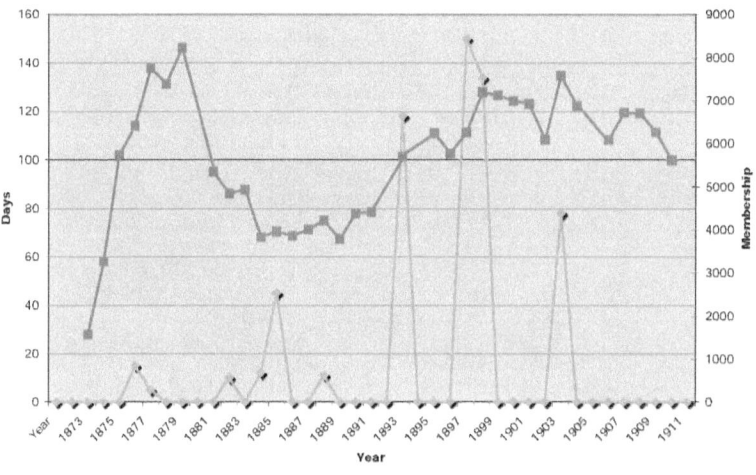

Source: "Report Prepared by the Bureau of National Guards for the War College," 1908, Document #3135, Box 57, Bureau of Militia Affairs, RG 168.7, National Archives; *Biennial Report . . . 1877 and 1878*; *Biennial Report . . . 1889 and 1890*; *Biennial Report . . . 1893 and 1894*; *Biennial Report . . . 1897 and 1898*; *Biennial Report . . . 1899 and 1900*; *Biennial Report . . . 1903 and 1904*. The dramatic decrease in membership in 1880 and 1881 is the result of legislatively mandated consolidation of the ING. The 1901 decrease is a result of the recovery from the mobilizations and demobilizations that resulted from the Spanish American War. In both cases, the size of the ING was affected by official restructuring of the ING, and by neither a sudden falloff of interested recruits nor a wave of current members quitting.

Appendix F

Selected ING Officers, 1874–90: Military Histories of Officers with Five to Six Years of Service in Their Current Rank

Name	Rank	Organization	Location	Military History	Yrs in Rank
Bowler, H. S.	Captain	B	Chicago		5.9
Harris, Bush W.	Captain	B—8th Infantry	Newton	Captain	5.9
Vickery, John A.	Captain	I—5th Infantry	Jacksonville	Captain Private 1876. 1st Lieutenant 9/9/1888	5.9
Matthews, Frederick L.	Colonel	Staff—ING	Springfield	Surgeon general *War service*— Private Co C 57th Penn Volunteer Infantry 9/1861. 1st Sergeant 10/1861. 2nd Lieutenant 6/26/1862. POW 7/1862. Paroled and unfit for service 10/1862. Major in Union League Regiment for the protection of western Penn 7/1/1863 to 30 days.	5.9
Carter, Charles C.	Major	Staff—6th Infantry	Rock Island	Major and surgeon Corporal Co A 6th Infantry 11/30/1877. Sergeant 5/20/1881. 2d Lieutenant 8/2/1882. 1st Lieutenant 3/12/1883.	5.8
Hiltman, John W.	Captain	A—1st Cavalry	Chicago	Captain Private 5/20/1880. 1st Lieutenant 2/21/1880.	5.7
Cheney, Charles E.	Captain	Staff—2nd Infantry	Chicago	Captain and chaplain	5.7
Blanchard, Sidney R.	Captain	D—4th Infantry	Ottawa	Captain Private 8/6/1877. Sergeant 9/1/1877. 1st Sergeant 4/1879. 2nd Lieutenant 8/23/1880.	5.7
Skelly, George M.	Captain	Staff—5th Infantry	Springfield	Captain and inspector of rifle practice Private Co C, 5th Infantry 7/1875. QM 5th Infantry 2/9/1878.	5.7
Holtkamp, Henry	1st Lieutenant	I—3rd Infantry	Galena	First Lieutenant Private 7/26/1877. Sergeant 8/14/1877. 2nd Lieutenant 5/25/1879.	5.6
Chenoweth, Frederick W.	Captain	I—1st Infantry	Chicago	Captain Private Co C 1st Infantry 7/26/1877. Corporal 2/2/1882. Sergeant 11/14/1882. 1st Lieutenant Co I 1st Infantry 9/26/1884.	5.6

cont.

Name	Rank	Organization	Location	Military History	Yrs in Rank
Pierce, Frederick C.	Colonel	Governor's staff	Rockford	Colonel and aide-de-camp 1st Lieutenant Co H 3d Infantry 1/11/1883. Capt 8/4/1883.	5.6
McIntire, Arthur C.	Colonel	Governor's staff	Mendota	Colonel and aide-de-camp	5.6
Bogardus, Charles	Colonel	Governor's staff	Paxton	Colonel and aide-de-camp *War Service—* Private Co A 151st NY Volunteer Infantry 8/1862. 1st Lieutenant 151st NY Volunteer Infantry 8/13/1862. Capt Captain12/12/1862. Lieutenant Colonel 11/5/1864. Brevet Colonel for "gallant and Meritorious service before Petersburg, Virginia." to rank from 4/2/1865	5.6
Smith, Augustus B.	Colonel	Governor's staff	Lewistown	Colonel and aide-de-camp *War Service—* Captain Co K 103rd Ill Volunteer Infantry then AAIG 1st Div 15th Army Corps. Served 3 yrs.	5.6
Kohler, Hjalmar	Colonel	Governor's staff	Moline	Colonel and aide-de-camp *Swedish National Guard—* Instructing officer for 2 yrs.	5.6
Otey, Clinton	Colonel	Governor's staff	Harrisburg	Colonel 1st Lieutenant Co H 11th Infantry 5/13/1879. Captain10/25/1880. Transferred to Co G 9th Infantry 5/1882. Discharged 5/1/1885	5.6
Mulock, Michael B.	1st Lieutenant	A—3rd Infantry	Streator	First lieutenant Private 6/19/1878. 1st Sergeant 8/31/1880. 2nd Lieutenant 11/1/1882.	5.5
Saint Clair, Jacob N.	Captain	Staff—3rd Infantry	Streator	Captain Private 7/18/1877. 1st Lieutenant 11/1/1882. 2nd Lieutenant 10/6/1881.	5.5
Fash, Charles	3rd Lieutenant	Sherman Zouaves	Knoxville		5.4
Eads, Theodore	2nd Lieutenant	Sherman Zouaves	Knoxville		5.4
Wright, George O.	1st Lieutenant	Sherman Zouaves	Knoxville		5.4
Tate, Thomas B.	Captain	Sherman Zouaves	Knoxville		5.4

cont.

Appendix F

Name	Rank	Organization	Location	Military History	Yrs in Rank
Smith, William F.	Captain		Springfield	A. C. S.	5.4
Smailes, William	Colonel	Staff—3rd Infantry	Elgin	Lieutenant colonel Captain 8/1/1877. *War service*— Private Co A 36th Ill Volunteer Infantry.	5.4
Evans, Henry H.	Colonel	Regimental staff	Aurora	Aide-de-camp	5.4
Sheets, Benjamin F.	Colonel	Regimental staff	Oregon	Aide-de-camp	5.4
Barkley, James H.	Colonel	Regimental staff	Springfield		5.4
Hilliard, Hiram	Brigadier General	Com-in-chief staff	Springfield	Adjutant general	5.4
Barnum, James H.	2nd Lieutenant	E	Petersburg		5.3
Lawler, Thomas G.	Captain	B	Rockford		5.3
Smailes, William	Captain	E	Elgin		5.3
Elder, John	Captain	C	Carthage		5.3
Black, Thomas G.	Major		Clayton	Brigade surgeon	5.3
Hughes, I Simpson	Major	Staff	Springfield	Major and surgeon Major and surgeon 6th Infantry 8/27/1881	5.3
Meserve, Arthur G.	Major	Staff—4th Infantry	Robinson	Major and surgeon Captain and assist Surgeon 3/19/1883	5.3
Fort, William J.	Lieutenant. Colonel	Staff	Lacon	Lieutenant colonel and judge advocate Private Co H 7th Infantry 3/21/1878. Captain and inspector rifle practice 7th Infantry 8/1/1879. *War service*— On duty in QM dept as agent from 9/1/1862 to 10/1865	5.3
Wood, Benson	Colonel	Regimental staff	Effingham	Judge advocate general	5.3
Reid, David O.	Colonel	Regimental staff	Moline	Aide-de-camp	5.3
Munn, Sylvester W.	Colonel	Regimental staff	Joliet	Aide-de-camp	5.3
Edgar, William H.	Colonel	Regimental staff	Jerseyville	Aide-de-camp	5.3
Golden, Thomas J.	Colonel	Regimental staff	Marshall	Aide-de-camp	5.3

cont.

Name	Rank	Organization	Location	Military History	Yrs in Rank
Brazee, C. M.	Colonel	Regimental staff	Rockford		5.3
Moore, James H.		Regimental staff	Sycamore	Chaplain	5.3
Davis, Frank B.	Captain	C	Chicago		5.2
Reece, Jasper N.	General		Springfield		5.1
O'Conner, P. J.	Captain	B	Chicago		5
Quirk, Daniel	Captain	E	Chicago		5
Hawes, Charles W.	Captain	A	Rock Island		5
Dunne, William P.	Major	Regimental staff	Chicago	Surgeon	5
Mills, Charles F.	Lieutenant. Colonel		Springfield	A. A. G.	5

Source: Officer Rosters in *Biennial Report . . . 1873 and 1874* through *Biennial Report . . . 1889 and 1890*.

Appendix G

Illinois Volunteer Forces: Service beyond the United States, 1898–99

Regiment	Mustered In	Foreign Service	Arrival FC	U.S. Return	Mustered Out
1st	13 May, 1898	Cuba	9 July, 1898	29 August, 1898	17 November, 1898
2nd	16 May, 1898	Cuba	13 December, 1898	3 April, 1899	26 April, 1899
3rd	7–10 May, 1898	Puerto Rico	31 July, 1898	9 November, 1898	13–24 January, 1899
4th	19–20 May, 1898	Cuba	7 January, 1899	5 April, 1899	2 May, 1899
5th	4–9 May, 1898	None			16 October, 1898
6th	11 May, 1898	Puerto Rico	25 July, 1898	13 September, 1898	25 November, 1898
7th	18 May, 1898	None			20 October, 1898
8th	12–21 July, 1898	Cuba	16 August, 1898	15 March, 1899	3 April, 1899
9th	4–11 July, 1898	Cuba	5 January, 1899	21 April, 1899	20 May, 1899
1st Cavalry	20–21 May, 1898	None			11 October, 1898
Battery A	12 May, 1898	Puerto Rico	4 August, 1898	13 September, 1898	25 November, 1898

Source: *Adjutant General's Office, Statistical Exhibit of Strength of Volunteer Forces Called into Service during the War with Spain, with Losses from All Causes* (Washington: Government Printing Office, 1899). Reproduced on the U.S. Army Center of Military History, Historical Resources Branch Web Page, http://www.army.mil/cmh-pg/spanam/spanhtm.htm.

Appendix H

Illinois Volunteer Forces: Enlisted Losses while in Service, 1898–99

Reg't	Transferred	Discharged for Disability	Discharged by General Court Martial	Discharged by Order	Killed in Action	Died of Wounds Rec'd in Action	Died of Disease	Died of Accident	Drowned	Suicide	Murdered or Homicide	Deserted	Total Losses	Total on Muster Out Roll
1st	5	9	0	9	0	0	84	0	0	0	0	0	107	1292
2nd	86	70	1	163	0	0	22	0	0	0	0	2	344	1350
3rd	21	10	0	20	0	0	42	0	0	0	0	1	94	1317
4th	55	54	0	210	0	0	24	1	0	0	0	4	348	1308
5th	1	10	0	9	0	0	17	0	0	0	0	7	44	1256
6th	21	11	1	4	0	0	22	0	0	0	0	1	60	1284
7th	53	5	0	13	0	0	2	0	0	0	0	6	79	1339
8th	0	6	3	27	0	0	16	2	0	0	1	9	64	1244
9th	31	46	1	113	0	0	27	2	0	0	0	4	224	1095
1st Cav.	12	14	0	11	0	0	16	1	0	0	0	6	60	1218
Bat. A	0	4	0	3	0	0	2	0	0	0	0	0	9	173
Totals	285	239	6	582	0	0	274	6	0	0	1	40	1433	12,876

Source: Adjutant General's Office, *Statistical Exhibit of Strength of Volunteer Forces Called into Service during the War with Spain, with Losses from All Causes* (Washington: Government Printing Office, 1899). Reproduced on the U.S. Army Center of Military History, Historical Resources Branch Web Page, http://www.army.mil/CMH-PG/documents/spanam/ws-stat.htm. Accessed 3/21/05.

Appendix I

State and Federal Appropriations per Guardsman, by State, 1897

State	State Allocation	Federal Allocation	Present Aggregate Strength	$ per man
Alabama	$24,000.00	$9,488.73	2,552	$13.11
Arkansas	None	$6,99.90	961	$7.18
California	$111,800.00	$7,763.00	3836	$31.17
Colorado	$62,689.00	$3,450.45	890	$74.31
Connecticut	$140,000.00	$5,175.67	2,779	$52.24
Delaware	$3,000.00	$2,587.23	390	$14.33
Florida	$12,000.00	$3,450.45	1,088	$14.20
Georgia	$15,000.00	$11,213.96	3,193	$8.21
Idaho	$255.00	$2,587.83	594	$4.74
Illinois	$90,000.00	$20,702.70	6,288	$17.61
Indiana	$45,999.00	$12,939.19	2,821	$20.89
Iowa	$50,200.00	$11,213.96	2,441	$25.16
Kansas	$34,150.00	$8,626.12	1,506	$28.40
Kentucky	$7,000.00	$11,213.96	1,597	$11.41
Louisiana	$21,000.00	$6,900.00	1,994	$13.99
Maine	$32,447.83	$5,175.67	1,367	$27.52
Maryland	$45,000.00	$6,900.00	1,732	$29.97
Massachusetts	$264,000.00	$12,939.00	5,227	$52.98
Michigan	$73,286.11	$12,076.57	2,524	$33.82
Minnesota	$50,000.00	$7,763.51	1,935	$29.85
Mississippi	$4,400.00	$7,763.51	1,769	$6.88
Missouri	$10,000.00	$14,664.41	2,51?	$9.83
Montana	$22,400.00	$2,587.83	406	$61.54
Nebraska	$15,000.00	$6,900.90	1,199	$18.27
Nevada	None	$2,587.00	400	$6.47
New Hampshire	$30,000.00	$3,450.45	1,390	$24.07
New Jersey	$171,645.17	$8,626.12	4,258	$42.34
New York	$448,000.00	$31,054.05	13,242	$36.18
North Carolina	$6,000.00	$9,488.73	1,410	$10.98
North Dakota	$11,000.00	$2,587.83	530	$25.64
Ohio	$317,235.24	$19,840.00	6,229	$54.11
Oregon	$30,000.00	$3,450.45	1,540	$21.72
Pennsylvania	$350,000.00	$27,603.60	8,250	$40.92
Rhode Island	$67,074.20	$3,450.20	1,268	$55.62
South Carolina	$10,000.00	$7,763.51	3,530	$5.03
South Dakota	$300.00	$3,450.45	795	$4.72
Tennessee	$8,000.00	$10,351.35	2,379	$7.71
Texas	$5,000.00	$12,939.18	3,000	$5.98
Utah	$3,500.00	$2,587.83	974	$6.25
Vermont	$18,000.00	$3,450.45	800	$26.81
Virginia	$11,732.91	$10,351.35	3,006	$7.34
Washington	$20,000.00	$3,450.45	1,051	$22.31
West Virginia	$15,000.00	$3,175.67	892	$20.38
Wisconsin	$110,000.00	$10,351.35	2,620	$45.94
Wyoming	$5,000.00	$2,587.83	510	$14.88
Arizona	$300.00	$2,000.00	442	$5.20
District of Columbia	$27,525.00	$8,000.00	1,339	$26.53
New Mexico	$1,600.00	$3,000.00	429	$10.72
Oklahoma	None	$1,412.35	550	$2.57
....				
Alaska	—	—	—.	—
Total	$2,799,549.46	$400,000.00	112,082	

Source: Computed from *Proceedings of the First Annual Convention, Interstate National Guard Association*, 1897, Appendix.

Appendix J

Maps Showing Distribution of Illinois Militia Companies, by City, 1874 and 1876

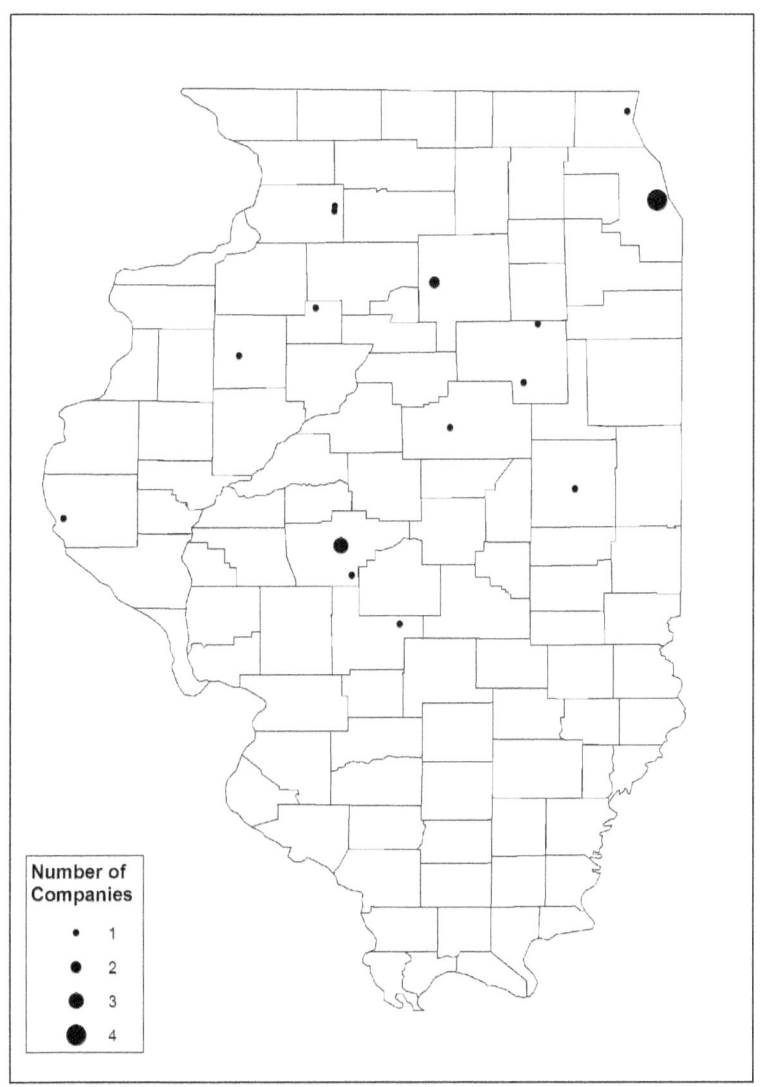

Figure J.1
1874 Distribution of State Militia Companies in Illinois by City
Source: *Biennial Report . . . 1813 and 1874; Biennial Report . . . 1875 and 1876.*

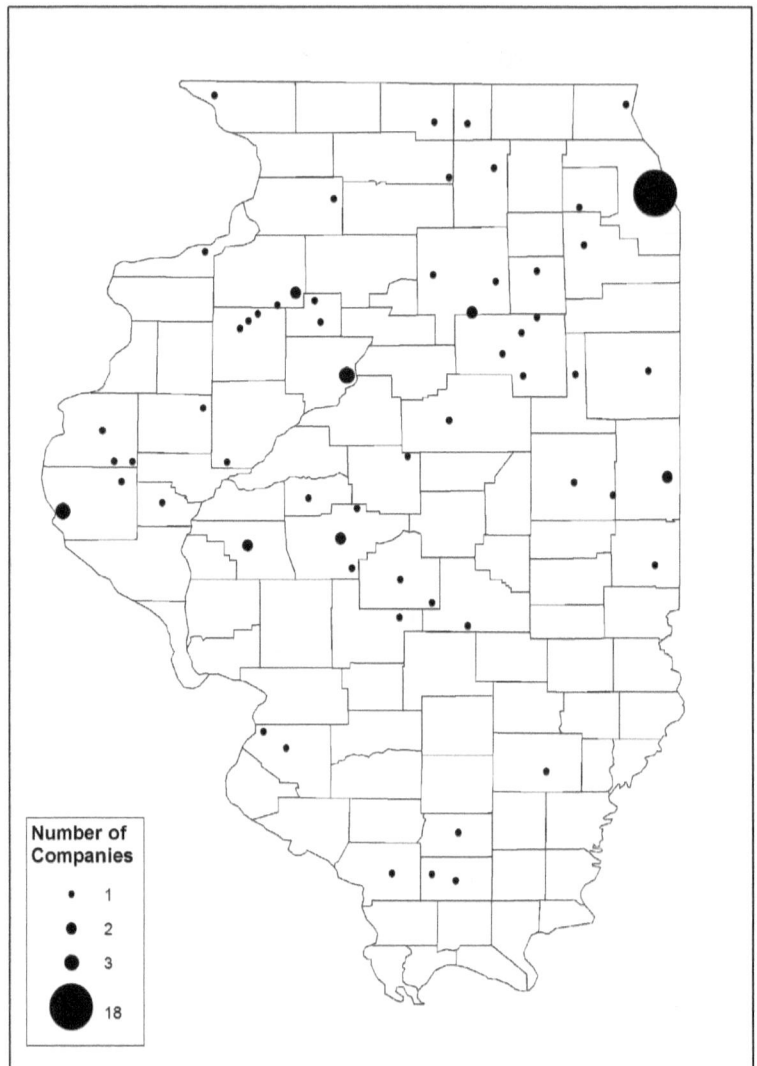

Figure J.2
1876 Distribution of State Militia Companies in Illinois by City
Source: *Biennial Report . . . 1813 and 1874; Biennial Report . . . 1875 and 1876.*

Notes

Notes to Introduction

1. Manhood and masculinity have come under increasing historical scrutiny in the last twenty years, yielding an outpouring of recent work that uses manhood and gender as one important element in understanding why men behaved the way the did at various times and places. One of the best early works is J. A. Mangan and James Walvin, eds., *Manliness and Morality: Middle-Class Masculinity in Britain and America, 1800–1940* (New York: St. Martin's Press, 1987). Two other important older studies are Mark C. Carnes, *Secret Ritual and Manhood in Victorian America* (New Haven, CT: Yale University Press, 1989), and Mary Ann Clawson, *Constructing Brotherhood Class, Gender and Fraternalism* (Princeton, NJ: Princeton University Press, 1989), both focusing on discussions of nineteenth-century American fraternalism. E. Anthony Rotundo, *American Manhood: Transformations in Masculinity from the Revolution to the Modern Era* (New York: Basic Books, 1993), and Michael Kimmell, *Manhood in America, A Cultural History* (New York: The Free Press, 1996), remain the most thorough surveys of the ways manhood was understood and expressed in the American past. More recently, scholars such as Gail Bederman, *Manliness and Civilization: A Cultural History of Gender and Race in the United States, 1880–1917* (Chicago: The University of Chicago Press, 1995); Kim Townsend, *Manhood at Harvard: William James and Others* (New York: W.W. Norton, 1996); Judy Hilkey, *Character Is Capital: Success Manuals and Manhood in Gilded Age America* (Chapel Hill: University of North Carolina Press, 1997); Kristin L. Hoganson, *Fighting for American Manhood: How Gender Politics Provoked the Spanish-American and Philippine-American Wars* (New Haven: Yale University Press, 1998); Amy S. Greenberg, *Cause for Alarm; The Volunteer Fire Department and the Nineteenth-Century City* (Princeton: Princeton University Press, 1998); and Clifford Putney, *Muscular Christianity: Manhood and Sports in Protestant America, 1880–1920* (Cambridge, MA: Harvard University Press, 2001), among others, have explored ways that the ideas and ideals of manhood were debated and framed during the chaotic times at the turn of the nineteenth century.

2. Some works that provide an overview of these issues are Mary P. Ryan, *Women in Public: Between Banners and Ballots, 1825–1880* (Baltimore: The

Johns Hopkins University Press, 1990; reprint, Johns Hopkins Paperbacks edition, 1992); Alan Trachtenberg, *The Incorporation of America: Culture and Society in the Gilded Age* (New York: Hill and Wang, 1982); Robert Wiebe, *The Search for Order, 1877–1920* (New York: Hill and Wang, 1967); Michael Schudson, *The Good Citizen: A History of American Civic Life* (Cambridge, MA: Harvard University Press, 1998). For the antebellum guard see Marcus Cunliffe, *Soldiers and Civilians: The Martial Spirit in America, 1775–1865* (Boston: Little, Brown and Company, 1968).

3. Jerry Cooper, *The Rise of the National Guard, the Evolution of the American Militia, 1865–1920* (Lincoln: University of Nebraska Press, 1997). Michael D. Doubler, *Civilian in Peace, Soldier in War* (Lawrence: University Press of Kansas, 2003), picks up on William Riker, *Soldiers of the States: The Role of the National Guard in American Democracy* (Washington, DC: Public Affairs Press, 1957; reprint, New York: Arno Press, 1979), 21–40 (page citations are to the reprint edition), to argue that there is a strong connection between strike duty and the resurgence of the National Guards in the late nineteenth century.

4. Gerald F. Linderman, *Embattled Courage: The Experience of Combat in the American Civil War* (New York: The Free Press, A Division of Macmillan, Inc., 1987); Gerald F. Linderman, *The Mirror of War: American Society and the Spanish American War* (Ann Arbor: University of Michigan Press, 1974). The classic expression of this in the 1890s is Stephen Crane, *The Red Badge of Courage* (1895).

5. David W. Blight, *Race and Reunion. The Civil War in American Memory* (The Belknap Press of Harvard University Press, 2001).

6. Ira Berlin et al., *Slaves No More: Three Essays on Emancipation and the Civil War* (New York: Cambridge University Press, 1992); Eric Foner, *A Short History of Reconstruction* (New York: Harper & Row, 1990).

7. Cooper, *Rise of the National Guard*, 70–72.

8. Cooper, *Rise of the National Guard*, 104; Willard B. Gatewood, Jr., *Black Americans and the White Man's Burden, 1898–1903* (Chicago: University of Illinois Press, 1975).

9. Cooper, *Rise of the National Guard*, 47–49. Between 1870 and 1899 the Pennsylvania militia served in nine strike situations, and between 1877 and 1899 the Ohio NG eight, and the New York NG, just six—in comparison to the ING's fifteen incidents of strike service.

10. Cooper, *Rise of the National Guard*, 49.

11. U.S. Const, Art 1, §8.

12. Militia Act of 1792, Second Congress, Session I. Chapter XXVIII, Passed May 2, 1792, providing for the authority of the President to call out the Militia.

13. Organization tables are the paper structure of company, regiment, division. That is the number of men and officers in each and their relation to each other.

14. U.S. Serial Set: House of Representatives 763 (46–2) 1936, 2–6.

15. Cooper, *Rise of the National Guard*.

16. See *Revised Statutes—Illinois 1874* (Springfield: Hurd, 1874), 1007–8; *Revised Statutes—Illinois 1882* (Springfield: Hurd, 1882), 1043–51; *Revised*

Statutes—Illinois 1889, (Springfield: Hurd, 1889), 1299–1307; *Revised Statutes—Illinois 1897* (Springfield: Hurd, 1897), 1525–1536; *Revised Statutes—Illinois 1899* (Springfield: Hurd, 1899), 1632–45; *Revised Statutes—Illinois 1905* (Springfield: Hurd,1905), 1918–42.

17. See Russell Weigley, *The History of the American Army* (New York: The Macmillan Company, 1967); Riker; John K. Mahon, *History of the Militia and the National Guard* (New York: The Free Press, 1983); John Shy, *A People Numerous and Armed: Reflections on the Military Struggle for American Independence*, Revised ed. (Ann Arbor: Ann Arbor Paperbacks, University of Michigan Press, 1990).

18. Mahon, 18. See also Weigley, ch. 1; Cunliffe; Riker.

19. Mahon, 110.

20. Cooper, *Rise of the National Guard*, 153–56.

21. Mahon uses "militia" until the 1870s and then uses the phrase "militia/national guard." Jim Dan Hill equates George Washington and other Revolutionary War generals with modern National Guard officers being inducted into national service. Hill also identifies the earliest volunteer companies, for example, New England's Minutemen with today's National Guard. See Jim Dan Hill, *The Minute Man in Peace and War: A History of the National Guard* (Harrisburg, PA: The Stackpole Company, 1964), 5, 11. Cooper uses "militia" until the post–Civil War period when he adopts "National Guard."

22. Weigley discusses recruitment and personnel supply throughout his volume on the American Army. See also Allan R. Millett and Peter Maslowski, *For the Common Defense: A Military History of the United States of America*, Revised and Expanded ed. (New York: The Free Press, 1994).

23. Cunliffe, ch. 6.

24. Kenneth M. Stampp, *America in 1857* (New York: Oxford University Press, 1990), 146.

25. Doubler, ch. 2; Cunliffe, chs. 6, 7; Susan G. Davis, *Parades and Power, Street Theater in Nineteenth-Century Philadelphia* (Philadelphia: Temple University Press, 1986; reprint, Berkeley: University of California Press, 1988), ch. 3 (page citations are to the reprint edition).

26. Hill, 99–121; Mahon, 108–11; Cooper, *Rise of the National Guard*, 34. See also Charles Johnson, *African American Soldiers in the National Guard: Recruitment and Deployment during Peacetime and War* (Westport, CT: Greenwood Press, 1992).

27. The two notable exceptions were New York and Connecticut, both of which had begun to rationalize their large state militia systems before the Civil War and continued development, albeit slowly, even during this period of slacking interest and enthusiasm. See Mahon, ch. 8; Cooper, *Rise of the National Guard*, 103–4.

28. Cooper, *Rise of the National Guard*, ch. 8; Doubler, ch. 4.

29. *Fourth Annual Report of the Adjutant General of Illinois. December 1872. Submitted to Governor John M. Palmer by Adjutant General J. Dilger, Dec. 31, 1872* (Springfield, IL: 1872); *Biennial Report of the Adjutant General of Illinois, Transmitted to the Governor and Commander-in-Chief. For 1873 and 1874* (Springfield, IL: 1874); *Biennial Report of the Adjutant General of Illinois to the*

Governor and Commander in Chief, 1879 and 1880 (Springfield, IL: Philips Bros, State Printers, 1880).

30. See Cunliffe and Davis.

31. *Biennial Report . . . 1873 and 1874* (Springfield, IL: 1874), 32.

32. *Biennial Report of the Adjutant General of Illinois, Transmitted to the Governor and Commander-in-Chief. For 1875 and 1876* (Springfield: D. W. Lusk, State Printer and Binder, 1877), 29–33.

33. *Biennial Report . . . 1875 and 1876*, 33–34.

34. Minute Book: Co. "I" 7th Inf., ING, Record Group 301.106, Illinois State Archives, 28.

35. W. T. Goode, *The Eighth Illinois* (Chicago: The Blakely Printing Company, 1899), 5.

36. *Fourth Annual Report . . . December 1872* (Springfield, IL: 1872), 1–2.

37. *The Chicago Tribune*, Monday 26 September 1881, 1. *The Chicago Tribune*, Tuesday, 27 September 1881, 9.

38. *Biennial Report . . . 1875 and 1876*, 23–43.

39. Descriptive List, Illinois National Guard, First Infantry, 1880–1904, Miscellaneous, RS 301.96, Illinois State Archives. (See appendix A.)

40. The majority of the membership were laborers, factory workers, or skilled tradesmen. A breakdown of all 463 members of Company A over the years between 1898 and 1916 demonstrates that at least in Dekalb, the soldier-citizen model continued to exert a strong hold on men across a range of working-class backgrounds. (See appendix B).

41. See twelve-issue run of *The Illinois Cavalryman*.

42. *Biennial Report of the Adjutant General of Illinois Transmitted to the Governor and Commander-in-Chief. For 1877 and 1878* (Springfield: Weber, Magie & Co., State Printers, 1878), 51–52. The Sixteenth Battalion included Companies A and B in Chicago, as well as the Clark County Guards of Marshall, and in October gained the Cumberland County Guards of Greenup. Evidence suggests these last two companies were not African American, as they are listed as "Independent," though under the Sixteenth Battalion's officers and staff, and in 1880 they are assigned with letter designations to the Seventeenth Battalion. There is no evidence to corroborate this one way or another, but based on the organization charts it appears that for technical purposes these two white, independent companies were subject to the orders of the black major of the Sixteenth Battalion, though it is extremely unlikely that attempt was made to place them under his command. See also Goode, ch. 1.

43. In 1892 most officers in all grades had served for three years or less in the current position. These patterns appear consistent over time; in 1882 the number of Captains with three, six, or nine years of service in the ING almost exactly matches the 1892 figures.

44. Thomas W. Scott, Adjutant General of Illinois, to Lieutenant Colonel E. M. Weaver, Chief, Division of Militia Affairs, Washington, DC, April 1, 1908, Document #111 April 3 1908, filed with Document #91, Box 45, Record Group 168.7, National Archives. Illinois actually had a low annual percentage of enlisted discharges (20 percent) and officer discharges (15 percent) relative to the rest of the State National Guard organizations: 23 out of

50 states reporting lost over 33 percent of their enlisted personnel each year. See the chart "Data Relative to Length of Service and Instruction of the Militia," Nov. 30, 1908, Document #91, Box 45, Division of Militia Affairs, Record Group 168.7, National Archives.

45. Mahon, 108–24.

46. See *Fourth Annual Report, 1872; Biennial Report . . . 1873 and 1874; Biennial Report . . . 1875 and 1876; Biennial Report . . . 1877 and 1878; Biennial Report . . . 1879 and 1880; Biennial Report of the Adjutant General of Illinois to the Governor and Commander-in-Chief. For 1881 and 1882* (Springfield: H.W. Rokker, State Printer and Binder, 1883); *Biennial Report of the Adjutant General of Illinois to the Governor and Commander-in-Chief. 1887 and 1888* (Springfield: Springfield Printing Co., State Printers, 1889); *Biennial Report of the Adjutant General of Illinois to the Governor and Commander-in-Chief. 1889 and 1890* (Springfield: H.W. Rokker, State Printer and Binder, 1891); *Biennial Report of the Adjutant General of Illinois to the Governor and Commander-in-Chief. 1891 and 1892* (Springfield: H.W. Rokker, State Printer and Binder, 1893); *Biennial Report of the Adjutant General of Illinois to the Governor and Commander-in-Chief. 1893 and 1894* (Springfield: Ed. F. Hartman, Printer and Binder, 1895); *Biennial Report of the Adjutant General of Illinois to the Governor and Commander-in-Chief. 1895 and 1896* (Springfield: Phillips Bros., State Printers, 1897); *Biennial Report of the Adjutant General of Illinois to the Governor and Commander-in-Chief. 1897–1898* (Springfield: Phillips Bros., State Printers, 1899); *Biennial Report of the Adjutant General of Illinois to the Governor and Commander-in-Chief. 1899–1900* (Springfield: Phillips Bros., State Printers, 1900); *Biennial Report of the Adjutant General of Illinois to the Governor and Commander-in-Chief. 1901–1902* (Springfield: Phillips Bros., State Printers, 1903); *Biennial Report of the Adjutant General of Illinois to the Governor and Commander-in-Chief. 1903–1904* (Springfield: Illinois State Journal Co., State Printers, 1904); *Biennial Report of the Adjutant General of Illinois to the Governor and Commander-in-Chief. 1905–1906* (Springfield: Phillips Bros., State Printers, 1907); *Biennial Report of the Adjutant General of Illinois to the Governor and Commander-in-Chief. 1907–1908* (Springfield: Illinois State Journal Co., State Printers, 1909); *Biennial Report of the Adjutant General of Illinois to the Governor and Commander-in-Chief. 1909–1910* (Springfield: Illinois State Journal Co., State Printers, 1914); *Biennial Report of the Adjutant General of Illinois to the Governor and Commander-in-Chief. 1911–1912* (Springfield: Illinois State Journal Co., State Printers, 1914); the reports on the *Militia Force of the United States* by the Adjutant General United States Army submitted to Congress and published in the Senate and House Executive Documents, Serial Sets; *Proceedings of the First Annual Convention. Interstate National Guard Association. Held at Planter's Hotel, St. Louis, Missouri, December 7–8, 1897* (St. Louis, Missouri: 1897), Appendix; "Allotment of Balance of unallotted funds ($84,451.00)," June 2, 1908, Document #25382, Box 140, Bureau of Militia Affairs, RG 168.7, National Archives; "Expenditures from the appropriation under section 1661, R.S., and from the $700,000.00 appropriation in Act approved June 12, 1906, for the participation of the Militia in Army Camps of Instruction, July to September, 1906," 1908, Bureau of Militia Affairs, RG 168.7, National Archives; "Data Relative to Length of Service and Instruction

of the Militia," Nov. 30, 1908, Document #91, Box 45, Bureau of Militia Affairs, RG 168.7, National Archives; "Tabulation Showing the Authorized Strength of the Organized Militia of the several States and Territories on January 21, 1903, and also the actual strength of the Same as Determined by the recent Special Inspections, the dates of completion of which range from the first of May to the last of June 1903," Oct. 17, 1903, Card # 506151, Box 27, Bureau of Militia Affairs, RG 168.4, National Archives; "untitled," July 24, 1909, Document #8801, Box 83, Bureau of Militia Affairs, RG 168.7, National Archives; "Balances, June 1, 1911, prior to allotment of unexpended balance," June 6, 1911, Document #25382, Box 140, Bureau of Militia Affairs, RG 168.7, National Archives; "List of Appropriations made by Various States and Territories for the Support of the Organized Militia," 1899[?], Near the back, with 1899 material, Box 23, Bureau of Militia Affairs, RG 168.2, National Archives; "Expenditures from the appropriation under section 1661, revised statutes, and from the appropriation: encampment and Maneuvers, Organized Militia, in connection with the joint maneuvers of Mobile troops during the calendar year 1908," 1908, Bureau of Militia Affairs, RG 168.7, National Archives.

47. *Fourth Annual Report, 1872; Biennial Report . . . 1873 and 1874; Biennial Report . . . 1875 and 1876; Biennial Report . . . 1877 and 1878; Biennial Report . . . 1879 and 1880; Biennial Report . . . 1881 and 1882; Biennial Report . . . 1887 and 1888; Biennial Report . . . 1889 and 1890; Biennial Report . . . 1891 and 1892; Biennial Report . . . 1893 and 1894; Biennial Report . . . 1895 and 1896; Biennial Report . . . 1897–1898; Biennial Report . . . 1899–1900.*

48. *Biennial Report . . . 1877 and 1878*, 1–12; *Biennial Report . . . 1881 and 1882*, 4–5; *Biennial Report . . . 1887 and 1888*, 3; *Proceedings of the Convention . . . 1879*, 8–11; *Proceedings of the Third Annual Convention of the National Guard Association of the United States, held at Philadelphia, March 7 and 8, 1881*, 3–7 (Copy bound with the proceedings of the first convention, in the possession of the NGAUS Library); *Proceedings of the First Annual Convention. Interstate National Guard Association. Held at Planter's Hotel, St. Louis, Missouri, December 7–8, 1897*, 10 (Bound typewritten copy of the minutes, bound in Vol. II [sic], held in the NGAUS Library, Washington, DC). See also the comments by Brigadier-General Milton Moore, "The National Guard as Part of the Military Forces of the United States," in *Proceedings, First, Fifth, and Sixth Conventions* (1898), 121; and Colonel E. R. Bliss, "Address of Welcome," in *Souvenir of the Banquet to the Interstate National Guard Association by the Illinois National Guard* (Chicago: R. R. Donnelley & Sons Company, 1899), 14.

49. See the following for examples of articles on strike interventions in which the neutrality of the guard is the central thesis: Andrew Birtle, "Governor George Hoadly's use of the Ohio National Guard in the Hocking Valley Coal Strike of 1884," *Ohio History* 91 (1982): 37–57; and Brian M. Linn, "Pretty Scaly Times: The Ohio National Guard and the Railroad Strike of 1877," *Ohio History* 94 (1984): 171–81. See also Cooper, *Rise of the National Guard*, ch. 3.

Notes to Chapter 1

1. *State Register*, 13 March 1875; *Daily State Journal*, 13 March 1875

2. See, for example, Bederman; Sarah Deutsch, *Women and the City, Gender, Space and Power in Boston, 1870–1940* (Oxford: Oxford University Press, 2000); Rebecca Edwards, *Angels in the Machinery: Gender in American Party Politics from the Civil War to the Progressive Era* (New York: Oxford University Press, 1997); Julie Saville, *The Work of Reconstruction: From Slave to Wage Laborer in South Carolina, 1860–1870* (New York: Cambridge, 1996); Evelyn Nakano Glenn, *Unequal Freedom: How Race and Gender Shaped American Citizenship and Labor* (Cambridge: Harvard University Press, 2002).

3. The literature on manhood was once limited to a discussion of literate, nineteenth-century men, these men having been responsible for producing the bulk of the writing on the issue, but recently scholars have tackled manhood in a variety of environments. See Greenberg; Madelon Powers, *Faces along the Bar; Lore and Order in the Workingmen's Saloon, 1870–1920* (Chicago: University of Chicago Press, 1998). See also, E. F. Parsons (2000), "Risky Business: The Uncertain Boundaries of Manhood in the Midwestern Saloon," *Journal of Social History* 34(2): 283–307; Paul Michael Taillon, "'What We Want is Good, Sober Men:' Masculinity, Respectability, and Temperance in the Railroad Brotherhoods, c. 1870–1910," *Journal of Social History* 36, no. 2 (2002): 319–38; Julia Grant, "A 'Real Boy' and not a Sissy: Gender, Childhood and Masculinity, 1890–1940," *Journal of Social History* 37, no. 4 (2004): 829–51; and Mike O'Brien, "Manhood and the Militia Myth: Masculinity, Class and Militarism in Ontario, 1902–1914," *Labour/Le Travail* 42, Fall 1998 (1998): 115–41; Matthew Conner, "Minstrel-Soldiers: The Construction of African-American Identity in the Union Army," *Prospects* 26 (2001): 109–36.

4. In *Citizen-Soldiers and Manly Warriors* (Rowman & Littlefield Publishers, Inc., 1999), R. Claire Snyder examines the theoretical and performative aspects of the identity of citizen-soldiers and the construction of "armed masculinity."

5. *Biennial Report . . . 1873 and 1874*, 29–30. The number of new members is actually greater than 1200, as between 1870 and 1874 at least four companies, representing about 200 men in total, disbanded, and so the 1874 figure includes the men who replaced those who left.

6. *Biennial Report . . . 1875 and 1876*, 2–6.

7. *Chicago Times*, 15 October 1874. A vote taken during the general convention of the Army of the Tennessee defeated a resolution to allow soldiers as well as officers into the society. *Daily State Journal*, 16 October 1874, *Illinois State Register*, 15 October 1874. The private military-styled companies of the fraternal organizations are examples of the types of private organization that did not seek affiliation with the state.

8. *Daily State Journal*, 16 October 1874, *Illinois State Register*, 15 October 1874.

9. *Daily State Journal*, 16 October 1874, *Illinois State Register*, 15 October 1874.

10. For antebellum militias, see Cunliffe, ch. 11; Davis, 66–72; and Ryan, *Women in Public*.

11. Jerry Cooper, *Rise of the National Guard*, ch. 2; Doubler, chs. 2, 3.

12. Davis, 66–72.

13. *Daily State Journal*, 16 October 1874.

14. *Illinois State Register*, 15 October 1874.

15. Chas. T. Headenburg, ed., *Souvenir History. Governor's Guard. Company C, Fifth Infantry, Illinois National Guard, 1866–1902* (Springfield: Journal Company, Printers, 1902), 15, 19.

16. *Daily State Journal*, 16 October 1874.

17. This expansion of the types of groups that were able to use the parade to seize or claim public and therefore political space is one of the main contentions of Ryan, *Women in Public*, 53–54.

18. *State Register*, 9–13 March 1875; *Daily State Journal*, 10–13 March 1875.

19. Ryan, *Women in Public*, 30–37.

20. *State Register*, 13 March 1875; *Daily State Journal*, 13 March 1875

21. *State Register*, 13 March 1875; *Daily State Journal*, 13 March 1875

22. *State Register*, 13 March 1875; *Daily State Journal*, 13 March 1875

23. This is not meant to discount the very real possibilities that the "Governor's Guard" might have been mostly made up of sons of "good" families. However, the speeches of both Emma Hickox and Governor Beveridge assume a common significance for militia membership that does not seem specific to this single company; rather, this company is a sterling example of a general principle.

24. Cunliffe, 230–35; Davis, 47; and Ryan, 31–35.

25. *State Register*, 13 March 1875; *Daily State Journal*, 13 March 1875.

26. John Alexander Logan. *The Volunteer Soldier of America. By John A. Logan. With Memoir of the author and Military reminiscences from General Logan's private journal* (Chicago and New York: R. S. Peale & Company, 1887).

27. *Biennial Report . . . 1873 and 1874* (Springfield: D.W. Lusk, State Printer and Binder, 1875), 28.

28. Cunliffe, 218–30.

29. Adjutant General of the United States Army, *Militia Force of the United States*, 43rd Congress, 1st sess., 1874, S. Exdoc. 41, Serial 1580, 2. *Biennial Report. . . . 1873 and 1874*, 28. Why Illinois officials failed to report these companies to Washington remains a mystery whose only solution seems to be that the Governor and his staff simply didn't think they were significant. Also, some companies never chose to seek affiliation with the state, preferring to remain purely private social organizations, albeit with military-styled uniforms, drills, and parades. See Henry Barrett Chamberlin, "A Sketch of the Oakland Rifles," in *Historical Sketch of the Oakland Rifles and Company "C," 4th Infantry I.N.G* (1889).

30. *Biennial Report . . . 1873 and 1874*, 28; *Fourth Annual Report . . . 1872*, 1–2.

31. *The Chicago Times*, Thursday, 25 February 1875, 3–4.

32. Cunliffe, 241–47. Also, recall the Zouaves from Atlanta in *Gone with*

the Wind by Margaret Mitchell. The year 1860 was also the year that Ellsworth came to the attention of Abraham Lincoln, accompanying him to Washington as a bodyguard and receiving a 2nd Lieutenant's commission in the professional army. Ellsworth was shot and killed just after the firing on Fort Sumter while attempting to remove a Confederate flag from a Washington, DC, hotel and was briefly immortalized as the Union's "First Martyr."

33. That the Zouave Cadets were remembered is in no doubt: "Chicago once sent out an independent company which beat the world. . . ." (*The Chicago Times*, Thursday, 29 July 1875), 5.

34. *Fourth Annual Report . . . 1872*, 3–4.

35. R. S. Bunzey, *History of Companies I and E, Sixth Regt., Illinois Volunteer Infantry from Whiteside County* (Morrison, IL: 1901), 22–23.

36. Holdridge O. Collins, *History of the Illinois National Guard, From the Organization of the First Regiment in September, 1874, to the Enactment of the Military Code in May, 1879* (Chicago: Black & Beach, 1884), 27–28.

37. Collins, 28; *Biennial Report . . . 1875 and 1876*.

38. Membership in the Illinois militia had fallen by the end of 1874 to around 850 men, but then this number more than doubled to over 2,000 during 1875 alone.

39. *Biennial Report . . . 1875 and 1876*, 12–20.

40. Critics insisted that the First Regiment was formed to oppose socialist demonstrations in Chicago and that the Bohemian Rifles were formed to oppose the First Regiment. This is both a Chicago-centric view and one that insists that militias served only overt class and political interests; it does not place these Chicago organizations within a broader statewide or national context. Richard Schneirov, *Labor and Urban Politics, Class Conflict and the Origins of Modern Liberalism in Chicago, 1864–97* (Chicago: University of Illinois Press, 1998), 59.

41. *The Chicago Times*, Thursday, 29 July 1875, 5.

42. *Biennial Report . . . 1875 and 1876*, General Order #3, 1875.

43. *The Chicago Times*, 5 July 1876.

44. *Biennial Report . . . 1875 and 1876*, 8–12, 28–35. Maxwell did feel that interest in the regiment would revive after the elections.

45. Schneirov, 59.

46. Schudson, 155–68.

47. *Biennial Report . . . 1873 and 1874*, 32.

48. This desire on the part of many men to tie themselves visibly to their communities can be viewed negatively as well as positively. Certainly in 1874 and 1875 members of the People's Party and other socialist groups in Chicago viewed the new First Regiment as little more than a creature of the Chicago Citizen's Association, calling it "the Businessmen's Militia." Schneirov, 59.

49. Henry L. Turner, *Souvenir Album and Sketch Book, First Infantry I.N.G. of Chicago* (Chicago: Knight & Leonard Company, 1890), 7.

50. Hubbard's father, Guerdon S. Hubbard, Sr., was one of the first traders to make a fortune during the early years of Chicago's history. See Guerdon Stonstall Hubbard, *The Autobiography of Guerdon Stonstall Hubbard. Pa-Pa-Ma-Ta-Be "The Swift Walker." With an Introduction by Caroline M. McIlvanie* (Chicago: The Lakeside Press, 1911).

51. Collins, 1–9.

52. *Biennial Report* . . . *1875 and 1876*, 12.

53. It is not clear where or when Sherman picked up his nominal rank of "General." He may be Francis T. Sherman, Major in the 12th IL USV Cavalry, and later Colonel of the 88th IL USV Infantry during the Civil War. There was also a Frank Sherman who was asked to lead a volunteer company gathered in the aftermath of the Chicago Fire in 1871. http://www.sos.state.il.us/departments/archives/databases.html. Accessed 3/21/05.

54. *The Chicago Times*, Thursday, 29 July 1875, 5.

55. Collins, 1–9.

56. *Harper's Weekly*, 21 August 1875, quoted in Collins, 19.

57. *The Chicago Times*, Thursday, 29 July 1875, 5.

58. Schneirov, *Labor and Urban Politics*, 59.

59. The Citizen's Association was specifically intended to oppose "the baser sort" and put "the best men" in power. See Schneirov, *Labor and Urban Politics*, 58; and Carl Smith, *Urban Disorder and the Shape of Belief. The Great Chicago Fire, the Haymarket Bomb, and the Model Town of Pullman* (Chicago: University of Chicago Press, 1995), 109.

60. Report of the Committee of the Chicago Citizens Association, quoted in Collins, 12.

61. Kimmel, ch. 4. See also Rotundo, ch. 10, and Elliot J. Gorn, *The Manly Art: Bare-Knuckle Prize Fighting in America* (Ithaca, NY: Cornell University Press; Reprint edition, 1989), ch. 3. See also Putney.

62. Report of the Committee of the Chicago Citizens Association, quoted in Collins, 12.

63. "Our Volunteer Troops," *Chicago Daily Tribune*, 20 December 1874, 8.

64. "Our Volunteer Troops," *Chicago Daily Tribune*, 20 December 1874, 8.

65. Collins, 18. These figures were presented to the regiment 29 May 1875.

66. *Biennial Report* . . . *1873 and 1874*, 28. The Ellsworth Zouaves charged $12.00 in annual dues in 1874, more than double any other company, which implies reasonably high resources on the part of the members.

67. Collins, 16–19.

68. Collins, 16–19; *Harper's Weekly*, 21 August 1875, quoted in Collins, 19.

69. *The Chicago Times*, Thursday, 29 July 1875, 5.

70. *The Chicago Times*, Thursday, 29 July 1875, 5.

71. Kimmel, ch. 4.

72. Cunliffe, chs. 7, 8; Kimmel, 81–89; Rotundo, 251–55; and Gorn, 138–49.

73. According to Schneirov, *Labor and Urban Politics*, 59, the Bohemian Rifles were formed in response to the First Regiment because the German socialists believed that the First Regiment had been formed for the sole purpose of intimidating their constituency. Whether or not this was their intent, the Bohemian Rifles were accepted into the state militia and, formally at least, were given the same support and encouragement as all the other new companies that entered the state militia in 1875 and 1876.

74. *Biennial Report*. . . . *1875 and 1876*, 33–34.

75. *Biennial Report* . . . *1875 and 1876*, 33–34.

76. Goode, Harry Stanton McCard, *History of the eighth Illinois United States Volunteers* (Chicago: E.F. Harman & Co., Publishers, 1899).

77. For a brief survey of the failures of Reconstruction and the consequent limitation of the rights of African Americans, see Eric Foner, *A Short History of Reconstruction* (New York: Harper & Row, 1990). For Illinois specifically, see Roberta Senechal, *The Sociogenesis of a Race Riot: Springfield Illinois, in 1908* (Chicago: University of Illinois Press, 1990); Felix L. Armfield, "Fire on the Prairies: The 1895 Spring Valley Race Riot," *Journal of Illinois History*, 2000, 3(3): 185–200; Caroline A. Waldron, "'Lynch Law Must Go!' Race, Citizenship and the Other in an American Coal Mining Town," *Journal of American Ethnic History*, 2000, 20(1): 50–77; Sundiata Keita Cha-Jua, "'A Warlike Demonstration': Legalism, Violent Self-Help, and Electoral Politics in Decatur, Illinois, 1894–1898," *Journal of Urban History*, 2000, 26(5): 591–629; Shirley J. Portwood, "'We Lifted Our Voices in Thunder Tones': African American Race Men and Race Women and Community Agency in Southern Illinois, 1895–1910," *Journal of Urban History*, 2000, 26(6): 740–58; Dennis B. Downey, "'A Many-Headed Monster': The 1903 Lynching of David Wyatt," *Journal of Illinois History*, 1999, 2(1): 2–16; Christopher K. Hays, "The African American Struggle for Equality and Justice in Cairo, Illinois, 1865–1900," *Illinois Historical Journal*, 1997, 90(4): 265–84; Anna R. Paddon and Sally Turner, "African Americans and the World's Colombian Exposition," *Illinois Historical Journal*, 1995, 88(1): 19–36.

78. In 1870 the state reported to the federal government that there was no active militia. By 1880 there were over 8,000 active members of the state militia—and thousands more had passed through in the intervening decade—the average member spending slightly less than three years in a militia company. *Fourth Annual Report; Biennial Report . . . 1873 and 1874; Biennial Report . . . 1879 and 1880*.

79. James M. McPherson, *Battle Cry of Freedom: The Civil War Era*, Oxford History of the United States, Vol. 6 (New York: Oxford University Press, 1988), 564. See Berlin et al. for ways in which Freedmen viewed their military service as a vital aspect of winning citizenship rights; also see Saville.

80. Goode, 5.

81. "Arms Furnished to a Colored Military Company," *The Chicago Tribune*, 24 July, 1869.

82. *Fourth Annual Report . . . 1872*, 1–2.

83. *Illinois State Register*, 15 Ocotber 1874.

84. Collins, 17. The Relief and Aid Society had a longstanding commitment toward the prevention of a creation of a welfare class, which resulted in a number of policies designed to judge those most fit to receive aid and deny it to any who did not meet their standards for being only temporarily distressed. For further information on the Relief and Aid Society see Karen Sawislak, "Smoldering City," *Chicago History* 17, nos. 3 and 4 (1988–89): 70.

85. *The Chicago Times*, Thursday, 25 February 1875, 3–4. The last company, the Hannibal Zouaves, was very likely the same as the Hannibal Guards, one of the first African American companies in Chicago. The only reason for saying this is the use of the name Hannibal, but this name was a very popular one for African American companies because of the famous North African

General Hannibal who challenged the Roman Empire. Also, because it was used in Chicago for an African American company, it is difficult to believe that any white company would have attempted to co-opt the name. The confusion would have been greater than any community would have sought to bear. This remains, of course, only speculation, and there is no conclusive evidence one way or another.

86. Goode, 5–6.

87. *Biennial Report* . . . *1873 and 1874*, 28; *The Chicago Tribune*, 20 December 1874.

88. *Biennial Report* . . . *1873 and 1874*, 35.

89. *Biennial Report* . . . *1875 and 1876*, 10; *Biennial Report* . . . *1877 and 1878*, 8; *Biennial Report* . . . *1879 and 1880*, 4–6; *Biennial Report* . . . *1881 and 1882*, 7; *Biennial Report* . . . *1887 and 1888*, 5.

90. U.S. Serial Set, H.misdoc. 191 (42–2) 1526, Statement from the Ordnance Department, dated 4/15/1872.

91. *Biennial Report* . . . *1873 and 1874*, 25–27.

92. U.S. Serial Set, S.exdoc. 22 pt 2 (45–2) 1780, 11. It is unclear what happened to the annual distributions which by 1878 were around $10,000 for Illinois; presumably the debt should have been closer to $45,000. There is a hint later on that instead of retiring the debt, from 1875 forward the Governor chose to request rifles for the rapidly growing state forces and leave off "paying" on the charges; see *The Chicago Times*, Thursday 29 July 1875, 5: "he [the Governor] secured for the regiment the newest and best arms known to modern warfare." The only place Governor Beveridge could have gotten the rifles was from the U.S. government, as he had no budget for a purchase of such magnitude for the militia.

93. Cooper, *Rise of the National Guard*, chs. 2, 3, 4.

94. See Cooper, *Rise of the National Guard*; and Jerry Cooper with Glen Smith, *Citizens as Soldiers: A History of the North Dakota National Guard* (Fargo: The North Dakota Institute for Regional Studies, North Dakota State University, 1986), in which he demonstrates that this was true across the nation.

95. *Biennial Report* . . . *1873 and 1874*, 28, 31.

96. *Biennial Report* . . . *1873 and 1874*, 31.

97. *Biennial Report* . . . *1875 and 1876*, 23–43.

98. *Biennial Report* . . . *1875 and 1876*, 29–33.

99. Collins, 30.

100. *Biennial Report* . . . *1875 and 1876*, 2–6.

101. William Barney, *The Passage of the Republic: An Interdisciplinary History of Nineteenth-Century America* (Lexington: D.C. Heath and Company, 1987), ch. 8.

102. Cooper, 28–29.

Notes to Chapter 2

1. *Biennial Report* . . . *1893 and 1894*, iv.

2. Turner, 5.

3. See Descriptive List, Illinois National Guard, First Infantry, 1880–1904, Miscellaneous, RS 301.96, Illinois State Archives. See appendix A.

4. "The Citizen Soldiery," *National Guardsman: A Journal Devoted to the Interests of the National Guard of the U.S.*, 1, no. 1 (August 1, 1877): 1.
5. Turner, 5.
6. Greenberg, 163–65.
7. Quoted in Cooper, *Rise of the National Guard*, 76.
8. Minute Book: Company "I" 7th Inf., ING, Record Group 301.106, Illinois State Archives, 22–23.
9. Minute Book, Company "I," 26.
10. Minute Book, Company "I," 28.
11. Minute Book, Company "I," 29–30.
12. Minute Book, Company "I," 30–34.
13. Minute Book, Company "I," 36–41. The "masked ball" did not earn any money for the company, probably as a result of the rental fee for the masks—"from the lady in Peoria."
14. Minute Book, Company "I," 39.
15. Minute Book, Company "I," 40–47.
16. Minute Book, Company "I."
17. Bunzey, 29.
18. *Biennial Report . . . 1887 and 1888*; see Orders and Circulars.
19. Cooper, *Rise of the National Guard*, 39.
20. Bunzey, 13, 355–56.
21. Minute Book, Company "I," 50.
22. Minute Book, Company "I," 51.
23. Minute Book, Company "I," 51–55.
24. Minute Book, Company "I," 55–56.
25. Minute Book, Company "I," 55–57.
26. Minute Book, Company "I," 57–58.
27. Minute Book, Company "I," 66–68.
28. Minute Book, Company "I," 69.
29. Minute Book, Company "I," 83.
30. See Minute Book, Company "I." The minute book is not clear on this point, but it is an obvious explanation for the rise and fall of this company.
31. *Biennial Report . . . 1881 and 1882*, 28. The ING was radically downsized in 1882, but Company I, seemingly going well until the cancellation of "True Blue," left the ING in 1881. Again the loss of the first Captain is probably the best explanation.
32. For example, see "Militia Notes" column in *The Chicago Tribune*, 5 July 1880, 8; Newspaper photo, header "When Cavalry officers gave tea for Mrs. Tanner and Friends at Camp Lincoln" in "the Family Album," clipping in the Camp Lincoln Vertical File, Sangamon Valley Collection, Lincoln Library, 325 South 7th Street, Springfield, IL; Newspaper photo, header "Sunday Visitors at Old Camp Lincoln, about 1901," clipping in the Camp Lincoln Vertical File, Sangamon Valley Collection; Newspaper clipping dated "1896" (and headlining Governor Altgeld) from a scrapbook in the Camp Lincoln Vertical File, Sangamon Valley Collection; newspaper clipping dated "around 1901" (and headlining Sunday Visitors) from a scrapbook in the Camp Lincoln Vertical File, Sangamon Valley Collection.
33. Headenburg, 27.

34. Headenburg, 27.
35. Turner, 73.
36. Turner, 60.
37. Horace W. Bolton, *History of the Second Regiment, Illinois Volunteer Infantry from Organization to Muster Out* (Chicago: R.R. Donnelley & Sons Company, 1899), 22.
38. *Inter Ocean*, 7 July 1875.
39. See Minute Book: Company "I," 39–48, April and May 1877 entries.
40. *Inter Ocean*, 20 May 1879.
41. *Chicago Daily Tribune*, 15 February 1884; 21 October 1892.
42. Chamberlin, 19.
43. Minute Book, Company "D" 7th Infantry, ING ("The Washington Guards"), RG 301.105, Illinois State Archives, minutes of 5 June 1877.
44. Minute Book, Company "D," minutes of 31 July 1877.
45. Minute Book, Company "D," minutes of 21 May 1879.
46. "Military Ball," *The Chicago Tribune*, 15 February 1884, 8.
47. "A Swell Affair," *Aurora Evening Post*, 7 March 1894, 1; "It Was a Gala Night," *Aurora Daily Beacon*, 7 March 1894, 1.
48. Chamberlin, 23.
49. Chamberlin, 23.
50. Chamberlin, 23.
51. Turner, 155.
52. Turner, 157
53. Chamberlin, 19.
54. Turner, 66.
55. Chamberlin, 23.
56. Turner, 66. It turned out that the company took in $165.00 at the ball but spent $875.00.
57. "To Soldier Guests," *Chicago Daily Tribune*, 21 October 1892, 1.
58. *New York Times*, 21 October 1892.
59. *Chicago Daily Tribune*, 21 October 1892, 2.
60. *Illinois State Journal*, 17 July 1898.
61. Chamberlin, 29; Headenburg, 35.
62. Headenburg, 35.
63. Headenburg, 35.
64. *Chicago Defender*, 17 October 1914
65. *Chicago Defender*, 26 December 1914
66. John R. Skinner, *History of the Fourth Illinois Volunteers in their relation to the Spanish-American War for the Liberation of Cuba and other Island Possessions of Spain* (Logansport, IN: Press of Wilson, Humphreys & Co., 1899), 378–79.
67. Skinner, 380–81.
68. Skinner, 384.
69. Davis, 66–72. Davis argued that volunteer military companies filled with men of "good families" marching in antebellum Philadelphia parades of the 1820s and 1830s defined an elite form of patriotism and patriotic display and simultaneously constituted themselves as patriotism's chief interpreters. Davis also argues that militia company performances at ceremonial tasks were

their most significant activity. While this may have been true for antebellum Philadelphia volunteer companies, it is not the contention of this chapter.

70. Davis, 66–72.

71. Davis offers a scale to evaluate parades from "respectable" to "rowdy"— generally meaning "organized" to "spontaneous," though of course in practice there was much bleeding from one end to the other and most parades ended up somewhere in between. Also, both Davis and Ryan, *Women in Public*, note the connection between the creation of new public ceremonial moments, both unique and those destined to become traditional, and the commemoration or identification of historic moments in the history of the young republic. Davis, 19; Ryan, ch. 1. See also Schudson, 155–68.

72. Cunliffe, ch. 7. Ryan, *Women in Public*, ch. 1.

73. *The Chicago Tribune*, Tuesday 27 September 1881, 9. Roy Turnbaugh, "Ethnicity, Civic Pride, and Commitment: The Evolution of the Chicago Militia," *Journal of the Illinois State Historical Society* 72, no. 2 (1979): 111–27.

74. Ryan, *Women in Public*, ch. 1; see also Mary Ryan, "The American Parade: Representations of the Nineteenth-Century Social Order," in *The New Cultural History*, ed. Lynn Hunt (Berkeley: University of California Press, 1989), 131–53.

75. See Ryan, ch. 5; Cunliffe, ch. 7.

76. *The Chicago Tribune*, Monday, 5 July 1880, 8.

77. *Chicago Daily Tribune*, Wednesday, 5 July 1882, 1–2.

78. *The Chicago Tribune*, Thursday, 5 July 1883, 2.

79. Bunzey, 42, 44.

80. *Grand Rapids Daily Democrat*, 5 July 1885, quoted in Headenburg, 27.

81. John F. Kutlowski and Kathleen Smith Kutlowski, "Commissions and Canvasses: The Militia and Politics in Western New York, 1800–1845," *New York History* 63, Spring (1982): 5–38.

82. See John Whiteclay Chambers II and G. Kurt Piehler, *Major Problems in American Military History* (Houghton Mifflin, 1999), ch. 5. For example, a "General Frank T. Sherman" was involved with the First Infantry in Illinois, but the only Frank T. Sherman from Illinois who served in the Civil War finished out his service in the rank of Colonel. http://www.sos.state.il.us/departments/archives/databases.html. Accessed 3/21/05.

83. Turner, 8.

84. Charles Diehl to Fred W. Bleike, Nov. 3, 1927, Folder 1, Charles Diehl Collection, Chicago Historical Society.

85. Turner, 8; Collins, 18–19.

86. Collins, 16–19; *Harper's Weekly* 21 August 1875, quoted in Collins, 19.

87. Edward M. Coffman, *The Old Army: A Portrait of the American Army in Peacetime, 1784–1898* (New York: Oxford University Press, 1986).

88. Headenburg, 15, 19.

89. Headenburg, 19, 23, 27.

90. Headenburg, 23; *Biennial Report . . . 1877 and 1878*, 111. According to the report of E. N. Bates, Brig. Gen. Commanding Second Brigade, ING, the Springfield companies were in service only five days, July 27–July 31, in East St. Louis.

91. McCard, 82.

92. *Biennial Report* . . . *1877 and 1878*, 51–52.

93. *Biennial Report* . . . *1891 and 1892*, 24, 35. It is difficult to completely track developments. Major Scott of the Sixteenth resigned September 23, 1881, but no company of the Sixteenth is on the disbanded list, and the officers are not otherwise listed as resigning. However, the commissioning of Alexander Brown of the Chicago Light Infantry (Colored) which took place on July 12, 1882, is not mentioned in the 1881–82 report either. *Biennial Report* . . . *1885 and 1886*, 95.

94. "The Sixteenth Battalion," *Chicago Daily Tribune*, 14 November 1881, 9; "The Colored Militia," *Chicago Daily Tribune*, 25 April 1882, 8; 1 May 1882, 10; 4 May 1882, 2, 8.

95. *Biennial Report* . . . *1885 and 1886*, 95.

96. *Biennial Report of the Adjutant General of Illinois to the Governor and Commander-in-Chief. For 1883 and 1884* (Springfield: H.W. Rokker, State Printer and Binder, 1884), 55. It is unclear why it did not make the 1882 or July 1883 rosters, because the company officers' commissions date from July 1882.

97. Goode, 6. It is not known when or why the McLean County organization folded or the Springfield Company lost steam. However, the records of all companies in the state forces suggest that African American companies must have suffered from the same difficulties of financing, enthusiasm, and membership problems that plagued most companies across the state.

98. The state always had long lists of companies seeking a place in the ING, and they were granted places whenever an older company was mustered out of an existing regiment—something that happened quite frequently. Obviously the state military authorities had no intention of similarly substituting a black company into the ranks, though such a case did exist in Massachusetts. Johnson, 31. Company L of the Sixth Massachusetts Infantry was African American, though the rest of the regiment was white. The regiment was mobilized with Company L in 1898. Company L joined the 6th in 1878.

99. "Ninth Battalion Mustered In," *Chicago Daily Tribune*, 23 August 1890, 3.

100. *The Guardsman* seems to have been a locally published journal for National Guard members in Illinois. No extant issues have been located. Chamberlin appears to have been white, as was George W. Bristol, later a Captain with the 1st Infantry ING, who succeeded him as an instructor and teacher with the 9th Battalion. Goode, 13–17. The 1st Regiment was the wealthiest and most socially prestigious regiment in Chicago and, perhaps, in the ING. Their support for the African American guard organization, while probably not crucial, set the tone for how other whites, within and without the ING, would view the efforts of the 9th Battalion to enter the ING.

101. Goode, 25.

102. "Colored Men Get into the I.N.G.," *Chicago Daily Tribune*, 15 September 1895.

103. Goode, 7, 13–17.

104. *Biennial Report* . . . *1895 and 1896*, 155–56.

105. *Biennial Report* . . . *1895 and 1896*, 139.

106. Under Illinois state law, no groups beyond the state militia could march publicly in uniform with weapons unless they had specific permission to do so granted by the Governor.

107. St. Clair Drake and Horace R. Cayton, *Black Metropolis; a Study of Negro Life in a Northern City,* 1962 ed., vol. 1 (New York: Harper & Row, Publishers), 8, 46–57. For population figures see *The Statistics of the Population of the United States . . . Compiled, from the Original Returns of the Ninth Census (June 1, 1870)* (Washington, DC: GPO, 1872), 24; *Statistics of the Population of the United States at the Tenth Census (June 1, 1880)* (Washington, DC: GPO, 1883), 3; *Report of the Population of the United States at the Eleventh Census: 1890* (Washington, DC: GPO 1895), xcviii; *Twelfth Census of the United States, Taken in the Year 1900: Population* (Washington, DC: United States Census Office, 1901), cxv.

108. *Chicago Daily Tribune,* 10, 11, 12, 15, 16, 18, 19 July 1896; 9, 10, 11, 12, 15, 16, 17, July 1897.

109. See "Report of Captain Eben Swift, U.S. Army to the War Department, Washington, D.C., A Statement of the Condition of the Illinois National Guard in 1897," in *Biennial Report . . . 1897 and 1898,* 47–63; and the "Statement of Governor John R. Tanner concerning the Court Martial Report of Major John C. Buckner, 9 November 1897," in *Biennial Report . . . 1897 and 1898,* 762.

110. "Photograph, Random set of men from the First Division of Illinois National Guard; Chicago (Ill.), " ca. 1895, Photographer—D. H. Spencer, ICHi-26577, Chicago Historical Society, Prints & Photographs Department, 1601 N. Clark Street, Chicago, IL.

111. Goode, 13.

112. For example, the Chicago papers referred to African Americans, in association with their ING organizations, as "ladies and gentlemen." *Inter Ocean,* 20 May 1879.

113. Ryan, *Women in Public,* 64–68; Ryan, "The American Parade," 131–53.

114. See Berlin, 230–33; Saville, 172.

115. "Their Night to Celebrate," *Chicago Daily Tribune,* 31 March 1887; "Thirty Years of Freedom Program," *Chicago Daily Tribune,* 26 April 1896.

116. Davis, 66–72.

117. *The New York Times,* Saturday, 24 September 1881, 1.

118. *The New York Times,* Monday, 26 September 1881, 1.

119. *The Chicago Tribune,* Monday, 26 September 1881, 1.

120. *The New York Times,* Sunday, 25 September 1881, 1.

121. *The New York Times,* Thursday, 22 September 1881, 5.

122. *The Chicago Tribune,* Tuesday, 27 September 1881, 9.

123. *The Chicago Tribune,* Tuesday, 27 September 1881, 9.

124. *The Chicago Tribune,* Tuesday, 27 September 1881, 9. If the reporter's guess was correct, between 600 and 800 veterans marched beside the militia. As President Garfield had been a Mason, in Chicago the Masons were given the honor of escorting the catafalque, or funeral car. The other four divisions of the Chicago procession consisted of the Odd-Fellows (the 3rd); the Knights of Pythias (the 4th); city officials, including companies of police, firemen, and post office employees (the 5th); and various civil and ethnic societies, totaling some 9,100 (the 6th).

125. *The Chicago Tribune*, Tuesday, 27 September 1881, 4, 9.

126. *The Chicago Tribune*, Tuesday, 27 September 1881, 4. The boosterism, while pardonable, hardly gives credit to the nine divisions that marched in the funeral cortege in Cleveland. See *The Chicago Tribune*, Monday, 26 September 1881, 1.

127. Ryan, *Women in Public*, 53–54.

128. For other organizations with a wide range of members, see Carnes; Clawson; Taillon.

129. Memorial Day was initially the product of southern women who took a day in the spring when the local flower season was at its peak to decorate the graves of the men who died in the Civil War. In the north the idea was taken up by the various veteran associations as they honored fallen comrades. Matthew Dennis, *Red, White, and Blue Letter Days: An American Calendar* (Ithaca: Cornell University Press, 2002), ch. 5.

130. *The Chicago Tribune*, Thursday, May 31, 1883.

131. "Flowers for Heroes," *Chicago Daily Tribune*, 27 May 1894, 7; "In a Memorial Pageant," Chicago Daily Tribune, 1 June 1897, 7.

132. Headenburg, 31.

133. Chamberlin, 11–25. The Oakland Rifles were an unaffiliated, private military company that worked as a feeder group to Company C, Fourth Infantry, providing them a pool of potential members and a large supply of active supporters.

134. Headenburg, 23

135. See Ryan, *Women in Public*, 42–43. See also John Bodnar, *Remaking America: Public Memory, Commemoration, and Patriotism in the Twentieth Century* (Princeton, NJ: Princeton University Press, 1993); and David Waldestreicher, *In the Midst of Perpetual Fetes: The Making of American Nationalism, 1776–1820* (Chapel Hill: University of North Carolina Press, 1997).

136. See chapter 7 of this book for a detailed history of the struggles for public funding by the ING.

137. The literature on these subjects is vast; however, there are good general synthesis works. See, for example, Ava Baron, *Work Engendered: Toward a New History of American Labor* (Ithaca: Cornell University Press, 1991); Ann Douglas, *The Feminization of American Culture* (New York: Knopf, 1977); T. Jackson Lears, *No Place of Grace: Anti-Modernism and the Transformation of American Culture* (New York: Pantheon Books, 1981); David Montgomery, *The Fall of the House of Labor: The Workplace, the State, and American Labor Activism, 1865–1925* (Cambridge University Press, 1987); Roy Rosenzweig, *Eight Hours for What We Will: Workers and Leisure in an Industrial City, 1870–1920* (New York: Cambridge University Press, 1983); Trachtenberg; Wiebe.

138. Schneirov, *Labor and Urban Politics*, 59.

139. Bunzey, 39–41.

Notes to Chapter 3

1. Bunzey, 357.
2. Cooper, *The Rise of the National Guard*, 44; Doubler, 95–96.
3. Montgomery.
4. Cooper, 49.
5. Riker; Schneirov, *Labor and Urban Politics*, 59, reaches a similar conclusion but via a different route, noting the rise of a "business man's militia" in Chicago just before the push to write a new militia bill and assuming causation from the coincidence of timing.
6. One example can be found in William Leach, *Land of Desire: Merchants, Power, and the Rise of a New American Culture* (New York: Pantheon, 1993), 58. "It was here that the greatest midwestern department stores bestrided the city's center and that Marshall Field periodically called out the National Guard to crush the unions." Marshall Field was indeed a powerful figure in Chicago, and one who supported the wealthy and fashionable First Regiment—though apparently neither of the other two regiments in town nor the African American companies. But he never "called out" the ING because he had no authority to do so. Only the governor at the request of the Mayor of Chicago or the Sheriff of Cook County could call out the ING for any purpose in Illinois, and the bulk of ING strike service actually took place far outside of Cook County anyway, in places where Marshall Field had little or no authority. Also, the ING was never once ordered to "crush the unions"; nor were any unions crushed. While Leach's hyperbole about the powers of Marshall Field is a little over the top, similar sentiments about the nature of the National Guards as an organization totally responsive to elite control are fairly widely held. See also Smith, Philip S. Foner, *The Great Labor Uprising of 1877* (New York: Monad Press, 1977), conclusion; Riker, ch. 4; Trachtenberg, ch. 3; Eugene E. Leach, "The Literature of Riot Duty: Managing Class Conflict In the Streets," *Radical History Review* 56 (1993): 23–50.
7. For histories of the militias see Cooper, *Rise of the National Guard*; Doubler; Martha Derthick, *The National Guard in Politics* (Cambridge, MA: Harvard University Press, 1965); Mahon; Hill. Many labor historians have alluded to the rise of militias and National Guards in the late nineteenth century, but few have focused on it, taking the connection between strikes and the formation of National Guard units as a given rather than a debatable proposition. See, for example, Schneirov, *Labor and Urban Politics*, and Schneirov et al. Older books that assume a direct relationship between industry and the National Guards include Bruce; Jeremy Brecher, *Strike!* (San Francisco: Straight Arrow Books, 1972); Philip Foner; and Samuel Yellen, *American Labor Struggles* (New York: S. A. Russell, 1956).
8. *Biennial Report . . . 1893 and 1894*, Section VI.
9. Disagreements could, of course, reach further than state v. county or city. In 1894 President Cleveland intervened and sent federal troops into Chicago, a move that infuriated both the mayor of the city and Governor John P. Altgeld, neither of whom felt that the situation warranted the presence of state troops, let alone the U.S. Army. See *Biennial Report . . . 1893 and 1894*, xl–xliv.

10. David Montgomery, "Strikes in Nineteenth-Century America," *Social Science History* 4, no. 1 (1980): 81–104; Robert Rienders, "Militia and Public Order in Nineteenth-Century America," *American Studies (Great Britain)* 11, no. 1 (1977): 81–101.

11. The classic example of pro-corporate behavior by the National Guards is during the Colorado mine strike in 1914. Colorado National Guard troops fired into a tent city constructed by striking miners and killed at least two women and eleven children. The Colorado National Guard troops had a history of close support for mine owners and operators, and they were condemned by National Guardsmen in other states for their actions. There is also strong evidence to suggest that these particular Colorado National Guardsmen were one and the same men hired by the mine operators as private guards, reformed into a CNG regiment in order to shift the cost onto the shoulders of Colorado taxpayers. See articles in the *National Guard Magazine* for May, June, and July 1914. See also Cooper, 149–50. In Montgomery, *Fall of the House of Labor*, 343–47, this is the only episode in his entire book in which he mentions the National Guards at all; otherwise they are entirely absent from his story—leaving the impression that this was a representative rather than an aberrant National Guard.

12. Schneirov, *Labor and Urban Politics*, 59; Smith, 104–5.

13. The Relief and Aid Society had a longstanding commitment to the prevention of a creation of a welfare class, which resulted in a number of policies designed to judge those most fit to receive aid and deny it to any who did not meet their standards for being only temporarily distressed. See Schneirov, *Labor and Urban Politics*; and Smith, 104. For further information on the Relief and Aid Society see Karen Sawislak, *Smoldering City: Chicagoans and the Great Fire, 1871–1874* (Chicago: University of Chicago Press, 1996).

14. *The Chicago Times*, Thursday, 25 February 1875, 3–4.

15. Collins, 17.

16. Schneirov, *Labor and Urban Politics*, 59; Collins, 17.

17. *The Chicago Times*, Thursday, 25 February 1875, 3–4; Collins, 17.

18. *The Chicago Times*, Thursday, 25 February 1875, 3–4.

19. *The Chicago Times*, Thursday, 29 July 1875, 5.

20. Collins, 17; *The Chicago Times*, Thursday, 29 July 1875, 5. Notice that Collins fails to suggest that any credit should belong equally to all the companies that mobilized for action.

21. For more recent studies of the 1877 strikes see Brian P. Luskey, "Riot and Respectability"; David O. Stowell, *Streets, Railroads, and the Great Strike of 1877* (Chicago: University of Chicago Press, 1999). For material specifically on Chicago in 1877 see Schneirov, *Labor and Urban Politics*, and Smith. Montgomery, *Fall of the House of Labor*, does not discuss the 1877 strikes in particular but does give some general reference material for national conditions for labor and capital in the 1870s and 1880s relevant for situating the events of 1877.

22. Railroad strikers were generally very careful to keep passenger trains running as long as they could, as they did not want to jeopardize their generally favorable public support on the issue of the family wage. See Bruce; Montgomery; Philip Foner.

23. Bruce, chs. 7, 8.
24. Schneirov, *Labor and Urban Politics*, 69–76; Smith, 106–11. See also Bruce, chs. 7–11. Brecher, ch. 1.
25. Schneirov, *Labor and Urban Politics*, 69–76; Smith, 106–11. See also Bruce, ch. 12. Bruce indicated his opinion about the changing tenor of the labor movements as the strikes spread across the country and from railroad line to railroad line by titling his chapter on the events in Chicago and St. Louis "Marxists and the Mob."
26. Collins, 64.
27. Schneirov, *Labor and Urban Politics*, 69–76; Smith, 106–11. See also Bruce, ch. 12.
28. Collins, 64.
29. Schneirov, *Labor and Urban Politics*, 69–76; Smith, 106–11; Bruce, 191–93.
30. Bessie Louise Pierce, *A History of Chicago. Vol. III, The Rise of a Modern City, 1871–1893* (New York: Alfred A Knopf, 1957), 346, 351. Pierce reflects a relentlessly pro-Republican view onto the political history of Chicago and regards Heath as one of the best progressive mayors.
31. *Biennial Report . . . 1877 and 1878*, 103.
32. *Biennial Report . . . 1877 and 1878*, 104.
33. *Biennial Report . . . 1877 and 1878*, 103. The companies were later disbanded and mustered out of state service.
34. Bruce, 242; Schneirov, *Labor and Urban Politics*, 69–76; Smith, 106–11.
35. Schneirov, *Labor and Urban Politics*, 69–76; Smith, 106–11. See also Bruce, ch. 12.
36. *Biennial Report . . . 1877 and 1878*, 106
37. *Biennial Report . . . 1877 and 1878*, 105–7.
38. Bruce, 251; Collins, 69; Schneirov, *Labor and Urban Politics*, 69–76; Smith, 106–11. General Ducat's report does not mention the volleys fired by the Second Regiment. The historian of the Second Regiment, Horace Bolton, recorded only that it "was called out to aid in repressing 'The Railroad Riots,' when their dash and coolness in dispersing the armed and desperate crowds which terrorized the city, fully established its reputation as an efficient and valuable organization." Bolton, 14.
39. *Biennial Report . . . 1877 and 1878*, 108.
40. *Biennial Report . . . 1877 and 1878*, 111, Report of General Bates, Brig. General Commanding Second Brigade, I.N.G. to General Ducat, dated August 10, 1877.
41. *Biennial Report . . . 1877 and 1878*, 111–12.
42. *Biennial Report . . . 1877 and 1878*, 108.
43. *Biennial Report . . . 1877 and 1878*, 109.
44. Mark A. Lause, "'The Cruel Striker War': Rail Labor & the Broken Symmetry of Galesburg Civic Culture 1877–1888," *Journal of the Illinois State Historical Society* 91, no. 3 (1998): 81–112, 92.
45. *Biennial Report . . . 1877 and 1878*, 108–13.
46. "The Colored Troops," *Chicago Daily Tribune*, 5 August 1877.
47. *Chicago Daily Tribune*, 8 February 1879.

48. *Biennial Report . . . 1877 and 1878*, 114–15.

49. It is not entirely clear why these sorts of confrontations didn't take place during coal-mine strike-policing expeditions in Illinois. The best hypothesis is that the locations of the strikes, one center city and the other outside the city limits, affected the nature and composition of the crowds, with a primary difference being that the crowds that formed during coal strikes seemed not to have contained workers from other industries or shops, a pattern more typical of large rail strikes.

50. See active duty reports in *Biennial Report . . . 1877 and 1878*; *Biennial Report . . . 1889 and 1890*; *Biennial Report . . . 1893 and 1894*; and *Biennial Report . . . 1897 and 1898*.

51. See reports on active duty in *Biennial Report . . . 1877 and 1878*; *Biennial Report . . . 1889 and 1890*; *Biennial Report . . . 1893 and 1894*; *Biennial Report . . . 1897 and 1898*; *Biennial Report . . . 1899 and 1900*; and *Biennial Report . . . 1903 and 1904*. See also "J. H. Barkley, Colonel Commanding the Fifth Regiment, ING, to Brigadier General J.N. Reece, Commanding the Second Brigade, ING. Springfield, IL, 6 June 1883," 1883, 1883 Strike File, Governor Hamilton's Correspondence, J. H. Barkley, RG 100.19, Illinois State Archives.

52. Birtle, 37–57, argues that the National Guard could take a "non-partisan" stance in regard to the disputing parties while policing strike-related situations and nevertheless end up with the public impression that their presence had ultimately served the ends of management when the strikes collapsed without securing their aims.

53. Michael Biggs, "Strikes as Sequences of Interaction, The American Strike Wave of 1886," *Social Science History* 2002 26(3): 583–617. See also *Biennial Report . . . 1885 and 1886*.

54. For example, there was no state-supported summer camp training in 1890 due to budget shortfalls. *Biennial Report . . . 1889 and 1890*, 5. See also Illinois' Writers Project, "Camp Lincoln," *Journal of the Illinois State Historical Society* 34, no. 3 (1941): 281–302.

55. *The Chicago Tribune*, 25 May 1883, 26 May 1883, 27 May 1883, 29 May 1883, 30 May 1883, 1 June 1883. *The Chicago Tribune* has a long reputation as an "anti-labor" newspaper, but the chronology of the strike they reported matches the chronology Colonel Barkley reported to Adjutant General Reece. Barkley to Reece, 6 June 1883.

56. Barkley to Reece, 6 June 1883.

57. In the traditional mines, after the shaft was dug and the lifts installed, it was up to each miner to work his own section of coal as assigned by the mine foreman, either a "room," or along a "long wall." In Illinois most mines were some variation of the "room" arrangement. Once the miner had a "room," it was up to him to make the cuts at the base of the coal seam (this was the part of the job known as mining), bore holes, lay in blasting powder, set off the explosion, gather up the fallen coal, load it into the car, and haul it to the opening to his "room" for the car drivers to pick up to take to the surface. The individual miner was also responsible for his own safety, including not only the results of his actual "work" but for the general area surrounding him as well. Miners ensured the structural stability of their "room" through timbering and

laid the track into the "room" that the coal cars ran along. Most of the work was done with the miner's personal tools and supplies, including powder and blasting caps. For this work, miners were paid by the weight of the raised coal, excluding any shale or slate and pieces too small to make the grade. In "machine mines" a cutting machine developed in the early 1870s was used to make cuts under the coal seam, after which the miner continued to work in the usual way. The introduction of the cutting machine changed work relationships throughout the mines in which they were introduced through a slow and heavily contested process of de-skilling. Piece rates continued after the introduction of machine cutters, however, and productivity remained roughly equal overall for machine and traditional pick mines. The price and productivity of an individual mine were, however, dependent on the quality and type of coal in the region, and so there were regional variations in price and productivity between machine and traditional mines. See general studies of coal mining practices, for example, Keith Dix, *Work Relations in the Coal Industry: The Hand-Loading Era, 1880–1930* (West Virginia: Institute for Labor Studies, 1977); Price V. Fishback, *Soft Coal, Hard Choices: The Economic Welfare of Bituminous Coal Miners, 1890–1930* (New York: Oxford University Press, 1992). For work more specific to Illinois, see John H. M. Laslett, *Nature's Noblemen: The Fortunes of the Independent Collier in Scotland and the American Midwest, 1855–1889* (Los Angles: Institute of Industrial Relations, University of California, 1983).

58. Report by the Governor of Illinois to the 33rd General Assembly, Concerning the Use of the State Militia in Support of the Civil Authorities, in Madison and St. Clair Counties, in May, 1883. "J. D. Miner, Caseyville to Governor Hamilton of Illinois, 31 May, 1883," 1883, May 23–31, 1883, Governor Hamilton's Correspondence, J. D. Miner, RG 100.19, Illinois State Archives.

59. Nationally the unit of measurement was generally one ton, but in Illinois the standard piece unit was one bushel. Shale and slate are two of the most common types of coal with too many impurities to be used effectively as a fuel source.

60. J. D. Miner to Governor Hamilton, 31 May 1883. Disagreements over the weighing process were endemic to coal mining because the miners were perennially suspicious that they were being shortchanged by the mine operators. See Fishback, ch. 5. There were also some complaints about the stiff penalties for loading "dirty" coal (coal with too many impurities), but these again were perennial labor-management conflicts in the coal mining industry.

61. "Telegram from B. Lowman, Sec'y, Belleville, Illinois to Governor Hamilton, 3 May 1883," 1883, 1883 Strike File, Governor Hamilton's Correspondence, B. Lowman, RG 100.19, Illinois State Archives. "We the miners have held a meeting & are fully determined to stand by our resolutions that were passed by us, by advice of our attorneys R.A. Halbert and Ed B――s."

62. Barkley to Reece, 6 June 1883, 7.

63. "Governor Hamilton, Springfield to E. J. Crandall, Collinsville, Illinois 26 May 1883," 1883, Strike File 1883, Governor Hamilton's Correspondence, Governor Hamilton, RG 100.19, Illinois State Archives. The Governor sent this message via telegraph, collect.

64. Barkley to Reece, 6 June 1883, 7.
65. Barkley to Reece, 6 June 1883, 7–9.
66. Barkley to Reece, 6 June 1883, 10.
67. Barkley to Reece, 6 June 1883, 10.
68. "Powder and Ball," *Chicago Daily Tribune*, 29 May 1883.
69. Barkley to Reece, 6 June 1883, 10.
70. Barkley to Reece, 6 June 1883, 11–14. Certainly the militia officers, including Colonel Barkley, felt satisfied that they had made themselves perfectly clear to the engineer and that he had quite deliberately ignored their requests and then instructions and even the repeated remonstrations of the ING officer riding in the engine with him as they approached the mine. *The Chicago Tribune*, 29 May 1883, 30 May 1883.
71. Barkley to Reece, 6 June 1883, 11–14.
72. *The Chicago Tribune*, 29 May 1883, 30 May 1883, 1 June 1883
73. "Geo. W. Parker, President and General Manager of the St. Louis, Alton & Terre Haute Rail Road, to E. F. Leonard, Secretary, Springfield, IL, 24 May 1883," 1883, Strike File 1883, Governor Hamilton's Correspondence, Geo. W. Parker, RG 100.19, Illinois State Archives. Parker recounts a tale of an attempted sabotage of a railroad trestle, which he blames on the strikers.
74. Barkley to Reece, 6 June 1883, 1–2.
75. On his arrival, Barkley had presented himself with a letter of introduction to a Dr. Wadsworth, who in turn introduced Barkley to J. M. Pearson, a Justice of the Peace. Both Wadsworth and Pearson signed the telegraph to Governor Hamilton requesting state intervention in Madison County. Barkley to Reece, 6 June 1883.
76. *Biennial Report . . . 1893 and 1894*, VI.
77. Barkley to Reece, 6 June 1883. Telegram quoted on 2–3.
78. "Labor Troubles," in *The Chicago Tribune*, 27 May 1883, 3. Earlier reports published in the *Tribune* assumed that Sheriff Hotz was the individual who requested state aid. See *The Chicago Tribune*, 25 May 1883.
79. Barkley to Reece, 6 June 1883, 4.
80. In 1922, the company town was much less common in Illinois than in some other coal mining regions (more than 90 percent of Illinois coal miners lived in independent towns), and it seems that this was the case from the beginning of the exploitation of the coalfields. This may account for the relative freedom of county officials to implicitly oppose the mine operators. See Fishback, 164.
81. Barkley to Reece, 6 June 1883, 4.
82. Barkley to Reece, 6 June 1883, 4.
83. Barkley to Reece, 6 June 1883, 4.
84. See active duty reports in *Biennial Report . . . 1889 and 1890; Biennial Report . . . 1893 and 1894; Biennial Report . . . . 1899 and 1900*.
85. See active duty reports in *Biennial Report . . . 1889 and 1890; Biennial Report . . . 1893 and 1894; Biennial Report . . . 1899 and 1900*.
86. *Biennial Report . . . 1885 and 1886*, 20–33.
87. Lause, 81–112.
88. *Biennial Report . . . 1893 and 1894*, XV–XVII; *Biennial Report . . . 1885 and 1886*, 21.

89. *Biennial Report* . . . *1885 and 1886*, 27–28.
90. "J. D. Miner, Caseyville to Governor Hamilton of Illinois, 31 May 1883," 1883, May 23–31, 1883, Governor Hamilton's Correspondence, J. D. Miner, RG 100.19, Illinois State Archives.
91. Miner to Hamilton, 31 May 1883.
92. Jas. K Magie, *Plain Talk*, 73.
93. *Biennial Report* . . . *1889 and 1890*, 154–75; *Biennial Report* . . . *1893 and 1894*, 103–36.
94. Barkley to Reece, 6 June 1883.
95. Miner to Hamilton, 31 May 1883.
96. "News Clipping included in the letter, Joseph J. Reifgraby Chairman of the Mass=and Indignation=Meeting of St. Louis Citizens to Governor Hamilton of Illinois, 9 June 1883," 1883, File June 10–15, 1883, Governor Hamilton's Correspondence, Joseph J. Reifgraby, RG 100.19, Illinois State Archives.
97. All but one recent study of the history of the militia/national guards nationwide generally assume a direct link between the rise in national and statewide strikes and the growth of the state national guards in these decades. See Cooper, *Rise of the National Guard*, for the one that does not. See Doubler; Derthick; Mahon; Riker. Hill also rejects a connection between strike duty and militia resurgence.

Notes to Chapter 4

1. Address of Lieut. J. H. Parker, *Souvenir of the Banquet*, 45.
2. Cooper, *Rise of the National Guard*, ch. 4.
3. Cooper, *The Rise of the National Guard*, 44–45. Nineteen of forty-four state militias had no record of strike duty at all in this period.
4. Rotundo; Kimmell; Bederman; Philip J. Deloria, *Playing Indian* (New Haven: Yale University Press, 1998); Schudson; Glenn; Warren Goldstein and Elliot J. Gorn, *A Brief History of American Sports* (New York: Hill and Wang, 1993).
5. Major William Gilham, *Manual of Instruction for the Volunteers and Militia of the United States. By William Gilham* (Philadelphia: C. Desilver, 1861).
6. See a collection of drill cards printed in 1882 by the New Hampshire National Guard, National Archives and Records Administration, Record Group 168.2, "Pre-Federal Correspondence," Box 21.
7. *Fourth Annual Report*; *Biennial Report* . . . *1873 and 1874*; *Biennial Report* . . . *1875 and 1876*; *Biennial Report* . . . *1877 and 1878*; *Biennial Report* . . . *1879 and 1880*; *Biennial Report* . . . *1881 and 1882*; *Biennial Report* . . . *1883 and 1884*; *Biennial Report* . . . *1885 and 1886*; *Biennial Report* . . . *1887 and 1888*; *Biennial Report* . . . *1889 and 1890*; *Biennial Report* . . . *1891 and 1892*; *Biennial Report* . . . *1893 and 1894*; *Biennial Report* . . . *1895 and 1896*; *Biennial Report* . . . *1897 and 1898*; *Biennial Report* . . . *1899 and 1900*; *Biennial Report* . . . *1901 and 1902*; *Biennial Report* . . . *1903 and 1904*.
8. Bunzey, 13; Cooper, *Rise of the National Guard*, ch. 4.

9. William R. King, "The Military Necessities of the United States, and the best Provisions for Meeting Them," *Journal of the Military Service Institution of the United States* 5, no. 20 (1884): 355–91; Otho E. Michaelis, "The Military Necessities of the United States, and the Best Provisions for Meeting Them," *Journal of the Military Service Institution of the United States* 5, no. 24 (1885): 272–91; George R. Price, "The Necessity for Closer Relations Between the Army and the People, and the Best Method to Accomplish the Result," *Journal of the Military Service Institution of the United States* 6, no. 24 (1885): 303–30; General William T. Sherman, "The Militia," *Journal of the Military Service Institution of the United States* 6, no. 21 (1885): 1–26; Arthur L. Wagner, "The Military Necessities of the United States, and the Best Provisions for Meeting Them," *Journal of the Military Service Institution of the United States* 5, no. 24 (1884): 237–71; Alexander S. Webb, "The Military Service Institution: What it is doing; What it may do; Its relations to the National Guard," *Journal of the Military Service Institution of the United States* 5, no. 27 (1884): 1–28; Walter Merriam Pratt, *Tin Soldiers, The Organized Militia and What it Really Is* (Boston: The Gorham Press, 1912), 164.

10. *Biennial Report . . . 1875 and 1876*, 23–42; *Biennial Report . . . 1877 and 1878*, 56–72; *Biennial Report . . . 1879 and 1880*, 50–91, *Biennial Report . . . 1881 and 1882*, Inspector General's Report.

11. See Kutlowski and Kutlowski, 5–38, for a discussion of militia service records and elective offices. The Kutlowskis suggest that among other factors, the impression of military service conferred on retired militia officers who carried their rank with them out of the National Guard was a significant advantage to men attempting to climb the ladder of political influence.

12. Only a small number of National Guard officers ever advocated a role for the militias specifically giving priority to strike interventions or even considered introducing tactics or training for the militias as a riot control force. Even when any consideration was given to the issue, theorists of riot control generally envisioned a *military* response. The theorists described the crowds which militia companies would face as "the enemy," and they gave thought to the most efficient ways of killing large numbers of the "mob" at once and imposing martial law on the affected cities. See Eugene Leach, 23–50, for a discussion of the work of a small group of National Guard officers who saw in riot control a serious mission for the state militias and advocated training and preparation for such duties. Even here, however, curious distinctions arose. Most of the riot control literature that Leach writes about is focused on the strike in the large urban environment. At least in the Midwest, most strike intervention took place in largely rural settings with much smaller crowds of people and smaller bodies of militia than anticipated in the literature Leach surveys. The doctrine that the regulars articulated for dealing with labor-related civil disorder also assumed a military-style response as opposed to a police-style approach to maintaining order. The militias followed the regulars, up to and including adopting what consideration the professional army gave to the business of riot control. As a result of this dichotomy, Leach's thesis that this literature speaks as much to certain middle-class fears as any actual strike intervention practices is all the more persuasive.

13. Cooper, *Rise of the National Guard*, chs. 6, 7.

14. See "Comment by General Fry" in General William T. Sherman, "The Militia," *Journal of the Military Service Institution of the United States* 6, no. 21 (1885): 1–26. General Fry runs down a list of the various attempts to change the 1792 federal militia law in only the first twenty-five years of its existence, and their failure, beginning in 1803 and then in 1806, 1809, 1810, 1816, 1817, 1819, 1822, 1826, and 1829. Fry offers his list as proof that the defects of the 1792 law were obvious from the beginning and that the defects had never induced Congress to take any action to improve matters for the organization and disciplining of the militias.

15. The few state militia organizations that survived the aftermath of the Civil War, in New York, Connecticut, and Massachusetts primarily, were explicitly modeled on the Union Army in organization and drill. Cooper, *Rise of the National Guard*, 25–26.

16. Turner, 12; *Chicago Daily Tribune*, 20 December 1874.

17. Collins, 14.

18. *Biennial . . . 1875 and 1876*, 2–6. State militias, including the Illinois militia, tended to award staff and senior line positions higher rank than the regulars, thus establishing the happy position of being able to create far more majors, colonels, and generals than they otherwise could have supported on their relatively small enlisted bases. As a result, when states came to consider active duty pay, they found that if they created "equivalency" charts—state militia ranks equal the rank in the regulars corresponding to similar job responsibilities—they could then use regular army pay standards much more economically.

19. Collins.

20. Cooper, *Rise of the National Guard*, 81–83.

21. *Biennial Report . . . 1887 and 1888*, 40–41; *Chicago Daily Tribune*, 28 January 1888.

22. Minute Book: Company "I" 7th Inf. Several entries discuss target shooting and target shooting matches; the strong implication is that they are practicing somewhere locally.

23. See Cooper, *Rise of the National Guard*; Cosmas, *An Army for Empire: The United States Army in the Spanish American War* (Columbia: University of Missouri Press, 1971), ch. 1; Doubler, 112. See also Riker, ch. 4; and Derthick, ch. 2, for more information on the general development of the militias during these decades.

24. *Biennial Report . . . 1897 and 1898*, 727.

25. *Biennial Report . . . 1873 and 1874*; *Biennial Report . . . 1875 and 1876*; *Biennial Report . . . 1877 and 1878*; *Biennial Report . . . 1879 and 1880*; *Biennial Report . . . 1881 and 1882*; *Biennial Report . . . 1887 and 1888*; *Biennial Report . . . 1889 and 1890*.

26. Emory Upton's famous critique of the state militias was developed in the 1870s and 1880s. Emory Upton, *The Military Policy of the United States*, 3rd ed. (Washington, DC: Government Printing Office, 1912).

27. See Cooper, *Rise of the National Guard*, 89–91. The first federal inspections of the Illinois National Guard took place in 1885 and 1886. "Report of Inspection of 2nd Brigade, Illinois National Guard, 1885," September 10, 1885, Document #ACP 5844, AGO 7840, Box 23, Theo. Schwan, RG 168.2,

National Archives; "Capt. Gains Lawson, 25th Infantry, Fort Snelling, Minn, to the Adjutant General US Army, Washington, DC; August 12, 1886," 1886, filed as "Miss[issippi] 1886," Box 23, Capt. Gains Lawson, RG 168.2, National Archives. See also Derthick and Mahon for information about developments in training in the 1890s and early part of the twentieth century.

28. Cooper, *Rise of the National Guard*, 89.
29. *Proceedings of the First Annual Convention.*
30. Cooper, *Rise of the National Guard*, 89–90.
31. Theo. Schwan to The Adjutant General, U.S. Army, September 10, 1885, Box 23, RG 168.2 5844 ACP 1885, 7840 AGO 1885, National Archives and Records Administration; Gaius Lawson to The Adjutant General, U.S. Army, August 12, 1886, Box 23, RG 168.2 "Misc 1886."
32. See the 1908 Act, but in brief the new Militia Bureau in the War Department was responsible for overseeing the disbursement of federal funds to the various state organizations.
33. *Biennial Report . . . 1885 and 1886*, Report of U.S. Army on Encampments.
34. Theo. Schwan, Col. 7th Inf., "Report of the condition and recent course of instruction of the 1st brigade of the Illinois National Guard." National Archives and Records Administration, Record Group 168.2, "Pre-Federal Period, Correspondence," 1885–1886, Box 22.
35. See Cooper, *The Rise of the National Guard*; Doubler. See also Millett and Maslowski, chs. 8, 10.
36. Report of Charles Fitzsimons, Brigadier General, First Brigade, I.N.G. to Brigadier General J. N. Reece, Adjutant General. October 29, 1895, published in *Biennial Report . . . 1891–1892*, 129.
37. *The Chicago Tribune*, Friday, 21 October 1892.
38. *The New York Times*, 20 October 1892.
39. *Biennial Report . . . 1891 and 1892*, 130.
40. *Biennial Report . . . 1891 and 1892*, 130–31.
41. *Biennial Report . . . 1891 and 1892*, 130–32.
42. *Biennial Report . . . 1891 and 1892*, 133.
43. Bunzey, 42; *The Chicago Tribune*, 19, 21, 22 October 1892.
44. *Biennial Report . . . 1893 and 1894*, iv.
45. *Biennial Report . . . 1893 and 1894*, xlvi.
46. *Biennial Report . . . 1893 and 1894*, iv.
47. Cary Ray Papers, "The First Infantry Illinois National Guard "The Dandy First" As military escort to the Chicago and Southern States Association, to the Southern Cotton States and International Exposition, Atlanta, Georgia, November 1895"; Blight, 272.
48. See Record Group 168, National Guard Bureau, National Archives and Records Administration, covering federal returns and correspondence from 1885 until 1916.
49. Cooper, 38–39.
50. Beginning in the 1880s, some ING regiments began experimenting with signal corps, bicycle corps, and hospital corps. Bolton, 21.
51. Bunzey, 20–21.
52. "Camp Lincoln," 281–302. Summer camp could be postponed during

years of heavy active duty, for policing strike-affected regions, or for national service, or for lack of funds. For example, there was no summer camp in 1898 or 1915, two summers when the entirety of the ING was called into federal service, and in 1890 when there was no money. *Biennial Report . . . 1897 and 1898, Biennial Report . . . 1889 and 1890.* Capt. Gains Lawson, 25th Infantry, Fort Snelling, Minn, to the Adjutant General U.S. Army, Washington, DC; August 12, 1886, 1886, filed as "Miss[issippi] 1886," Box 23, Capt. Gains Lawson, RG 168.2, National Archives, 1.

53. *Biennial Report . . . 1887 and 1888*, 84; *Biennial Report . . . 1891 and 1892*, 78, 109–10; *Biennial Report . . . 1895 and 1896*, 19; *Biennial Report . . . 1899 and 1900*, 98.

54. "Report of Captain J.B. Babacock, 5th U.S. Cavalry, On the Encampment of the Illinois National Guard in 1892," in *Biennial Report . . . 1891 and 1892*, 59.

55. "Report of Major Jacob Kline, Captain, 18th U.S. Infantry, on the Encampments, 1887," *Biennial Report . . . 1887 and 1888*, 104. See also encampment inspection reports in all *Biennial Reports* and the report of Capt. Gains Lawson, 25th Infantry, Fort Snelling, Minn, to the Adjutant General U.S. Army, Washington, DC.

56. *Biennial Report . . . 1895 and 1896*, 19; *Biennial Report . . . 1899 and 1900*, 98.

57. See Capt. Lewis Green to Chief, Division of Militia Affairs, 10 September 1909, Document 8237-B, Box 78, RG 168.7, NARA; A.L. Miles to Chief, Division of Militia Affairs, 8 May 1913, Document 39615, Box 181, RG 168.7, NARA.

58. M. C. Kerth to Illinois Adjutant General, 21 April 1909, Document 5950-2,3, Box 67, RG 168.7, NARA.

59. Extracts from Capt. Eben Swift's Report, in *Biennial Report . . . 1895 and 1896*, 108.

60. Bolton, 22.

61. Newspaper photo, header "When Cavalry officers gave tea for Mrs. Tanner and Friends at Camp Lincoln" in "the Family Album," clipping in the Camp Lincoln Vertical File, Sangamon Valley Collection, Lincoln Library, 325 South 7th Street, Springfield, IL.

62. Newspaper photo, header "Sunday Visitors at Old Camp Lincoln, about 1901," clipping in the Camp Lincoln Vertical File, Sangamon Valley Collection. Original in Guy Mathis Collection, ALPML.

63. Newspaper clipping dated "1896" (and headlining Governor Altgeld) from a scrapbook in the Camp Lincoln Vertical File, Sangamon Valley Collection.

64. "Camp Lincoln," 281; newspaper clipping dated "around 1901" (and headlining Sunday Visitors) from a scrapbook in the Camp Lincoln Vertical File, Sangamon Valley Collection.

65. See Bunzey, 39–41; Headenburg, 35.

66. Bunzey, 39.

67. "Camp Lincoln," 297–98.

68. Guy Mathis Collection, Militia pictures, ALPML.

69. "Life in Camp Lincoln," *Chicago Daily Tribune*, 19 July 1896, 18

70. Bunzey, 21.

71. Cary T. Ray Papers, "Resume of Service."

72. ING Photographs, Chicago Historical Society; Guy Mathis Collection, Militia pictures, ALPML; photographs in the Camp Lincoln Vertical File, Sangamon Valley Collection.

73. Bunzey, 21.

74. Guy Mathis Collection, ALPML.

75. For example, in 1890 Senator W. D. Washburn of Minnesota donated a trophy to be awarded to the winner of a marksmanship competition between teams representing Wisconsin, Michigan, Iowa, Minnesota, and Illinois. If one team won the trophy three times in a row, the trophy became theirs permanently. Illinois won the competitions in 1891 and 1892. The third competition was held in 1903; the Illinois State Rifle team won that meet as well, and the trophy became theirs permanently. See *Biennial Report . . . 1891 and 1892*, 5; *Biennial Report . . . 1903 and 1904*, 7.

76. Goldstein and Gorn, 140.

77. Minute Book: Company "I" 7th Inf., ING, Record Group 301.106, Illinois State Archives, 39–48, April and May 1877 entries.

78. Minute Book: Company "I" 7th Inf., ING, Record Group 301.106, Illinois State Archives, 39–48, April and May 1877 entries. Turner.

79. Minute Book: Company "I" 7th Inf., ING, Record Group 301.106, Illinois State Archives, 39–48, April and May 1877 entries; Turner; see individual company histories.

80. *The Chicago Tribune*, Friday, May 14, 1875.

81. *The Chicago Tribune*, Friday, May 14, 1875.

82. Bunzey, 22.

83. See Bunzey; Bolton; Headenburg; and Turner.

84. *The Chicago Tribune*, Friday, May 14, 1875.

85. Headenburg, 27; Bunzey, 22.

86. See the individual company histories in Turner, *Souvenir Album and Sketch Book*.

87. See 4/24/1878 entry in Minute Book: Company "I," 39.

88. *The Chicago Tribune*, 5 July 1883, 2.

89. Turner, 66. *The Chicago Tribune*, July 5, 1878.

90. Turner, 60.

91. Bunzey, 22. See the individual company histories in Turner, *Souvenir Album and Sketch Book*.

92. Cooper, *Rise of the National Guard*, 80.

93. For more on the technological advancements and the changes in practice they demanded, see James L. Abrahamson, *America Arms for A New Century: The Making of a Great Military Power* (New York: The Free Press—A Division of Macmillan Publishing, Inc, 1981); Thomas C. Leonard, *Above the Battle: War Making in America from Appomattox to Versailles* (1978); Millett and Maslowski; James Sefton, *The United States Army and Reconstruction, 1865–1877* (Greenwood Press Reprint, 1980); Robert M. Utley, *Frontier Regulars*; Weigley, *The History of the American Army*; Russell F. Weigley, *Towards an American Army; Military Thought from Washington to Marshall* (New York: Columbia University Press, 1962); Paul Wellman, *Indian Wars of the West* (Dorset House Publishing Co. Inc., 1954).

94. See the Adjutant General reports in *Fourth Annual Report; Biennial Report . . . 1873 and 1874; Biennial Report . . . 1875 and 1876; Biennial Report . . . 1877 and 1878; Biennial Report . . . 1879 and 1880; Biennial Report . . . 1881 and 1882; Biennial Report . . . 1883 and 1884; Biennial Report . . . 1885 and 1886; Biennial Report . . . 1887 and 1888; Biennial Report . . . 1889 and 1890; Biennial Report . . . 1891 and 1892; Biennial Report . . . 1893 and 1894; Biennial Report . . . 1895 and 1896; Biennial Report . . . 1897 and 1898; Biennial Report . . . 1899 and 1900; Biennial Report . . . 1901 and 1902; Biennial Report . . . 1903 and 1904; Biennial Report . . . 1905 and 1906; Biennial Report . . . 1907 and 1908; Biennial Report . . . 1909 and 1910; Biennial Report . . . 1911 and 1912;* for the general history of the slow growth of state rifle ranges, replacement of old weapons with new, accounting practices for ammunition expended and saved, etc., and, most important, the ever-expanding office of the Inspector General of Rifle Practice.

95. "What the Militia Needs," *Chicago Daily Tribune*, 4 June 1887.

96. Bunzey, 13.

97. *Biennial Report . . . 1897 and 1898*, 18.

98. Address of Lieut. J. H. Parker, *Souvenir of the Banquet*, 45.

99. See reports on Rifle Practice in *Fourth Annual Report; Biennial Report . . . 1873 and 1874; Biennial Report . . . 1875 and 1876; Biennial Report . . . 1877 and 1878; Biennial Report . . . 1879 and 1880; Biennial Report . . . 1881 and 1882; Biennial Report . . . 1883 and 1884; Biennial Report . . . 1885 and 1886; Biennial Report . . . 1887 and 1888; Biennial Report . . . 1889 and 1890; Biennial Report . . . 1891 and 1892; Biennial Report . . . 1893 and 1894; Biennial Report . . . 1895 and 1896; Biennial Report . . . 1897 and 1898; Biennial Report . . . 1899 and 1900; Biennial Report . . . 1901 . . . 1902; Biennial Report . . . 1903 and 1904; Biennial Report . . . 1905 and 1906; Biennial Report . . . 1907 and 1908; Biennial Report . . . 1909 and 1910; Biennial Report . . . 1911 and 1912.*

100. Bolton; Bunzey; Chamberlin; Collins; Headenburg; Turner.

101. Colonel E. R. Bliss, "Address of Welcome," in Turner, 14.

102. *The Chicago Tribune*, 3 July 1880.

103. "President Wants Real, Not Parade Soldiers," *New York Times*, 23 January 1906, 4.

104. See "Letter Book Company 'G' 4th Inf., ING, " RG 301.101, Illinois State Archives; "Letter Book Company 'M' 6th Inf., Illinois National Guard, " RG 301.102, Illinois State Archives.

105. Walter Merriam Pratt, *Tin Soldiers, The Organized Militia and What it Really Is* (Boston, The Gorham Press, 1912), 165.

106. Pratt, 165–66.

107. Jas. K. Magie, *Plain Talk about Politics and Politicians of Illinois: with Facts and Figures Concerning the State Expenditures* (Chicago: J. Sampson & Company, Printers and Binders, 1882), 73. See also Cunliffe.

108. A. L. Mills, Chief of the Division of Militia Affairs, to Adjutant General of Illinois, 2 February 1914, Document 43398, Box 189, RG 168.7, NARA.

109. Address of Lieut. J. H. Parker, *Souvenir of the Banquet*, 45.

Notes to Chapter 5

1. *Souvenir of the Banquet*, preface, 5. The quotations acknowledge the Rudyard Kipping poem "The White Man's Burden," written in 1899 as a response to the American takeover of the Philippines after the Spanish American War.

2. Graham A. Cosmas, *An Army for Empire: The United States Army in the Spanish American War* (Columbia: University of Missouri Press, 1971), 133–36, argues that National Guard officers and their supporters in Congress were directly responsible for the large calls for volunteer troops—200,000 strong and to be recruited by the states— and that the army did not need and could not adequately provide for under their existing logistical practices. Millett and Maslowski, 289, repeat the same assertion.

3. Eleanor Hannah, "A Place in the Parade: Citizenship, Manhood, and African American Men in the Illinois National Guard, 1870–1917," *Journal of Illinois History*, Vol. 5, No. 2, Summer 2002: 82–108.

4. Under the provisions of the Volunteer Law of April 22, 1898, Congress authorized 3,000 volunteers to be recruited, organized, and officered directly by the federal government (separately from the 120,000 men to be drawn from the states, via the state National Guards, into the United States Volunteers). The famous First United States Volunteer Cavalry, or the "Rough Riders," were raised under provisions of this law. On May 10, when the war objectives changed again, Congress authorized another 10,000 federal volunteers as the United States Volunteer Infantry, under the direct control of the regular army—i.e., no recourse to state Governors or Congressmen. The federal volunteers were supposed to be raised from men theoretically "immune" to tropical disease, thus the nickname "Immunes." The regiments were given recruiting areas largely in the South with this end in view. Four of the federal infantry regiments raised as part of the 10,000 federal volunteers were filled by African American men, officered largely by white regular army officers. The Ninth Infantry USV, or "Immunes," were part of this group. See Cosmas, 133–36; Millett and Maslowski, ch. 9.

5. For general sources on the Spanish American War see Cosmas; G. J. A. O'Toole, *The Spanish War: An American Epic, 1898* (New York: W.W. Norton & Company, 1984); David F. Trask, *The War with Spain in 1898* (New York: Macmillan Publishing Co., 1981). For information relating to the regular army prior to the war see Abrahamson; Millett and Maslowski.

6. Linderman, *Mirror of War*.

7. Hoganson.

8. Millet and Maslowski, 290. In all, over 200,000 men volunteered to serve in the Spanish American War.

9. Paper read before Annual Association National Guard Missouri, Adjutant-General's Office, Jan. 1, 1898. Brigadier-General Milton Moore, "The National Guard as Part of the Military Forces of the United States," in *Proceedings, First, Fifth, and Sixth Conventions* (1898), 121. In possession of the NGAUS Library.

10. Millett and Maslowski, 280. Observers accepted, often grudgingly, the idea of state militias as they developed in the 1870s and 1880s in the position

of reserve army because they believed that it would be virtually impossible to significantly alter the status quo. Alterations in the reserve system were believed impossible because (1) the people of the United States would never accept a large standing army, (2) there were no serious military threats to the security of the national boundaries to worry the population and so Congress, (3) the public was totally uninterested in military matters, (4) any changes were perceived to be a threat to the power and authority of state governors and to certain prerogatives of the state governments, and finally (5) the growing political power of the activist officers in the emerging National Guards. For secondary commentary see Abrahamson; Coffman; Cosmas; O'Toole; Trask; Russell F. Weigley, *Towards and American Army: Military Thought from Washington to Marshall* (New York: Columbia University Press, 1962). See the following late nineteenth-century journal articles for views of the Guards: King, "The Military Necessities of the United States"; Michaelis, "The Military Necessities of the United States"; Price, "The Necessity for Closer Relations Between the Army and the People"; Sherman, "The Militia"; Wagner, "The Military Necessities of the United States, and the Best Provisions for Meeting Them"; Webb, "The Military Service Institution: What it is doing; What it may do." In particular, see also Upton, *The Military Policy of the United States*, for a contemporary, and hostile, view of the guards from the professional officer ranks.

11. "Strength of the National Guard," *Chicago Daily Tribune*, 20 January 1892.

12. See Charles H. Brown, *The Correspondent's War: Journalists in the Spanish-American War* (New York: Charles Scribner's Sons, 1967).

13. *Biennial Report . . . 1897 and 1898*, 21–22. Message of John R. Tanner, Governor to the House of Representatives, Springfield, Feb. 17, 1898.

14. *Biennial Report . . . 1897 and 1898*, 21.

15. See Brown.

16. *The Daily Inter-Ocean*, 18, 20 February 1898.

17. See Cosmas; O'Toole. The American report merely concluded that the *Maine* sank as a result of an external explosion. The Spanish report concluded that the *Maine* sank as the result of an internal explosion, a conclusion shared by U.S. naval damage-control experts under Admiral Rickover who reexamined all the available data in 1976 and concluded that the *Maine* sank as the result of a spontaneous combustion of some coal with particular impurities that was stored in lockers next to the boiler room, and once the fire burned down the wall between the storage chamber and the boiler, the steam engine exploded, sinking the ship.

18. Millett and Maslowski, 289.

19. Cosmas, particularly chs. 1, 3, 4. Cosmas offers some evidence of influential individual National Guardsmen on Capitol Hill in 1898, but he overstates the case for the "powerful National Guard lobby." He is, after all, referring to the same group who had been completely unable to secure any significant new legislation on their own behalf beyond a small increase in their federal budget in almost twenty years of agitation on the issue, and they got the increase in 1887—eleven years before the war. See Doubler, 113–15, and Cooper, *Rise of the National Guard*, 91–93.

20. Cooper, *Rise of the National Guard*, 98–105.

21. "Telegram from the Secretary of War, Russell A. Alger to the Governor of Illinois, 25 April 1898," *Biennial Report . . . 1897 and 1898*, 22.

22. Cosmas, 12–3, chs. 4, 5, 6; Trask, ch. 7.

23. O'Toole, 195. Seventy-seven percent of the volunteers were rejected on physical grounds, and 90 percent of those seeking commissions in the volunteer forces were rejected as well.

24. *Biennial Report . . . 1897 and 1898*, 24.

25. *Biennial Report . . . 1897 and 1898*, 32.

26. *Biennial Report . . . 1897 and 1898*, 28.

27. *Biennial Report . . . 1897 and 1898*, 25.

28. *Biennial Report . . . 1897 and 1898*, 28. See also Cosmas and Trask for their discussions of the difficulties of supplying the troops in the first weeks of the war. The limited supplies on the market only exacerbated the problems because the Army itself was not in the habit of stockpiling even such less perishable items as tents, clothing, and munitions.

29. Troops were also being mustered for an expedition for the Philippines, but those troops were drawn from the western states and gathered in San Francisco.

30. *Biennial Report . . . 1897 and 1898*, 27.

31. *Biennial Report . . . 1897 and 1898*, 37.

32. *Illinois State Journal*, 15, 28, 29, July 1898.

33. *Biennial Report . . . 1897 and 1898*, 38.

34. Bunzey; Cosmas, 230–36.

35. *Biennial Report . . . 1899 and 1900*, 8–9.

36. *Biennial Report . . . 1899 and 1900*, 4.

37. Cosmas, 251–52; Doubler, 131.

38. "1st Illinois Volunteer Infantry, Morning Reports," bound book, RG 94, National Archives.

39. Cosmas, 251.

40. Cosmas, 251–52.

41. "1st Illinois Volunteer Infantry, Morning Reports," bound book, RG 94, National Archives; and Thomas Miller Meldrum, *The Cuban Campaign of the First Infantry Illinois Volunteers, April 25–September 9 1898* (Chicago: T.M. Meldrum, 1899).

42. Kendrick to Scriven, Kendrick Collection, manuscripts division, CHS.

43. *Biennial Report . . . 1897 and 1898*, 39–40; McCard, 87.

44. *Biennial Report . . . 1897 and 1898*, 39; McCard, 87.

45. Cary T. Ray to Charles Belt, 17 November 1898, Memoirs, Folder 2, Ray Collection.

46. See Johnson for a state-by-state breakdown of African American troops in state militias and National Guards from 1870 through WWII.

47. "Negroes Wish to Go," *Chicago Daily Tribune*, 22 May 1898, 2.

48. McCard, 83.

49. Goode, 65–69.

50. *Biennial Report . . . 1897 and 1898*, 39.

51. Goode, 36–47; McCard, 83–85; *Biennial Report . . . 1897and 1898*, 39.

52. *Biennial Report . . . 1897and 1898*, 39.

53. McCard, 85.

54. "John C. Bruckner Is Striving to Get a Command," *Chicago Daily Tribune*, 27 May 1898.

55. *Illinois State Journal*, 15 July 1898.

56. *Biennial Report . . . 1897 and 1898*, 39–40; McCard, 87.

57. "1st Illinois Volunteer Infantry, Morning Reports."

58. Goode, 44–45. The editors of the *Illinois Record* protested this belief earlier, after the 10th Cavalry was ordered to Cuba, 9 April 1898.

59. According to the following: *Adjutant General's Office, Statistical Exhibit of Strength of Volunteer Forces Called into Service during the War with Spain, with Losses from All Causes* (Washington, DC: Government Printing Office, 1899). Reproduced on the U.S. Army Center of Military History, Historical Resources Branch Web Page, http://www.army.mil/cmh-pg/spanam/spanhtm.htm, and *Adjutant General's Office, Statistical Exhibit of Strength of Volunteer Forces Called Into Service During the War With Spain, with Losses From All Causes* (Washington, DC: Government Printing Office, 1899). Reproduced on the U.S. Army Center of Military History, Historical Resources Branch Web Page, http://www.army.mil/CMH-PG/documents/spanam/ws-stat.htm, accessed on 3/21/05. Only sixteen men of the Eighth Illinois died of disease, fewer than any other Illinois regiment that saw service outside of the United States.

60. Gatewood, "An Experiment in Color," 307–8.

61. The *New York Times* carried a brief notice of adjustment problems for the Eighth in San Luis on August 20, but there were no later national reports of trouble for the Eighth.

62. McCard, 90–96; Goode, chs. 7, 8, 9.

63. McCard, 88–91.

64. Goode, 212–14.

65. McCard, 95. It was fairly common for some officers' wives to join their husbands' regiments during garrison duty in Cuba and Puerto Rico. For example, several wives of the senior officers of the 2nd Illinois USV Infantry spent time in Cuba. See H. W. Bolton, ed., *History of the Second Regiment Illinois Volunteer Infantry from Organization to Muster-Out* (Chicago: R.R. Donnelley & Sons Company, 1899).

66. "Excerpt from a letter by Dr. Curtis, 1st Lt, 8th Ill. USV," reprinted in Goode, 233–34.

67. McCard, 91–92; *Correspondence Relating to the War with Spain . . . from April 15, 1898, to July 30, 1902* (Washington, DC: Government Printing Office 1902), 246.

68. McCard, 91–92.

69. McCard, 92.

70. Goode, 171. Goode includes a quote that the soldiers of the 8th believed to have been uttered by General Leonard Wood: "The soldiers of the Eighth were made up of the scums and slums of Chicago, or the state of Illinois." Unfortunately for the 8th in this case, Wood was successfully maneuvering to be made the governor-general of all of occupied Cuba. Goode responded to the insult with "They were the scums of Chicago because they had Negro officers, we infer. Many thanks to General Wood."

71. Goode, 238.

72. Goode, 238.
73. Goode, 238.
74. Goode, 237.
75. Goode, 278; McCard, 95.
76. McCard, 92, 95.
77. Bolton, 23.
78. Skinner, 286.
79. See the photographs reproduced in Meldrum, *The Cuban Campaign*.
80. John F. Kendrick to Margaret Scriven, 28 September 1958, John Kendrick Collection, Chicago Historical Society. Other memoirs of members of the First Regiment and their service in Cuba held at the Chicago Historical Society include those of Cary T. Ray, Horace Mellum, and Nicholas Budinger.
81. Address of Lieut. J. H. Parker, *Souvenir of the Banquet*, 45.
82. Skinner, 386
83. Bunzey, 37.
84. Bolton, 433.
85. Bunzey, 352.
86. Goode, 5.
87. McCard, 5.
88. McCard, 81.
89. *Souvenir of the Banquet*, 27.
90. In lieu of their first goal of obtaining a completely federalized reserve army, members of the regular army often proposed a system for reorganizing the National Guards to make them more efficient and useful by their standards. In the 1880s a favorite organizing strategy was to have one regiment per congressional district and to legislate a three-party payer system—federal, state, and local—to carry the significant cost increases that reformers felt would be necessary to properly outfit, supply, and train the new "reserves." For example, see "Comment by General Fry" in Sherman. Fry refused to accept the viability of the militias and reiterated a commitment to the establishment of an entirely federalized reserve under the authority of Congress to raise an army, and he rejected the notion that the militia could ever be a useful or efficient body of reserve troop training. See also Price and Wagner. National Guard leadership also advocated different missions for the militias. Guardsmen along the Eastern Seaboard tended to be content with the idea of the militias as coastal defense alone, whereas Guardsmen from the interior states, like Illinois, tended to advocate a much more aggressive role for the Guard at home and also abroad as a reserve army. See Derthick, chs. 1, 2. However, very few Guardsmen advocated a primary role for the Guards as state strike police.
91. Upton, *The Military Policy of the United States*.
92. The federal appropriation for the militias doubled in 1887 from $200,000 to $400,000 as a response to National Guard Association (est. 1879) lobbying. Cooper, *Rise of the National Guard*, ch. 3.
93. Upton. See also Magie, 73.

Notes to Chapter 6

1. "Report of C.C. Craig, Capt, Artillery Battalion, Btty B, ING," in *Biennial Report . . . 1899 and 1900*, 160.
2. *Chicago Daily Tribune*, 20 January 1892.
3 See Montegomery; Schnierov et al., Introduction.
4. Cooper, *Rise of the National Guard*, 49. The ING intervened in fifteen strikes (nine in the coalfields) between 1878 and 1899, the Ohio National Guard in eight, and the New York National Guard in six; the Pennsylvania National Guard troops intervened in only four strikes after 1877.
5. See "J. H. Barkley, Colonel Commanding the Fifth Regiment, ING, to Brigadier General J.N. Reece, Commanding the Second Brigade, ING. Springfield, IL, 6 June 1883, " 1883, 1883 Strike File, Governor Hamilton's Correspondence, J. H. Barkley, RG 100.19, Illinois State Archives.
6. Brackett, William S., *The Rising Menace Against the Peace of American Society*, delivered December 8, 1892.
7. Brackett, 16.
8. Brackett, 19.
9. Smith, ch. 10.
10. *The Chicago Tribune*, 30 May 1883.
11. Bolton, 17.
12. Bolton, 19.
13. Cary T. Ray Papers, "Resume of Service" File 1, Collection of the Chicago Historical Society.
14. "Report of C.C. Craig," *Biennial Report . . . 1899 and 1900*, 157–60.
15. Ray Papers, "Resume of Service."
16. Bolton, 20.
17. Bunzey, 24.
18. Bunzey, 24
19. Ray Papers, "Resume of Service."
20. Caroline Waldron Merithew and James R. Barrett, "'We Are All Brothers in the Face of Starvation': Forging an Interethnic Working Class Movement in the 1894 Bituminous Coal Strike," *Mid-America* 83, no. 2 (2001): 121–54, 133. See also Montgomery, "Strikes in Nineteenth-Century America."
21. Merithew and Barrett, 138–39; "Occasions on which the Organized Militia has been called out in aid of Civil Authorities," Report Prepared by the Bureau of National Guards for the War 1908, Document #3135, Box 57, Bureau of Militia Affairs, RG 168.7, NARA.
22. *Biennial Report . . . 1893 and 1894*, XIV–XXVIII.
23. Merithew and Barrett, 142.
24. Merithew and Barrett, 148.
25. "Occasions on which the Organized Militia has been called out in aid of Civil Authorities," 1908.
26. Schneirov et al., 9.
27. For a basic overview of the issues and the events of the strike intervention in Chicago, see the following in *Biennial Report . . . 1893 and 1894*: Report of the Adjutant General, XIV–XXVIII; Altgeld's Protests and the

President's Replies, XL–XLIV; Reports by various officers about the Chicago strike intervention, 103–38. For a detailed analysis of the U.S. Army involvement see Jerry M. Cooper, *The Army and Civil Disorder: Federal Military Intervention in Labor Disputes, 1872–1900* (Westport, CT: Greenwood Press, 1980); Robert W. Coakley, "The Role of Federal Military Forces in Domestic Disorders," ed. D. F. Trask, *Army Historical Series* (Washington, DC: U.S. Government Printing Office, 1988); Montgomery, *The Fall of the House of Labor*; Schneirov et al.

28. *Biennial Report . . . 1893 and 1894*, XL–XLIV. See also Cooper, *Rise of the National Guard*; Cooper, *The Army and Civil Disorder*; Coakley; and Schneirov et al.

29. Ray Papers, "Resume of Service."

30. *Biennial Report . . . 1893 and 1894*, XV–XVI.

31. *Biennial Report . . . 1893 and 1894*, XVI.

32. *Biennial Report . . . 1893 and 1894*, XVII. "Moving the Trains" generally consisted of guarding, with however many men were necessary, each train as it left the train yards and proceeded out of town far enough to pick up speed sufficient to prevent any sensible person or persons from personally blocking the tracks. "Guarding" was when the engine and cars were surrounded by ING troops facing outward toward the crowds. The guards moved with the train, keeping it surrounded and forcing individuals who might be blocking the tracks to clear them until open track was reached. In his article "'Honest Men and Law-Abiding Citizens': The 1894 Railroad Strike in Decatur," Sampson claims that Altgeld "over-reacted" to the strike and that militia intervention in Decatur was not necessary.

33. *Biennial Report . . . 1893 and 1894*, 100. Report of Frank P. Wells, Lt. Col. 5th Inf, Decatur, July 30, 1894.

34. *Biennial Report . . . 1893 and 1894*, 92–98. Report of J.S. Culver, Colonel 5th Inf, Springfield, October 5, 1894.

35. Montgomery; Schneirov et al.

36. See "Governor Altgeld's Protests Against the use of Federal Troops in Illinois During the Late Strikes and the President's Replies," in *Biennial Report . . . 1893 and 1894*, XL–XLIV.

37. Robert D. Sampson, "'Honest Men and Law-Abiding Citizens': The 1894 Railroad Strike in Decatur," *Illinois Historical Journal* 1992 85(2): 74–88.

38. Merithew and Barrett, 142.

39. Merithew and Barrett, 142; Smith; Ray Papers, "Resume of Service."

40. "Report of Adjutant General H. Hilliard to Governor Cullom, 9/30/1878, in *Biennial Report . . . 1877 and 1878*, 1.

41. "Report of Adjutant General Thomas Scott to Governor Denenn, 10/1/1906," *Biennial Report . . . 1903 and 1904*.

42. Cooper, *Rise of the National Guard*, ch. 3.

43. This observation comes from reading the coverage of several strikes in *The Chicago Tribune* and the *Illinois State Journal*, including editorials, front page articles, wire service notes, and back page follow-up pieces. See, for example, *The Chicago Tribune*, frequent coverage daily between 28 May–6 June, 1883, on Collinsville and Belleville; and 30 September–20 October, 1898, on Virden and Pana.

44. Barkley to Reece, 6 June 1883, 8.

45. "Governor Hamilton, Springfield to Fred Ropiequet, Sheriff, Belleville, Illinois, 27 May 1883," 1883, Strike File 1883, Governor Hamilton's Correspondence, Governor Hamilton, RG 100.19, Illinois State Archives.

46. "Governor Hamilton, Springfield to E. J. Crandall, Collinsville, Illinois 26 May 1883," 1883, Strike File 1883, Governor Hamilton's Correspondence, Governor Hamilton, RG 100.19, Illinois State Archives. The Governor sent this message via telegraph, collect.

47. "Report of Adjutant General Alfred Orendorff to Governor Altgeld, October 1, 1894," in *Biennial Report . . . 1893 and 1894*, VII–VIII.

48. "Report of Adjutant General Alfred Orendorff to Governor Altgeld, October 1, 1894," in *Biennial Report . . . 1893 and 1894*, VIII.

49. Notwithstanding General Order No. 8, the commander of the strike intervention in La Salle encamped his men on mine-owned property, though apparently well away from the actual mine and mine buildings. See "Report of Col. Fred Bennitt, 3rd Inf, ING to Adjutant General Orendorff, 1 June 1894," *Biennial Report . . . 1893 and 1894*, 42; *Biennial Report . . . 1889 and 1890*, 154–75.

50. *Illinois State Journal*, 30 September 1898.

51. "L.E. Bennitt, Col. 4th Inf, ING to Brig. Gen'l J. N. Reece, Carterville, 11 July 1899," *Biennial Report . . . 1889 and 1890*.

52. Josiah Fletcher, "Letter to the Editor II; The Army and the People," *Journal of the Military Service Institution of the United States (JMSI)* 7, no. 25 (1886): 103; William R. King, "The Military Necessities of the United States, and the Best Provisions for Meeting Them *JMSI* 5, no. 20 (1884): 355–91; Otho E. Michaelis, "The Military Necessities of the United States, and the Best Provisions for Meeting Them," *JMSI* 5, no. 24 (1885): 272–91; General E. L. Molineux, "Riots in Cities and their Suppression," *JMSI* 4, no. 16 (1883): 335–70; Elwell S. Otis, "The Army in Connection with the Labor Riots of 1877," *JMSI* 5, no. 24 (1885): 292–323; George R. Price, "The Necessity for Closer Relations Between the Army and the People, and the Best Method to Accomplish the Result," *JMSI* 6, no. 24 (1885): 303–30; General William T. Sherman, "The Militia," *JMSI* 6, no. 21 (1885): 1–26; Arthur L. Wagner, "The Military Necessities of the United States, and the Best Provisions for Meeting Them," *JMSI* 5, no. 24 (1884): 237–71; Alexander S. Webb, "The Military Service Institution: What it is doing; What it may do; Its relations to the National Guard," *JMSI* 5, no. 27 (1884): 1–28; R. W. Young, "Legal and Tactical Considerations Affecting the Employment of the military in the Suppression of Mobs; Chapter Three. Martial law," *JMSI* 9, no. 33 (1888): 95–116

53. *Biennial Report . . . 1893 and 1894*, 103–38; *Biennial Report . . . 1889 and 1890*, 154–75. Merithew and Barrett, 142; Ray Papers, "Resume of Service."

54. *Biennial Report . . . 1897 and 1898; Biennial Report . . . 1899 and 1900*.

55. "Report of J.S. Culver, Colonel 5th Inf, ING to Adjutant General Orendorff, 5 October 1894," in *Biennial Report . . . 1893 and 1894*, 95.

56. Strikers and bystanders were killed and wounded by ING rifle fire in 1883 (one killed and one wounded) and 1894 (at least six killed and many

more wounded). *Biennial Report* . . . *1883 and 1884; Biennial Report* . . . *1893 and 1894,* 95.

57. "Report of A. Ducat, Major General, Commanding ING," in *Biennial Report* . . . *1877 and 1878.*

58. *Chicago Tribune,* 30 May 1883.

59. *Biennial Report* . . . *1883 and 1884; Biennial Report* . . . *1893 and 1894,* 95.

60. *Biennial Report* . . . *1889 and 1890,* 154–75; *Biennial Report* . . . *1893 and 1894,* 103–36.

61. *Illinois State Journal,* 2 October 1898.

62. *Illinois State Journal,* 2 July 1898, 17 July 1898.

63. *Illinois State Journal,* 27 July 1898.

64. *Illinois State Journal,* 13, 14, 15, August 1898.

65. *Illinois State Journal,* 15 September 1898.

66. *Illinois State Journal,* 18 September 1898.

67. *Illinois State Journal,* 29, 30 September, 1 October 1898.

68. *Biennial Report* . . . *1897 and 1898,* 41–42; Thomas Scott, Illinois Adjutant General to Chief of Division of Militia Affairs, January 25, 1909, NARA, RG 168.7, Box 57, Document 4369-A.

69. *Illinois State Journal,* 8 October 1898; Pana/Virden strike photographs, ALPML; *Biennial Report* . . . *1899 and 1900.*

70. *Illinois State Journal,* 23 September 1898.

71. For studies of the role of African American strikebreakers and the reactions to them, see Ronald L. Lewis, "Job control and Race Relations in the Coal Fields, 1870–1920," *The Journal of Ethnic History* 12, no. 4: 35–64; Mark A. Lause, "'The Cruel Striker War' Rail Labor & the Broken Symmetry of Galesburg Civic Culture 1877–1888," *Journal of the Illinois State Historical Society* 91, no. 3 (1998): 81–112; and Merithew and Barrett, 142–52.

72. *Illinois State Journal,* 23, 24, 26, 27 September 1898.

73. *Illinois State Journal,* 10 October 1898.

74. "Report of C.C. Craig, Capt, Artillery Battalion, Btty B, ING," in *Biennial Report* . . . *1899 and 1900,* 157–60. See also Lewis, "Job Control and Race Relations."

75. "C.C. Craig, Capt. Artillery Btty B, ING to AG Reece, Galesburg, 9 November 1898," in *Biennial Report* . . . *1899 and 1900,* 160.

76. *The Chicago Tribune,* 13 October 1898.

77. *The Chicago Tribune,* 15 October 1898; see also *The Chicago Tribune,* 26 October 1898.

78. *The Chicago Tribune,* 13 October 1898.

79. Lewis, "Job Control and Race Relations."

80. *The Chicago Tribune,* 15 October 1898; see also *The Chicago Tribune,* 26 October 1898.

81. *Illinois State Journal,* 24, 28, 30 November 1904.

82. *Illinois State Journal,* 3 December 1904.

83. *Illinois State Journal,* 21 December 1904.

84. *Biennial Report* . . . *1905 and 1906,* 5.

85. *Biennial Report* . . . *1885 and 1886,* 20–33.

86. Schneirov et al., 1–14.

87. *The Chicago Tribune*, 15 October 1898; see also *The Chicago Tribune*, 26 October 1898.

88. The mine operators did so anyway and were promptly rewarded with the riots that all had predicted. When the militia was sent to intervene, they pointedly refused to guard African American strikebreakers or arrest strikers. *Biennial Report . . . 1889 and 1890*, 154–75. *Illinois State Journal*, 10 October, 1898.

89. *Illinois State Journal*, 2 October 1898.

90. Eric Arnesen, "Specter of the Black Strikebreaker: Race, Employment, and Labor Activism in the Industrial Era," *Labor History* 44, no. 3 (2003): 319–35.

91. *Illinois State Journal*, 8 October 1898.

92. This practice changed over time, and in 1898 and 1899 Illinois militia spent months occupying strike-torn regions. See appendix H.

93. See Lause, "Cruel Striker War."

94. *Illinois State Journal*, 15 September 1898, 1 December 1904.

95. *Biennial Report . . . 1889 and 1890*, 154–75.

96. *Illinois State Journal*, 2 October 1898.

97. *Illinois State Journal*, 2, 4 October 1898.

98. *Illinois State Journal*, 4 October 1898.

99. *Illinois State Journal*, 3 December 1904.

100. Anthony Roland DeStefanis, *Guarding capital: Soldier Strikebreakers on the long road to the Ludlow Massacre*, PhD Dissertation, The College of William and Mary, 2004.

101. Cosmas, Millett, and Maslowski.

102. See sections of the AGs' introductory reports titled "In Aid of the Civil Authorities," in *Biennial Report . . . 1893 and 1894*; and *Biennial Report . . . 1889 and 1890*. According to Merithew and Barrett, coal strikes did get more violent beginning in 1894.

103. See the several reports of strike duty beginning on page 154 in *Biennial Report . . . 1889 and 1890*.

104. "Report of Adjutant General J. N. Reece to the Governor, Oct. 1, 1900," in *Biennial Report . . . 1899 and 1900*, 7. AG Reece went on to note that the militia accounts were overdrawn by $128,000 because of strike service in 1898 and 1899.

105. Alfred Orrendorf to T.B. Needles, Chairman House Committee Appropriations, 14 February 1895, copy in Governor's Correspondence, Illinois State Archives.

106. See Barkley to Reece, 6 June 1883, *Chicago Daily Tribune*, 29 May 1883. See also Eugene E. Leach, "Literature of Riot Duty."

Notes to Chapter 7

1. *Proceedings of the Third Annual Convention of the Interstate National Guard Association*, 163–64.

2. This process is very similar to the processes of state building described in Theda Skocpol, *Protecting Soldiers and Mothers: The Political Origins of Social*

Policy in the United States (Cambridge: The Belknap Press of Harvard University Press, 1992).

3. Collins, 17.
4. Collins, 18.
5. *Biennial Report . . . 1875 and 1876*, 30.
6. Collins, 46–57; Schneirov, *Labor and Urban Politics*, 59, suggests that this bill represented a "stunning triumph of Chicago's top citizens in creating new state administrative apparatus and centralizing political power." This view is quite Chicago-centric and overlooks how relatively little Ducat received in light of what he requested.
7. Collins, 46–47, Circular of Oct., 15, 1876 reprinted in full; 38–47 for information on the proposed bill.
8. Collins, 38–39.
9. Collins, 39–40.
10. "State Affairs," *Chicago Daily Tribune*, 30 March 1877.
11. Collins, 46–57.
12. Collins, 46–57.
13. *Revised Statutes. Illinois 1874* (Springfield: Hurd, 1874), 1007.
14. *Biennial Report . . . 1877 and 1878*, 15–17.
15. *Biennial Report . . . 1877 and 1878*, 10.
16. Collins, 57.
17. *Biennial Report . . . 1881 and 1882*, 5–7. Then–Adjutant General I. H. Elliot used his opening statement in the Biennial Report to explain that this appropriation (The Military Code of Illinois, Article 10, provided for a 0.01 mil property tax to supply militia funds—see *Revised Statutes. Illinois, 1882*) was at least $20,000 short of meeting the obligations imposed by the 1879 Military Code. *Biennial Report . . . 1887 and 1888*, 13.
18. *Biennial Report . . . 1895 and 1896*, 7–8.
19. *Biennial Report . . . 1911 and 1912*, 144. And this was long after the federal outlay for the National Guards had moved in the millions annually.
20. See Adjutant General's reports at the front of each of the biennial reports issued between 1874 and 1912.
21. For more on late-nineteenth-century attitudes against state government spending, see Cooper, *Rise of the National Guard*, 42–43; Schneirov, *Labor and Urban Politics*, 329–35.
22. *Chicago Daily Tribune*, 6 June 1883, 13 March 1887.
23. *Chicago Daily Tribune*, 3 July 1889.
24. *Biennial Report . . . 1875 and 1876*, 7.
25. *Biennial Report . . . 1875 and 1876*, 7.
26. Schneirov, *Labor and Urban Politics*, 59. Schneirov argues that the "Businessmen's Militia"—his name for the First Illinois—was formed solely in response to these events. Schneirov ignores militia companies elsewhere in the city and around the state and so does not read the First Illinois as part of a larger militia phenomenon. In 1874 Chicago was home to another regiment's worth of companies—most were gathered together the following year into the Second Regiment—and to scattered and small African American companies as well. There were also a steadily growing number of companies scattered throughout the state. See appendix J.

27. *Biennial Report . . . 1875 and 1876,* 7.
28. *Biennial Report . . . 1875 and 1876,* 8.
29. *Biennial Report . . . 1875 and 1876,* 8–9. There was great controversy at the time over the role that Hilliard would play in pushing for the 1879 legislation, with some observers feeling that he did all but scuttle the bill over a disagreement about the size and type of responsibilities that would be given the Adjutant General. See Collins.
30. *Biennial Report . . . 1877 and 1878,* 1–12. Hilliard did not get anywhere near so princely a sum as $200,000 annually, but he did get an annual appropriation in the next militia act.
31. *Biennial Report . . . 1881 and 1882,* 4–5.
32. *Biennial Report . . . 1881 and 1882,* 5. Elliot's opening line of his argument is almost as interesting: "It is not my province to discuss in this report the necessity of what is known as a National Guard in the United States, but . . ."; he then goes on to do a bit of that anyway, which is why his other sentence is more interesting.
33. *Biennial Report . . . 1881 and 1882,* 5–6.
34. *Biennial Report . . . 1881 and 1882,* 3.
35. *Biennial Report . . . 1881 and 1882,* 3.
36. *Biennial Report . . . 1895 and 1896,* 3–18.
37. *Biennial Report . . . 1897 and 1898,* 15.
38. *Biennial Report . . . 1897 and 1898,* 15.
39. In 1908 the Adjutant General of Illinois estimated that over the preceding five years the ING lost on average 20 percent of its almost 6,000 strong membership annually. That meant that every year ING officers needed to recruit on average 1,200 new members. Thomas W. Scott, Adjutant General of Illinois to Lieutenant Colonel E. M. Weaver, Chief, Division of Militia Affairs, Washington DC, April 1, 1908, Record Group 168.7, Box 45, #111 April 3, 1908, Filled with #91, National Archives and Records Administration.
40. See Kutlowski and Kutlowski, 5–38, for a discussion of militia service records and elective offices. The Kutlowskis suggest that among other factors the impression of military service conferred on retired militia officers who carried their rank with them out of the National Guard was a significant contribution to men attempting to climb the ladder of political influence. See also Cunliffe; Douglass; Ryan; Schneirov, *Labor and Urban Politics;* Hannah, "A Place in the Parade," 82–108.
41. Schneirov, *Labor and Urban Politics;* Schneirov et al.
42. *Journal of the Senate, 1879,* 1003–4.
43. For information on Torrence, see *Chicago Daily Tribune,* 29 January 1882; 31 January 1882.
44. *Chicago Inter Ocean,* 28 March 1893.
45. *The Chicago Tribune,* 15 September 1895.
46. Roger D. Bridges, "Equality Deferred: Civil Rights for Illinois Blacks, 1865–1885." Journal of the Illinois State Historical Society 1981 74(2): 82–108.
47. Willard Gatewood Jr., "An Experiment in Color. The Eighth Illinois Volunteers, 1898–1899," *Journal of the Illinois State Historical Society* 1972 65(3): 293–312.

48. "General Orders No. 22, November 9, 1897," in *Biennial Report . . . 1897 and 1898*, 755–62; Johnson, 56–57. *Illinois Record*, 13 November 1897, 19 March 1898.

49. "General Orders No. 22," in *Biennial Report . . . 1897 and 1898*, 755–62. *The Illinois Record*, 13 November 1897, 19 March 1898. See Also Gatewood, "An Experiment in Color."

50. Gatewood, "An Experiment in Color," 296–98.

51. "Buckner on the Carpet," *Chicago Daily Tribune*, 27 July 1897.

52. *Illinois Record*, 19 March 1898.

53. *Illinois Record*, 19 March 1898, 9 July 1898. Goode, 36–47.

54. *Chicago Daily Tribune*, 27 May 1898.

55. All of the relevant correspondence is reprinted in Willard B. Gatewood, Jr., *"Smoked Yankees" and the Struggle for Empire* (Urbana, IL: University of Illinois Press, 1971) 179–235. It is worth noting that skin color played at least a part in some of the controversy as John Marshall was very light-skinned and had blue eyes, fair enough some said to pass for white if he wanted to. The complaints of the men in Cuba focused on food, being kept in camp, the heat, tropical illnesses, and Marshall's extremely exacting standards for behavior, which resulted in some 200 courts-martial for disciplinary infractions while the unit was stationed in San Luis.

56. *Illinois Record* 26 November 1898, 4 February 1899.

57. Gatewood, "An Experiment in Color," 312. In 1913 Marshall was charged with filing a time card for his game warden duties the same week he also filed to receive pay for attending ING summer camp, and he had to resign from the Eighth in some disgrace.

58. See, for example, Captain Lewis D. Greene to The Chief, Division of Militia Affairs, War Department, Washington, DC, 10 September 1909, NARA RG 168.7 Box 78 #8237-B filed with #8071, BR 1906, Inspection reports, BR 1908 inspection reports, Report of 12 Sept 1910, NARA RG 168.7 box 103 #14286-D.

59. *Biennial Report . . . 1907 and 1908*, 263–93. See also Roberta Senechal, *The Sociogenesis of a Race Riot. Springfield, Illinois, in 1908* (Urbana, IL: University of Illinois Press, 1990).

60. *Biennial Report . . . 1907 and 1908*, 270.

61. "Confidential sheet to accompany Field Inspection Report of 8th Illinois Infantry, in camp at Camp Lincoln, Springfield, Illinois, Aug. 31st to Sept. 6th, 1913." RG 168.7 Box 189, #43389, filed with #41592, National Records Administration, Washington, DC.

62. "Confidential sheet to accompany Field Inspection Report of 8th Illinois Infantry, in camp at Camp Lincoln, Springfield, Illinois, Aug. 31st to Sept. 6th, 1913." RG 168.7 Box 189, #43389, filed with #41592, National Records Administration, Washington, DC.

63. *Chicago Daily Tribune*, 8 February 1879; Gatewood, "An Experiment in Color."

64. See *Chicago Daily Tribune*, 1 August 1881, for a call for ING officers to create just such a body to see to their concerns.

65. *Chicago Daily Tribune*, 7 December 1887.

66. *Chicago Daily Tribune*, 8 December 1887. The amendments that year

were bent toward increasing the abilities of officers to enforce discipline among the enlisted personnel.

67. Editorial, *The National Guardsman* Vol. 6, No. 2, June 1893, 1.

68. The laws also included a clause that prohibited any but recognized militia companies from parading with weapons unless they had a special license from the Governor. Militia Law of 1879 in *Revised Statues. Illinois 1882*.

69. *Illinois Statutes*. The Militia Law was rewritten or substantially amended in 1874, 1876, 1879, 1885, 1897, 1899, and 1903. See the General Orders published in the complete run of the biennial reports.

70. *Biennial Report . . . 1885 and 1886*; Illinois' Writers Project, "Camp Lincoln."

71. See General Orders and Circulars in *Biennial Report . . . 1883 and 1884*; *Biennial Report . . . 1885 and 1886*.

72. *Biennial Report . . . 1885 and 1886*, 4; *Biennial Report . . . 1887 and 1888*, 4.

73. See Collins; Turner; Headenburg; *Fourth Annual Report*; *Biennial Report . . . 1873 and 1874*; *Biennial Report . . . 1875 and 1876*; *Biennial Report . . . 1877 and 1878*; *Biennial Report . . . 1879 and 1880*; *Biennial Report . . . 1881 and 1882*; *Biennial Report . . . 1883 and 1884*; *Biennial Report . . . 1885 and 1886*; *Biennial Report . . . 1887 and 1888*; *Biennial Report . . . 1889 and 1890*; *Biennial Report . . . 1891 and 1892*; *Biennial Report . . . 1893 and 1894*; *Biennial Report . . . 1895 and 1896*; *Biennial Report . . . 1897 and 1898*; *Biennial Report . . . 1899 and 1900*; *Biennial Report . . . 1901 and 1902*; *Biennial Report . . . 1903 and 1904*; *Biennial Report . . . 1905 and 1906*; *Biennial Report . . . 1907 and 1908*; *Biennial Report . . . 1909 and 1910*; *Biennial Report . . . 1911 and 1912*. See also Roy Turnbaugh, "Ethnicity, Civic Pride, and Commitment: The Evolution of the Chicago Militia," *Journal of the Illinois State Historical Society* 72, no. 2 (1979): 111–27.

74. Turner, Collins, Headenburg, Chamberlin, Goode, Minute Book Company "I." Turner, Headenburg, Goode, and Chamberlin are all examples of fund-raising materials. See also Cooper, *Rise of the National Guard*, 60.

75. Robert M. Fogelson, *America's Armories: Architecture, Society, and Public Order* (Cambridge, MA: Harvard University Press, 1989).

76. *Biennial Report . . . 1895 and 1896*, 8. Some regiments owned or leased their own specialized armories, but these were privately constructed.

77. *Biennial Report . . . 1895 and 1896*, 8–9.

78. *Biennial Report . . . 1897 and 1898*, 19.

79. *Biennial Report . . . 1905 and 1906*, 6.

80. *Biennial Report . . . 1905 and 1906*, 5–6. Scott was unfortunately prescient. The state arsenal building burned down completely in the early 1930s.

81. *Biennial Report . . . 1907 and 1908*, 9.

82. *Biennial Report . . . 1907 and 1908*, 9.

83. Collection G1986:097, Prints and Photographs Division, Chicago Historical Society. The report emphasizes the terrible conditions the cavalry put up with. The armory was really just the offices in front of and over an old stable complex, with ladder stairs between levels, low Jerry-rigged hallways hung above the riding arena to provide access to company quarters in an old hay loft and storage areas, and poor stable conditions for the horses themselves—in short a giant fire-trap.

84. *Biennial Report . . . 1910 and 1911*, 3.

85. "*The Chicago Defender*, 17 October 1914," File 6, Notes . . . 1914–1915, Box 20, Vivian G. Harsh Research Collection of Afro American History and Literature, Chicago Public Library, Carter Woodson Branch. There was some disgruntlement in the black community over the eight-month lag between promised completion and actual opening of the new armory.

86. *Biennial Report . . . 1895 and 1896*, 8.

87. Bunzey, 13.

88. Headenburg, 31.

89. *Chicago Daily Tribune*, 22 May, 1881.

90. *Chicago Daily Tribune*, 15 April 1881.

91. Turner, 23–24. There is an extensive biographical essay on a major donor, Mr. Marshall Field, in the souvenir, who purchased the land and then gave the First Regiment a very generous 99-year lease on the property and the building they erected on it.

92. *Chicago Inter Ocean*, 25 April 1893

93. *Biennial Report . . . 1901 and 1902*, 17–19. See also Turner.

94. Bunzey, 355.

95. Bunzey 355–56.

96. *Biennial Report . . . 1901 and 1902*, 17.

97. Fogelson.

98. Fogelson, ch. 5.

99. *Historical and Pictorial Review—1940. National Guard and Naval Militia, State of Illinois* (Baton Rouge, LA: Army and Navy Publishing Company, Inc. 1940). Taken from typewritten copy held in the records of the Illinois National Guard files.

100. 8th Regiment Armory, Douglass Community Area, 1915, DN-0064686, Chicago Historical Society, Prints and Photographs Division.

101. Millett and Maslowski, ch 5.

102. "Springfield Girls Guests at Camp Lincoln in 1907"; "Mansion Tallyho Party Bound for Camp Lincoln," Camp Lincoln Vertical File, Sangamon Valley Collection, Lincoln Library, Springfield, Illinois.

103. "The Volunteers of America. Proceedings of the Convention of National Guards, St. Louis, October 1, 1879," in *The Volunteers of America. Proceedings of the Convention of National Guards, St. Louis, October 1, 1879*,1–2; *Proceedings of the Third Annual Convention of the National Guard Association of the United States, held at Philadelphia, March 7 and 8, 1881*. Even though the printed title reads "Third Annual Convention," the opening remarks of General Wingate of New York read, "I have much pleasure in informing you that since the last convention of this association met in St. Louis in, in October, 1879 . . . ," 3.

104. *The Volunteers of America*. The proposed militia bill indicates a close relationship with the regular army via regulation and boards of inspection and training made up of representatives of both the National Guards and the regular army. This proposed bill also mandated an organizational plan that assigned to each congressional representative a minimum of 700 uniformed militia as the basis for receiving federal aid. Seven hundred men would be either a minimum strength regiment or a maximum strength battalion organization.

105. *The Volunteers of America*, 1–2.
106. *Proceedings of the Third Annual Convention*, 14.
107. *Proceedings of the Third Annual Convention*, 24–26.
108. *Proceedings of the Third Annual Convention*, 3–7.
109. *Proceedings of the Third Annual Convention*, 5.
110. *Proceedings of the First Annual Convention. Interstate National Guard Association. Held at Planter's Hotel, St. Louis, Missouri, December 7–8, 1897.* Initially there was much debate over how much to ask for—$1 million, $2 million, $5 million—but the convention members settled on $1 million as the most feasible project.
111. *Proceedings 1897*, 10. Derthick comments on the "vague" notions that INGA and the NGAUS held about their goals and their future, but I think these statements, twenty years apart, are far more notable for their singleness of purpose and the clarity, if not the feasibility, of the vision.
112. *The Volunteers of America*, 1–3.
113. *Proceedings of the Third Annual Convention of the Interstate National Guard Association of the United States, held on Tuesday and Wednesday, Jan. 23–24, 1900, in the House of Representative, at Indianapolis, Ind. Gen. J. N. Reece, of Illinois, presiding; Col. C.E. Bleyer, of Illinois, Secretary* (Indianapolis, IN: 1900), 164.
114. *Proceedings of the Third Annual Convention of the Interstate National Guard Association*, 163–64.
115. *Proceedings of the Fourth Annual Convention of the Interstate National Guard Association of the United States, held at Washington D.C., January 20, 21, 22, 1902*, 209–10.
116. For discussions of the Federalization, or Nationalization, of the Guard over the first quarter of the twentieth century see Cooper, *Rise of the National Guard*, chs. 5, 6; Derthick; Doubler; Hill; Mahon; Riker.
117. For extended analysis of these bills see Louis Cantor, "Elihu Root and the National Guard: Friend or Foe?," *Military Affairs* 33 (1969): 361–73; Elbridge Colby, "Elihu Root and the National Guard," *Military Affairs* 23 (1959): 28–34; Russell F. Weigley, "The Elihu Root Reforms and the Progressive Era," in *Command and Commanders in Modern Warfare*, ed. William Geffen (Washington, DC: Office of Air Force History, 1971), 11–27. See also Cooper, *Rise of the National Guard*, Riker, Mahon, Derthick, and Hill.
118. Cooper, chs. 5, 6; *Proceedings of the Third Annual Convention of the Interstate National Guard Association*, 163–64; *Proceedings of the Fourth Annual Convention of the Interstate National Guard Association of the United States, held at Washington D.C., January 20, 21, 22, 1902* (Washington, DC: 1902), 209–10.
119. See Proceedings INGA for 1897, 1898, 1900.
120. Cooper, *Rise of the National Guard*, 111–27.
121. "Memories," Folder 2, Ray Collection.
122. A. L. Mills, Chief of the Division of Militia Affairs, to Adjutant General of Illinois, 2 February 1914, Document 43398, Box 189, RG 168.7, NARA.
123. *American Military History* (U.S. Army Center of Military History, 1988), 354–57.

124. See front page editorial cartoon in the *Illinois Cavalryman*, 5 August 1916. The cartoon features a wounded soldier from the fighting in Europe, front and center, and on the distant edge of the picture is a small line of tents marked "Mexican Border."

125. *Illinois Cavalryman*, 12 August 1916.

126. See complete run (twelve issues) of the *Illinois Cavalryman*.

Bibliography

Manuscript Collections

RG 94: National Archives.
RG 168: National Archives.
"Camp Lincoln Vertical File." In *Sangamon Valley Collection:* Lincoln Library, 325 South 7th Street, Springfield, IL.
"Descriptive Book, Co "A," 3rd Infty, Ing." Regional History Center, Northern Illinois University.
RG 100.19: Illinois State Archives.
RG 301.96: Illinois State Archives.
RG 301.105: Illinois State Archives.
RG 301.106: Illinois State Archives.
Prints and Photos, Chicago Historical Society.
Cary T. Ray Papers, Charles Diehl Papers, John Kendrick Papers, Nicholas Budinger Papers, Manuscript Collections, Chicago Historical Society.
Audiovisual Collection, Abraham Lincoln Presidential Museum and Library.

Published Reports

Fourth Annual Report of the Adjutant General of Illinois. December 1872. Submitted to Governor John M. Palmer by Adjutant General J. Dilger, Dec. 31, 1872 (Springfield, IL: 1872).
Biennial Report of the Adjutant General of Illinois, Transmitted to the Governor and Commander-in-Chief. For 1873 and 1874 (Springfield, IL: 1874).
Revised Statutes. Illinois (Springfield: Hurd, 1874).
Biennial Report of the Adjutant General of Illinois, Transmitted to the Governor and Commander-in-Chief. For 1875 and 1876 (Springfield: D.W. Lusk, State Printer and Binder, 1877).
Biennial Report of the Adjutant General of Illinois Transmitted to the Governor and Commander-in-Chief. For 1877 and 1878 (Springfield: Weber, Magie & Co., State Printers, 1878).
"The Volunteers of America. Proceedings of the Convention of National Guards, St. Louis, October 1, 1879," in *The Volunteers of America.*

Proceedings of the Convention of National Guards, St. Louis, October 1, 1879 (St. Louis: John J. Daly & Co., Printers, 1879).
Biennial Report of the Adjutant General of Illinois to the Governor and Commander-in-Chief, 1879 and 1880 (Springfield: Philips Bros, State Printers, 1880).
Proceedings of the Third Annual Convention of the National Guard Association of the United States, held at Philadelphia, March 7 and 8, 1881 (Philadelphia: 1881).
Biennial Report of the Adjutant General of Illinois to the Governor and Commander-in-Chief. For 1881 and 1882 (Springfield: H.W. Rokker, State Printer and Binder, 1883).
Biennial Report of the Adjutant General of Illinois to the Governor and Commander-in-Chief. For 1883 and 1884 (Springfield: H.W. Rokker, State Printer and Binder, 1884).
Biennial Report of the Adjutant General of the Illinois to the Governor and Commander-in-Chief. For 1885 and 1886 (Springfield: H.W. Rokker, Printer and Binder, 1887).
Biennial Report of the Adjutant General of Illinois to the Governor and Commander-in-Chief. 1887 and 1888 (Springfield: Springfield Printing Co., State Printers, 1889).
Biennial Report of the Adjutant General of Illinois to the Governor and Commander-in-Chief. 1889 and 1890 (Springfield: H.W. Rokker, State Printer and Binder, 1891).
Biennial Report of the Adjutant General of Illinois to the Governor and Commander-in-Chief. 1891 and 1892 (Springfield: H.W. Rokker, State Printer and Binder, 1893).
Biennial Report of the Adjutant General of Illinois to the Governor and Commander-in-Chief. 1893 and 1894 (Springfield: Ed F. Hartman, Printer and Binder, 1895).
Biennial Report of the Adjutant General of Illinois to the Governor and Commander-in-Chief. 1895 and 1896 (Springfield: Phillips Bros., State Printers, 1897).
Proceedings of the First Annual Convention. Interstate National Guard Association. Held at Planter's Hotel, St. Louis, Missouri, December 7–8, 1897 (St. Louis, Missouri: 1897).
Biennial Report of the Adjutant General of Illinois to the Governor and Commander-in-Chief. 1897–1898 (Springfield: Phillips Bros., State Printers, 1899).
Biennial Report of the Adjutant General of Illinois to the Governor and Commander-in-Chief. 1899–1900 (Springfield: Phillips Bros., State Printers, 1900).
Biennial Report of the Adjutant General of Illinois to the Governor and Commander-in-Chief. 1901–1902 (Springfield: Phillips Bros., State Printers, 1903).
Biennial Report of the Adjutant General of Illinois to the Governor and Commander-in-Chief. 1903–1904 (Springfield: Illinois State Journal Co., State Printers, 1904).

Biennial Report of the Adjutant General of Illinois to the Governor and Commander-in-Chief. 1905–1906 (Springfield: Phillips Bros., State Printers, 1907).

Biennial Report of the Adjutant General of Illinois to the Governor and Commander-in-Chief. 1907–1908 (Springfield: Illinois State Journal Co., State Printers, 1909).

Biennial Report of the Adjutant General of Illinois to the Governor and Commander-in-Chief. 1909–1910 (Springfield: Illinois State Journal Co., State Printers, 1914).

Biennial Report of the Adjutant General of Illinois to the Governor and Commander-in-Chief. 1911–1912 (Springfield: Illinois State Journal Co., State Printers, 1914).

Biennial Report of the Adjutant General of Illinois to the Governor and Commander-in-Chief. 1907–1908. (Springfield: Illinois State Journal Co., State Printers, 1909).

Biennial Report of the Adjutant General of Illinois to the Governor and Commander-in-Chief. 1909–1910. (Springfield: Illinois State Journal Co., State Printers, 1914).

Biennial Report of the Adjutant General of Illinois to the Governor and Commander-in-Chief. 1911–1912. (Springfield: Illinois State Journal Co., State Printers, 1914).

Primary Published Sources

Bliss, Colonel E. R. "Address of Welcome." In *Souvenir of the Banquet to the Interstate National Guard Association by the Illinois National Guard*, 14. Chicago: R. R. Donnelley & Sons Company, 1899.

Bolton, H. W. *History of the Second Regiment Illinois Volunteer Infantry from Organization to Muster-Out*. Chicago: R.R. Donnelley & Sons Company, 1899.

Brigadier-General Milton Moore, Commanding 1st Brigade, N.G.M. "The National Guard as Part of the Military Forces of the United States." In *Annual Association National Guard Missouri*. Missouri, 1898.

Bunzey, R. S. *History of Companies I and E, Sixth Regt., Illinois Volunteer Infantry from Whiteside County*. Morrison, Illinois, 1901.

Chamberlin, Henry Barrett. "A Sketch of the Oakland Rifles." In *Historical Sketch of the Oakland Rifles and Co. "C," 4th Infantry I.N.G*, 11–25, 1889.

Collins, Holdridge O. *History of the Illinois National Guard, from the Organization of the First Regiment in September, 1874, to the Enactment of the Military Code in May, 1879*. Chicago: Black & Beach, 1884.

Fletcher, Josiah. "Letter to the Editor Ii; the Army and the People." *Journal of the Military Service Institution of the United States* 7, no. 25 (1886): 103.

Goode, W. T. *The Eighth Illinois*. Chicago: The Blakely Printing Company, 1899.

Headenburg, Chas. T. *Souvenir History. Governor's Guard. Company C,*

Fifth Infantry, Illinois National Guard, 1866–1902. Springfield: Journal Co., Printers, 1902.

Hubbard, Guerdon Stonstall. *The Autobiography of Guerdon Stonstall Hubbard. Pa-Pa-Ma-Ta-Be "the Swift Walker." with an Introduction by Caroline M. Mcilvanie.* Chicago: The Lakeside Press, 1911.

Illinois, Adjutant General. *Fourth Annual Report of the Adjutant General of Illinois. December 1872. Submitted to Governor John M. Palmer by Adjutant General J. Dilger, Dec. 31, 1872.* Springfield, IL, 1872.

King, William R. "The Military Necessities of the United States, and the Best Provisions for Meeting Them." *Journal of the Military Service Institution of the United States* 5, no. 20 (1884): 355–91.

Logan, John Alexander. *The Volunteer Soldier of America. By John A. Logan. With Memoir of the Author and Military Reminiscences from General Logan's Private Journal.* Chicago and New York: R. S. Peale & Company, 1887.

Magie, Jas. K. *Plain Talk About Politics and Politicians of Illinois: With Facts and Figures Concerning the State Expenditures.* Chicago: J. Sampson & Company, Printers and Binders, 1882.

McCard, Harry Stanton. *History of the Eighth Illinois United States Volunteers.* Chicago: E.F. Harman & Co., Publishers, 1899.

Meldrum, Thomas Miller. *The Cuban Campaign of the First Infantry Illinois Volunteers, April 25–September 9 1898.* Chicago: T. M. Meldrum, 1899.

Michaelis, Otho E. "The Military Necessities of the United States, and the Best Provisions for Meeting Them." *Journal of the Military Service Institution of the United States* 5, no. 24 (1885): 272–91.

Molineux, General E. L. "Riots in Cities and Their Suppression." *Journal of the Military Service Institution of the United States* 4, no. 16 (1883): 335–70.

Moore, Brigadier-General Milton. "The National Guard as Part of the Military Forces of the United States." In *Proceedings, First, Fifth, and Sixth Conventions,* 121, 1898.

Otis, Elwell S. "The Army in Connection with the Labor Riots of 1877." *Journal of the Military Service Institution of the United States* 5, no. 24 (1885): 292–323.

Parker, J. H. "Address of Lieut. J. H. Parker." In *Souvenir of the Banquet to the Interstate National Guard Association by the Illinois National Guard.* Chicago: R.R. Donnelly & Sons Company, 1899.

Pratt, Walter Merriam. *Tin Soldiers, the Organized Militia and What It Really Is.* Boston: The Gorham Press, 1912.

Price, George R. "The Necessity for Closer Relations between the Army and the People, and the Best Method to Accomplish the Result." *Journal of the Military Service Institution of the United States* 6, no. 24 (1885): 303–30.

Sherman, General William T. "The Militia." *Journal of the Military Service Institution of the United States* 6, no. 21 (1885): 1–26.

Skinner, John R. *History of the Fourth Illinois Volunteers in Their Relation to the Spanish-American War for the Liberation of Cuba and Other Island Possessions of Spain.* Logansport, IN: Press of Wilson, Humphreys & Co., 1899.

Turner, Henry L. *Souvenir Album and Sketch Book, First Infantry I.N.G. Of Chicago.* Chicago: Knight & Leonard Co., 1890.

Upton, Emory. *The Military Policy of the United States*. 3rd ed. Washington: Government Printing Office, 1912.
Wagner, Arthur L. "The Military Necessities of the United States, and the Best Provisions for Meeting Them." *Journal of the Military Service Institution of the United States* 5, no. 24 (1884): 237–71.
Webb, Alexander S. "The Military Service Institution: What It Is Doing; What It May Do; Its Relations to the National Guard." *Journal of the Military Service Institution of the United States* 5, no. 27 (1884): 1–28.
Young, R. W. "Legal and Tactical Considerations Affecting the Employment of the Military in the Suppression of Mobs; Chapter Three. Martial Law." *Journal of the Military Service Institution of the United States* 9, no. 33 (1888): 95–116.

Secondary Published Sources

Abrahamson, James L. *America Arms for a New Century: The Making of a Great Military Power*. New York: The Free Press—A Division of Macmillan Publishing, Inc., 1981.
Adler, Jeffrey S. "'We've Got a Right to Fight; We're Married': Domestic Homicide in Chicago, 1875–1920." *Journal of Interdisciplinary History* 34, no. 1 (2003): 27–49.
Armfield, Felix L. "Fire on the Prairies: The 1895 Spring Valley Race Riot." *Journal of Illinois History* 3, no. 3 (2000): 185–200.
Arnesen, Eric. "Specter of the Black Strikebreaker: Race, Employment, and Labor Activism in the Industrial Era." *Labor History* 44, no. 3 (2000): 319–35.
———. *Brotherhoods of Color: Black Railroad Workers and the Struggle for Equality*. Cambridge, MA: Harvard University Press, 2001.
Bakhtin, Mikhail. *Rabelais and His World*. Trans. Hélène Iswolsky. Bloomington: Indiana University Press, 1984.
Barney, William. *The Passage of the Republic: An Interdisciplinary History of Nineteenth-Century America*. Lexington: D.C. Heath and Company, 1987.
Baron, Ava. *Work Engendered; toward a New History of American Labor*. Ithaca: Cornell University Press, 1991.
Barrett, Caroline Waldron and James R. Merithew. "'We Are All Brothers in the Face of Starvation': Forging an Interethnic Working Class Movement in the 1894 Bituminous Coal Strike." *Mid-America* 83, no. 2 (2001): 121–54.
Beattie, Peter M. *The Tribute of Blood: Army, Honor, Race and Nation in Brazil, 1864–1945*. Durham, NC: Duke University Press, 2001.
———. "Beyond Machismos. Recent Examinations of Masculinities in Latin America." *Men and Masculinities* 4, no. 3 (2002): 303–8.
Bederman, Gail. *Manliness and Civilization: A Cultural History of Gender and Race in the United States, 1880–1917*. Chicago: The University of Chicago Press, 1995.
Bérube, Alan. *Coming out under Fire; the History of Gay Men and Women in World War Two*. New York: Plume Books, 1991.

Biggs, Michael. "Strikes as Sequences of Interaction: The American Strike Wave of 1886." *Social Science History* 26, no. 3 (2002): 583–617.

Birtle, Andrew. "Governor George Hoadly's Use of the Ohio National Guard in the Hocking Valley Coal Strike of 1884." *Ohio History* 91 (1982): 37–57.

Blight, David W. *Race and Reunion. The Civil War in American Memory*. Cambridge, MA: The Belknap Press of Harvard University Press, 2001.

Block, Sharon. "Rape without Women: Print Culture and the Politicization of Rape, 1765–1815." *Journal of American History* 89, no. 3 (2002): 849–68.

Bodnar, John. *Remaking America: Public Memory, Commemoration, and Patriotism in the Twentieth Century*. Princeton, NJ: Princeton University Press, 1993.

Brackett, William S. *The Rising Menace against the Peace of American Society*, December 8, 1892.

Brecher, Jeremy. *Strike!* San Francisco: Straight Arrow Books, 1972.

Brown, Charles H. *The Correspondent's War: Journalists in the Spanish-American War*. New York: Charles Scribner's Sons, 1967.

Bruce, Robert. *1877: Year of Violence*. c1959 ed. Chicago: Quadrangle Paperbacks, 1970.

The Bureau of National Affairs, Inc. "Supreme Court Proceedings." *The United States Law Week: Supreme Court Proceedings*, 17 April 1990, 3649–50.

Butler, Judith. *Gender Trouble: Feminism and the Subversion of Identity*. 10th Anniversary Edition. Oxford, UK: Routledge, 1999.

Carnes, Mark C. *Secret Ritual and Manhood in Victorian America*. New Haven, CT: Yale University Press, 1989.

Cha-Jua, Sundiata Keita. "'A Warlike Demonstration': Legalism, Violent Self-Help, and Electoral Politics in Decatur, Illinois, 1894–1898." *Journal of Urban History* 26, no. 5 (2000): 591–629.

Chambers, John Whiteclay and G. Kurt Piehler. *Major Problems in American Military History*: Houghton Mifflin, 1999.

Chauncey, George. "Christian Brotherhood or Sexual Perversion? Homosexual Identities and the Construction of Sexual Boundaries in the World War One Era." *Journal of Social History* 19, no. 2 (1985): 189–211.

Clawson, Mary Ann. *Constructing Brotherhood: Class, Gender and Fraternalism*. Princeton, NJ: Princeton University Press, 1989.

Coakley, Robert W. *The Role of Federal Military Forces in Domestic Disorders*, Army Historical Series. Ed. David F. Trask. Washington, DC: U.S. Government Printing Office, 1988.

Coffman, Edward M. *The Old Army: A Portrait of the American Army in Peacetime, 1784–1898*. New York: Oxford University Press, 1986.

Connell, R. W. *Gender & Power*. Stanford, CA: Stanford University Press, 1987.

Conner, Matthew. "Minstrel-Soldiers: The Construction of African-American Identity in the Union Army." *Prospects* 26 (2001): 109–36.

Cooper, Jerry. *The Rise of the National Guard: The Evolution of the American Militia, 1865–1920*. Lincoln: University of Nebraska Press, 1997.

———. *The Army and Civil Disorder: Federal Military Intervention in Labor Disputes, 1872–1900*. Westport, CT: Greenwood Press, 1980.

Cooper, Jerry and Glen Smith. *Citizens as Soldiers: A History of the North Dakota National Guard*. Fargo: The North Dakota Institute for Regional Studies, North Dakota State University, 1986.

Cosmas, Graham A. *An Army for Empire: The United States Army in the Spanish American War*. Columbia: University of Missouri Press, 1971.

Cronon, William. *Nature's Metropolis: Chicago and the Great West*. Paperback ed. New York: W.W. Norton & Company, 1992.

Cunliffe, Marcus. *Soldiers and Civilians: The Martial Spirit in America, 1775–1865*. Boston: Little, Brown and Company, 1968.

Davis, Susan G. *Parades and Power, Street Theatre in Nineteenth-Century Philadelphia*. Philadelphia: Temple University Press, 1986.

Dearinger, Ryan L. "Violence, Masculinity, Image and Reality on the Antebellum Frontier." *Indiana Magazine of History* 100, no. 1 (2004).

Deloria, Philip J. *Playing Indian*. New Haven: Yale University Press, 1998.

Dennis, Matthew. *Red, White, and Blue Letter Days: An American Calendar*. Ithaca: Cornell University Press, 2002.

Derthick, Martha. *The National Guard in Politics*. Cambridge, MA: Harvard University Press, 1965.

Deutsch, Sarah. *Women and the City, Gender, Space and Power in Boston, 1870–1940*. Oxford: Oxford University Press, 2000.

Dix, Keith. *Work Relations in the Coal Industry: The Hand-Loading Era, 1880–1930*. West Virginia: Institute for Labor Studies, 1977.

Doubler, Michael D. *Civilian in Peace, Soldier in War*. Lawrence: University Press of Kansas, 2003.

Douglas, Ann. *The Feminization of American Culture*. New York: Knopf, 1977.

Downey, Dennis B. "'A Many-Headed Monster': The 1903 Lynching of David Wyatt." *Journal of Illinois History* 2, no. 1 (1999): 2–16.

Drake, St. Clair and Horace R. Cayton. *Black Metropolis; a Study of Negro Life in a Northern City*. Vol. 1. 1962 ed. New York: Harper & Row, Publishers, 1962.

Edwards, Rebecca. *Angels in the Machinery: Gender in American Party Politics from the Civil War to the Progressive Era*. New York: Oxford University Press, 1997.

Eisenhower, John S. D. *Intervention! The United States and the Mexican Revolution, 1913–1917*. New York: Norton, 1993.

Faragher, John Mack. *Sugar Creek: Life on the Illinois Prairie*. New Haven: Yale University Press, 1987.

Filene, Peter G. *Him/Her/Self: Sex Roles in Modern America*. 2nd ed. Baltimore: Johns Hopkins University Press, 1986.

Fishback, Price V. *Soft Coal, Hard Choices: The Economic Welfare of Bituminous Coal Miners, 1890–1930*. New York: Oxford University Press, 1992.

Fogelson, Robert M. *America's Armories: Architecture, Society, and Public Order*. Cambridge, MA: Harvard University Press, 1989.

Foner, Eric. *A Short History of Reconstruction*. New York: Harper & Row, 1990.
Foner, Philip S. *The Great Labor Uprising of 1877*. New York: Monad Press, 1977.
Freedman, Stephen. "Organizing the Workers in a Steel Company Town: The Union Movement in Joliet, 1870–1920." *Illinois Historical Journal* 79, no. 1 (1986): 2–18.
Gatewood, Willard B., Jr. "An Experiment in Color. The Eighth Illinois Volunteers, 1898–1899." *Journal of the Illinois State Historical Society* 65, no. 3 (1972): 293–312.
———. *Black Americans and the White Man's Burden, 1898–1903*. Urbana: University of Illinois Press, 1975.
———. *"Smoked Yankees": And the Struggle for Empire: Letters from Negro Soldiers, 1898–1902*. The University of Arkansas Press Reprint Series, Vol. 4. Ed. Willard B. Gatewood. Fayetteville: University of Arkansas Press; Reprint edition, 1987.
Glenn, Evelyn Nakano. *Unequal Freedom: How Race and Gender Shaped American Citizenship and Labor*. Cambridge and London: Harvard University Press, 2002.
Goldman, Hal. "Black Citizenship and Military Self-Preservation in Antebellum Massachusetts." *The Historical Journal of Massachusetts* 25, no. 2 (1997): 157–83.
Gorn, Elliot J. *The Manly Art: Bare-Knuckle Prize Fighting in America*. Ithaca, NY: Cornell University Press, 1986.
Gorn, Elliot J. and Warren Goldstein. *A Brief History of American Sports*. New York: Hill and Wang, 1993.
Grant, Julia. "A 'Real Boy' and Not a Sissy: Gender, Childhood and Masculinity, 1890–1940." *Journal of Social History* 37, no. 4 (2004): 829–51.
Greenberg, Amy S. *Cause for Alarm: The Volunteer Fire Department in the Nineteenth-Century City*. Princeton: Princeton University Press, 1998.
Griffith, R. Marie. "Apostles of Abstinence: Fasting and Masculinity during the Progressive Era." *American Quarterly* 52, no. 4 (2000): 599–638.
Hall, John R., ed. *Reworking Class*. Ithaca, NY: Cornell University Press, 1997.
Haydu, Jeffery. "Business Citizenship at Work: Cultural Transposition and Class Formation in Cincinnati, 1870–1910." *American Journal of Sociology* 107, no. 6 (2002): 1424–68.
Hays, Christopher K. "The African American Struggle for Equality and Justice in Cairo, Illinois, 1865–1900." *Illinois Historical Journal* 90, no. 4 (1997): 265–84.
Higham, John. *Strangers in the Land: Patterns of American Nativism, 1860–1925*. Rev. ed. New York: Athenaeum, 1973.
Hilkey, Judy. *Character Is Capital: Success Manuals and Manhood in Gilded Age America*. Chapel Hill: University of North Carolina Press, 1997.
Hill, Jim Dan. *The Minute Man in Peace and War: A History of the National Guard*. Harrisburg, PA: The Stackpole Company, 1964.

Historical and Pictorial Review—1940. National Guard and Naval Militia, State of Illinois. Baton Rouge, LA: Army and Navy Publishing Company, Inc., 1940.

Hofstadter, Richard. *The Age of Reform: From Bryan to F.D.R.* New York: Vintage Books, 1955.

Hoganson, Kristin L. *Fighting for American Manhood: How Gender Politics Provoked the Spanish-American and Philippine-American Wars.* New Haven: Yale University Press, 1998.

Ira, Berlin et al. *Slaves No More: Three Essays on Emancipation and the Civil War.* New York: Cambridge University Press, 1992.

Johnson, Charles. *African American Soldiers in the National Guard: Recruitment and Deployment during Peacetime and War.* Westport, CT: Greenwood Press, 1992.

Kammen, Michael. *A Season of Youth: The American Revolution and the Historical Imagination.* New York: Alfred A. Knopf, 1978.

Karsten, Peter. "Militarization and Rationalization in the United States, 1870–1914," in *The Militarization of the Western World,* ed. John R. Gillis. New Brunswick, NJ: Rutgers University Press, 1989.

Kasson, John F. *Houdini, Tarzan and the Perfect Man: The White Male Body and the Challenge of Modernity in America.* New York: Hill and Wang, 2001.

Kimmell, Michael. *Manhood in America, a Cultural History.* New York: The Free Press, 1996.

Kutlowski, John F. and Kathleen Smith Kutlowski. "Commissions and Canvasses: The Militia and Politics in Western New York, 1800–1845." *New York History* 63, Spring (1982): 5–38.

Laslett, John H. M. *Nature's Noblemen: The Fortunes of the Independent Collier in Scotland and the American Midwest, 1855–1889.* Los Angeles: Institute of Industrial Relations, University of California, 1983.

Lause, Mark A. "'The Cruel Striker War' Rail Labor & the Broken Symmetry of Galesburg Civic Culture 1877–1888." *Journal of the Illinois State Historical Society* 91, no. 3 (1998): 81–112.

Leach, Eugene E. "The Literature of Riot Duty: Managing Class Conflict in the Streets." *Radical History Review* 56 (1993): 23–50.

Leach, William. *Land of Desire: Merchants, Power, and the Rise of a New American Culture.* New York: Pantheon, 1993.

Lears, T. Jackson. *No Place of Grace: Anti-Modernism and the Transformation of American Culture.* New York: Pantheon Books, 1981.

Leonard, Thomas C. *Above the Battle: War Making in America from Appomattox to Versailles.* New York: Oxford University Press, 1978.

Lewis, Ronald L. "Job Control and Race Relations in the Coal Fields, 1870–1920." *The Journal of Ethnic History* 12, no. 4 (1988): 35–64.

Linderman, Gerald F. *The Mirror of War: American Society and the Spanish American War.* Ann Arbor: University of Michigan Press, 1974.

———. *Embattled Courage: The Experience of Combat in the American Civil War.* New York: The Free Press, A Division of Macmillan, Inc., 1987.

Linn, Brian M. "Pretty Scaly Times: The Ohio National Guard and the Railroad Strike of 1877." *Ohio History* 94, no. summer–autumn (1984): 171–81.

Linn, Brian McAllister. *The Philippine War 1899–1902*. Lawrence: University Press of Kansas, 2000.
Luskey, Brian P. "Riot and Respectability: The Shifting Terrain of Class Language and Status in Baltimore during the Great Strike of 1877." *American Nineteenth Century History [Great Britain]* 4(3): 61–96. 43, no. 3 (2003): 61–96.
Mahon, John K. *History of the Militia and the National Guard*. New York: Macmillan Publishing Company, 1983.
Mangan, J. A. and James Walvin, eds. *Manliness and Morality: Middle-Class Masculinity in Britain and America, 1800–1940*. New York: St. Martin's Press, 1987.
McPherson, James M. *Battle Cry of Freedom: The Civil War Era*. Oxford History of the United States, Vol. 6. New York: Oxford University Press, 1988.
Millett, Allan R. and Peter Maslowski. *For the Common Defense: A Military History of the United States of America*. Revised and expanded ed. New York: The Free Press, 1994.
Mirola, William A. "Shorter Hours and the Protestant Sabbath. Religious Framing and Movement Alliances in Late-Nineteenth-Century Chicago." *Social Science History* 23, no. 3 (1999): 395–443.
Mitchell, Reid. *The Vacant Chair. The Northern Soldier Leaves Home*. New York: Oxford University Press, 1993.
Montgomery, David. "Strikes in Nineteenth-Century America." *Social Science History* 4, no. 1 (1980): 81–104.
———. *The Fall of the House of Labor: The Workplace, the State, and American Labor Activism, 1865–1925*. New York: Cambridge University Press, 1987.
Morgan, H. Wayne, ed. *The Gilded Age, a Reappraisal*. Syracuse, NY: Syracuse University Press, 1963.
Fraser, Nancy and Linda Gordon. "A Genealogy of Dependency: Tracing a Keyword of the U.S. Welfare State." *Signs: Journal of Women in Culture and Society* 19, no. 2 (1994): 309–36.
Nelson, Dana D. "The Haunting of White Manhood: Poe, Fraternal Ritual and Polygenesis." *American Literature* 69, no. 3 (1997): 515–46.
Frankel, Noralee and Nancy S. Dye, eds. *Gender, Class, Race and Reform in the Progressive Era*. Lexington: The University Press of Kentucky, 1991.
O'Brien, Mike. "Manhood and the Militia Myth: Masculinity, Class and Militarism in Ontario, 1902–1914." *Labour/Le Travail* 42, no. Fall 1998 (1998): 115–41.
O'Toole, G.J.A. *The Spanish War: An American Epic, 1898*. New York: W.W. Norton & Company, 1984.
Parsons, Elaine Frantz. "Risky Business: The Uncertain Boundaries of Manhood in the Midwestern Saloon." *Journal of Social History* 34, no. 2 (2000): 283–307.
Pierce, Bessie Louise. *A History of Chicago. Vol Iii, the Rise of a Modern City, 1871–1893*. New York: Alfred A Knopf, 1957.

Portwood, Shirley J. "'We Lifted Our Voices in Thunder Tones': African American Race Men and Race Women and Community Agency in Southern Illinois, 1895–1910." *Journal of Urban History* 26, no. 6 (2000): 740–58.
Powers, Madelon. *Faces along the Bar: Lore and Order in the Workingman's Saloon, 1870–1920*. Chicago: University of Chicago Press, 1998.
Price, Robert K. and Kenneth M. Nelson. "Debating Manliness: Thomas Wentworth Higginson, William Sloane Kennedy and the Question of Whitman." *American Literature* 73, no. 3 (2001): 497–524.
Illinois' Writers Project. "Camp Lincoln." *Journal of the Illinois State Historical Society* 34, no. 3 (1941): 281–302.
Putney, Clifford. *Muscular Christianity: Manhood and Sports in Protestant America*. Cambridge, MA: Harvard University Press, 2001.
Rienders, Robert. "Militia and Public Order in Nineteenth-Century America." *American Studies (Great Britain)* 11, no. 1 (1977): 81–101.
Riker, William. *Soldiers of the States: The Role of the National Guard in American Democracy*. Washington, DC: Public Affairs Press, 1957.
Roediger, David R. *The Wages of Whiteness: Race and the Making of the American Working Class*. London and New York: Verso, 1991.
Rosenzweig, Roy. *Eight Hours for What We Will; Workers and Leisure in an Industrial City, 1870–1920*. New York: Cambridge University Press, 1983.
Rossel, Jorg. "Industrial Structure, Union Strategy and Strike Activity in American Bituminous Coal Mining, 1881–1894." *Social Science History* 26, no. 1 (2002): 1–32.
Rotundo, E. Anthony. *American Manhood: Transformations in Masculinity from the Revolution to the Modern Era*. New York: Basic Books, 1993.
Ryan, Mary. "The American Parade: Representations of the Nineteenth-Century Social Order." In *The New Cultural History*, ed. Lynn Hunt, 131–53. Berkeley: University of California Press, 1989.
Ryan, Mary P. *Women in Public: Between Banners and Ballots, 1825–1880*. Baltimore: The Johns Hopkins University Press, 1990.
Sampson, Robert D. "'Honest Men and Law-Abiding Citizens': The 1894 Railroad Strike in Decatur." *Illinois Historical Journal* 85, no. 2 (1992): 74–88.
Saville, Julie. *The Work of Reconstruction: From Slave to Wage Laborer in South Carolina, 1860–1870*. New York: Cambridge University Press, 1996.
Sawislak, Karen. "Smoldering City." *Chicago History* 17, no. 3 and 4 (fall and winter) (1988–89).
Schneirov, Richard. "Chicago's Great Upheaval of 1877." *Chicago History* 9, no. 1 (1980): 2–17.
———. *Labor and Urban Politics*. Urbana: University of Illinois Press, 1998.
Schneirov, Richard, Shelton Stromquist, and Nick Salvatore, eds. *The Pullman Strike and the Crisis of the 1890s*. Urbana: University of Illinois Press, 1999.
Schudson, Michael. *The Good Citizen: A History of American Civic Life*. Cambridge, MA: Harvard University Press, 1998.

Scott, Joan Wallach. *Gender and the Politics of History*. New York: Columbia University Press, 1988.
Sefton, James. *The United States Army and Reconstruction, 1865–1877*. Westport, CT: Greenwood Press, Reprint, 1980.
Senechal, Roberta. *The Sociogenesis of a Race Riot: Springfield, Illinois in 1908*. Urbana: University of Illinois Press, 1990.
Shy, John. *A People Numerous and Armed: Reflections on the Military Struggle for American Independence*. Revised ed. Ann Arbor: Ann Arbor Paperbacks, University of Michigan Press, 1990.
Skocpol, Theda. *Protecting Soldiers and Mothers: The Political Origins of Social Policy in the United States*. Cambridge: The Belknap Press of Harvard University Press, 1992.
Smith, Carl. *Urban Disorder and the Shape of Belief: The Great Chicago Fire, the Haymarket Bomb, and the Model Town of Pullman*. Chicago: The University of Chicago Press, 1995.
Snyder, R. Claire. *Citizen-Soldiers and Manly Warriors: Military Service and Gender in the Civic Republican Tradition*. New York: Rowman & Littlefield, 1999.
Stampp, Kenneth M. *America in 1857*. New York: Oxford University Press, 1990.
Stansell, Christine. *City of Women: Sex and Class in New York, 1789–1860*. New York: Knopf, 1986.
Stowell, David O. *Streets, Railroads, and the Great Strike of 1877*. Chicago: University of Chicago Press, 1999.
Summers, Mark Wahlgren. "'To Make the Wheels Revolve We Must Have Grease': Barrel Politics in the Gilded Age." *Journal of Policy History* 14, no. 1 (2002): 49–72.
Taillon, Paul Michael. "'What We Want Is Good, Sober Men': Masculinity, Respectability, and Temperance in the Railroad Brotherhoods, c. 1870–1910." *Journal of Social History* 36, no. 2 (2002): 319–38.
Townsend, Kim. *Manhood at Harvard: William James and Others*. New York: W.W. Norton, 1996.
Trachtenberg, Alan. *The Incorporation of America: Culture and Society in the Gilded Age*. New York: Hill and Wang, 1982.
Trask, David F. *The War with Spain in 1898*. New York: Macmillan Publishing Co., 1981.
Turnbaugh, Roy. "Ethnicity, Civic Pride, and Commitment: The Evolution of the Chicago Militia." *Journal of the Illinois State Historical Society* 72, no. 2 (1979): 111–27.
Turner, Anna R. and Sally Paddon. "African Americans and the World's Colombian Exposition." *Illinois Historical Journal* 88, no. 1 (1995): 19–36.
Utley, Robert M. *Frontier Regulars: The United States Army and the Indian, 1866–1891*. Paperback ed. Lincoln: University of Nebraska Press, 1984.
Waldestreicher, David. *In the Midst of Perpetual Fetes: The Making of*

American Nationalism, 1776–1820. Chapel Hill: University of North Carolina Press, 1997.

Waldron, Caroline A. ""Lynch Law Must Go!" Race, Citizenship and the Other in an American Coal Mining Town." *Journal of American Ethnic History* 20, no. 1 (2000): 50–77.

Watt, William J. "The Origins of a Modern Militia." In *Indiana's Citizen Soldiers: The Militia and National Guard in Indiana History*, ed. William J. Watt and James R. Spears. Indianapolis: The Indiana State Armory Board, 1980.

Weigley, Russell. *The History of the American Army*. New York: The Macmillan Company, 1967.

———. *Towards and American Army; Military Thought from Washington to Marshall*. New York: Columbia University Press, 1962.

Wellman, Paul. *Indian Wars of the West*. New York: Dorset House Publishing Co., Inc., 1954.

Wiebe, Robert. *The Search for Order, 1877–1920*. New York: Hill and Wang, 1967.

Winter, Thomas. *Making Men, Making Class: The YMCA and Workingmen, 1877–1920*. Chicago: University of Chicago Press, 2002.

Yellen, Samuel. *American Labor Struggles*. New York: S. A. Russell, 1956.

Index

Page numbers in italics refer to photographs.

Abbey Mine, 93–95, 98, 168
adjutant general (AG), 37, 190, 199, 200
Adkins, W. G., 161
African Americans: Braidwood strike, 89; Civil War, 2–3, 21, 35, 153, 154; creation of companies, 9, 11–12, 34–36, 38, 273n26; discrimination, 195–98; financing of companies, 246n97; history, 3–4, 66–70; Massachusetts National Guard, 246n98; names of companies, 242n85; New Year's ball, 56; presence in National Guard, 59, 146; public performances, 42, 75; Sixteenth Battalion, 234n42; Spanish American War, 134–35, 137, 149, 152–54; strike breakers, 171–72, 175–78, 182, 271n88; strike duty, 89–90; support from whites, 247n100; Zouave companies, 26. *See also* Eighth Illinois; Ninth Battalion
alcohol abuse, 99–101
Alger, Russell A., 139
Alpine Hunters, 25, 82
Altgeld, John P., 68, 162, 165, 166, 177, 194, 195, 250n9
Alton, Ill., 88
American Railway Union, 160–61, 164

Anthony, Deputy, 96, 100
armories, 42–43, 48, 55–56, 187, 188, 193, 199, 200–206
Army of the Tennessee, 19, 237n7
Arnesen, Eric, 178
Atlanta, Ga., 65

balls (dances), 44, 46–49, 54–56, 106, 118, 199, 206. *See also* social events
Baltimore, 84, 85
Baltimore and Ohio Railroad, 84
Bardowsky, Frank, 163
Barkley, Colonel, 94–98, 100, 101, 178, 181, 254n70, 254n75
Bates, E. N., 246n90
Battery A, 141, 143, 180
Battery B, 141, 172, 174, 180
Battery D, 72, 202
Beard, George J., 196
Beardstown Guards, 125
Belknap, Secretary of War, 21
Belleville, Ill., 94, 95, 160
Bell, General, 208
Beveridge, John L.: appeal to manhood and citizenship, 17–18, 238n23; *Color Guard*, 22–24; commissioning of Ducat, 39; First Regiment (Chicago), 29, 32–33, 64; military career, 108; militia code, 187–88; Relief and Aid Society, 83
Billings, Josh, 47
Bloomington, Ill., 12

Bohemian companies, 38
Bohemian Guards, 86
Bohemian Rifles, 28, 33–34, 239n40, 240n73
Bolton, Horace, 50, 151, 152, 160–61, 251n38
Brackett, William S., 159–60
Braidwood, Ill., 88–90
Breckenridge, General, 150–51
Bristol, George W., 68, 246n100
Bronzeville, 56
Brotherhood of Locomotive Engineers, 84
Brown, Alexander, 67, 246n93, 246n96
Buckner, John C., 68, 147, 194–96
Bunzey, Rufus S., 121–22, 152, 161
Bureau of Militia Affairs, 212
Burnham and Root, 202
Burning, Mr., 49
"Business Militia," 273n26. *See also* First Regiment (Chicago)
Byram, Frank C., 74

Cadets, 36, 66. *See also* Hannibal Guards; Hannibal Zouaves
Caldwell, Allen, 46
Camp Alger, 141
Camp Cuba Libre, 141
Camp Lincoln, 109; cost, 190; establishment, 116; exercises, 117; photographs, 69, *119, 120, 121, 122*; purchase, 199
Camp Tanner, 144, 147
Camp Thomas, 141
Canada, 207, 208
Card, Lieutenant, 72
Carrizal, Mexico, 213
Carterville, Ill., 162–63, 169, 176
cavalrymen, 199, 207
centennial celebrations, 26–28, 40
Centralia, Ill., 71, 162
Chamberlain, Henry Barret, 53, 67–68, 246n100
Chicago: armories, 200–202; centennial celebration, 27; Cleveland's sending of troops to, 250n9; Columbian Exhibition parade, 112–13; composition of regiments, 43; domestic order, 81–83; Garfield funeral parade, 71–72; Memorial Day celebration, 73; militia code meeting, 186–88, 272n6; militia companies, 25–26, 66–70, 273n26; politics, 195; public order, 191; regiments at summer camp, 117; strikes, 83–87, 89–92, 164–66. *See also* First Regiment (Chicago)
Chicago & Southern States Association, 114
Chicago and Eastern Illinois Railroad Company, 165
Chicago Citizens' Association, 30–31, 239n48, 240n60
Chicago Defender, 198
Chicago Evening Post, 152
Chicago Inter Ocean, 50, 138, 194–98
Chicago Light Infantry, 67
Chicago Times, 30, 32, 33
Chicago Tribune: balls, 54; Columbian Exhibition parade, 112–13; Fourth of July celebrations, 60; funding, 190; Garfield funeral parade, 72; Hibernian Rifles, 194; Ninth Battalion, 67; organization of companies, 29; participation in 1875 Chicago parade, 30; reputation, 252n55; strikes, 90, 96; subscription drive, 30, 31; weapons training, 127
Chicago-Virden Coal Company, 172
Chickamauga, Ga., 141, 142, 144
Chile, 137
citizenship: African Americans, 35, 70, 154; appeals to, 13, 17–18, 21, 38; displays, 41; federal service, 215–16; issue, 1–3; parades, 42, 70–73, 75–77; public order, 79. *See also* citizen-soldiers; patriotism
citizen-soldiers, 23–24, 102, 107, 135, 137, 188. *See also* citizenship
Civil War: African Americans, 2–3, 21, 35, 153, 154; manhood, 134, 135, 151; Memorial Day celebrations, 73; patriotism, 22–24; sig-

nificance, 2–3, 9–10; veterans, 108–9, 257n15
Clan-na-Gael Guards, 25, 82, 194
Clark County Guards (Marshall), 66, 234n42
Clark, E. G., 74
Cleveland, Grover, 161, 164, 166, 250n9
Cleveland, Ohio, 70–71
coal, measurement, 94, 253nn59–60
Coldwater, Mich., 71
Collins, Charles, 22
Collins, Holdridge, 29, 31, 82, 83, 85, 186, 193–94
Collinsville, Ill., 93–100, 168
Colorado National Guard, 162, 180, 250n11
Color Guard, 21–22
Company A: organization, 29
Company A, Fifteenth Battalion: Garfield funeral parade, 71
Company A, First Infantry: competition, 125, 126; social events, 50
Company A, Second Regiment (Chicago): public performance, 60–61
Company A, Sixteenth Battalion, 66, 234n42
Company A, Third Infantry (Dekalb): composition, 11, *218*, 234n38
Company B: organization, 29
Company B, Second Regiment (Chicago): public performance, 60–61
Company B, Sixteenth Battalion, 66, 234n42
Company C: composition, 12, 36; organization, 29
Company C, Fifth Infantry: armory, 202; balls, 55; funeral parades, 74; Grand Rapids courthouse, 61–63, 66; Memorial Day celebration, 73. *See also* Governor's Guard
Company C, First Infantry: ball, 54; competition, 125, 126
Company C, Fourth Infantry, 248n133; funeral parades, 74; women, 53–54
Company D: organization, 29; Ray with, 212
Company D, Seventh Infantry: women, 51
Company E: First Regiment (Chicago), 30
Company E, First Infantry: social events, 50
Company E, Sixth Infantry: Spanish American War, 143
Company F, Fifth Regiment, 160
Company F, First Regiment (Chicago), 30
Company F, Fourth Regiment, 176
Company G, 32
Company G, First Infantry: competition, 125
Company H, 32
Company H, Fifth Regiment, 165
Company H, First Infantry: competition, 125
Company I, First Infantry, *163*
Company I, Seventh Infantry. *See* Mason City Guards
Company I, Sixth Infantry: armories, 201–2; armory, 203–4; parades, 61; Spanish American War, 143; summer camp, 120
Company M, Illinois National Guard, 60, 148
competition, 122–32. *See also* drills; marksmanship
Confederate Army, 9
Confidence, Ill., 95
Congress: authority, 6–7; funding, 114, 208, 210; militia law, 210–11, 277n104; professionalism of National Guard, 108, 110, 111, 213, 257n14; Spanish American War, 133, 262n2, 262n4; structure of state militias, 9
Connecticut National Guard, 200, 233n27, 257n15
Corbin, H. C., 142, 145, 150
Cosmas, Graham, 139, 144
Cotton States and International Exhibition, 114

court-martials, mock, 120
Craig, Captain, 170, 174, 179
Crandall, E. J., 95, 168
Crandall Mining Company, 95, 168
crowd dispersal tactics, 169–70. See also riots
Cuba, 134, 144–45, 148–51, 180, 196, 274n55. See also Spanish American War (1898–99)
Cullom, Shelby, 65, 86, 89, 90, 187–89
Culver, J. S., 142, 165–66, 169–70
Cumberland County Guards (Greenup), 66, 234n42
Curtis, Dr., 149

Daily State Journal, 21
"Dandy First," 203. See also First Regiment (Chicago)
Danville, Ill., 165–66
Davenport, Iowa, 71
Davis, Susan, 70
Decatur, Ill., 61, 71, 165
Decoration Day, 125
Delany, Martin, 194
Delavan, Ill. company, 165
Delaware Blues, 49
Delaware Guards, 49
Des Moines, Iowa, 71
Dick Act (1903), 114, 210–11
Dick, Charles, 210
Diehl, Charles, 63–64
Dilgar (adjutant general), 37
Douglass, Frederick, 35
drills: attendance, 38; citizenship, 42; competition, 106, 124–26; deemphasis, 130; description, 105–6; First Regiment (Chicago), 33; fund-raising, 47, 49–51, 199, 206; military training, 103; mock, 120; professionalism, 115; public image, 59–63; regular Army, 110; regulation, 39; shift away from, 104–5, 122–23, 128, 213; summer camp, 116–17; Zouave companies, 25
Dubuque, Iowa, 71
Ducat, Arthur C.: centennial celebration, 27; commissioning, 39; militia code, 186–87, 191, 272n6; politics, 194; professionalism of militia, 108–9; review of First Regiment (Chicago), 32, 64; strikes, 86–90, 170
The Dutch Recruit, 47, 48
dysentery, 144–45

East St. Louis, 85, 88–90, 93, 99, 177
Eighth Illinois: armory, 55–56, 201, 205, 205; discrimination, 195–98; officers, *197*; parades, 66, 150; politics, 196; Spanish American War, 4, 134, 143, 146–51, 153, 194–96, 265n59. See also Ninth Battalion
Elliot, I. H., 191–92, 273n32
Ellsworth, Elmer, 25, 239n32
Ellsworth Zouaves, 32. See also Company G
equipment, 139–41, 199, 264n28
ethnic groups, 33–36, 59, 89–90, 182. See also specific groups
Evansville, Ind., 71, 126
Ewers, E. P., 150–51
Ewert, Theodore, 179

Fieldhouse, Walter, 204
Field, Marshall, 202–3, 249n6, 276n91
Fifer, Joseph, 67
Fifteenth Amendment, 70
Fifth Army Corps, 143, 144
Fifth Regiment, 94–96, 141–43
First Battalion of Whiteside County Militia, 25
First Cavalry, 11, 71, 118, 141, 143, 201, 205, 276n83
First Division, Illinois National Guard, 69
First Illinois Cavalry, 214
First Illinois: Spanish American War, 143
First Infantry Association, 202–3
First Infantry: camp, 207; flag, 52–53; football team, *45*; Garfield funeral parade, 72; history, 64; occupations, *217*; parades, 63–64; regular

Army veterans, 108; Spanish American War, *146*; women, 53
First Regiment (Chicago): armories, 42–43, 202–5; centennial celebrations, 26–27; composition, 11; creation, 239n40, 240n73, 273n26; dedications, 114; funding, 30–31, 37, 186; image, 239n48, 246n100; manhood, 43–44; marksmanship, 127; Marshall Field's support, 249n6; Ninth Battalion, 69; organization, 25, 28–33; political identity, 28; professionalism, 108; public image, 64–65; railroad strikes, 86; Relief and Aid Society, 82, 83; Spanish American War, 141, 144–45, 148, 151–52; strike duty, 161. *See also* Ninth Battalion
First United States Volunteer Cavalry ("Rough Riders"), 262n4
Fitzhugh, Harrison G., 74
Fitzsimons, Charles, 113–14, 137
flags, 52–53
Fogelson, Robert, 204
Foner, Eric, 35
Fourth Illinois, USV, 56–57, 141, 143, *145*
Fourth of July, 60–61
France, 214–15
Freeport Company, 60–61
Fry, General, 257n14, 266n90
funding: armories, 42; federal, 109, 110, 114–15, 128, 185–86, 206–12, *228*, 267n92; First Regiment (Chicago), 30–31, 37, 186; history, 9; Mason City Guards, 11; militia companies, 36–39; per man, 209, 228; social events, 42, 44–51, 58, 76–77; sources, 12–14, 105–6; state, 4–5, 109, 128, 186–93, 199–206, 209, *228*
funeral parades, 70–75

Galesburg, Ill., 71, 85, 87, 89
Garfield, James A., 70–73, 248n124
Gate City Guards, 65
Gatewood, Willard, 194–95
General Order No. 4, 39
General Order No. 8, 168
German Catholic Church Society, 19
German immigrants, 59
Gilham, William, 105
Goldstein, Warren, 123
Gone with the Wind (Mitchell), 239n32
Goode, W. T., 67, 69, 147, 150, 153, 266n70
Gorn, Elliot, 123
Governor's Guard: *Color Guard*, 21–22; composition, 238n23; manliness and citizenship, 18; Memorial Day celebration, 73; parades, 19, 21, 65–66, 74; social events, 49–50. *See also* Company C, Fifth Infantry
Grand Army of the Republic, 32, 63, 64, 73
Grand Army Zouaves, 25
Grand Rapids, Mich., 61–63, 66
Grant, Ulysses S., 19–21, 26, 36, 65
Great Britain, 207, 208
Guánica, 143
Gunn, W. H., 22

Hall, Charles E., 195
Hamilton, Governor, 95, 97, 100–101, 168, 178
Hannibal Guards, 11–12, 36, 89, 242n85. *See also* Cadets; Hannibal Zouaves
Hannibal Zouaves, 25, 36, 50, 82, 242n85. *See also* Cadets; Hannibal Guards
Harper's Weekly, 30, 32, 64
Harris Guards, 125
Harrison, Carter, 202
Havana Guards, 49, 125
Hayes, Rutherford B., 65
Headenburg, Charles, 49–50, 55
Heath, Monroe, 86–88
Henderson (miner), 100–101
Hibernian Rifles, 68, 194. *See also* Seventh Regiment
Hickox, Emma, 22, 23, 238n23
Higgins, Adjutant General, 28, 37–38

Hilliard, Hiram, 39, 86, 90, 108–9, 188–92, 273nn29–30
Hilton, Charles, 192–93, 200
Homestead, Pa., 176
Hopkins, John P., 164–66
Hotz, Sheriff, 97, 98, 181
Houston Light Guard, 126
Hubbard, Guerdon S., Jr., 29
Hubbard, Guerdon S., Sr., 240n50
Hubbard, Theodore C., 66
Hudek, Prokop, 33–34
Hurt, John S., 49

Illinois Cavalryman, 11, 214
Illinois Day parade, 114
Illinois General Assembly, 109, 186–89, 192, 199–201, 213. *See also* Illinois (state)
Illinois Guardsman, 67, 246n100
Illinois National Guard Association, 198
Illinois National Guard (ING): advantages of membership, 43; deaths and injuries at hands of, 170, 270n56; discharges, 12, 235n44; distribution, 191, 229–30; expenditures, 199–206; federalization, 104–5, 141–43, 185–86, 212–13, 226; inspection reports, 39, 110–12, 117, 150, 258n27, 277n104; legislation, 83; lobbyists, 211; organization, 39, 232n13; professionalism, 107–12, 114–15, 128, 156, 210, 213; purposes, 188, 190–93; retention of members, 109–10; self-presentation, 42, 132; size and diversity, 10–15, 21, 33–36, 59, 162, 191, 221, 243n31, 273n39; social rank, 22–24; Spanish American War, 135, 141–43, 226; study, 3–5; terms of enlistment, 188. *See also* Illinois State Guard
Illinois Naval Militia, 205
Illinois (state): budget (1878), 38, 242n85; funding of National Guard, 4–5, 12–14, 47–48, 186, 199–201; legislation, 7, 83, 108, 187–89; strike duty, 80. *See also* Illinois General Assembly
Illinois State Fair, 65
Illinois State Guard, 26–28, 30–31, 108. *See also* Illinois National Guard (ING)
Illinois State Journal, 54–55, 55, 148
Illinois State Rifle team, 127
Immel, Kate, 51
Indiana National Guard, 142, 156, 162
Indianapolis, 71
Industrial University at Champaign, 19
Inspector General of Illinois, 108, 199
Inter-State Competitive Drill, 126
Interstate National Guard Association (INGA), 114, 132, 139, 208–12, 277n111
Iowa National Guard, 162
Irish companies, 27, 30, 38, 59, 75, 194. *See also* First Regiment (Chicago)
Irish Rifles, 25, 82

Jackson, Mich., 71
Jackson, Robert, 149
Jacobs, W. V., 51
Johnson, James H., 197
Joliet, Ill., 71, 88

Kendrick, John F., 152
Kinsley, H. M., 68
Knights of Pythias, 248n124

L. & N. Railroad, 95–97
La Crome, Wis., 71
Lanham, Deputy Sheriff, 98
Lansing, Mich., 71
La Salle (commander), 269n49
LaSalle County, 162
Law and Order (pro-slavery) party, 9
Lawton, Henry W., 150
lectures, 47, 49, 199, 206
Leiter, Joseph, 176, 177
Lincoln, Abraham, 19–21, 26, 36, 65, 70, 239n32

Lincoln, Ill. company, 165
Logan, John, 24
Long Branch, N.J., 70
Ludlow Massacre, 180
Lukins, Fred W., 175

machine mines, 93–95, 97, 253n57
Madison County (Ill.), 93–97, 168
Madison, Wis., 27
Magie, Jas., 100
Maine, U.S.S., 137–38, 263n17
malaria, 144–45
manhood: appeals to, 13, 17–24; Civil War, 134, 135, 151; concept, 1–3; definition, 104–5; displays, 41, 42–44, 75–77; federal service, 215–16; growth of National Guard, 102; historical analysis, 231n1, 237n3; marksmanship, 129–32; military training, 185; Spanish American War, 135, 151–55; women, 53–54
The Manual of Instruction for the Volunteers and Militia of the United States: With Numerous Illustrations (Gilham), 105, 106, 107
marksmanship: competition, 14, 104–5, 112, 123–25, 128, 260n75; federal oversight, 213; importance, 126–28; manhood, 129–32; Mason City Guards, 257n22; training, 109; Zouave companies, 25
Marshall, John, 134, 147–50, 154, 196, *197*, 198, 274n55, 274n57
martial law, 178–81
Martinsburg, W.Va., 84
Maryland National Guard, 71, 162, 200
Mason City Guards, 11, 48–51, 73, 125, 243n31, 257n22
Masons, 72, 248n124
Massachusetts National Guard, 3–4, 71, 115, 246n98, 257n15
Mathis, Guy, 122
Matoon Gazette, 56–58
Matoon, Ill., 89
Maxwell, H. B., 27–28, 34
McAuliffe, John, 85

McCard, Harry, 66, 149, 153–54
McClurg, Lieutenant Colonel, 82
McKinley, President, 133, 134, 140
McLean County Guards, 12, 25, 36, 246n97
Memorial Day, 73–75, 125, 248n129
Merritt, General, 50, 118
Mexican border service, 10, 213–16
Michigan National Guard, 156, 162
Michigan Southern Depot, 86
"The Mid-Summer Picnic of '98" (Kendrick), 152
Miles, Nelson A., 112–13, 143
military rank: assumption, 62; examination, 115; Garfield funeral parade, 72–73; militia code, 189; organization, 108, 257n18; retired militia, 107, 256n11, 273n40
military training: cost, 185; emphasis at summer camp, 116–18; evolution, 105–12, 115, 193; federal service, 213–15; methods, 103–5. *See also* drills; summer camp
"militia," 233n21
militia act (1792), 108, 110, 232n12, 257n14
Militia Act of 1879, 189, 192, 194, 275n68, 277n104
Militia Act of 1903, 114, 210–11
militia code: (1845), 39; politics, 193–94; pursuit of better, 186–91; weapons, 66. *See also* militia law; *specific laws*
militia companies: active, 241n78; definition, 7–8; distribution, 229–30; funding, 36–39; growth, 18, 39–40, 237n5, 239n38; history and significance, 1–2, 5–16; lack of federal representation, 238n29; organization, 24–33, 108, 155–56, 266n90; physical benefits, 32–33; regulations, 199. *See also* Illinois National Guard (ING); National Guard
militia law: (1796), 210; (1903), 114, 210–11; (1908), 111, 258n32; lobby, 135, 264n19. *See also* militia code; *specific laws*

Miller, Edward S., *197*
mine company towns, 254n80
Miner, J. D., 99
miner strikes, 88–93; (1894), 162–64; (1897–99), 171–78; Colorado, 250n11; Madison and St. Clair counties, 93–101; precipitating events, *220*; responses, 168–69; violence, 99–101
mines, 253n57. *See also* machine mines
Minonk, Ill., 162
Minute Men, 7, 233n21
Missouri, 9
Missouri National Guard, 136
mobs, 182, 204–5. *See also* riots
Moline, Ill., 61, 73, 125
Molly Maguires, 84
Monmouth Guards, 60, 148
Monmouth, Ill., 73
Montgomery Light Guards, 25, 82
Moore, Milton, 136
Moore, R. B., 50, 89–90
Morrison, Ill., 71, 203–4
Morrison Military Club, 204
Morton, Thomas J., 160
Mount Vernon, Ill., 71
Mulligan Zouaves, 25, 82
Muscatine, Ill., 125

National Guard: definition, 8, 233n21; federalization, 6–7; history and significance, 1–2; influence on state legislatures, 110; law, 6–7; organization, 10, 266n90; purposes, 13–14, 102, 133–36; self-image, 132. *See also* Illinois National Guard (ING); militia companies
National Guard Association, 110, 111, 135, 185–86
National Guard Association of the United States (NGAUS), 139, 206–9, 277n111
The National Guardsman, 43, 198
Nelson, James S., *197*
New Hampshire National Guard, 105
New York 69th, 27

New York National Guard, 71, 159, 189, 200, 206, 232n9, 233n27, 257n15, 267n4
New York State, 4
New York Times, 54, 113
Ninth Battalion, 12, 67–69, 137, 146–47, 194–95. *See also* Eighth Illinois
Ninth "Immunes" USV, 134, 149–50, 262n4
Normal, Ill., 65
Northcott (acting governor), 178

Oakland Rifles, 52, 54, 74, 248n133
Oak Ridge Cemetery, 19–21, 36, 65, 73
Oakwood Cemetery, 114
O'Brien, M. F., 55
occupations, 11, 38–39, *217*, *218*
Odd-Fellows, 248n124
officers: African American, 150, 154; authority, 188, 262n2, 273n40; First Regiment (Chicago), 31; histories, *222–25*; marksmanship, 128; professionalism, 107–9, 111; regulations, 199; strike duty, 158–60, 166–67, 178–79, 181, 183, 184; summer camp, 117; terms of service, 12, 109, 234n43, 235n44
Oglesby, Richard J., 99
Ohio National Guard, 3–4, 71, 156, 162, 209, 232n9, 267n4
Orrendorff, Alfred, 165
Ottawa, Ill., 73, 125

Palma Soriano, 149
Palmer, Governor, 36
Pana Coal Company, 171, 172
Pana, Ill., 158, 161–63, 171–72, *173*, 176–79; strikes, 181
parades: African Americans, 35; atmosphere, 245n71; attendance, 38; Buckner's court-martial, 195; competition, 125; deemphasis, 130; display of citizenship, 42, 70–73, 75–77; Eighth Illinois, 66, 150; First Regiment (Chicago),

32; Fourth of July, 60–61; funeral, 70–75; importance, 44, 199; manhood, 18–21; mock, 120; participation in 1875 Chicago, 30; patriotism, 20, 21, 58–63, 70–73, 245n69; problems, 112–14; public image, 63–66, 75, 106; summer camp, 118; weapons, 275n68. *See also* social events
Paris, Ill., 71
Parker, General, 214
Parker, George, 97, 254n73
Parker, H. P., 132
Parker, J. H., 152
Parsons, Albert, 85
patriotism: centennial celebrations, 27–28; growth of National Guard, 102; military performance, 33; parades, 20, 21, 58–63, 70–73, 245n69; social events, 41–42; Springfield, 22–24. *See also* citizenship
Paxton, Ill., 71
Pearson, J. M., 254n75
Pekin, Ill., 163
Pennsylvania coal fields, 84
Pennsylvania National Guard, 4, 71, 159, 200, 232n9, 267n4
Penwell Coal Company, 171
Peoria, Ill., 26, 85, 89, 165
Pershing, John J., 213, 214
Philadelphia, 26–27, 85, 245n69
Philippines, 154, 180, 264n29
physical benefits, 32–33
Picnic Island, Port Tampa, 144
Pittsburgh, 84, 85
police, 80–81, 92, 94–99, 158–60, 174–75, 178–83
political identity, 27–28, 75, 193–98, 206, 211–12
Ponce, 143
Pontiac, Ill., 26
"Pony Clubs," 121
Porter, James H., 195
Potter, E. A., 113
Pratt, Walter Merriam, 131
presidential authority, 211
public image, 22–24, 58–66, 75, 106, 122, 245n69
Puerto Rico, 134, 142, 143, 180
Pullman strike, 158, 160–61, 164–67

Quincy, Ill., 26

race, 33–36, 59, 89–90, 177–78, 182, 197. *See also* African Americans
railroad strikes, 83–91, 177, 251n22, 268n32. *See also* Pullman strike
Rand, W. C., 52
Rantoul Guards, 25
Ray, Cary T., 122, 145, 161, 165, 212
Reading, Pa., 85
Reece, Jasper, 138, 140–41, 181, 208–9, 271n104
Reinecker Mine, 95–97, 100–101, 254n70
Relay House, 88
Relief and Aid Society, 36, 81–83, 191, 241n84, 250n13
Republican Party, 194–96
reserve system, 7, 8, 133–36, 155–56, 207, 209–11, 213–16, 263n10, 266n90, 277n104
Rickover, Admiral, 263n17
Riddle, Francis A., 155
rifle companies, 9
rifle ranges, 109, 112. *See also* marksmanship
riots, 4, 91, 190–91, 197. *See also* crowd dispersal tactics; mobs
"The Rising Menace Against the Peace of American Society" (Brackett), 159–60
Rock Falls Zouaves, 25
Rockford, Ill., 65, 73
Rock Island, Ill., 60–61, 71, 125
Roosevelt, Theodore, 130, 212
Root, Elihu, 210
Ropiequet, Sheriff, 95, 97, 99, 168
"Rough Riders," 262n4
Ryan, Mary, 73

San Francisco, 27, 71
Sanitation District, 90
San Juan, 143, 144
San Luis, 134, 149–50, 274n55

Santiago, 149
Savannah girls, 56–58
Schwan, Theodore, 112
Scottish members, 59, 72
Scott, Samuel, 72, 246n93
Scott, Thomas W., 200–201, 273n39
Second Brigade, 88
Second Infantry, Illinois National Guard: armory, 202; Garfield funeral parade, 71; social events, 50
Second Regiment (Chicago): composition, 11, 273n26; funding, 39
Second Regiment, Illinois State Guard, 27; armory, 205; budget, 186; marksmanship, 127; political identity, 28; railroad strikes, 86, 87, 251n38; Spanish American War, 141, 143, 152
Seventh Regiment, 141, 143, 194, 205. *See also* Hibernian Rifles
Shaffer, J. H., 207
Shafter, General, 144
Shays's Rebellion, 79
Sheridan Guards, 25
Sheridan, Philip H., 32, 64, 110
Sherman, Frank T., 29, 65, 240n53
Sherman Guards, 19, 20
Sherman, William T., 110
Siboney, 145
Sixteenth Battalion, 12, 66–67, 72, 234n42, 246n93
Sixth Infantry, 71–72, 141, 143, 152, 197
Skinner, John, 56, 151, 152
social class, 33–36, 59
social events: fund-raising, 42, 44–51, 58, 76–77, 199–200; manhood, 75–77; patriotism, 41–42; women, 42, 51–58. *See also* balls (dances); parades
Socialists, 81, 239n40, 239n48
Soldiers' Orphans Home (Normal, Ill.), 65
Souvenir Album and Sketch Book: First Infantry I.N.G. of Chicago, 43, 53
Souvenir History: Governors Guard: Company C, Fifth Infantry, Illinois National Guard, 65
Spanish American War (1898–99), 133–56; decision to use National Guard, 136–40; development of National Guard, 6, 10, 114, 156, 193, 216; Eighth Illinois, 4, 134, 143, 146–51, 153, 194–96, 265n59; First Regiment (Chicago), 141, 144–45, 148, 151–52; Fourth Illinois, 56–57, 141, 143, *145*; Illinois National Guard troops sent, 141–43, 226; illness, 144–45, 148–49, 152; legislation for raising troops, 211; lessons of occupation, 180; manhood, 135, 151–55; marksmanship, 127–28; precipitation, 137–38; preparation, 136–41; rejection of volunteers, 264n23; women, 54
Springfield Fire Department, 19
Springfield, Ill.: armory and arsenal, 200–202; Beveridge in, 17–18; gathering of troops for Spanish American War, 140; militia code, 188; parades, 18–21, 26, 36, 65, 70; Pullman strike, 166; race riots, 197–98; representation at Grand Rapids, 61–63; summer camp, 116, 117
Springfield *Illinois Record*, 195, 196
Springfield Zouaves, 12, 19, 20, 26, 36, 65. *See also* Governor's Guard
Spring Valley, Ill., 163–64
Spy of Shenandoah, 49
State Arsenal and Armory, 201
St. Clair County (Ill.), 93–97, 99
Sterling City Guards, 19, 25
Sterling, Ill., 61
St. Louis, Alton & Terre Haute Rail Road Company, 97
St. Louis convention, 206–8
stockyards, 90
Streator, Ill., 88
strike duty, 79–81; (1870–99), 232n9; (1878–99), 267n4; attitudes toward, 78–79, 158–62, 164; avoidance, 157–58; Company C,

66; costs, 92–93; deaths, 100–101; history, 12–14, 78–79, 255n97; intervention requests, 97–101; martial law, 178–81; neutrality, 92, 102, 252n52; pay, 161; professionalism, 110; responsibilities, 4, 91, 166–70, 178, 181–84, 256n12; statistics, *219*; tactics, 167–70; time spent on, 162, 170, 180, *221*. *See also* miner strikes; railroad strikes; strikes

strikes: guard development, 40; types, 90–93, 252n49. *See also* miner strikes; railroad strikes

Sublette Guards, 60

summer camp: appropriations, 199, 207; Buckner's courts-martial, 195–96; Dick Act, 210–11; federal oversight, 213; military training, 103, 110, 115–18; postponement, 259n52; socializing, 118–22; standardization, 109

"The Summer Guards of St. Louis," 50–51

Swain, E. D., 207

Sycamore, Ill., 26

Tampa, Fla., 141, 144

Tanner, Mrs. John R., 118

Tanner, John R.: development of National Guard, 193; inauguration, 50; politics, 195–96; recognition of Eighth Illinois, 134; Spanish American War, 137–40, 142, 145, 147, 148, 153, 154; strikes, 168–69, 175–79, 182

Terre Haute, Ind., 125

Third Infantry, *119*, 141–43, *218*

Tilton, Ill., 170

Torrence, Joseph T., 90, 194

Trinity Episcopal Church Ladies Guild, 51

Trout, Amos, 46, 49

Troy, Ill., 94, 95

"True Blue," 49

Turner, Henry L., 43, 53, 54, 63

Turnley, Henry, 149, 153–54

Twenty-third Kansas USV, 134, 150

uniforms, 36, 37, 108, 109, 139, 199

Union Army, 2–3, 9, 21, 35, 108–9, 153, 257n15. *See also* United States Army

union organization, 177, 249n6

Union Stock Yards, 90

United Mine Workers, 172, 178

United States Army: attitudes toward militias, 110–12, 115; Dick Act, 210–11; identification with, 206, 212, 277n104; military training, 106, 107; organization of National Guard, 266n90; rank, 189; reserve system, 7, 8; Spanish American War, 133, 134, 138–39, 144, 154, 180, 262n2; strike duty, 86, 87, 164; uniforms, 109. *See also* Union Army

United States Volunteers, 4, 56, 134–36, 140, 144, 147

United States War Department: Dick Act, 210–11; financial support, 37, 258n32; permanence of militias, 110; relationship with National Guard, 212, 213; Spanish American War, 134, 140–42, 144, 145, 147–49

University Cadets, 19, 20

Upton, Emory, 258n26

U.S. Constitution, 6–7

Vance, J. M., 99, 192

Van Patten, Philip, 85

Viegard, Mr., 47, 49

Villa, "Pancho," 213

Virden, Ill., 158, 161, 170, 172–79, *173, 174,* 181

Virginia Guards, 125

Virginia National Guard, 206

volunteer militia: competition, 123; definition, 7–10; federal service, *226*; funding, 186; losses in service, 145, *227*; organization, 24–25, 207; reasons for joining, 59; rejection, 264n23. *See also* militia companies

Wadsworth, Dr., 254n75

Wagar, Claron S., 151
"Walker Brothers," 47
Warning to Illinois Girls, 56–58
Washburn, W. D., 260n75
Washington, D.C., 71
watermelon theft, 120
Waymen, Bishop, 20
weapons: militia code, 66, 247n106; parades, 275n68; quality, 37; Spanish American War, 139; strike duty, 81, 98, 169–70, 179. *See also* marksmanship
Welch, "Andy," 51
Wesley, Allen A., *197*
West Virginia National Guard, 162
Wheeler, General, 50
Wheeler, H. A., 114, 118, 200
Wheeler, Lloyd, 72
Whitewater, Wis., 71

Williams, Quartermaster, 72
Wilson, Woodrow, 21, 65, 213
Wingate, General, 208
Wisconsin National Guard, 159
Wolf, H. M., 49
women, 42, 51–58, 96, 182
Wood, Leonard, 266n70
Workingmen's Party of the United States, 84–85
World War I, 10, 135, 213–16

Yates, Richard, 176–77, 179
Young, Charles G., 147

Ziegler, Ill., 158, 167, 176–77, 179, 181, 183
Zouave companies: drills, 39, 125; popularity, 25–26; reputation, 239n32. *See also specific companies*

www.ingramcontent.com/pod-product-compliance
Lightning Source LLC
Chambersburg PA
CBHW020942230426
43666CB00005B/132